THE PENGUIN CLASSICS
FOUNDER EDITOR (1944–64): E. V. RIEU
PRESENT EDITORS
Betty Radice and Robert Baldick

FRANÇOIS-MARIE AROUET (1694–1778), who later took the name of VOLTAIRE, was the son of a notary, and educated at a Jesuit school in Paris. Although his father wished him to study law, he determined on a literary career. Gaining an introduction to the intellectual life of Paris, he soon won a not altogether enviable reputation as a writer of satires and odes, for the suspicion of having written a satire on the Regent resulted in six months' imprisonment in the Bastille. On his release his first tragedy, *Œdipe*, was performed (1718) in Paris with great success; and soon after he published a national epic poem he had written in prison, *La Henriade* (1724), which placed him with Homer and Virgil in the eyes of his contemporaries. After a second term in the Bastille Voltaire spent the years 1726–9 in England, and returned to France full of enthusiasm for the intellectual activity and the more tolerant form of government he had found there. His enthusiasm and his indictment of the French system of government are expressed in his *Philosophical Letters* (1733), whose sale was forbidden in France. The next fifteen years were spent at the country seat of his mistress, Madame Du Châtelet, where he wrote his most popular tragedies and *Zadig*, a witty Eastern tale, and started work on his *Century of Louis XIV*. After Madame Du Châtelet's death in 1749, Voltaire visited the court of Frederick the Great, and while there completed his historical work, *Essay on Customs* (*Essai sur les moeurs et l'esprit des nations*), and began his *Philosophical Dictionary*, but he and Frederick did not agree for long, and in 1753 he left Prussia. France was still unsafe, and after two years' wandering he settled near Geneva. During his last, most brilliant, twenty years, he wrote *Candide*, his dialogues, and more tales, and published his *Philosophical Dictionary* (1764) in 'pocket' form, while conducting a ceaseless attack on what he called the 'infamous thing', i.e. all manifestations of tyranny and persecution by a privileged orthodoxy in Church and State. He died aged eighty-four after a triumphant visit to Paris, from which he had been exiled for so long.

THEODORE BESTERMAN is the founder and director of the Institut et Musée Voltaire housed in Voltaire's own home of Les Délices, Geneva. He is the author of the standard biography, *Voltaire* (1969), founder and editor of *Studies on Voltaire and the Eighteenth Century*. Recognized as the foremost authority on Voltaire, he has received many honours at home and abroad.

VOLTAIRE

PHILOSOPHICAL DICTIONARY

edited and translated by

THEODORE BESTERMAN

PENGUIN BOOKS

Penguin Books Ltd, Harmondsworth, Middlesex, England
Penguin Books Inc., 7110 Ambassador Road, Baltimore, Maryland 21207, U.S.A.
Penguin Books Australia Ltd, Ringwood, Victoria, Australia

—

This translation first published 1971

—

Copyright © Theodore Besterman, 1971

—

Made and printed in Great Britain
by Richard Clay (The Chaucer Press) Ltd,
Bungay, Suffolk
Set in Monotype Garamond

INTRODUCTION[1]

1

FIRST planned in Berlin in 1752 during the last months of Voltaire's bitter-sweet stay with Frederick of Prussia, the *Dictionnaire philosophique* was never long out of his thoughts. The first edition finally saw print in 1764. Its impact was immediately felt, the most perceptible though least important result being that it was condemned by all the establishments, religious and governmental, drawing from Voltaire the usual flood of protestations and disavowals. However, also as usual, these disavowals were accompanied by new editions of the 'alphabetic abomination', containing additions which obviously could have come from no other pen than his. Voltaire was always willing to play the formal game of denial, as required by the rules, under which a protestation of not guilty was accepted as evidence of innocence unless someone could produce positive evidence of guilt. But though Voltaire gleefully played this charade of 'as if', he never withdrew a word he had written or an opinion he had advanced. In short, the book was condemned by the authorities, but read by all, that is, by the few who could read and the still fewer who had access to books.

The *Dictionnaire philosophique* is not what we now understand by a dictionary, least of all a dictionary of philosophy, for its alphabetical arrangement is little more than a literary *trompe l'œil*. This epoch-making little book is in fact a series of essays on a wide variety of subjects, sometimes arranged under convenient headings arranged in alphabetical sequence, but sometimes placed under deliberately misleading or even provocative catchwords. Thus, under '*Catéchisme chinois*', the reader will find nothing whatever about Chinese catechism, but instead a far-reaching demonstration of the superiority of ethics over religion.

To say further that the *Dictionnaire* is even less a treatise on

1. The chapter devoted to the *Dictionnaire philosophique* in my *Voltaire* (1969) was originally written as the present introduction and was extracted from it.

philosophy than a dictionary is not a paradox but, in our time, a necessary explanation. This gloss was not needed in the eighteenth century: the contemporary reader of a new work which, though anonymous, showed on every page the unmistakable hallmark of the Délices and of Ferney, and the title-page of which bore the words *Dictionnaire philosophique*, knew exactly what to expect. For in the language of Voltaire and his friends the term 'philosophy' was used in such a context in the sense of what we now call 'free thought' or 'rationalism' – either one a better and more accurate term than the now fashionable 'humanism', a word as vague as it is ambiguous[1]. What we today understand by 'philosophy' was usually referred to by Voltaire as 'metaphysics'. As for our 'metaphysics', he stigmatized it as nonsense.

What is certain is that the *Dictionnaire philosophique* is poles apart from the academic or even the systematic. Voltaire wrote what his genius impelled him to write, and if the result did not happen to be a play or an epigram, a letter or a poem, a controversial pamphlet or a work in several volumes, that is, if it was a fairly short piece in prose, he would sometimes print it as a pamphlet or even a leaflet, but more often he would file it in a series of folders marked *Mélanges*. Out of these folders Voltaire built up his innumerable volumes of essays, published both separately and as parts of his various, ever more voluminous sets of collected works. When, however, these writings were of a certain type, consciously hortatory or propagandist, they found their way, from 1752 until the end of his life, into volumes eventually destined to be entitled *Dictionnaire philosophique portatif* (from 1764), *Opinion par alphabet* (this title never appeared in print), *La Raison par alphabet* (from 1769), *Dictionnaire philosophique* (from 1770), *Questions sur l'encyclopédie*[2] (from 1770).

1. But of course the eighteenth-century, specialized use of *philosophe* in French can be as misleading as the *humanism* of twentieth-century English. Every time it occurs the translator has to determine whether it is being used in its general or special sense, that is, whether to translate it as 'philosopher' or 'freethinker'.

2. This title should always be written thus, for it means *Encyclopedic questions* not *Questions on the Encyclopédie*, that is, the *Encyclopédie* of which Diderot was the architect.

Voltaire's wider object in publishing these works is evident, and he made his specific purpose clear beyond a peradventure in a lapidary remark on the great *Encyclopédie*: 'Twenty folio volumes will never make a revolution. It is the little portable volumes of thirty *sous* that are to be feared. Had the gospel cost twelve hundred sesterces the Christian religion would never have been established.'[1]

Voltaire acted on this conviction. His alphabetical essays, dialogues, skits and other papers, and even more the mixed volumes containing them, vary in tone and emphasis, but they quickly became enormously popular in their collected forms, and went into numerous editions, some of them prepared under Voltaire's supervision, but most often pirated by the booksellers. These editions are interrelated in such a complicated way that it would be a considerable critical and bibliographical enterprise to disentangle the various states of many of the texts. So one cannot but sympathize with Condorcet and Beaumarchais. When, after the great man's death, they were preparing the Kehl edition of his works they were confronted with a vast mass of miscellaneous material, most of it in print, but some left by Voltaire only in manuscript. Unwilling or unable to cope with it logically, or even, it must be said, intelligently, and finding that a good deal of it could be forced into an alphabetical semblance, they poured as much as they could into a vast cornucopia for which they purloined the label *Dictionnaire philosophique*.

It is true that in adopting this desperate procedure they followed up to a point Voltaire's own example, for he was decidedly casual in such matters, like most of his contemporaries. Yet Beaumarchais and his collaborators went far beyond anything authorized by Voltaire's practices. Indeed the title they used was the less justified in that they included a great deal of not even ostensibly alphabetical material, and even a complete book (the *Lettres philosophiques*), to say nothing of many long essays and contributions published in or intended for Diderot's *Encyclopédie*. For good measure they also went

1. Best. 12362 (5 April 1762); references of this kind are to my edition of *Voltaire's Correspondence* (1953–65; Definitive edition, 1968–).

so far as to throw in lexicographic notes written for the
Dictionnaire de l'Académie.

II

The original *Dictionnaire philosophique* was repeatedly condemned by the civil and religious authorities in several
countries. Thus, when the *procureur général* (public prosecutor)
of Geneva, Jean Robert Tronchin, was asked in 1764 by the
city council to give his opinion of Voltaire's book, his very
long report (Best. 11255) described it as a 'deplorable monu-
ment of the extent to which intelligence and erudition can be
abused'. Among the terms the *procureur* used to describe the
Dictionnaire are 'baneful paradoxes', 'indiscreet researches',
'audacious criticism', 'errors, malignity and indecency',
'contagious poison', 'temerarious, impious, scandalous,
destructive of revelation', and so on, and so on. The book was
to the end included in the unlamented official Roman index
of forbidden books. This fate was only to be expected, and
indeed it can almost be said to have been invited, for Voltaire
deliberately planned the *Dictionnaire* as a 'revolutionary' book,
in which the most 'liberal' ideas were to be expressed openly
and lucidly, and made available to all who could read.
Dangerous undertaking! Did not the presence of the *Dictionnaire* among the books of the chevalier de La Barre contribute
to his frightful execution?

Such being Voltaire's general purpose, let us see whether
more precise intentions in launching the *Portatif* can be
determined. Here is the list of the articles contained in the
first edition of 1764 (in French these are of course in alphabetical sequence): Abraham; Soul; Friendship; Love; Socratic
love; Self-love; Angel; Anthropophagi; Apis; Apocalypse;
Atheist; Atheism; Baptism; Beautiful; Beauty; Beasts; Good,
sovereign good; Good (all is); Limits of human understanding;
Character; Certain, certainty; Chain of events; Chain of
created beings; the Heaven of the ancients; Circumcision;
Body; China; Chinese catechism; Japanese catechism;
Catechism of the clergy; Christianity (historical researches on);

Convulsions; Criticism; Destiny; God; Equality; Hell; State, government (which is the best?); Ezekiel; Fables; Fanaticism; Falsity of human virtues; End, final causes; Folly; Fraud; Glory; War; Grace; History of the Jewish kings and parlipomena; Idol, idolator, idolatry; Flood; Jephte, or sacrifices of human blood; Joseph; Freewill; Laws; Civil and ecclesiastic laws; Luxury; Matter; Wicked; Messiah; Metamorphosis; Metempsychosis; Miracles; Moses; Fatherland; Peter; Prejudices; Religion; Resurrection; Solomon; Feeling; Dreams; Superstition; Tyranny; Tolerance; Virtue.

It is clear that Voltaire's preoccupations in the first *Dictionnaire philosophique* were overwhelmingly theological and philosophical. Indeed, although we have seen that it is not a systematic treatise, the *Portatif* does contain preponderantly philosophical writing in the widest sense. This is evident in the articles themselves even more than in their titles, which do not always define very exactly the texts that follow them. Thus even such essays as 'Friendship' and 'Beautiful' have religious or ethical overtones. And this tendency is strongly confirmed by the second edition of 1765, in which Voltaire added articles entitled *Abbé*; Confession; Dogmas; False intelligence; Faith; War; Idea; Letters, men of letters; Martyr; Paul; Priest; Sect; Superstition II; Theist; Theologian.

Voltaire's treatment of these religious subjects is above all scientific: that is, he was concerned to establish the truth. Here and elsewhere his first question is always: did an alleged event really occur? This fact explains what so many people find disconcerting: the destructiveness of Voltaire's writings on religion. This kind of approach, thanks very largely to Voltaire himself, is no longer necessary, for since then theologians have learned the subtle art of selective symbology. Educated laymen, of course, learned it even more quickly. One of the bitterest complaints made by the *procureur général* of Geneva was that Voltaire quoted from the *Bible* passages which 'taken literally would be unworthy of Divine Majesty'. Tronchin was mercifully unconscious of the fact that he had himself swallowed a large dose of the 'contagious 'poison' of Voltaire's thought, and been affected by it to an extent amply revealed by his innocent confession, for it was then quite exceptional even to envisage the possibility that there could be things in holy writ considered 'unworthy of Divine Majesty'. When the *Dictionnaire* was first published men were still so naïve and so logical as to believe that sacred and inspired scriptures must be taken to mean what they say, and that it is blasphemous to select for belief what one chooses to believe, and to ignore or 'interpret' the rest. The fundamental task of the freethinker was therefore to throw the light of reason into this murky situation, an undertaking well within Voltaire's capacity and knowledge, to say nothing of his courage.

In most cases it was of course impossible to determine positively whether or not a given Biblical narrative was historically true. But whether this could be done or not Voltaire then proceeded to a second inquiry: even if the Biblical story is true, were the events depicted good? In other words, Voltaire added an ethical judgement to a primary scientific evaluation. The whole of his work is indeed an illustration of his notion of reason: the search for the true and the good. This general idea can be even more briefly subsumed: Voltaire's master idea, one can almost speak of an obsession, was the idea of justice, for to him that which is just is that which is true and good. It is not too much to say that Voltaire was also obsessed by man's ignorance of himself, his world and his universe.

These being Voltaire's guiding principles, and his interests being universal, it was inevitable that the range of subjects treated in the *Dictionnaire philosophique* should steadily widen, until it finally took in nearly everything of 'philosophical' interest in the widest possible sense. Thus Voltaire's little 'portable' finally came to have profound influence on men's thinking in all fields of reflection and public policy.

The very first words of the first edition of the *Dictionnaire philosophique* characterize the whole: 'Abraham is one of the names famous in Asia Minor and in Arabia, like Thoth among the Egyptians, the first Zoroaster in Persia, Hercules in Greece, Orpheus in Thrace, Odin among the northern nations, and so many others whose fame is greater than the authenticity of their history.' This opening paragraph appears to us so simple, so direct, so innocuous, only because we have completely absorbed the Voltairean idiom and mode of thought. In the middle of the eighteenth century all readers were staggered, and most of them were horrified, to find so distinguished a Biblical personage as Abraham quietly classed, without fuss or apology, with pagan and even mythological figures who are described as more famous than authentic. Voltaire then added that he of course excluded from this category the Jews, about whose history he felt as he must, since it had manifestly been written by the holy ghost in person. This double irony emphasized what was being denied, and it served also to underline the revolutionary nature of the comparative and critical method of religious investigation.

Voltaire goes on to explain that he is concerned only with the Arabs (meaning the Mohammedans), who boast of their descent from Abraham. Yet, as he shows all that is doubtful about this claim, he cannot but help demonstrate also the doubtful historicity of the Jewish patriarch, and the mistakes and contradictions of the references to him in the *Bible*. Of course Voltaire does not expect the reader to follow him blindly: he concludes his article on Abraham (all the rest was added later, at different dates) by referring the reader to the many volumes written to resolve the difficulties. 'They are all written by delicate wits and discerning minds, excellent philosophers, unprejudiced, no pedants.'

Such was always, in a literary sense, Voltaire's method: he tried to ascertain the facts, then drew ethical conclusions from them, and finally presented these conclusions with the lucidity and elegant irony which were the secrets of his unique style. In the *Dictionnaire philosophique* Voltaire did indeed follow his own precepts: 'I think the best way to fall on the infamous is to seem to have no wish to attack it; to disentangle a little chaos of antiquity; to try to make these things rather interesting; to make ancient history as agreeable as possible; to show how much we have been misled in all things; to demonstrate how much is modern in things thought to be ancient, and how ridiculous are many things alleged to be respectable; to let the reader draw his own conclusions' (Best. 11140, 9 July 1764).

No wonder Alembert begged for another copy of the 'dictionary of Satan' which had issued from the 'printing press of Beelzebub'; and that Grimm widely distributed this 'precious *vade mecum* which all the elect should carry in their pockets'. Voltaire, I repeat, was of course obliged to disavow the book, which he did frequently and fervently. His view was always that the infamous should be crushed but that the hand which did the crushing should remain unknown (unpublished letter of 25 November 1764). His friends agreed, for it appeared to them obvious from internal evidence that the *Dictionnaire* had at least four authors, Beelzebub, Astaroth, Lucifer and Asmodeus, whom the angelic doctor (saint Thomas Aquinas) had so ably demonstrated not to be consubstantial one with the other.

III

The complex bibliographical history of the *Dictionnaire philosophique* has been sketched above.[1] The present volume presents a carefully eclectic text. It is broadly speaking a translation of everything that Voltaire himself printed in successive editions under the title of *Dictionnaire philosophique* or *Dictionnaire philosophique portatif*. Whatever he published under different collective titles has generally been excluded, but when he merely revised the text of the *Dictionnaire* to a minor extent, by way of correction, verbal modification, or the like, the final readings have been adopted.

I have translated direct from the original editions. However, these contain a good many textual defects, most of which have persisted and have even been aggravated in the subsequent editions. I have put these right wherever I have spotted

1. Further details are provided by J. Vercruysse, 'Les Œuvres alphabétiques de Voltaire', *Revue de l'université de Bruxelles* (octobre 1969–janvier 1970), pp. 1–10.

them; usually I have done this silently, but sometimes I have pointed out the changes in the footnotes. However, this is a translation, not a critical edition.

Hardly any adequate English translations of the great French eighteenth-century masterpieces have been made. It is not particularly surprising that this generalization includes the *Dictionnaire philosophique*. What is surprising is that such attempts at translation as have been made have got progressively worse. Indeed the most recent one, published in New York in 1962, contains blunders so numerous and so gross that the mind boggles. Still, it must be admitted that it is not easy to translate Voltaire, especially in his ironical mood, above all because of his masterful manipulation of indirection, vocabulary[1] and word order. A rendering of such a work as the *Dictionnaire philosophique* must be strictly faithful to the meaning and savour of the original, and must also try to recapture as much as possible of Voltaire's inimitable style.

However, it is really too elementary a mistake to reproduce certain features slavishly. Thus the punctuation of the published *Dictionnaire*, especially in its proliferation of semi-colons and colons, has no resemblance to that used by Voltaire in his manuscripts, and not infrequently makes nonsen e of the text. It is thus clearly absurd to perpetuate the often misleading whims of a compositor in editing these early editions, let alone in translating them. I have therefore rationalized the punctuation of the original editions of the *Dictionnaire* to bring it into line with Voltaire's own style and practice. Specifically, I have inserted a good many full-stops and commas into the innumerable un-Voltairean snake-like sentences divided by semi-colons which disfigure all the editions, and which translators have conveyed even into English.

Similar remarks apply to the erratic use of italics and capitals. Finally, in a few cases I have corrected the paragraphing when the compositor ran different subjects together, or vice versa.

1. See, for instance, Jeanne R. Monty, 'Notes sur le vocabulaire du *Dictionnaire philosophique*', *Studies on Voltaire and the Eighteenth Century* (1966), xli. 71–86.

In order to preserve the French sequence of the articles the original titles have been preserved.

IV

One is struck by Voltaire's high standards of accuracy. It is true that modern notions of textual fidelity were unknown in the eighteenth century. The words Voltaire places within quotation marks are not always accurate or even direct quotations. They are seldom so inaccurate as those made by Montesquieu or Diderot, but still every quotation has to be checked, especially as Voltaire often quoted from memory. On the other hand, it will be found that often, when Voltaire has been criticized by the devout for misquoting the *Bible*, he has in fact faithfully translated the Latin Vulgate, which he regarded (wrongly, as we now know) as the best available text. So far as may be I have substituted the translations of the Revised version, but often this is not possible, as explained in the notes; see, for instance, note 6 on '*Ame*'.

However, when it comes to objective facts, Voltaire can seldom be faulted. Even his references to sources are usually accurate, a rare thing in the eighteenth century. Yet the interest of Voltaire's *Dictionnaire philosophique* is in its ideas, not in the worldwide range of facts incidentally adduced. It would therefore be unprofitable, and indeed well-nigh impossible, to attempt anything in the nature of detailed factual annotation. The reader who is curious to know whether the language of Chaldea was really very different from that of Shechem must look to the critical edition now being prepared for the *Complete Works of Voltaire*. Here he will find only the minimum of textual notes and indispensable factual explanations, in addition to occasional remarks on the intellectual content of this enormously influential little book.

Abbé

'Where are you going, *monsieur l'abbé*?'[1] etc. Do you realize that *abbé* means *father*? If you become one you do a service to the state, you undoubtedly do the work a man can do: a thinking being will be born to you. There is something divine in this act.

But if you are *monsieur l'abbé* merely because you have been tonsured, and in order to wear a dog-collar and a short cloak, and to wait for a modest benefice, you do not deserve the name of *abbé*.

The ancient monks gave this name to the superior they elected. The abbot was their spiritual father. How the passage of time changes the meaning of words! The spiritual abbot was a poor man in charge of a few other poor men: but the poor spiritual fathers have since had incomes of 200 or 400,000 *livres*[2]; and there are poor spiritual fathers in Germany today who have regiments of guards.

A poor man who has taken a vow of poverty which leads him to become a monarch! It has already been said, it must be repeated a thousand times, that this is intolerable. The law complains of this abuse, religion is indignant at it, and those

1. This is an agreeable example of one of Voltaire's methods of attack: raking fire from an invisible position. This apparently innocent example of the use of a term he was about to define was in fact the first line of a popular ditty:

> *Où allez-vous, monsieur l'abbé?*
> *Vous allez vous casser le nez.*
> *Vous allez sans chandelle,*
> *Eh bien?*
> *Pour voir les demoiselles,*
> *Vous m'entendez bien.*

'Where are you going, *monsieur l'abbé*? You'll come a cropper since you are going to see the girls in the dark, if you see what I mean.'

2. The *livre* was the same as the franc, equivalent to about five of to-day's new francs, or one United States dollar.

who are really poor, without clothes and food, cry to heaven at the door of *monsieur l'abbé*.

But I hear *messieurs les abbés* of Italy, of Germany, of Flanders, of Burgundy, saying: 'Why should we not accumulate possessions and honours? Why should we not be princes? After all, bishops are. They were originally poor like us, they have enriched themselves, they have elevated themselves. One of them has become superior to kings. Allow us to imitate them as much as we can.'

You are right, gentlemen, overrun the country: it belongs to the strong or the crafty man who seizes it. You have profited from the times of ignorance, of superstition, of folly, to despoil us of our heritage and to trample us underfoot in order to fatten yourselves on the substance of the wretched: tremble lest the day of reason arrive.

Abraham

Abraham is one of the names famous in Asia Minor and in Arabia, like Thoth among the Egyptians, the first Zoroaster in Persia, Hercules in Greece, Orpheus in Thrace, Odin among the northern nations, and so many others whose fame is greater than the authenticity of their history. I speak here only of profane history; for that of the Jews, our teachers and our enemies, whom we believe and detest,[1] having manifestly been written by the holy ghost himself, we feel about it as we must. I refer here only to the Arabs. They boast that they descend from Abraham through Ishmael. They believe that this patriarch built Mecca and died in that city. The fact is that the race of Ishmael has been infinitely more favoured by god than the

1. This sort of thing is common form in Voltaire, and the legend of his anti-Semitism has persisted, and has most recently been given new life by Arthur Hertzberg, *The French Enlightenment and the Jews* (New York, 1968), p. 10, who regards Voltaire as 'the major link in Western intellectual history between the anti-Semitism of classical paganism and the modern age'. This judgement shows some failure to understand Voltaire's language and the intellectual atmosphere of the eighteenth century. Voltaire did not dislike the Jews on 'racial' grounds, but only because they were the people of the *Old Testament* and the precursors of Christianity.

race of Jacob. It is true that both races have produced thieves; but the Arab thieves have been prodigiously superior to the Jewish thieves. The descendants of Jacob conquered only a very small country, which they lost; and the descendants of Ishmael have conquered part of Asia, Europe and Africa, have established an empire vaster than that of the Romans, and have driven the Jews from their caves, which they called the promised land.

If we followed the methods of our modern history books it would be quite hard to believe that Abraham was the father of two such different nations. We are told that he was born in Chaldea, and that he was the son of a poor potter who earned his living by making little clay idols. It is scarcely credible that the son of this potter went to Mecca, 300 leagues away in the tropics, by way of impassable deserts. If he was a conqueror he no doubt aimed at the fine country of Assyria; and if he was only a poor man, as he is depicted, he founded no kingdoms in foreign parts.

Genesis relates that he was seventy-five years old when he departed from the land of Haran after the death of his father, the potter Terah; but the same *Genesis* also says that Terah, having begotten Abraham at the age of seventy, lived to the age of 205, and that Abraham did not leave Haran until after the death of his father. Either the author did not know how to arrange his narrative, or it is clear from *Genesis* itself that Abraham was 135 when he left Mesopotamia. He went from one idolatrous country to another idolatrous country called Shechem, in Palestine. Why did he go there? Why did he leave the fertile banks of the Euphrates for so distant, so sterile and so stony a region as Shechem? The Chaldean language must have been very different from that of Shechem, which was not a trading centre. Shechem is more than a hundred leagues from Chaldea. Deserts have to be traversed to get there. But god wanted him to make this journey, he wanted to show him the land which his descendants were to occupy several centuries later. The human mind has difficulty in grasping the reasons for such a journey.

Hardly had he arrived in the little mountainous country of

Shechem than famine obliged him to leave it. He went to Egypt to seek sustenance. It is 200 leagues from Shechem to Memphis. Is it natural to go so far to ask for grain, and that to a country whose language one does not understand? What strange journeys to undertake at the age of nearly 140!

He brought his wife Sarah to Memphis. She was extremely young, almost a child compared to him, for she was only sixty-five. As she was very beautiful he resolved to turn her beauty to account, and said to her: 'Pretend to be my sister, that it may go well with me for your sake.' He should rather have said: 'Pretend to be my daughter.' The king fell in love with the young Sarah, and gave the self-styled brother many sheep, oxen, asses, she-asses, camels, man-servants and maids: which proves that Egypt was already a very powerful, very civilized, and consequently very ancient kingdom, and that brothers who came and offered their sisters to the kings of Memphis were magnificently rewarded.

According to the scriptures the young Sarah was ninety when god promised her that Abraham, who was then 160, would give her a child that year.

Abraham, who loved to travel, went into the horrible desert of Kadesh with his pregnant wife, still young and still pretty. A king of this desert did not fail to fall in love with Sarah as had the king of Egypt. The father of the faithful told the same lie as in Egypt: he passed off his wife as his sister, and this again earned him a profit of sheep, oxen, men-servants and maids. We might say that Abraham grew very rich by means of his wife. The commentators have written a prodigious number of volumes to justify Abraham's conduct, and to reconcile his chronology. The reader must therefore be referred to these commentaries. They are all written by delicate wits and discerning minds, excellent philosophers, unprejudiced, no pedants.

For the rest, this name *Bram*, *Abram*, was famous in India and Persia: some learned men even allege that he was the same legislator as the one the Greeks called Zoroaster. Others say that he was the Brahma of the Indians, but this has not been proved. But what appears very reasonable to many scholars is that this Abraham was a Chaldean or a Persian. Later on the Jews boasted that they were descended from him, as the Franks descend from Hector, and the Bretons from Tubal. It is certain that the Jewish nation was quite a modern horde; that it did not establish itself near Phoenicia until very late; that it was surrounded by ancient peoples; that it adopted their language; that it took from them the very name of Israel, which is Chaldean, according to the testimony of the Jew Flavius Josephus himself. We know that it took even the names of the angels from the Babylonians; and finally that it was only after the Phoenicians that it gave god the name of Eloi or Eloa, Adonai, Jehovah or Hiao.

It probably knew the name of Abraham or Ibrahim only through the Babylonians; for the ancient religion of all the regions from the Euphrates to the Oxus was called *Kish-Ibrahim*, *Milat-Ibrahim*. All the researches made on the spot by the learned Hyde[1] confirm this.

The Jews thus treat history and ancient fables as their old-clothes-men treat their worn out garments: they turn them and sell them for new at the highest possible price.

It is a singular example of human stupidity that we should for so long have regarded the Jews as a nation which had taught everything to all others, although their historian Josephus himself admits the contrary.

It is difficult to pierce the darkness of antiquity; but it is evident that all the kingdoms of Asia flourished greatly before the vagabond horde of Arabs called Jews possessed a little corner of earth for its own, before it had a town, laws, and a settled religion. Thus, when we consider an ancient rite, an ancient opinion, established both in Egypt or Asia, and among the Jews, it is quite natural to suppose that this little people, new, ignorant, rude, still lacking the arts, copied as best it could the ancient, flourishing and industrious nation.

This is the principle to be followed in judging Judea, Biscay,[2] Cornwall, Bergamo the home of Harlequin, etc.

---

1. Thomas Hyde, the second edition (1760) of whose *Historia religionis veterum Persarum* (1700) was in Voltaire's library.
2. Voltaire means the Basques.

Triumphant Rome certainly in no way imitated Biscay, Cornwall or Bergamo; and a man must be a great ignoramus or a
great rascal to say that the Jews taught the Greeks.[1]

Adam

The pious Mme Bourignon[2] was sure that Adam was a
hermaphrodite, like the divine Plato's first men. God had
revealed this great secret to her; but as I have not received
the same revelations, I shall say nothing of them. The Jewish
rabbis have read the works of Adam; they know the name of
his teacher and of his second wife; but as I have not read
these works of our first parent, I shall not say a word about
them. Some very learned dolts are quite astonished to find,
when they read the *Vedas* of the ancient Brahmans, that the
first man was created in India, etc., that his name was Adimo,
which means the begetter; and that his wife was called Procriti,
which means life. They say that the sect of the Brahmans is
unquestionably more ancient than that of the Jews; that the
Jews could write in the Canaanite language only at a very late
epoch, since they settled very late in the little land of Canaan.
They say that the Indians were always inventors, and the Jews
always imitators, the Indians always ingenious and the Jews
always stupid. They say that it is hard to see how Adam, who
was ruddy and hairy, could have been the father of the
Negroes, who are as black as ink and have black wool on
their heads. What do they not say? As for me, I do not say a
word, I leave these researches to the reverend father Berruyer[2]
of the Society of Jesus: he is the greatest innocent I have ever

1. At the end of this article Voltaire attributed it to the learned Nicolas
Fréret; but this was merely part of his prudential campaign of pretence
that the *Dictionnaire philosophique* was a collective work. However, the
pretence was transparent, it deceived nobody, and was not seriously intended to deceive. It was part of the tacit conspiracy in which all were
involved including the authorities: the important thing was to maintain
the *appearance* of legality.

2. Antoinette Bourignon, a seventeenth-century visionary theologian.

3. Voltaire elsewhere called Joseph Isaac Berruyer's *Histoire du peuple de
dieu* (1728–53, 15 vols.) a 'bad novel' (Best. D5732).

known. His book was burned because the author seemed to ridicule the *Bible :* but I can certify that he did not realize what he was doing.

Ame: Soul

It would be a fine thing to see one's soul. *Know thyself* is an excellent precept, but it is only for god to put it into effect: who but he can know his own essence?

We call soul that which animates. We know little more about it, our intelligence being limited. Three fourths of mankind go no further, and do not worry about this thinking being; the remaining fourth seeks the answer; nobody has found it or will ever find it.

Wretched philosopher, you see a plant that grows, and you say *vegetation*, or even *vegetative soul*. You perceive that bodies have and communicate movement, and you say *force :* you see your gun-dog learn his work under your guidance, and you exclaim *instinct*, *sensitive mind*; you have complex ideas, and you say *wit*.

But for pity's sake what do you understand by these words? This flower grows, but is there a real being called *vegetation*? This body pushes another, but does it possess in itself a distinct being called *force*? This dog retrieves a partridge, but is there a being called *instinct*? Would you not laugh at a reasoner (were he the tutor of Alexander[1]) who told you: 'All animals live, therefore there is in them a being, a substantial form, which is life'?

If a tulip could talk, and told you: 'My vegetation and I are two beings, though obviously joined together', would you not ridicule the tulip?

Let us first see what you know, and of what you are sure: that you walk on your feet, that you digest with your stomach, that you feel with all your body, and that you think with your head. Let us see whether your reason alone could have given you enough understanding to conclude without supernatural help that you have a soul.

1. This is an allusion to Aristotle's animistic theories.

The first philosophers, whether Chaldeans or Egyptians, said: 'There must be something in us that produces our thoughts; this something must be very subtle; it's a breath, it's fire, it's ether, it's a quintessence, it's a faint simulacrum, it's an entelechy, it's a number, it's a harmony.' Finally, according to the divine Plato it is a compound of the *same* and the *other*. 'It is atoms in us that think,' said Epicurus after Democritus. But, my friend, how does an atom think? Admit that you have no idea.

We should undoubtedly adopt the view that the soul is an immaterial being; but you certainly cannot conceive what that immaterial being is. 'No,' reply the learned men, 'but we know that its nature is to think.' And how do you know that? 'We know it because it thinks.' Oh sages! I very much fear that you are as ignorant as Epicurus: it is the nature of a stone to fall because it falls; but I ask you who makes it fall.

'We know', they go on, 'that a stone has no soul.' Quite so, I agree with you. 'We know that a negation and an affirmation are not divisible, do not form parts of matter.' I am of your opinion. But matter, for the rest unknown to us, possesses qualities which are not material, which are not divisible. It has the god-given quality of gravitation towards a centre. Now this gravitation has no parts, is not divisible. The motor force of bodies is not a being composed of parts. Nor does the vegetation of organic bodies, their life, their instinct, constitute distinct beings, divisible beings; you can no more cut in two the vegetation of a rose, the life of a horse, the instinct of a dog, than you can cut in two a feeling, a negation, an affirmation. Thus your fine argument drawn from the indivisibility of thought proves nothing at all.

So what is it that you call your soul? What notion do you have of it? Without revelation you cannot, by your own means, admit anything other in you than an unknown ability to feel, to think.

Now tell me honestly, is this ability to feel and to think the same as that which makes you digest and walk? You will agree with me that it is not, for your understanding could say endlessly to your stomach: *Digest*, it would not obey if it

were ill; your immaterial being would in vain order your feet
to walk, they would stay where they were if they had the gout.

The Greeks saw clearly that thought often had nothing to
do with the play of our organs; they attributed an animal soul
to these organs, and to thought a finer, subtler soul, a *νοῦς*.

But behold, this soul of thought frequently has the ascend-
ancy over the animal soul. The thinking soul orders its hands
to grasp, and they grasp. It does not tell its heart to beat, its
blood to run, its chyle[1] to form; all these things happen without it: so here we have two very perplexed souls which are
hardly masters in their own house.

Now this first animal soul certainly does not exist: it is
nothing but the movement of your organs. Take careful note,
O man, that your feeble reason offers no more proof of the
existence of the other soul. You can know it only by faith.
You are born, you live, you act, you think, you are awake,
you sleep, without knowing how. God has given you the
faculty of thought as he has given you everything else; and
had he not told you in the epochs favoured by his providence
that you have an immaterial and immortal soul you would
not have the slightest proof of it.

Let us consider the fine system your philosophy has fabricated around these souls.

One claims that the soul of man is part of the substance of
god himself; another, that it is part of the great whole; a
third, that it is created from all eternity; a fourth, that it is
made, and not created; others assert that god forms them as
they are needed, and that they arrive at the moment of copulation. 'They lodge in the seminal animalculae,' cries one. 'No,'
says another, 'they occupy the fallopian tubes.' 'You are
mistaken,' says a newcomer, 'the soul waits six weeks for the
foetus to be formed, and then takes possession of the pineal
gland; but if it hits on an abortion it turns back and waits for
a better opportunity.' The latest opinion is that it inhabits
the *corpus callosum*[2]; this is the site assigned to it by La Pey-

1. Voltaire is using this technical term in its colloquial application to
the bile.

2. This is an inner part of the *cerebrum*.

ronie[1]; one has to be first surgeon to the king of France to regulate thus the soul's lodging. Nevertheless his *corpus callosum* has not had as great a career as the surgeon himself.

Saint Thomas, in his seventy-fifth and following questions,[2] says that the soul is a form *subsistante per se*, that it is all in all, that its essence differs from its power, that there are three vegetative souls, that is, the *nutritive*, the *augmentative*, the *generative*; that the memory of things spiritual is spiritual, and that the memory of things corporal is corporal; that the rational soul is a form 'immaterial in its functions, and material in its being'. Saint Thomas wrote two thousand pages just as forceful and as lucid, so he is the angel of the schoolmen.

Just as many systems have been created about the soul's feelings when it has left the body with which it felt; how it will hear without ears, smell without a nose, and touch without hands; which body it will afterwards resume, the one it had at the age of two or at eighty; how the I, the identity of the same person, will subsist; how the soul of a man become an imbecile at the age of fifteen, and dead imbecile at the age of seventy, will pick up the thread of the ideas it had at the age of puberty; by what feat of skill a soul whose leg had been cut off in Europe and which had lost an arm in America, will recover this leg and this arm, which, having been transformed into vegetables, had passed into the blood of some other animal. One would never be done if one wanted to give an account of all the extravagances this wretched human soul has imagined about itself.

What is very singular is that in all the laws of god's people there is not a word about the spirituality and the immortality of the soul. There is nothing in the decalogue, nothing in *Leviticus* nor in *Deuteronomy*.

It is quite certain, it is indubitable that Moses nowhere promised the Jews rewards and punishments in another life, that he never talked to them about the immortality of their

1. The surgeon François Gigot de La Peyronie, who specialized, among other things, in diseases of the brain.
2. Of the angelical doctor's *Summa theologica*, the authoritative textbook of the Roman church.

souls, that he never held out hopes of heaven, that he did not threaten them with hell: all is temporal.

Before he died he told them in his *Deuteronomy*:[1]

If you misbehave after you have had children and grandchildren you will be exterminated from the land and reduced to a few among the nations.

I am a jealous god, who punishes the iniquity of the fathers to the third and fourth generation.

Honour your father and mother so that you may live long.

You will have food without ever lacking any.

If you follow strange gods you will be destroyed . . .

If you obey you will have rain in the spring; and in the autumn wheat, oil, hay for your cattle, so that you may eat your fill.

Preserve these words in your hearts, in your hands, between your eyes, write them over your doors, so that your days be multiplied.

Do what I order you without adding or omitting anything.

If there arrives a prophet who foretells prodigies, and his prediction is true, and what he has said comes to pass, and he says to you: 'Come, let us follow strange gods . . .', kill him at once, and let every man strike him after you.

When the lord delivers the other nations to you, slaughter them all without sparing a single man, and have no pity for anyone.

Do not eat impure birds like the eagle, the griffin, the ixion, etc.

Do not eat animals that chew the cud and whose nails are not[2] cloven, like the camel, the hare, the porcupine, etc.

By observing all ordinances you will be blessed in the town and in the fields; the fruits of your belly, your land, your cattle will be blessed. . .

If you do not keep all the ordinances and all the ceremonies you will be cursed in the town and in the fields. . . . You will suffer famine, poverty: you will die of wretchedness, of cold, of poverty, of fever; you will have the mange, the itch, ulcers. . . . You will have boils in the knees and the calves of your legs.

The stranger will lend to you at interest, but you shall not lend

1. Voltaire sets out what follows as a direct quotation, but of course it is a typically eighteenth-century mosaic of more or less faithful bits and pieces, translated by him from the Vulgate; it would be quite misleading to render such an amalgam in the language of the *Bible*.

2. Voltaire misread the text.

to him at interest[1]. . . because you will not have served the Lord.

And you will eat the fruit of your belly, and the flesh of your sons and your daughters, etc.

It is obvious that everything is temporal in all these promises and in all these threats, and that not a word is to be found on the immortality of the soul and the future life.

Several illustrious commentators believed that Moses was perfectly aware of these two great dogmas; and they prove it by the words of Jacob who, thinking that his son had been devoured by wild beasts, said in his sorrow: 'I will descend with my son into the grave, *in infernum*, into hell', that is, I will die since my son is dead.[2]

They prove it further by passages in *Isaiah* and *Ezekiel*; but the Hebrews to whom Moses spoke could not have read either Ezekiel or Isaiah, who did not live until several centuries later.

It is quite useless to argue about the hidden opinions of Moses. The fact is that he never spoke in the public laws of a life to come, that he limited all punishments and all rewards to the present. If he knew of the future life, why did he not explicitly proclaim this great dogma? And if he did not know it, what was the object of his mission? This question has been put by a number of great personages; they reply that the master of Moses and of all men reserved to himself the right to explain to the Jews in his own time a doctrine they were incapable of understanding when they were in the desert.

If Moses had announced the dogma of the immortality of the soul, a large school of Jews would not always have opposed it; this great school of the Sadducees would not have been authorized in the state; the Sadducees would not have filled the highest offices; no great pontiffs would have been drawn from their ranks.

---

1. *Exodus* xxiii. 20 in fact permits lending upon usury to foreigners, forbidding it only between 'brothers'.

2. This interpretation of the Vulgate is confirmed by the Revised version, which reads: 'For I will go down to the grave to my son mourning', although the marginal note points out that the Hebrew word is *sheol*, the abode of the dead (*Genesis* xxxvii. 35).

It appears that it was not until after the foundation of Alexandria that the Jews divided themselves into three sects: the Pharisees, the Sadducees and the Essenes. The historian Josephus, who was a Pharisee, tells us in book XIII of his *Antiquities* that the Pharisees believed in metempsychosis; the Sadducees believed that the soul dies with the body; the Essenes, adds Josephus, held souls to be immortal: according to them souls descended into bodies, in aerial form, from the highest region of the air; they are carried back there by a violent attraction, and after death those that belonged to good people live beyond the ocean, in a land in which there is neither heat nor cold, nor wind, nor rain. The souls of the wicked go to a very different climate. Such was the theology of the Jews.

He who alone was to teach all men condemned these three sects; but without him we should never have been able to know anything about our soul, since philosophers have never had any settled notion of it, and since Moses, the world's only true legislator before our own, Moses, who spoke with god face to face and saw him only from behind, left men in profound ignorance about this great matter. It is therefore only for 1,700 years that we have been certain of the existence of the soul, and its immortality.

Cicero had nothing but doubts; his grandson and granddaughter were able to learn the truth from the first Galileans who came to Rome.

But before that time, and since then in all the rest of the world into which the apostles did not penetrate, every man must have said to his soul: 'Who are you? Whence do you come? What are you doing? Where are you going? I don't know what you are, but you think and feel, and were you to feel and think for a hundred thousand million years, you would never understand it better by your own intelligence, without the help of god.'

O man! This god has given you understanding in order to behave well, and not to penetrate the essence of the things he has created.

So thought Locke, and before Locke, Gassendi, and before

Gassendi a multitude of wise men; but we have novices who know all that these great men did not know.

Some cruel enemies of reason have dared to rise up against these truths acknowledged by all wise men. They have carried bad faith and impudence so far as to impute to the authors of this work[1] the assertion that the soul is matter. Persecutors of innocence, you know very well that we have said the exact contrary. You must have read these very words: 'But my friend how does an atom think? Admit that you know nothing about it.' So obviously you are slanderers.

Nobody knows what really is the being called *spirit*, to which even you give the material name of *spirit*, which means wind. It is impossible for limited beings like us to know whether our intelligence is substance or faculty: we cannot completely know either extended substance nor the thinking being nor the mechanism of thought.

We assure you, with the respected Gassendi and Locke, that we know nothing by ourselves of the creator's secrets. Are you then gods who know all? We repeat that it is only by revelation that we can know the nature and the destination of the soul. What then! Is this revelation not enough for you? You must certainly be enemies of the revelation on which we insist since you persecute those who expect everything from it, and who believe in it alone.

We repeat that we rely on the word of god; and you, enemies of reason and of god, you who blaspheme the one and the other, you treat the humble doubt and the humble submission of the philosopher as the wolf treated the lamb in Aesop's fables; you tell him: 'You spoke ill of me last year, I must suck your blood.' Such is your conduct. As you know, you have persecuted wisdom because you thought that the wise men despised you. It is well known that you have said so, you have felt your own merit, and you wanted to avenge yourself. Philosophy takes no revenge; she laughs peacefully at your vain efforts; she gently enlightens mankind,

1. That is, the *Dictionnaire philosophique* itself; the reader is reminded that some passages were added by Voltaire in the second and subsequent editions.

whom you want to brutalize so that they should become like you.

Amitié: Friendship

This is the marriage of the soul, it is a contract between two sensitive and virtuous persons. I say *sensitive* because a monk, a solitary, may not be at all wicked and live without knowing friendship. I say *virtuous* because the wicked have only accomplices, the voluptuous have companions in debauchery, self-seekers have associates, the politic assemble the factions, the typical idler has connections, princes have courtiers. Only the virtuous have friends. Cethegus was the accomplice of Catiline, and Maecenas the courtier of Octavius, but Cicero was the friend of Atticus.

What does this contract between two tender and honest minds contain? Its obligations are stronger or weaker according to the degree of sensibility of the friends and the number of services rendered, etc.

The enthusiasm of friendship was stronger among the Greeks and among the Arabs than among us. The tales these peoples have invented about friendship are admirable; we have none like them, we are a little cool in everything.

Friendship was a matter of religion and of legislation among the Greeks. The Thebans had the lovers' regiment: a fine regiment! Some have supposed that it was a regiment of sodomites. They are mistaken. This is to take the incidental for the essential. Friendship among the Greeks was prescribed by law and religion. Paederasty was unfortunately tolerated by custom. We must not impute shameful abuses to the law.

Amour: Love

Amor omnibus idem.[1] Here we must have recourse to the physical: it is the stuff of nature which the imagination has embroid-

1. Virgil, *Georgics* iii. 244: 'All feel the same love'.

ered. If you want to have some idea of love, look at the sparrows in your garden; look at your pigeons; contemplate the bull when he is presented to your heifer; look at this proud horse whom two of his grooms lead to the peaceful mare who awaits him and who turns aside her tail to receive him; see his eyes sparkle; listen to his neighing; contemplate these leaps, these curvettings, these erect ears, this mouth that opens with little convulsions, these nostrils that flare, this fiery breath that leaves them, this mane that rises and waves, this imperious movement with which he springs on to the object his nature has destined for him; but do not be envious, and reflect on the advantages enjoyed by the human species: in love they compensate all those that nature has given to animals: strength, beauty, lightness, speed.

There are even animals who know nothing of sexual pleasure. Scaled fishes are deprived of this consolation: the female drops millions of eggs in the slime; the male who encounter them passes over and fertilizes them with his seed, without caring to what female they belong.

Most of the animals that couple taste pleasure through only a single sense; and all is quenched as soon as this appetite is satisfied. Apart from you, no animal knows love-making; your whole body is sensitive; above all, your lips enjoy a voluptuousness that nothing wearies, and this pleasure belongs to your species alone; finally, you can have sexual intercourse at all times, and animals only at fixed times. If you reflect on these pre-eminent advantages you will say with the earl of Rochester: 'Love would cause a nation of atheists to adore the divinity.'

As men have received the gift of perfecting all that nature has granted them, they have perfected love. Cleanliness, self-care, make the skin more delicate and thus increase the pleasure of contact, and attention to its health renders the organs of voluptuousness more sensitive.

All the other feelings then enter into that of love, like metals that amalgamate with gold: friendship, respect, come to its aid; the skills of body and mind are still further bonds.

Nam facit ipsa suis interdum fœmina factis,
Morigerisque modis, et mundo corpore cultu,
Ut facile insuescat secum vir degere vitam.[1]

Above all, vanity tightens all these bonds. We applaud our choice, and crowding illusions are the ornaments of this structure the foundations of which have been laid by nature.

These are the things that raise you above the animals; but, if you taste so many pleasures unknown to them, what sorrows also of which the beasts have no idea! What is frightful for you is that in three quarters of the earth nature has poisoned the pleasures of love and the sources of life with an appalling disease to which only man is subject and which infects only his organs of generation.

This pestilence is not at all like so many other maladies that are the consequences of our excesses. It was not introduced in the world by debauchery. The Phrynes, the Laises, the Floras, the Messalinas were never attacked by it; it was born in islands on which men lived in a state of innocence, and spread thence in the ancient world.

If one could ever have accused nature of despising its work, of contradicting its plan, of acting against its intentions, it would have been in this instance. Is that the best of possible worlds? Come! it is true that Caesar, Antony, Octavius never had this disease; but was it not possible to save Francis I from being killed by it? No, it is said, matters were so ordained for the best: I should like to believe it, but it is sad for those to whom Rabelais dedicated his book.[2]

Amour nommé socratique: So-called Socratic love

How did it come about that a vice destructive of mankind if it were general, an infamous outrage against nature, is

1. 'Lucrèce, liv. V' says Voltaire: in fact Lucretius, *De rerum natura* iv. 1280–82: 'For a woman sometimes so arranges her conduct, by obliging ways and the good care of her body, that she accustoms one to live with her.'

2. The prologue of the first book of *Gargantua* is addressed to 'Very illustrious drinkers and, you, very precious poxed ones ...'

yet so natural? It appears to be the highest degree of deliberate corruption, and is nevertheless the ordinary lot of those
who have not yet had time to be corrupted. It has penetrated
unspoilt hearts that have not yet known ambition nor fraud
nor the thirst for wealth; it is blind youth that flings itself
into this disorder upon leaving childhood, by an instinct
still little understood.

The inclination of the two sexes for each other declares
itself early; but, whatever has been said of the women of
Africa and southern Asia, this inclination is generally much
stronger in the man than in the woman; this is a law that nature
has fixed for all animals. It is always the male that attacks the
female.

The young males of our species, brought up together,
feeling the force which nature begins to display in them,
and not finding the natural object of their instinct, fall back
on what resembles it. A young boy often resembles a beautiful girl for two or three years by the freshness of his com-
plexion, the brilliance of his colour, and the tenderness of
his eyes; if he is loved it is because nature is led astray:
homage is paid to the fair sex by attaching oneself to one who
has its beauties, and when his age has made this resemblance
vanish, the mistake ceases.

> *Citraque juventam*
> *Aetatis breve ver et primos carpere flores.*[1]

It is well known that this error of nature is much commoner
in mild climates than in the northern ice, because the blood
is more inflamed there and opportunity more common:
hence what seems merely a weakness in the young Alcibiades
is a disgusting abomination in a Dutch sailor and a Musco-
vite camp-follower.

I cannot suffer the allegation that the Greeks authorized
this abuse. The legislator Solon is cited because he said in

1. Ovid, *Metamorphoses* x. 84–5; here Voltaire, knowing that many
of his readers would recognize the passage, quoted only the end; lines
83–5: '[Orpheus] offered the example to the people of Thrace by giving
his love to tender boys, and enjoying the springtime and first flower of
their youth.'

two bad lines: 'You will cherish a handsome boy so long as his chin is beardless.' But was Solon in fact a legislator when he wrote these two ridiculous lines? He was young then, and when the debauchee became a sage, he did not include such an infamy among the laws of his republic; it is as if one accused Theodore Beza of having preached paederasty in his church because in his youth he addressed some verse to the young Candide, and said:

Amplector hunc et illam.[1]

Among his chitchat Plutarch makes one of the interlocutors say in the *Dialogue on Love* that women are not worthy of true love; but this text has been misused, for another interlocutor properly takes the women's part.

It is certain, so far as knowledge of antiquity can be, that Socratic love was not an infamous love: what has misled us is this word love. Those who were called 'a young man's lovers' were precisely like those who are today the companions of our princes. They were the children of honour: young men devoted to the education of a distinguished child, sharing the same studies, the same military labours, a martial and sacred institution which was misused as were nocturnal festivities and orgies.

The troop of lovers instituted by Laius was an invincible troop of young warriors bound by oath to give their lives for one another; and this is the finest thing ancient discipline ever produced.

It is useless for Sextus Empiricus and others to say that paederasty was prescribed by the laws of Persia. Let them cite the text of the law; let them produce the code of the Persians; even if they produced it I still would not believe it, I would say that the allegation is untrue because it is impossible. No, it is not in human nature to make a law that contradicts and outrages nature, a law that would annihilate

1. Many of his critics were scandalized by the line '*Amplector quoque, sic et hunc et illam*' ('So I love both him and her') which occurs in Théodore de Bèze's epigram *De sua in Candidam et Audebertum benevolentia*, Audebert being a fellow poet, Candide the girl he loved.

the human species if it were strictly observed. How many people have mistaken shameful and tolerated practices in a country for the laws of that country! Sextus Empiricus, who doubted everything, must really have doubted this jurisprudence. If he lived today and saw two or three young Jesuits take advantage of a few pupils, would he be entitled to say that the constitutions of Ignatius of Loyola permit them to behave like this?

The love of boys was so common in Rome that there was no thought of punishing this nonsense, in which everybody indulged heedlessly. Octavius Augustus, that debauched and cowardly murderer, who dared to exile Ovid, approved of Virgil when he sang Alexis, and Horace when he composed little odes for Ligurinus; but the ancient law called *Scantinia*,[1] which prohibited paederasty, always survived; the emperor Philip again enforced it and chased out of Rome the little boys who traded in it. Finally, I don't believe that there has ever been a civilized nation which has legislated against morality.[2]

1. The *Lex Scantinia* 'against sexual abomination' was named after a first-century B.C. legislator.

2. This footnote was added by Voltaire in 1769; still later he replaced the dots at the beginning by 'nonconformists': *Messieurs* the . . . ought to be condemned to present the police every year with a child of their own making. The *abbé* Desfontaines was on the point of being roasted in the place de Grève for having taken advantage of some little climbing-boys who were sweeping his chimney. Some patrons[3] saved him. A victim was needed: Deschaufours[4] was roasted in his place. That was going too far; *est modus in rebus*:[5] the punishment should fit the crime; what would Caesar, Alcibiades, Nicomedas, king of Bithynia, Henry III, king of France, and so many other kings have said?

When they burned Deschaufours they based themselves on the *Etablissements de saint Louis*, translated into French in the fifteenth century. 'If anyone is suspected of . . .[6] he shall be taken to the bishop; and if it is proved

3. Pierre François Guyot Desfontaines was saved from the stake by Voltaire himself.

4. Etienne Benjamin Des Chaufours was burnt for sodomy in 1726, just after Desfontaines had his lucky escape.

5. 'There is a middle way in all things.'

6. This word Voltaire never supplied, but it was '*bougrerie*', 'buggery'.

Amour-propre: Self-love

A vagabond grandly asked for alms near Madrid. A passer-by said to him: 'Aren't you ashamed to carry on this infamous trade when you can work?' 'Sir,' replied the beggar, 'I am asking for your money, not for advice'; then he turned his back, preserving all his Castilian dignity. This gentleman was a proud vagabond; it took little to wound his vanity. He asked for alms out of self-love, and could not bear to be reprimanded by another self-love.

A missionary travelling in India met a fakir loaded with chains, as naked as a monkey, lying on his stomach, and having himself whipped for the sins of his fellow countrymen the Indians, who gave him a few farthings. 'What self-renunciation!' said one of the spectators. 'Self-renunciation!' answered the fakir. 'Know that I have myself lashed in this world only to pay you back in the other, when you will be horses and I a horseman.'

Those who have said that self-love is the basis of all our feelings and of all our actions were therefore quite right in India, in Spain, and in all the habitable world: and just as no one writes to prove to men that they have faces, there is no need to prove to them that they have self-love. This self-love is the instrument of our conservation; it resembles the instrument that perpetuates the species: it is necessary, it is dear to us, it gives us pleasure, and it must be hidden.

---

against him, he shall be burnt, and all his goods belong to the baron, etc.' But saint Louis did not say what should be done to the baron if the baron is suspected of . . . and *if it is proved against him*. It should be noted that by the word . . . saint Louis means heretics, who were then given no other name. It was by a misunderstanding that Deschaufours, a gentleman of Lorraine, was burned in Paris. Despréaux[1] was quite right to compose a satire against misunderstandings; they have done much more harm than people think.

1. Now better known as Boileau.

Ange: Angel

Angel, in Greek, *messenger*; we shall hardly know more of them when we learn that the Persians had *Peris*, the Hebrews *Malakim*, the Greeks their *Daimonoi*.

But what we shall perhaps find more instructive is the fact that one of mankind's first notions has always been to place intermediary beings between divinity and us. It is these demons, these genii that antiquity invented. Princes were seen to intimate their orders through messengers, therefore divinity also sends its couriers: Mercury, Iris were couriers, messengers.

The Hebrews, the only people guided by divinity itself, at first gave no names to the angels god finally deigned to send them. They borrowed the names given to them by the Chaldeans[1] when the Jewish nation was captive in Babylonia, Michael and Gabriel were first named by Daniel, a slave of that people. The Jew Tobit, who lived at Nineveh, knew the angel Raphael, who travelled with his son to help him collect some money which the Jew Gabael owed him.

In the laws of the Jews, that is, *Leviticus* and *Deuteronomy*, there is not the slightest reference to the existence of angels, let alone their worship. Moreover, the Sadducees did not believe in angels.

But they are talked about a great deal in the histories of the Jews. The angels were corporeal. They had wings on their backs, as the Gentiles pretended that Mercury had on his heels. Sometimes they hid their wings under their clothes. How could they have lacked bodies since they drank and ate, and the inhabitants of Sodom wanted to commit the sin of paederasty with the angels who visted Loth?

The ancient Jewish tradition, according to Maimonides, acknowledges ten degrees, ten orders of angels: 1. The

---

1. It is very rare indeed to find anything obscure in Voltaire, but here for once the meaning is not clear: '*ils empruntèrent les noms que leur donnaient les Chaldéens*' may mean that the Jews took Chaldean names or that the Chaldeans gave these names to the angels.

chaios acodesh, pure, saintly. 2. The *ofamin*, swift. 3. The *oralim*, the strong. 4. The *chasmalim*, the flames. 5. The *seraphim*, sparks. 6. The *malachim*, angels, messengers, deputies. 7. The *eloim*, the gods or judges. 8. The *ben eloim*, children of the gods. 9. *cherubim*, images. 10. *ychim*, the animated.

The story of the fall of the angels is not in the books of Moses; the first reported witness to it is that of the prophet Isaiah, who, apostrophizing the king of Babylon, exclaimed: 'What has become of the extorter of tribute? The pines and the cedars rejoice in his fall; how are you fallen from heaven, oh Hellel, star of the morning?'[1] This Hellel has been translated by the Latin word *Lucifer*; then the name of Lucifer was given allegorically to the prince of the angels who battled in heaven; and finally this name, which means phosphorus and dawn, has become the name of the devil.

The Christian religion is based on the fall of the angels. Those who rebelled were thrown down from the spheres they inhabited into the hell at the centre of the earth, and became devils. A devil in the shape of a serpent tempted Eve, and damned mankind. Jesus came to redeem mankind and to triumph over the devil, who still tempts us. Nevertheless this fundamental tradition is found only in the apocryphal book of *Enoch*, and even there in a form quite different from the accepted tradition.

In his 109th letter saint Augustine does not hesitate to endow both good and evil angels with slender and agile bodies. Pope Gregory II reduced to nine choirs, nine hierarchies or orders, the ten choirs of angels recognized by the Jews: they are the seraphim, cherubim, thrones, dominations, virtues, powers,[2] archangels and finally the angels who give that name to eight other hierarchies.

In their temple the Jews had two cherubim, each with

1. *Isaiah* xiv. 5, 8 and 12; the Lucifer of the Vulgate and the Authorized version appears as 'day star' in the Revised version; *lucifer* in classical Latin meant 'light-bringing' and, hence, the morning-star; φωσφορος is the equivalent Greek word.

2. Voltaire speaks of nine hierarchies, but only lists eight; here he accidentally omitted the principalities.

two heads, one of an ox and the other of an eagle, with six wings. Today we paint them in the image of a flying head, with two little wings below the ears. We paint the angels and archangels in the image of youth, with two wings on their backs. As for the thrones and dominations, nobody has yet taken it into his head to paint them.

Saint Thomas, in the second article of question 108, says that the thrones are as close to god as the cherubim and seraphim because it is on them that god is seated. Scotus has counted a thousand million angels. The ancient mythology of the good and evil genii having passed from the east to Greece and to Rome we hallow this view in accepting that every man has a good and an evil angel, one of whom helps and the other harms him from his birth until his death; but we do not yet know whether these good and evil angels pass continuously from one post to another, or whether they are relieved by others. On this matter consult the *Summa* of saint Thomas.

It is not precisely known where the angels live, whether it is in the air, in the void, or the planets: god has not wished us to know it.

Anthropophages: Cannibals

I have spoken of love. It is hard to pass from people who embrace each other to people who eat each other. It is only too true that there have been cannibals. Some have been found in America. There may still be some, and the cyclops were not the only ones in antiquity who sometimes fed on human flesh. Juvenal reports that among the Egyptians, so wise a people, so famous for its laws, so pious a people, who worshipped crocodiles and onions, the Denderites ate one of their enemy who had fallen into their hands. He does not tell this story on hearsay: this crime was committed almost under his eyes; he was then in Egypt, not far from Dendera. In this connection he cites the Gascons and the Sagantines, who formerly fed on the flesh of their countrymen.

In 1725 four savages were brought from the Mississippi to

Fontainebleau. I had the honour to converse with them. Among them was a lady of that country whom I asked whether she had eaten men. She replied very innocently that she had. I appeared a little scandalized. She excused herself by saying that it was better to eat one's dead enemy than to let him be devoured by beasts, and the victors deserved to have the preference.[1] We kill our neighbours in pitched or unpitched battle, and for the meanest rewards prepare meals for the crows and the worms. There is the horror, there is the crime. When one has been killed what does it matter whether one is eaten by a soldier or by a crow or a dog?

We respect the dead more than the living. We ought to respect both. Nations called civilized are right not to put their vanquished enemies on the spit, for if we were permitted to eat our neighbours we would soon eat our fellow countrymen, which would be a mixed blessing for the social virtues. But the civilized nations have not always been civilized; all were for long savage; and in the infinite number of revolutions this globe has undergone, the human species has sometimes been numerous, sometimes very rare. What is happening today to elephants, lions, tigers, whose numbers have much decreased, once happened to mankind. In times when a region was little inhabited by men, they had few arts, they were hunters. The habit of feeding on what they had killed readily caused them to treat their enemies like their stags and their boars. It was superstition that caused human victims to be immolated, it was necessity that caused them to be eaten.

Which is the greater crime, piously to assemble to plunge a knife into the heart of a young girl adorned with fillets, in honour of the divinity, or to eat a villain who has been killed in self-defence?

Nevertheless we have many more examples of girls and boys who have been sacrificed than of girls and boys who have been eaten. The Jews immolated them. This was called the anathema. It was a real sacrifice, and it is commanded in the

---

1. Voltaire tells substantially the same story in a letter of October 1737 (Best. D 1376) and in the *Essai sur les mœurs*, cxlvi, though in his letter he places it in 1723.

twenty-seventh chapter of *Leviticus* not to spare the living souls who had been devoted to god,[1] but it is nowhere prescribed that they should be eaten, they are merely threatened with this fate. And Moses, as we have seen, said to the Jews that, if they did not observe these ceremonies, not only would they have the itch but mothers would eat their children. It is true that in Ezekiel's time the Jews must have been in the habit of eating human flesh, for in chapter xxxix he predicts to them that god would make them eat not only the horses of their enemies but also the horsemen and the other warriors.[2] This is definite. And in fact why should the Jews not have been cannibals? It would have been the only thing the people of god lacked to be the most abominable on earth.

I have read in some anecdotes on the history of England in Cromwell's time that a tallow-chandler in Dublin sold excellent candles made of the fat of Englishmen. Some time after one of her customers complained that her candles were no longer so good. 'Alas,' she said, 'it's because we have been short of Englishmen this month.' I ask who were the guiltier, those who murdered Englishmen or this woman who made their grease into candles?

Antitrinitaires: Anti-trinitarians

There are heretics who might not be regarded as Christians. Nevertheless they recognize Jesus to be saviour and mediator; but they dare to maintain that nothing is more contrary to strict reason than what is taught among Christians about the trinity of persons in a single divine essence, the second of which was begotten by the first, and the third of which proceeds from the two others.

1. *Leviticus* xxvii. 29: 'None devoted, which shall be devoted of men, shall be ransomed; he shall surely be put to death.'
2. *Ezekiel* xxxix. 18–20: 'Ye shall eat the flesh of the mighty, and drink the blood of the princes of the earth. . . . And ye shall be filled at my table with horses and chariots, with mighty men, and with all men of war, saith the Lord GOD.' Of course in Voltaire's time it was still thought that if the *Bible* is the word of god its language must mean what it says.

That this unintelligible doctrine is nowhere found in scripture.

That no passage can be produced that authorizes it and to which, without in any way departing from the spirit of the text, a clearer, more natural meaning cannot be given, one more consistent with common sense and the basic and immutable truths.

That to maintain, as do their adversaries, that there are several distinct *persons* in the divine essence, and that it is not the eternal who is the only true god, but that the son and the holy ghost must be added to them, is to introduce the crudest and most dangerous error into the church of Jesus Christ, since it manifestly encourages polytheism.

That it implies a contradiction to say that there is only one god and that nevertheless there are three *persons*, each of which is truly god.

That this distinction, one essence and three persons, was never in scripture.

That it is obviously false, since it is certain that there are no fewer *essences* then *persons*, nor *persons* than *essences*.

That the three persons of the trinity are either three different substances, or accidents of the divine essence, or that same essence without distinction.

That in the first case three gods are created.

That in the second case god is composed of accidents and one worships accidents and metamorphoses accidents into persons.

That in the third case an indivisible subject is uselessly and groundlessly divided, and what is not distinguished in itself is distinguished into *three*.

That if it is said that the three *personalities* are neither different substances in the divine essence, nor accidents of that essence, one would have to be at some pains to convince oneself that they are anything.

That it must not be believed that the most rigid and the most convinced *trinitarians* themselves have any clear idea of the manner in which the three *hypostases* subsist in god without dividing his substance and consequently without multiplying it.

That saint Augustine himself, after he had advanced a thousand reasonings as false as they are obscure on this subject, was obliged to admit that nothing intelligible could be said about it.

Then they quote this father's words, which are in fact very singular: 'When it is asked', says he, 'what are the *three*, human language is found inadequate, and there are no terms to express them: yet it is said that there are *three persons*, not in order to say something, but because we must speak and not remain silent. *Dictum est tres personae, non ut aliquid diceretur, sed ne taceretur*'(*De Trinitate* V. ix).

That the modern theologians have not elucidated this matter any better.

That when they are asked what they understand by this word *person*, they explain it only by saying that it is a certain incomprehensible distinction that causes one to distinguish in a numerically single nature a father, a son and a holy ghost.

That the explanation they give of the terms *to beget* and *to proceed* is not more satisfactory since it comes down to saying that these terms indicate certain incomprehensible relationships between the three persons of the trinity.

That from all this we can gather that the basic argument between them and the orthodox turns on the question whether there are in god three distinctions of which we have no notion and between which there are certain relationships of which we do not have any notion either.

From all this they conclude that it would be wiser to abide by the authority of the apostles, who never spoke of the trinity, and to banish from religion for ever all terms which are not in the scriptures, such as *trinity, person, essence, hypostasis, hypostatic and personal union, incarnation, generation, procession,* and so many more like them, which, being absolutely meaningless, since they have no real representative being in nature, can provoke only false, vague, obscure and incomplete ideas in the understanding.[1]

1. Here Voltaire added 'Taken in large part from the article "Unitaire" of the Encylopédie'; but this also was part of his campaign of indirection.

Let us add to this article what dom Calmet says in his dissertation[1] on this passage from the epistle of *John* the evangelist: 'There are three who bear witness on earth, the spirit, and the water, and the blood: and the three agree in one. There are three who bear witness in heaven, the Father, the Word, and the Spirit; and these three are one.'[2] Dom Calmet admits that these two passages are not in any ancient *Bible*; and it would indeed have been strange if saint John had spoken of the trinity in a letter, without saying a single word about it in his gospel. No trace of this dogma is to be found in the canonical gospels, nor in the apocryphal ones. All these reasons could excuse the anti-trinitarians had the councils not taken their decisions. But as heretics make light of councils, we are at a loss to know how to confound them. Let us simply believe and hope that they believe.

Apis

Was the bull Apis worshipped at Memphis as a god, as a symbol, or as a bull? It seems likely that fanatics regarded him as a god, wise men as a simple symbol, and that the stupid worshipped the bull. Was Cambysis right to kill this bull with his own hand when he conquered Egypt? Why not? He showed fools that their god could be put on a spit without nature taking the trouble to avenge this sacrilege. Great things have been said about the Egyptians. I know of no more contemptible people. There must always have been a radical defect, in their character and their government, which has always made vile slaves of them. I agree that they conquered the earth in times almost unknown; but in historic times they have

1. The vast theological commentaries of the Benedictine Antoine Augustin Calmet were one of Voltaire's primary sources; although he properly ridiculed these works Voltaire had a warm personal regard for Calmet himself; his library included the *Commentaire littéral sur tous les livres de l'Ancien et du Nouveau testament* (1709-34, 25 vols.), and other works by him.

2. I *John* v. 8-7 in the Latin Vulgate; in the Revised version verse 7 appears as 'And it is the Spirit that beareth witness, because the Spirit is the truth.'

been subjugated by all those who cared to take the trouble, by the Assyrians, by the Persians, by the Greeks, by the Romans, by the Arabs, by the Mameluks, by the Turks, in short by everybody except our crusaders, who were even greater blunderers than the Egyptians were cowards. It was the Mameluk militia that beat the French. There are perhaps only two tolerable things about this nation: the first, that those who worshipped a bull never tried to compel those who worshipped a monkey to change their religion; the second, that they have always hatched chickens in ovens.

Their pyramids are praised; but they are the monuments of a nation of slaves. The whole people must have been made to work on them, for otherwise these ugly masses could never have been erected. What were they for? To preserve in a small chamber the mummy of some prince or some governor or some intendant, which his soul was to revive after a thousand years had passed. But if they hoped for this resurrection of bodies, why remove their brains before embalming them? Were the Egyptians to be resuscitated without brains?

Apocalypse

Justin Martyr, who wrote about the year 170 of our era, was the first who mentioned the *Apocalypse*[1]; he attributed it to the apostle John the evangelist. In his dialogue with Trypho, this Jew asks Justin whether he does not believe that Jerusalem would be restored one day. Justin replies that like all right-thinking Christians he thinks it will. 'There was among us', he says, 'a certain personage named John, one of the twelve apostles of Jesus; he predicted that the faithful would pass a thousand years in Jerusalem.'

This reign of a thousand years was an opinion long held by Christians. It was a period much favoured among the gentiles. The souls of the Egyptians recovered their bodies at the end of a thousand years. In Virgil souls in purgatory were tried during the same space of time, *et mille per annos*.[2] The new

1. Better known to English readers as the book of *Revelation*.
2. 'And for a thousand years.'

Jerusalem of a thousand years was to have twelve doors in memory of the twelve apostles; its form was to be square; its length, width and height were to be 12,000 *stadia*, that is, 500 leagues, so that the houses were also to be 500 leagues high. It would have been rather disagreeable to live on the top floor; still, this is what the *Apocalypse* says in chapter xxi.

Justin is the first who attributed the *Apocalypse* to saint John, but some people have challenged his testimony because in this same dialogue with the Jew Trypho he says that according to the narrative of the apostles when Jesus Christ went into the Jordan he made the waters of this river boil, and set them on fire, though this is not found in any of the apostles' writings.

The same saint Justin confidently cites the oracles of the sybils. What is more, he claims to have seen in the Egyptian Pharos the remains of the madhouses in which the seventy-two interpreters were confined in Herod's time. The testimony of a man who had the misfortune to see these madhouses seems to indicate that the author should have been locked up in them.

Saint Irenaeus, who came later, and who believed also in the millennium, says that he learned from an old man that saint John had written the *Apocalypse*. But saint Irenaeus has been reproached for having written that there must be only four gospels because there are only four parts of the world and four cardinal winds, and because Ezekiel saw only four animals. He calls this reasoning a demonstration. It must be admitted that Irenaeus certainly demonstrated as well as Justin saw.

In his *Electa* Clement of Alexandria mentions only an *Apocalypse* by saint Peter, to which great importance was attached. Tertullian, a great partisan of the millennium, not only asserts that saint John predicted this resurrection and this reign of a thousand years in the city of Jerusalem, but he also claims that this Jerusalem was already beginning to form in the air; all the Christians of Palestine, and even the pagans, had seen it for forty successive days at the end of the night; but unfortunately the city disappeared as soon as the day broke.

In his preface to the gospel of saint John and in his *Homilies* Origen cites the oracles of the *Apocalypse*; but he also cites the oracles of the sybils. Nevertheless saint Denis of Alexandria, who also wrote towards the middle of the third century, says in one of his fragments, conserved by Eusebius, that nearly all the doctors rejected the *Apocalypse* as a book devoid of reason; that this book had not been composed by saint John but by one Cerinthus, who borrowed a great name to give his dreams more weight.

The council of Laodicea, held in 360, did not include the *Apocalypse* among the canonical books. It was very singular that Laodicea, which was a church to which the *Apocalypse* was addressed, rejected a treasure destined for it, and that the bishop of Ephesus, who attended the council, also rejected this book by saint John, who was buried in Ephesus.

It was visible to all eyes that saint John still moved in his grave, and constantly made the earth rise and fall. Nevertheless the same people who were sure that saint John was not really dead were also sure that he had not written the *Apocalypse*. But those who believed in the millennium were unshakable in their opinion. Sulpicius Severus, in his *Sacred history*, book ix, calls insensate and impious those who did not accept the *Apocalypse*. Finally, after much hesitation, after opposition in council after council, the view of Sulpicius Severus prevailed. The matter having been elucidated, the church decided that the *Apocalypse* is incontestably by saint John: so there is no appeal.

Each Christian community has applied to itself the prophecies contained in this book; the English have found in it the revolutions of Great Britain; the Lutherans the troubles of Germany; the French protestants the reign of Charles IX and the regency of Catherine de Medicis. They are all equally right. Bossuet and Newton both wrote commentaries on the *Apocalypse*; but on the whole the eloquent declamations of the one and the sublime discoveries of the other have done them greater honour than their commentaries.

Arius

Here is an incomprehensible question that has exercised curiosity, sophistic subtlety, acrimony, intrigue, fury to dominate, rage to persecute, blind and bloody fanaticism, barbarous credulity, and has produced more horrors than the ambition of princes, though this has produced much. Is Jesus word? If he is word did he emanate from god in time or before time? If he emanated from god is he coeternal and consubstantial with him or is he of a similar substance? Is he distinct from him or is he not? Was he made or begotten? Can he beget in his turn? Has he paternity or the quality of production without paternity? Was the holy ghost made or begotten or produced or does he proceed from the father, from the son or from both? Can he beget, can he produce? If his hypostasis is consubstantial with the hypostasis of the father and the son, how is it possible for him not to do the same things as these two persons who are himself?

It was certainly necessary for these questions, so far above reason, to be determined by an infallible church.

Christians sophisticated, quibbled, hated each other, excommunicated each other because of some of these dogmas, so inaccessible to the human mind, before the times of Arius and Athanasius. The Egyptians and Greeks were cunning people, and split hairs in four; but this time they split one only in three. Alexandros, bishop of Alexandria, took it into his head to preach that god was necessarily individual, simple, a monad in the strictest sense of the word. This monad is triune.

The priest Arios or Arious, whom we call Arius, was quite scandalized by Alexandros's monad. He explained the matter differently. In part he quibbled like the priest Sabellius, who had quibbled like the Phrygian Praxeas, a great quibbler. Alexandros quickly assembled a little council of people who agreed with him, and excommunicated his priest. Eusebius, bishop of Nicomedia, took Arius's part: and the whole church was in flames.

I admit that the emperor Constantine was a scoundrel. I do not deny that he was a parricide who had smothered his wife in a bath, butchered his son, murdered his father-in-law, his brother-in-law and his nephew. I agree that he was a man bloated with pride and plunged in pleasure. He was a detestable tyrant like his children, *transeat*. But he had common sense. One does not become an emperor, one does not subjugate all one's rivals, without having reasoned clearly.

When he saw that the civil war of the scholastic skulls had been kindled, he sent the famous bishop Hosius[1] to the two belligerent parties with dehortatory letters. 'You are great fools,' he told them plainly in his letter, 'to quarrel about things you don't understand. It is unworthy of the gravity of your ministries to make so much noise about so trivial a matter.' By a 'trivial' matter Constantine did not refer to things touching the divinity, but to the incomprehensible efforts being made to explain its nature. The Arab patriarch who wrote the *History of the Church of Alexandria*[2] makes Hosius say, when presenting the emperor's letter:

My brethren, Christianity has hardly begun to enjoy peace, and you are about to plunge into eternal discord. The emperor is only too right to tell you that you are *quarrelling about a very trivial matter*. If the object of the dispute were essential, Jesus Christ, whom we all recognize as our legislator, would certainly have spoken of it. God would not have sent his son to earth in order not to teach us our catechism. Everything that he has not expressly told us is the work of men, and their lot is to err. Jesus has commanded you to love each other, and you begin by disobeying him in hating one another, in provoking discord in the empire. Pride alone gives birth to disputes, and Jesus, your master, has commanded you to be humble. None of you can know whether Jesus was made or begotten. And how does his nature concern you, so long as yours is

1. Hosius or Osius (Voltaire calls him Ozius) was a fourth-century bishop of Cordova; though he probably wrote the remarkable letter partially quoted by Voltaire, he himself, in extreme old age, was involved in the Athanasian schism.

2. This history of the Coptic church, the *Histoire de l'église d'Alexandrie* (Paris, 1677), was in fact composed by Johann Michael Wansleben from native sources.

to be just and rational. What does an empty science of words have in common with the morality which should guide your actions? You encumber doctrine with mysteries, you who are proper only to strengthen religion by virtue. Do you want the Christian religion to be only a mass of sophistries? Is that what Christ came for? Stop disputing; worship, build, humble yourselves, feed the poor, calm family quarrels instead of scandalizing the entire empire with your discord.

Hosius spoke to the headstrong. The council of Nicaea was assembled, and for 300 years there was civil war in the Roman empire. This war led to others, and for century after century, until our own days, there has been mutual persecution.

Athée, athéisme: Atheist, atheism

I

In former times anybody who possessed a secret in one of the crafts ran the risk of being taken for a sorcerer; every new sect was accused of butchering children in its mysteries; and every philosopher who turned aside from the jargon of the schools was accused of atheism by fanatics and rascals, and condemned by fools.

Anaxagoras dared to maintain that the sun is not guided by Apollo riding in a quadriga: and he was called an atheist and obliged to flee.

Aristotle was accused by a priest of atheism; and, not succeeding in having his accuser punished, retired to Chalcas. But what is most odious in the history of Greece is the death of Socrates. Aristophanes (whom the commentators admire because he was a Greek, forgetting that Socrates also was a Greek) was the first who accustomed the Greeks to regard Socrates as an atheist.

This comic poet, who was neither comic nor a poet, would not have been allowed in our society to write farces for the fair of Saint-Laurent: he appears to me to be lower and more contemptible than Plutarch[1] depicts him. This is

1. In his parallel between Aristophanes and Menander.

what the wise Plutarch says of this humbug: 'The language of Aristophanes betrays his wretched character: it consists of the lowest and most disgusting quips; even the people do not find him amusing, and to men of judgement and honour he is insupportable; his arrogance is unbearable and decent people detest his malignity.'

This then is the Tabarin[1] whom, by the way, mme Dacier,[2] the admirer of Socrates, dared to admire: this is the man who from afar prepared the poison with which infamous judges put to death the most virtuous man in Greece.

The tanners, cobblers and dressmakers of Athens applauded a farce[3] in which Socrates was shown hoisted in the air in a basket, announcing that there was no god, and boasting that he had stolen a coat while teaching philosophy. An entire people, whose bad government authorized such infamous liberties, well deserved what happened to it: to become slaves of the Romans and today of the Turks.

Let us pass over the whole period of time between the Roman republic and ourselves. The Romans, much wiser than the Greeks, never persecuted any philosopher for his opinions. This cannot be said of the barbarian peoples which succeeded the Roman empire. As soon as the emperor Frederick II quarrelled with the popes, he was accused of being an atheist and of being the author, with his chancellor de Vineis, of the book of the *Three Impostors*.[4]

When our great chancellor de L'Hospital[5] declared himself against the persecutions, he was at once accused of athe-

1. An early seventeenth-century strolling player, whose name is used as a synonym for buffoon.
2. Anne Lefèvre Dacier, a classical scholar whom Voltaire much admired notwithstanding what he says here.
3. Aristophanes's *The Clouds*.
4. Neither Frederick II nor his treacherous chancellor and friend Pietro della Vigna had anything to do with the *Traité des trois imposteurs*. This is an early eighteenth-century anti-religious work, in the Spinozist tradition, generally but implausibly attributed to Henri de Boulainvilliers.
5. Michel de L'Hospital; Voltaire much admired this liberal statesman, who did his best to defend the French Protestants against persecution.

ism, *Homo doctus, sed verus atheos.*[1] A Jesuit, as inferior to
Aristophanes as Aristophanes is inferior to Homer, a wretch
whose name has become ridiculous even among the fanatics,
in a word, the Jesuit Garasse,[2] found atheists everywhere:
this is what he called all those against whom he burst out.
He called Théodore de Bèze an atheist. It was he who misled the public about Vanini.[3]

Vanini's unhappy end does not move us with indignation
and pity like that of Socrates because Vanini was only a
foreign pedant without merit, but after all Vanini was not
an atheist, as has been alleged; he was precisely the opposite.
He was a poor Neapolitan priest, a preacher and theologian
by trade, a merciless argufier about quidities and universals,
*et utrum chimera bombinans in vacuo possit comedere secundas
intentiones.* But for the rest, there was not a drop of atheism in
him. His notion of god was theologically most sound and
correct. 'God is his principle and his end, father of the one and
the other, and needing neither the one nor the other; eternal
without being in time, present everywhere without being
anywhere. No past or future exists for him, he is everywhere
and beyond everything, governing everything, and having
everything, immutable, infinite without parts; his power is
his will', etc.

Vanini prided himself on reviving Plato's fine conception,
embraced by Averroes,[4] that god had created a chain of
beings, from the smallest to the greatest, whose last link is

1. *Note by Voltaire: Commentarium rerum Gallicarum*, xxviii.
2. François Garasse, a violent controversialist but a good man, was one
of Voltaire's favourite butts.
3. Lucilio Vanini, a precursor of Voltaire, whom the latter did not
properly appreciate. He was cruelly done to death for his opinions. I repeat that I do not consider it my business to intervene between Voltaire
and the reader. But here, for once, I must point out that Voltaire made
one of his rare basic mistakes by failing to appreciate that the *Amphitea-
trum aeternae providentiae divino-magicum* (1615), from which the quotation
is taken, is an ironical retraction of the kind of which Voltaire himself was
the master. His failure to come to terms with Vanini, who was in fact an
atheist, is a real tragedy in the history of ideas.
4. Averroes, more correctly Abūl-Walīd Muhammad ibn-Ahmad Ibn-
Muhammad ibn-Rushd, the Arab philosopher born in Cordova.

attached to his eternal throne: an idea, in truth, more sublime than true, but which is as far removed from atheism as being is from nothingness.

He travelled to make his fortune and to engage in disputations; but unfortunately disputation is the road that leads away from fortune; one makes as many irreconcilable enemies as one finds learned men or pedants with whom to argue. The misfortune of Vanini had no other cause; his heat and rudeness in dispute earned him the hatred of some theologians; and having had a quarrel with one Francon or Franconi, this Francon, the friend of his enemies, of course accused him of being an atheist who taught atheism.

This Francon or Franconi, aided by a few witnesses, had the barbarity to maintain during the trial what he had asserted. When cross-examined about what he thought of the existence of god, Vanini answered that, like the church, he worshipped one god in three persons. Picking up a straw he said: 'This trifle is enough to prove that there is a creator.' Then he pronounced a very fine discourse on vegetation and motion, and on the necessity for a supreme being without whom there would be neither motion nor vegetation.

Grammont,[1] the presiding judge, then at Toulouse, reports this discourse in his *History of France*, today quite forgotten; and this same Grammont, because of an incredible prejudice, alleges that Vanini said all this from 'vanity, or from fear, rather than from an inner conviction'.

On what can the *président* Grammont's rash and atrocious judgement be based? It is obvious that Vanini's answer should have secured his acquittal on the charge of atheism. But what happened? This unhappy foreign priest also dabbled in medicine. They found a big live toad which he kept at home in a vessel full of water, and of course he was accused of being a sorcerer. They alleged that this toad was the god he worshipped. An impious meaning was given to several passages in his books, which is very easy and very commonly done, by taking objections for replies, by interpreting

1. The président Gabriel Barthélemi de Grammont, author of *Historiarum Galliae ab excessu Henrici IV libri* XVIII (Tolosae, 1643).

malignantly some ambiguous phrases, by poisoning an innocent expression. The faction that oppressed him finally extorted from the judges the sentence that condemned the unhappy man to death.

To justify this death it was clearly necessary to accuse the wretched man of the most frightful things. The Minim and very minimal Mersenne[1] pushed lunacy so far as to print that Vanini 'left Naples with twelve of his apostles to convert all the nations to atheism'. How pitiful! How could a poor priest have had twelve men in his pay? How could he have persuaded twelve Neapolitans to travel at great expense, at the peril of their lives, to spread everywhere this abominable and revolting doctrine? Would a king be powerful enough to pay twelve preachers of atheism? Nobody before father Mersenne had put forward so enormous an absurdity. But it has been repeated after him, the newspapers, the historical dictionaries have been infected with it; and the world, which loves sensations, has believed this legend without question.

Bayle himself, in his *Pensées diverses*, speaks of Vanini as an atheist; he used this example to support his paradox 'that a society of atheists can exist'. He assures us that Vanini was a very moral man and that he was the martyr of his philosophic views. He is equally mistaken on both these points. The priest Vanini tells us in the *Dialogue* he wrote in imitation of Erasmus that he had had a mistress called Isabella. He was as bold in his writings as in his conduct, but he was not an atheist.

A century after his death the learned La Croze[2] and the writer who took the name of Philète[3] sought to justify him; but as nobody takes any interest in the memory of an unhappy

1. Marin Mersenne (1588–1648), a Minim Friar, whose erudition was matched only by the narrowness of his theology. The quoted passage occurs in Mersenne's *L'Impiété des déistes* (Paris, 1624). Voltaire's pun ('*le minime et très minime*') is not much less feeble in French.

2. Mathurin Veyssière de La Croze, primarily an orientalist, was a religious eccentric; Voltaire knew him well, and possessed his *Entretiens sur divers sujets* (Cologne [Amsterdam], 1733).

3. That is, Peter Friedrich Arpe, whose *Apologia pro Jul. Caesare Vanino* (Cosmopoli [Rotterdam], 1712) was in Voltaire's library.

Neapolitan, a very bad author, hardly anybody reads these apologies.

In his *Athei detecti*, the Jesuit Hardouin,[1] more learned than Garasse, accuses Descartes, Arnauld, Pascal, Nicole, Malebranche of atheism: fortunately they did not suffer Vanini's fate.

From all these facts I pass on to the ethical problem debated by Bayle, that is, *whether a society of atheists could exist.* Let us first observe on this point the enormous extent to which men contradict themselves when disputing: those who have argued with the greatest vehemence against Bayle's opinion, those who have denied with the greatest insults the possibility of a society of atheists, have since maintained with the same dauntlessness that atheism is the religion by which China is governed.

They are certainly mistaken about the Chinese government; all they had to do was to read the edicts of the emperors of this vast country, they would have seen that these edicts are sermons, which everywhere speak of a supreme being, ruler, avenger and remunerator.

But at the same time they are no less mistaken about the impossibility of a society of atheists; and I do not know how M. Bayle could have forgotten a striking example which could have made his cause victorious.

In what respect does a society of atheists seem impossible? It is because men who are unchecked are supposed to be incapable of living together; because the law is helpless against secret crimes; because a vengeful god is needed to punish in this world or the next the wicked who have avoided human justice.

It is true that the laws of Moses did not teach a future life, threatened no punishments after death, did not teach the first

---

1. Jean Hardouin was indeed a very learned Jesuit, but bizarre beyond the limits of sanity in his views; it was not only atheists he saw everywhere but also medieval monks, who, according to him, were the real authors of most classical writings. Unfortunately the anonymous pamphlet mentioned by Voltaire, *L'Athéisme découvert* (1715), though often attributed to Hardouin, is in fact by François de La Pillonière.

Jews the immortality of the soul; but the Jews, far from being atheists, far from seeking to avoid divine vengeance, were the most religious of all men. Not only did they believe in the existence of an eternal god, but they believed that he was always present in their midst; they were terrified of being punished in themselves, in their children, in their posterity to the fourth generation, and this check was very powerful.

But among the gentiles several sects had no such check: the sceptics doubted everything; the Academics suspended their judgement on everything; the Epicureans were convinced that the divinity could not meddle in human affairs, and at bottom acknowledged no divinity. They were certain that the soul is not a substance but a faculty that is born and perishes with the body; therefore they bore no yoke but that of morality and honour. The Roman senators and knights were true atheists, for the gods did not exist for men who neither feared them nor hoped for anything from them. Thus in Caesar's and Cicero's time the Roman senate was really an assembly of atheists.

In his harangue for Cluentius the great orator said to the assembled senate: 'What harm does death do him? We reject all the inept fables about hell. What then has death taken from him? Nothing but the feeling of pain.'

Caesar, Catalina's friend, wishing to save his friend's life from this same Cicero, did he not object that to put a criminal to death is not to punish him, that death is nothing, that it is only the end of our sufferings, that it is a happy moment rather than a disastrous one? Did not Cicero and the entire senate yield to this reasoning? The conquerors and legislators of the known world were thus clearly a society of men who had no fear of the gods, who were true atheists.

Bayle next inquires whether idolatry is more dangerous than atheism, whether it is a greater crime not to believe in the divinity than to have unworthy opinions about it. In this he shares the views of Plutarch: he believes that it is better to have no opinion than a bad one. But with all due deference to Plutarch it is obvious that it was infinitely better for the Greeks to fear Ceres, Neptune and Jupiter than to fear nothing at all. It is obvious that the sanctity of oaths is necessary, and that we must have confidence rather in those who think that a false oath will be punished, than in those who think that they can take a false oath with impunity. It is indubitable that it is infinitely more useful in a civilized city to have even a bad religion than none at all.

It would thus appear that Bayle should rather have inquired which is the more dangerous, fanaticism or atheism. Fanaticism is certainly a thousand times more baneful, for atheism does not inspire bloody passions, but fanaticism does; atheism does not discountenance crime, but fanaticism causes crimes to be committed. Let us suppose, with the author of the *Commentarium rerum Gallicarum*, that the chancellor de L'Hospital was an atheist. He enacted only wise laws and counselled only moderation and concord: the fanatics committed the massacres of saint Bartholomew. Hobbes was taken for an atheist. He led a calm and innocent life: the fanatics of his time deluged England, Scotland and Ireland with blood. Spinoza was not only an atheist, but he taught atheism: it was certainly not he who shared the judicial assassination of Barneveldt, it was not he who tore to pieces the two brothers de Witt and ate them on the grill.[1]

For the most part atheists are bold and misguided scholars who reason badly and who, unable to understand the creation, the origin of evil, and other difficulties, have recourse to the hypothesis of the eternity of things and of necessity.

The ambitious, the voluptuous, hardly have the time to reason, and to adopt a bad system; they have other things to do than to compare Lucretius with Socrates. This is the way things are nowadays.

It was not so in the Roman senate, which was almost entirely composed of men who were atheists in both theory

1. Certain cases of cruel injustice obsessed Voltaire throughout his life: prominent among them were the particularly atrocious ones of Johan van Oldenbarneveldt (1619) and Johan and Cornelius de Witt (1672). As for saint Bartholomew's day, Voltaire was ill every year on the anniversary of this official massacre of Protestants by Roman Catholics (24 August 1572).

and practice, that is, who believed neither in providence nor in the future life. This senate was an assembly of philosophers, voluptuaries and ambitious men, all very dangerous, and who destroyed the republic. Epicureanism persisted under the emperors: the senate's atheists had been sedition-mongers in the times of Sulla and Caesar; under Augustus and Tiberius they were atheist slaves.

I should want no dealings with an atheist prince who thought it useful to have me pounded in a mortar: I am quite sure that I would be pounded. If I were a sovereign I should want no dealings with atheist courtiers whose interest it was to have me poisoned: I should have to take antidotes at random every day. It is thus absolutely necessary for princes and peoples to have deeply engraved in their minds the notion of a supreme being, creator, ruler, remunerator and avenger.

There are atheist peoples, says Bayle in his *Pensées sur les comètes*. The Kaffirs, the Hottentots, the Topinamboos, and many other small nations have no god. That may be so, but it does not mean that they deny god. They neither deny nor affirm him: they have never heard of him. Tell them that there is one, and they will readily believe it. Tell them that everything happens in the nature of things, they also believe you. To allege that they are atheists is as relevant as to say that they are anti-Cartesians: they are neither for nor against Descartes. They are real children; a child is neither atheist nor theist, he is nothing.

What conclusion can we draw from all this? That atheism is a monstrous evil in those who govern; and also in learned men even if their lives are innocent, because from their studies they can affect those who hold office; and that, even if not as baleful as fanaticism, it is nearly always fatal to virtue. Above all, let me add that there are fewer atheists today than there have ever been, since philosophers have perceived that there is no vegetative being without germ, no germ without design, etc., and that grain is not produced by putrefaction.

Unphilosophical mathematicians have rejected final causes, but true philosophers accept them; and as a well-known

author has said, a catechist announces god to children, and
Newton demonstrates him to wise men.

II

If there are atheists, who is to be blamed if not the mercenary
tyrants of souls who, in revolting us against their swindles,
compel some feeble spirits to deny the god whom these
monsters dishonour? How often have the people's leeches
driven prostrated citizens to revolt against the king?[1]

Men fattened on our substance cry out to us: 'Be sure that
a she-ass spoke; believe that a fish swallowed up a man and
threw him on the shore three days later safe and sound;
don't doubt that the god of the universe ordered one Jewish
prophet to eat shit (Ezekiel), and another prophet to buy
two whores and to beget sons of whores on them (Hosea).[2]
These are the very words a god of truth and purity is made to
pronounce. Believe a hundred things either obviously
abominable or mathematically impossible: otherwise the
god of mercy will burn you in the fires of hell, not only for
millions of billions of centuries, but throughout all eternity,
whether you have a body or whether you have no body.'

These inconceivable stupidities revolt feeble and reckless
minds, as well as firm and wise minds. They say: 'Our
masters depict god for us as the most senseless and the most
barbarous of all kinds, therefore there is no god'; but they
ought to say: 'Therefore our masters attribute to god their
own absurdities and rages, therefore god is the opposite
of what they proclaim, therefore god is as wise and as good as
they allege him to be mad and wicked.' This is what wise
men conclude. But if a fanatic hears them, he denounces them
to a magistrate subservient to the priests; and this magistrate
has them burnt on a slow fire, believing that he is avenging
and imitating the divine majesty he violates.[3]

1. *Note by Voltaire:* See the article Fraud.
2. See *Ezekiel* iii. 15; *Hosea* i. 2.
3. As usual, Voltaire's polemical writings cannot be taken at their face
value; it is the present editor's opinion that Voltaire was himself for all
practical purposes an atheist; see my *Voltaire* (1969), chapter 17.

Babel

The great monuments have always been raised by vanity. It was out of vanity that men built the beautiful tower of Babel: 'Go to, let us build a tower, whose top may reach unto heaven, and let us make us a name; lest we be scattered abroad upon the face of the whole earth.'[1]

The enterprise was undertaken in the time of one Phaleg, who reckoned old Noah as his grandfather in the fifth degree. As can be seen, architecture and all its sister arts had made great progress in five generations. Saint Jerome, the same who had seen fauns and satyrs, had not seen the tower of Babel any more than I; but he asserts that it was 20,000 feet high. A mere trifle. The ancient *Yalkut*,[2] written by one of the most learned Jews, proves that its height was 81,000 Jewish feet, and there is no one who does not know that the Jewish foot was of about the same length as the Greek foot. This size is much more probable than Jerome's. This tower still exists; but it is no longer quite so high. Several very trustworthy travellers have seen it. I, who have not seen it, will no more speak of it than of my grandfather Adam, with whom I have not had the honour of conversing. But consult the reverend father dom Calmet: he is a man of delicate wit and profound philosophy; he will explain it all to you. I do not know why it is said in *Genesis* that Babel means confusion; for *Ba* means father in the oriental languages, and *Bel* means god; Babel means the city of god, the holy city. The ancients gave this name to all their capitals. But it is unquestionable that Babel means confusion, either because the architects were over-whelmed after having raised their structure to 81,000 Jewish feet, or because the languages became confused; and it is obviously since then that the Germans no longer understand the Chinese; for it is evident, according to the learned Bochart,[3] that originally the Chinese language was the same as high German.

1. *Genesis* xi. 4.
2. This was merely a rabbinically annotated text of the *Old Testament*.
3. The erratically erudite Samuel Bochart.

Baptême: Baptism

Baptism, Greek word meaning immersion. Men, who are always guided by their senses, easily imagined that what washes the body washes also the soul. There were great tanks for the priests and the initiates in the vaults under the Egyptian temples. From time immemorial the Indians have purified themselves in the water of the Ganges, and this ceremony is still in great vogue. It passed to the Hebrews: they baptized all the foreigners who embraced the Judaic law, and who would not submit to circumcision; above all the women, who were not made to undergo this operation except in Ethiopia, were baptized; it was a regeneration, which gave a new soul, as in Egypt. See, on this, Epiphanius, Maimonides and the *Gemara*.[1]

John baptized in the Jordan, and he even baptized Jesus, who, however, never baptized anyone, but who deigned to hallow this ancient ceremony. Every symbol is meaningless in itself, and god attaches his grace to the symbol he is pleased to choose. Baptism soon became the chief rite and the seal of the Christian religion. Nevertheless the first fifteen bishops of Jerusalem were all circumcised; it is not certain that they were baptized.

This sacrament was misused in the first centuries of Christianity; nothing was so common as to await the final agony in order to receive baptism. The example of the emperor Constantine is pretty good proof of that. This is how he reasoned: baptism purifies everything; I can therefore kill my wife, my son and all my relations; after which I shall have myself baptized and I shall go to heaven; and in fact that is just what he did. This was a dangerous example; little by little disappeared the custom of waiting for death before taking the plunge into the sacred bath.

The Greeks always conserved baptism by immersion. The Latins, having extended their religion into Gaul and Germany towards the end of the eighth century, and seeing that im-

1. Part of the *Talmud*, the most extensive exegesis of Jewish doctrine.

mersion could kill children in cold countries, substituted simple aspersion, for which they were often anathemized by the Greek church.

Saint Cyprian, bishop of Carthage, was asked if those who had simply had their whole bodies sprinkled were really baptized. He answered in his seventy-sixth letter that 'several churches do not believe that these sprinkled people are Christians; that as for himself he thinks that they are Christians, but that they have infinite less grace than those who have been immersed three times according to custom'.

With the Christians a man was initiated as soon as he was immersed; before this was done he was merely a catechumen. To be initiated it was necessary to have guarantors, sureties, who were given a name corresponding to *godfathers*, so that the church chould be sure that the new Christians would be faithful and would not divulge the mysteries. This is why in the first centuries the gentiles were usually as ill-instructed about the mysteries of the Christians as these were about the mysteries of Isis and Eleusis.

Cyril of Alexandria, in his tract against the emperor Julian, expresses himself thus: 'I would speak of baptism were I not afraid that my discourse might reach those who are not initiated.'

As early as the second century they began to baptize children; it was natural that the Christians should want their children to be provided with this sacrament, since they would have been damned without it. It was finally decided that it must be administered to them after a week because among the Jews this was the age at which they were circumcised. This is still the custom in the Greek church. Nevertheless in the third century the practice prevailed of being baptized only at death.

Those who died in the first week were damned, according to the strictest fathers of the church. But Peter Chrysologos, in the fifth century, invented limbo, a kind of mitigated hell, or, precisely, brink of hell, suburb of hell,[1] where go little children

---

1. Voltaire is referring to the derivation of the word from the Latin *limbus*, edge, border.

who die without baptism, and where resided the patriarchs before the descent of Jesus Christ into hell; so that the view that Jesus Christ descended to limbo and not into hell has prevailed since then.

It has been debated whether a Christian born in the deserts of Arabia could be baptized with sand: the reply was he could not; whether it was permitted to baptize with rose water: and it was decided that pure water was necessary, but that muddy water could be used. It is obvious that all the regulations depended on the prudence of the first pastors who established them.

THE STRICT UNITARIANS' CONCEPTION OF BAPTISM[1]

'To anyone who is willing to reason without prejudice it is evident that baptism is neither a mark of conferred grace nor a seal of alliance but a simple profession of faith.

'That baptism is not necessary, whether by necessity of precept or by necessity of means.

'That it was not established by Jesus Christ, and that Christians can dispense with it without running the slightest risk.

'That neither children nor adults should be baptized, nor indeed anyone.

'That baptism may have been useful in the first days of Christianity to those who were emerging from paganism, in order to publish their profession of faith and to be its authentic mark; but that at present it is absolutely useless, and completely immaterial.'

1. These sections were added by Voltaire in the 1767 edition, the first with the note 'Taken from the article "Unitaires" in the *Dictionnaire encyclopédique*'; the second with 'Taken from m. Boulanger'; the third with 'From m. *l'abbé* Nicaise'. The article 'Baptism' in the *Questions sur l'encyclopédie* is based on the present one, but in a much modified form.

IMPORTANT ADDITION[1]

In his immortal satire on *The Caesars* the emperor Julian, the philosopher, puts these words into the mouth of Constantius, son of Constantine: 'Whoever feels guilty of rape, murder, rapine, sacrilege, and of all the most abominable crimes, will be clean and pure as soon as I shall have washed him with this water.'

It was in fact this fatal doctrine that induced all the Christian emperors and all the great men of the empire to put off their baptism until death. They thought they had discovered the secret of living criminally and of dying virtuously.

ANOTHER ADDITION[1]

What a strange idea, inspired by the wash-pot, that a jug of water washes away all crimes! Now that all children are baptized because a no less absurd idea assumes them all to be criminals, they are all saved until they reach the age of reason and can become guilty. So butcher them as quickly as possible to assure them paradise. This conclusion is so logical that there existed a devout sect who went about poisoning or killing all newly baptized infants. These devotees reasoned perfectly. They said: 'We are doing these little innocents the greatest possible kindness; we are preventing them from being wicked and unhappy in this life, and we are giving them eternal life.'

Beau, beauté: Beautiful, beauty

Ask a toad what beauty is, absolute beauty, the *to kalon*. He will answer that it is his female, with two large round eyes sticking out of her little head, a large and flat snout, a yellow belly, a brown back. Question a Negro from Guinea; for him beauty is a black oily skin, sunken eyes, a flat nose.

Question the devil; he will tell you that the beautiful is a pair of horns, four claws, and a tail. Finally, consult the philosophers: their answer will be grandiloquent nonsense; they

1. See footnote on page 62.

ask for something conforming to the archetype of the beautiful in essence, to the *to kalon*.

I once went with a philosopher to see a tragedy. 'How beautiful it is!' said he. 'What do you find beautiful in it?' I asked him. 'It is', he said, 'because the author has attained his goal.' The next day he took some medicine that did him some good. 'It has attained its goal,' I told him; 'what a beautiful medicine!' He realized that one cannot say that a medicine is beautiful, and that before you can apply to anything the word *beauty* it must have aroused admiration and pleasure in you. He agreed that the tragedy had inspired these two feelings in him, and that this was the *to kalon*, the beautiful.

We made a journey to England: the same play was performed there, perfectly translated; it made all the spectators yawn. 'Oh, oh!' said he, 'the *to kalon* is not the same for the English as for the French.' After much reflection he concluded that beauty is decidedly relative, in the same way as that which is decent in Japan is indecent in Rome, and what is fashionable in Paris is not so in Peking; and he saved himself the trouble of composing a long treatise on the beautiful.

Bêtes: Animals

What a pitiful thing, what poor stuff it is to say that animals are machines deprived of knowledge and feeling, which always perform their operations in the same way, which learn nothing, which improve nothing,[1] etc.!

What! this bird which makes its nest semi-circular when it is attached to a wall, which builds it in a quarter-circle when it is in a corner, and makes it circular in a tree, this bird does everything in the same way? This gun dog you have trained for three months: does he not know more at the end of that time than he knew before your lessons? Does the canary immediately repeat the tune you are teaching him? Do you not spend much time in teaching him? Have you not seen that it makes mistakes and corrects itself?

1. This was the doctrine of Descartes.

Do you judge that I have feelings, memory, ideas because I speak to you? Well! I do not speak to you; you see me come home looking distressed, search anxiously for a paper, open the desk in which I remember having put it, find it, read it with joy. You judge that I have experienced the feeling of distress and that of pleasure, that I have memory and knowledge.

Judge in the same way this dog who has lost his master, who has searched for him with mournful cries in every path, who comes home agitated, restless, who runs up and down the stairs, who goes from room to room, who at last finds his beloved master in his study, and shows him his joy by the tenderness of his cries, by his leaps, by his caresses.

Barbarians seize this dog who so prodigiously surpasses man in friendship. They nail him to a table and dissect him alive to show you the mesenteric veins. You discover in him all the same organs of feeling that you possess. Answer me, mechanist, has nature arranged all the springs of feeling in this animal in order that he should not feel? Does he have nerves to be impassive? Do not assume that nature presents this impertinent contradiction.

But the leaders of this school inquire about the souls of animals. I do not understand this question: A tree has the faculty of receiving in its fibres the sap that circulates in it, of putting forth the buds of its leaves and of its fruit; will you ask me what is the soul of this tree? It has received these endowments; the animal has received those of feeling, of memory, of a certain number of ideas. Who has created all these endowments? Who has given all these faculties? He who has made the grass of the fields to grow, and who makes the earth gravitate towards the sun.

'The souls of animals are substantial forms,' said Aristotle; and after Aristotle the Arab school, and after the Arab school the angelic school,[1] and after the angelic school the Sorbonne, and after the Sorbonne nobody at all.

'The souls of animals are material,' exclaim other philosophers. Those have had no greater success than the others.

1. That is, saint Thomas Aquinas.

They were asked in vain what is a material soul; they had to agree that it is feeling matter: but what has given it this feeling? It is a material soul, that is, matter has given feeling to matter; they cannot break this circle.

Listen to other animals reasoning about animals. They allege that the soul is a spiritual being which dies with the body: but what proof have you of such a soul? What conception have you of this spiritual being which in reality has feeling, memory and its part of ideas and arrangements, but which will never know what a child of six knows? On what ground do you imagine that this being, which is not body, dies with the body? The greatest donkeys[1] are those who have alleged that this soul is neither body nor spirit. There's a fine system! By spirit we can only understand something unknown which is not body: hence the system of these gentlemen comes down to this, that the soul of an animal is a substance which is neither body nor something which is not body.

What can be the cause of so many contradictory errors? It is the habit men have always had of examining what a thing is before knowing whether it exists. The mobile tongue, the valve of a bellows, is called the soul of the bellows. What is this soul? It is a name I have given to this valve which descends, lets the air in, raises itself, and pushes it through a tube when I agitate the bellows.

Here we have no soul distinct from the machine. But what operates the animals' bellows? I have already told you; he who operates the stars. The philosopher who said, '*Deus est anima brutorum*',[2] was right; but he should have gone further.

Bien (souverain bien): Good (sovereign good)

Well-being is rare. Could not the sovereign good in this world be regarded as supremely chimerical? The Greek philosophers debated this question at length, as usual. Does it not

1. Voltaire makes an untranslatable pun: '*bêtes*' here means both animals and stupid people.
2. 'God is the soul of animals'; the philosopher cited was probably Voltaire himself.

seem, my dear reader, that you are witnessing beggars reasoning about the philosophers' stone?

The sovereign good! What a word! You might just as well have asked what is the sovereign blue or the sovereign stew, sovereign walking, sovereign reading, etc.

Everyone finds his good where he can and has as much of it as he can, in his own fashion and little enough.

> *Quid dem? quid non dem? Renuis tu quod iubet alter.*
> *Castor gaudet equis; ovo prognatus eodem*
> *Pugnis . . .*
>
> *Castor veut des chevaux, Pollux veut des lutteurs:*
> *Comment concilier de goûts, tant d'humeurs?*[1]

The greatest good is that which delights you so strongly that it makes you totally incapable of feeling anything else, just as the greatest evil is that which goes so far as to deprive us of all feeling. These are the two extremes of human nature, and these two moments are brief.

No extreme pleasures nor extreme sufferings can last a whole lifetime: the sovereign good and the sovereign evil are chimeras.

We have the beautiful fable of Crantor:[2] he makes Wealth, Pleasure, Health, Virtue compete at the Olympic games; each claims the apple. Wealth says: 'I am the sovereign good, for with me all goods are bought.' Pleasure says: 'The apple belongs to me, for wealth is sought only to have me.' Health asserts that without her there is no pleasure and that wealth is useless. Finally Virtue maintains that she is superior to the other three because with gold, pleasure and health one can become very wretched if one misbehaves. Virtue was given the apple.

The fable is very ingenious. It would have been even more so if Crantor had said that the sovereign good is the assembly

---

1. The first line of the Latin is Horace, *Epistles* II. ii. 63; 'What should I give them? what not? You refuse what the other orders.' The rest, very freely translated by Voltaire, is Horace, *Satires* II. i. 26–7: 'Castor delights in horses; [Pollux], born from the same egg, in fighting.'
2. A Greek moral philosopher of the fourth century B.C.

of the four rivals united, Virtue, Health, Wealth, Pleasure; but this fable does not resolve the absurd question of the sovereign good. Virtue is not a good, it is a duty: it is a different kind, of a superior order. It has nothing to do with painful or agreeable sensations. The virtuous man with the stone and gout, without help, without friends, lacking necessities, persecuted, put in chains by a voluptuous tyrant who is in good health is very unhappy; and the insolent persecutor, fondling a new mistress on his purple bed, is very happy. Say that the persecuted good man is preferable to his insolent persecutor; say that you love one and detest the other; but admit that the good man in chains is wild with rage. If the good man will not admit this he is deceiving you, he is a charlatan.

Bien (tout est): All is good

There was a fine row in the schools, and even among people who think, when Leibniz, paraphrasing Plato, built his edifice of the best of possible worlds, and imagined that all was for the best. He affirmed in the north of Germany that god could make only a single world. Plato had at least left him free to make five, because there are only five regular solids: the tetrahedron or three-faced pyramid with uniform base, the cube, the hexahedron, the dodecahedron, the icosahedron. But our world is not shaped like any of Plato's five bodies, he had allowed god a sixth manner.

That will do for Plato. Leibniz, who was certainly a better geometer than he, and a more profound metaphysician, did mankind the service of explaining that we ought to be entirely satisfied, and that god could do no more for us, that he had necessarily chosen, among all the possibilities, what was undeniably the best one.

'What will become of original sin?' they shouted at him. 'It will become what it can,' said Leibniz and his friends; but in public he wrote that original sin was necessarily part of the best of worlds.

What! to be chased from a place of delights, where we

would have lived for ever if an apple had not been eaten!
What! produce in wretchedness wretched children who will
suffer everything, who will make others suffer everything!
What! to undergo every illness, feel every sorrow, die in
pain, and for refreshment be burned in the eternity of centuries! Is this really the best lot that was available? This is not
too *good* for us; and how can it be good for god?

Leibniz realized that these questions were unanswerable:
so he wrote thick books in which he did not agree with himself.

A Lucullus in good health, dining well with his friends and
his mistress in the house of Apollo, can say laughingly that
there is no devil; but let him put his head out of the window
and he will see unhappy people; let him suffer a fever and he
will be unhappy himself.

I do not like to quote; it is usually a ticklish job: what
precedes and follows the passage quoted is passed over, and
one exposes oneself to a thousand quarrels. Still, I must
quote Lactantius, church father, who, in his chapter XIII,
of his *On the Wrath of God*[1] puts these words into the mouth of
Epicurus:

Either god wants to remove the evil from this world, and cannot,
or he can, and does not want to; or he neither wants to nor can; or
he wants to and can. If he neither wants to nor can, this is impotence,
which is contrary to the nature of god; if he can but does not want
to, this is wickedness, which is no less contrary to his nature; if he
neither can nor wants to this is at once wickedness and impotence;
if he wants to and can (which is the only one of these possibilities
fitting for god) whence then comes the evil which is on earth?

The argument is powerful; so that Lactantius answers it
very badly, saying that god wants evil but that he has given us
the wisdom with which one acquires the good. It must be
admitted that this answer is quite weak in comparison with the
objection, for it assumes that god could create wisdom only by
producing evil; besides our wisdom is pretty ridiculous!

1. The exact date of *De ira dei* is not known; Lactantius Firmianus
flourished *c.* 300.

The origin of evil has always been an abyss whose bottom nobody has been able to see. This is what reduced so many ancient philosophers and legislators to have recourse to two principles, one good, the other bad. Typhon was the bad principle of the Egyptians, Ahriman of the Persians. It is well known that the Manicheans adopted this theology; but as these people had never spoken to the good nor the bad principle, we should not take their word for it.

Among the absurdities with which this world overflows and which can be counted among our evils, it is not a trivial one to have imagined two all-powerful beings fighting each other to see which of them would put more of himself into this world, and entering into a treaty like the two doctors in Molière: Pass me the emetic, and I'll pass you the lancet.

Basilides[1] alleged as early as the first century of the church, following the Platonists, that god had entrusted the creation of the world to his lowest angels, and that these, not being skilful, arranged matters as we see them. This theological fable crumbles into dust before the terrible objection that it is not in the nature of an all-powerful and all-wise God to entrust the building of the world to incompetent architects.

Simon,[2] who appreciated the objection, met it by saying that the angel who directed the workshop was damned for having done his work so badly; but the burning of this angel does not remedy our ills.

Among the Greeks the adventure of Pandora does not meet the objection any better. The box in which all ills reside, and at the bottom of which hope remains, is certainly a charming allegory; but this Pandora was created by Vulcan only to avenge himself against Prometheus, who had made a man out of mud.

The Indians have no better solution: having created man god gave him a drug that ensured his permanent health; man loaded his donkey with the drug, the donkey was thirsty, the

1. Basilides was a second-century gnostic, one of the most important links between Persian dualism and Manicheism.
2. Probably Simon of Gitta as reported in the *Clementine homilies.*

serpent told him about a fountain; and while the donkey drank the serpent took the drug for himself.

The Syrians imagined that man and woman, having been created in the fourth heaven, took it into their heads to eat a pancake instead of the ambrosia which was their natural food. The ambrosia was exhaled through the pores, but after having eaten pancakes they had to go to stool. The man and woman begged an angel to tell them where the closet was. 'Well,' replied the angel, 'you see that little planet, though it is so small, which is about 60 million leagues from here; it is the universe's privy; hurry there.' They went there, they were left there, and since then our world has been what it is.

We must still ask the Syrians why god allowed man to eat the pancake, and so appalling a host of ills to descend on us in consequence.

I move quickly, before I get bored, from this fourth heaven to milord Bolingbroke. This man, who was undoubtedly a great genius, gave the celebrated Pope his notion of the *All is good*. It was in effect found later word for word in the posthumous works of lord Bolingbroke, and had previously been set out by lord Shaftesbury in his *Characteristics*. Read Shaftesbury's chapter on moralists; you will find these words in it:

Much is alleged in answer to show why nature errs, and how she came thus impotent and erring from an unerring hand. But I deny she errs. . . . 'Tis . . . from this order of inferior and superior things that we admire the world's beauty, founded thus on contrarieties: whilst from such various and disagreeing principles, a universal concord is established. . . . The vegetables by their death sustain the animals: and animal bodies dissolved, enrich the earth, and raise again the vegetable world. . . . The central powers, which hold the lasting orbs in their just poise and movement, must not be controlled to save a fleeting form, and rescue from the precipice a puny animal, whose brittle frame, however protected, must of itself so soon dissolve.[1]

1. *Characteristics: the Moralists* I. iii. (I have modernized the original text.) The intellectual descent from Shaftesbury to Pope through Bolingbroke has been much debated, but what Voltaire says here is still basically sound.

Bolingbroke, Shaftesbury and Pope, who embodied their ideas, do not resolve the question any better than the others: their *All is good* means nothing more than that all is controlled by immutable laws. Who does not know that? You tell us nothing new when you observe, as all little children have done, that flies are born to be eaten by spiders, spiders by swallows, swallows by shrikes, shrikes by eagles, eagles to be killed by men, men to kill one another, and to be eaten by worms, and then, all but one in a thousand, by devils.

Here we have a clear and fixed order among every kind of animal. There is order everywhere. When a stone is formed in my bladder it is by means of admirable mechanics: calculous juices pass little by little into my blood, they filter into the kidneys, pass through the ureters, deposit themselves in my bladder, and assemble there by an excellent Newtonian attraction; the stone is formed, gets bigger, I suffer pains a thousand times worse than death, by the most elegant arrangement in the world. A surgeon, having perfected the art invented by Tubalcain,[1] comes to thrust a sharp and cutting iron into the perineum, and takes hold of my stone with his pincers. It breaks under his efforts by a necessary mechanism; and by the same mechanism I die in frightful torments. *All this is good*, all this is the evident consequence of inalterable physical principles. I agree with them, and I knew it as well as you did.

If we were without feeling there would be no reason to object to this cause and effect. But that is not the point. We are inquiring whether there are any perceptible evils, and whence they come. 'There are no evils,' says Pope in his fourth essay on the *All is good*; 'or, if there are particular evils, they form the common good.'[2]

A strange general good! composed of the stone, the gout, all crimes, all suffering, death and damnation.

The fall of man is the plaster we stick on all these particular

1. Tubalcain, the descendant of Cain, was 'the forger of every cutting instrument of brass and iron' (*Genesis* iv. 22).
2. Pope's most lapidary rendering of this view is 'All partial Evil universal Good' (*Essay on man*, i. 292).

diseases of the body and the soul, which are called 'general health'. But Shaftesbury and Bolingbroke derided original sin; Pope does not refer to it; it is obvious that their system undermines the Christian religion at its foundations, and explains nothing at all.

Nevertheless this system has recently been approved by several theologians who readily accept contradictions. Capital! we must not begrudge anybody the consolation of reasoning as best he can about the deluge of evils by which we are inundated. It is right to allow the incurable to eat what they like. It has even been claimed that this system is consoling. 'God', says Pope, 'sees perish with equal eye the hero and the sparrow, an atom or a thousand planets precipitated into ruin, the formation of a soap-bubble or a world.'[1]

Here, I must admit, we have a pleasant consolation. Do you not find a great palliative in the prescription of lord Shaftesbury, who says that god is not going to upset his eternal laws for so puny an animal as man? It must at least be admitted that this puny animal has the right to cry out humbly, and to seek to understand, in crying, why these eternal laws are not made for the well-being of every individual.

This system of *All is good* represents the author of nature only as a powerful and maleficent king, who does not care, so long as he carries out his plan, that it costs four or five hundred thousand men their lives, and that the others drag out their days in want and in tears.

So far from the notion of the best of possible worlds being consoling, it drives to despair the philosophers who embrace it. The problem of good and evil remains an inexplicable chaos for those who seek in good faith. It is an intellectual exercise for those who argue: they are convicts who play with

1. *Essay on man*, i. 87–90, reads:

> 'Who sees with equal eye, as God of all,
> A hero perish, or a sparrow fall,
> Atoms or systems into ruin hurled,
> And now a bubble burst, and now a world.'

The difference is not trivial, for Voltaire, unlike Pope, has included creation in god's indifference.

their chains. As for the unthinking mass, it rather resembles fish who have been moved from a river to a reservoir. They do not suspect that they are there to be eaten in lent: nor do we know anything by our own resources about the causes of our density.

Let us put at the end of nearly all chapters on metaphysics the two letters used by Roman judges when they could not understand a lawsuit: *N. L., non liquet*, this is not clear.

Bornes de l'esprit humain: Limits of the human mind

They are everywhere, poor doctor. Do you want to know how it is that your arm and your foot obey your will, and your liver does not obey it? Do you seek to know how thought is formed in your puny understanding, and this child in the uterus of this woman? Those like you have written ten thousand volumes on this subject; they have found a few qualities of this substance: children know them as well as you do. But at bottom, what is this substance? and what is it you have named mind from the Latin word meaning *breath*,[1] unable to do any better because you have no idea what it is?

Consider this grain of wheat I throw into the earth, and tell me how it rises to produce a stalk bearing an ear. Teach me how the same earth produces an apple at the top of this tree and a chestnut on the neighbouring tree. I could compose for you a folio volume of questions to which you would have to reply only with four words: *I do not know*.

And yet you have taken your degrees, and your gown is furred, and so is your cap,[2] and you are called *master*. And this other conceited upstart who has bought an office thinks that he has bought the right to judge and to condemn what he does not understand.

1. The point is lost in translation: the French and Latin words are *esprit* and *spiritus*; but *esprit* has several meanings for which English has different words; spirit, mind, wit, etc.
2. Formerly the quantity and quality of fur on his cap and gown indicated the wearer's academic rank.

Montaigne's motto was: *What do I know?* and yours is: *What do I not know?*

Caractère: Character

From the Greek word *impression, engraving*. It is what nature has engraved in us. Can we efface it? Vast question. If I have a hooked nose and two cat's eyes I can hide them with a mask. Can I do better with the character nature has given me? A man born violent, choleric, presented himself before François I, king of France, to complain of an injustice. The prince's countenance, the respectful conduct of the courtiers, the very place in which he found himself, made a powerful impression on this man; he unconsciously lowered his eyes, his rough voice softened, he presented his request humbly. One would believe him to be naturally as gentle as are (at least at this moment) the courtiers in whose midst he is even disconcerted; but if François I is good at reading faces he will easily realize in his eyes, lowered but alight with hidden fire, in the taut muscles of his face, in his lips pressed against each other, that this man is not so gentle as he is obliged to appear. This man followed him to Pavia, was captured with him, and taken to prison in Madrid with him; the majesty of François I no longer made the same impression on him; he became familiar with the object of his respect. One day, while pulling off the king's riding boots, and pulling them badly, the king, soured by his misfortune, became angry: my man sent the king to the devil, and threw his boots out of the window.

Sixtus V[1] was by nature petulant, obstinate, haughty, impetuous, vindictive, arrogant: his character appears to have been softened by the ordeal of his novitiate. As he began to enjoy some reputation in his order, he lost his temper with an attendant and felled him with his fist. When inquisitor in Venice he exercised his office with insolence. Become cardinal he was possessed *della rabbia papale*.[2] This rage subdued his

---

1. Few men of such bad character can boast such great achievements as this sixteenth-century pope.
2. That is, the furious ambition to become pope.

nature; he buried his person and his character in obscurity; he shammed humility and ill-health; he was elected pope: in this instant was restored all the elasticity so long restrained by policy; he was the proudest and most despotic of sovereigns.

Naturam expellas furca, tamen ipsa redibit.[1]

Chassez le naturel, il revient au galop.

Religion, morality put a curb on the power of nature; they cannot destroy it. The drunkard in a cloister, reduced to one glass of cider with each meal, will no longer get drunk, but he will always love wine.

Age weakens the character; it is a tree that produces nothing but a few degenerate fruits, but they are still of the same kind; it gets to be covered with knots and moss, it becomes worm-eaten, but it is still an oak or a pear tree. If we could change our character we would give ourselves one, we would be the masters of nature. Can we give ourselves something? Do we not receive everything? Try to arouse continuous activity in an indolent mass, to freeze with apathy the boiling soul of the impetuous, to inspire a taste for music and poetry into one who lacks taste and an ear: you will no more succeed than if you undertook to give sight to one born blind. We perfect, we mitigate, we hide what nature has placed in us; but we place nothing in ourselves.

A farmer was told: 'You have too many fish in this pond, they will not thrive; there are too many animals in your fields, there is not enough grass, they will lose weight.' After this exhortation it so happened that pike ate half my man's carp, and wolves half of his sheep; the rest fattened. Will he congratulate himself on his management? This countryman is you yourself; one of your passions devours the others and you think you have triumphed over yourself. Do we not really all resemble the old general of ninety who, coming across some young officers who were causing a disturbance with some

---

1. Horace, *Epistles* I. x. 24, inaccurately quoted: 'Nature will always return even if you expel her with a pitchfork.' The French adaptation is from Philippe Néricault Destouches's drama *Le Glorieux* III. v.

women of the town, said in a temper: 'Gentlemen, is this the example I give you?'

Carême, questions sur le carême:
Lent, questions on lent

Did the first men who bethought themselves to fast adopt this regimen on the prescription of a doctor because they had had indigestion?

Was the lack of appetite we feel when we are sad the first source of the fast-days prescribed by sad religions?

Did the Jews take the custom of fasting from the Egyptians, all of whose rites they imitated, even flagellation and the scapegoat?

Why did Jesus fast for forty days in the desert whence he was carried off by the devil, by the *Knathbull*? Saint Matthew remarks that after this lent he was hungry[1]; he was therefore not hungry during this lent?

Why does the Roman church consider it a crime to eat terrestrial animals during the days of abstinence, and a good action to be served soles and salmon? The rich papist who has had five hundred *francs*' worth of fish on his table will be saved; and the poor man, dying of hunger, who ate four *sous*' worth of pickled pork, will be damned!

Why must we ask our bishop's permission to eat eggs? If a king commanded his people never to eat eggs, would he not be regarded as the most ridiculous of tyrants? What strange aversion do bishops have against omelettes?

Will anybody believe that among the papists there have been tribunals imbecile enough, despicable enough, barbarous enough, to condemn to death wretched citizens who had committed no other crime than to eat horseflesh in lent? The fact is only too genuine: I have in my hands a judgement of this kind. What is strange is that the judges who delivered such verdicts thought themselves superior to the Iroquois.

Idiotic and cruel priests! on whom do you impose lent? Is

1. *Matthew* iv. 2.

it on the rich? They take good care not to observe it. Is it on the poor? They keep lent the whole year. The wretched farmer hardly eats meat and has no money to buy fish. Fools that you are, when will you correct your absurd laws?

Catéchisme chinois: Chinese catechism

a conversation of Ku-Su, disciple of Confucius, with prince Koo, son of the king of Loo, tributary of the Chinese emperor Gnen-Van, 417 years before our common era[1]

FIRST CONVERSATION

KOO: What am I to understand when I am told to worship heaven (Chang-ti)?

KU-SU: It's not the material sky that we see; for this sky is simply the air, and this air is composed of all the exhalations of the earth: it would be a most absurd folly to worship vapours.

KOO: Still, I wouldn't be surprised if we did. It seems to me that men have committed even greater follies.

KU-SU: That's true; but you're destined to govern; you must be wise.

KOO: So many peoples worship heaven and the planets!

KU-SU: The planets are nothing but earths like ours. The moon, for instance, might just as well worship our sand and our mud, as we ourselves to kneel to the sand and the mud of the moon.

KOO: What is meant when people say: heaven and earth, going up to heaven, to be worthy of heaven?

KU-SU: They say an extremely silly thing.[2] There is no heaven; every planet is surrounded by its atmosphere, as by a shell, and revolves in space around its sun. Every sun is the centre of several planets which travel continuously around it:

1. Voltaire added another of his imaginative attributions: '*Translated into Latin by father Fouquet former ex-Jesuit*. The manuscript is in the Vatican library no. 42759'.

2. *Note by Voltaire:* See the article 'Ciel'.

there is neither high nor low, neither ascent nor descent. You will appreciate that if the inhabitants of the moon said that one ascends to the earth, that one must become worthy of the earth, they would be talking extravagantly. In the same way we say something meaningless when we say that we must become worthy of heaven; it's as if we said: we must become worthy of the air, worthy of the constellation of the dragon, worthy of space.

KOO: I think I understand you; we should worship only the god who made heaven and earth.

KU-SU: Certainly, we should worship only god. But when we say that he has made heaven and earth, we are piously uttering very poor stuff. For if by heaven we understand the prodigious space in which god lit so many suns and made so many worlds revolve, it is much more ridiculous to say *heaven and earth* than to say *mountains and a grain of sand*. Our globe is infinitely less than a grain of sand in comparison with these millions of billions of universes in whose presence we vanish. All we can do is to join our feeble voices here with those of the innumerable beings who render homage to god in the abyss of infinite space.

KOO: So we were badly deceived when we were told that Fo descended among us from the fourth heaven in the shape of a white elephant.

KU-SU: These are stories the bonzes tell children and old women: we should worship nobody but the eternal author of all beings.

KOO: But how can one being have made the others?

KU-SU: Consider this star; it is fifteen hundred thousand million *lis* from our little globe; it emits rays which produce on your eyes two angles equal at the apex; they produce the same angles on the eyes of all animals. Isn't this clearly a design? Isn't this an admirable law? And who constructs if not a workman? Who makes laws if not a legislator? Therefore there is a workman, an eternal legislator.

KOO: But who made this workman? and how is he made?

KU-SU: Prince, I was walking yesterday near the vast palace built by the king your father. I heard two crickets, one of whom said to the other: 'What a monstrous edifice!' 'Yes,' said the other, 'and, glorious that I am, I admit that someone more powerful than the crickets built this prodigy; but I've no conception of that being; I see that he is, but I don't know what he is.'

KOO: I assure you that you are a better educated cricket than I am; and what I like about you is that you don't pretend to know what you don't know.

SECOND CONVERSATION

KU-SU: So you agree that there is an all-powerful being, self-existent, supreme artisan of all nature?

KOO: Yes; but if he is self-existent nothing can limit him; he is therefore everywhere; he exists in all matter, in all my own parts?

KU-SU: Why not?

KOO: So I am myself part of the divinity?

KU-SU: Perhaps that does not follow. This piece of glass is imbued by light in all its parts; but is it on that account light itself? It is only sand, and nothing more. All is in god, no doubt; that which animates everything must be everywhere. God is not like the emperor of China, who lives in his palace and sends orders by kolaos. Since he exists it is necessary that his existence fills the whole of space and all his creation; and since he is in you this is a continuous warning not to do anything for which you might blush before him.

KOO: What must we do to dare to contemplate ourselves thus before the supreme being without repugnance and without shame?

KU-SU: Be just.

KOO: And what else?

KU-SU: Be just.

KOO: But the sect of Laokium[1] says that there is neither justice nor injustice, neither vice nor virtue.

1. Or rather, Lao-Tse, the reputed founder in the sixth century B.C. of Taoism, and the author of the *Tao teh king*; Voltaire returns to him in the fourth conversation. The reader must hold fast to the fact that when

KU-SU: Does the sect of Laokium say that there is neither health nor illness?

KOO: No, it does not advance so great an error.

KU-SU: The error of thinking that there is neither health of the soul nor illness of the soul, neither virtue nor vice, is as great and more deadly. Those who have said that everything is indifferent are monsters: is it indifferent whether one nourishes one's son or crushes him on a stone, whether one helps one's mother or plunges a dagger into her heart?

KOO: You make me shudder; I detest the sect of Laokium; but justice and injustice have so many shades of meaning! One is often quite uncertain. Who knows exactly what is permitted and what is prohibited? Who could unhesitatingly fix the limits that separate good and evil? What rule can you give me to distinguish them?

KU-SU: The rules of my master Confucius: 'Live as you would wish to have lived when you come to die. Treat your neighbour as you want him to treat you.'

KOO: These maxims, I admit, should be the code of mankind; but when I am dying what will it matter to me to have lived virtuously? How will it benefit me? When this clock is destroyed will it be happy that it rang the hours well?

KU-SU: This clock doesn't feel, doesn't think; it can't feel remorse as you do when you feel guilty.

KOO: But if, after having committed several crimes, I succeed in no longer feeling remorse?

KU-SU: Then you would have to be snuffed out; and be sure that among men who don't like to be suppressed some would be found to render you incapable of committing new crimes.

KOO: Thus god, who is in them, would allow them to be wicked after having allowed me to be wicked?

KU-SU: God has given you reason; neither you nor they should abuse it. Not only will you be unhappy in this life, but who has told you that you won't also be so in another?

Voltaire wrote knowledge of the far east was scanty and inaccurate: the *Tao teh king* was not in any real sense known in the west until 1832. However, the validity of Voltaire's arguments is not affected by his very imperfect knowledge of e.g. Taoism.

KOO: And who has told you that there is another life?

KU-SU: The moment there is any doubt you should behave as if there is one.

KOO: But if I'm sure that there isn't one?

KU-SU: I defy you to prove it.

THIRD CONVERSATION

KOO: You are pressing me, Ku-Su. To make it possible for me to be rewarded or punished when I'm no more, it's necessary that something that feels and thinks subsists in me. Now, since nothing of me had any feeling or thought before my birth, why should there be any after my death? What could be this incomprehensible part of myself? Will the buzzing of this bee remain when the bee is no more? Does the vegetation of this plant remain when it has been uprooted? Is not vegetation a word used to signify the inexplicable manner in which the supreme being has wished the plant to draw the juices of the earth? In the same way soul is a word invented to denote feebly and obscurely the springs of our life. All animals move; and this ability to move is called *active force*; but this force is not a distinct being. We have passions, memory, reasons; but these passions, this memory, this reason are clearly not separate things; they aren't beings extant in us; they aren't little people having a distinct existence; they are generic words, invented to fix our ideas. Hence the soul which denotes our memory, our reason, our passions, is itself nothing but a word. Who causes movement in nature? It is god. Who makes all the plants vegetate? It is god. Who enables animals to move? It is god. Who makes thought in man? It is god.

If the human soul[1] were a little person enclosed in my body, directing its movements and ideas, would that not signify in the eternal artisan an impotence and a device unworthy of him? Was he then incapable of making automata having in themselves the ability to move and to think? You have taught me Greek, you have made me read Homer. Vulcan appears to me to have been a divine blacksmith since he made golden

1. *Note by Voltaire:* See the article Ame.

tripods which went on their own to the council of the gods, but this Vulcan would seem to me a wretched charlatan if in the structure of these tripods he had hidden one of his boys who moved them without anyone noticing it.

There are frigid dreamers who have regarded as a fine idea the notion that the planets are turned by spirits who push them ceaselessly, but god has not been reduced to this pitiful expedient. In a word, why use two springs when one will do? You dare not deny that god has the power to animate the little-known being we call *matter*. Why then should he use another agent to animate it?

There is much more. What could this soul be that you give so generously to my body? Whence would it come? When would it come? Would it be necessary for the creator of the universe to lie constantly in wait for the coupling of men and women, to note attentively the moment at which a seed leaves the body of a man and enters that of a woman, and then quickly to send a soul into this seed? And if this seed die, what would then become of the soul? It would then have been created uselessly, or it would await another opportunity.

This strikes me as a strange occupation for the master of the world; and not only must he pay continual attention to the copulations of mankind, but he must do as much with all animals; for like us they all have memory, ideas, passions; and if a soul be necessary to constitute these feelings, this memory, these ideas, these passions, god must work perpetually to forge souls for elephants and fleas, for owls, for fish and for bonzes.

What impression do you want to give me of the architect of so many millions of worlds were he obliged to carry out so many repairs to keep his creation going?

These are a very few of the reasons that can make me doubt the existence of the soul.

KU-SU: You reason in good faith; and this virtuous sentiment would be agreeable to the supreme being even if it were mistaken. You can make a mistake, but you don't try to deceive yourself, and so you can be excused. But reflect that you have put forward nothing but doubts, and that these doubts are dreary. You must agree that there are more consoling probabilities. It is hard to be annihilated. Hope to live. You know that a thought is not matter, you know that it has no connection with matter; why then would you find it so difficult to believe that god has placed in you a divine principle which, being indissoluble, cannot be subject to death? Dare you say that it is impossible that you should have a soul? Clearly not, and if it is possible, is it not highly probable that you have one? Could you reject so fine a system, one so necessary to mankind? And what difficulties would put you off?

KOO: I'd like to embrace that system, but I'd like to have it proved. I can't believe when I have no evidence. I'm always struck by the grand idea that god has made everything, that he is everywhere, that he permeates everything, that he gives everything movement and life; and if he is in all parts of my being, as he is in all parts of nature, I don't see why I need a soul. What use have I for that little subordinate being when I am animated by god himself? What good would this soul do me? We do not derive our ideas from ourselves, for we nearly always have them in spite of ourselves, we have them when we are asleep, everything happens in us without our interference. The soul would say in vain to the blood and the animal spirits[1]: 'Please flow in this fashion for my sake.' They will always circulate in the manner god has prescribed for them. I prefer to be the machine of a god who is proved rather than the machine of a soul whose existence I doubt.

KU-SU: Very well! if god himself animates you, never sully with crimes this god who is within you; and if he has given you a soul, may this soul never offend him. In one system as in the other you have a will, you are free. That is to say, you have the power to do what you will. Use this power to save the god who gave it to you. It is a good thing that you are a philosopher, but it is necessary for you to be just. You will be so even more when you believe that you have an immortal soul.

Deign to answer me: isn't it true that god is sovereign justice?

1. This was the name then given to the impulses transmitted by the nerves.

KOO: Certainly; and if it were possible for him to cease to be so (which is a blasphemy) for my part I should like to act with equity.

KU-SU: Isn't it true that it will be your duty when you are on the throne to reward virtuous actions and to punish criminals? Would you wish god not to do what you are yourself bound to do? You know that in this life there are and always will be unrewarded virtue and unpunished crime. It is therefore necessary that good and evil be judged in another life. It is this idea, so simple, so natural, so general, that has installed in so many nations the belief in the immortality of our souls and in the divine justice that judges them when they have abandoned their mortal remains. Is there a system more rational, more agreeable to the divinity, and more useful to mankind?

KOO: Why then have several nations not embraced this system? You know that we have in our province about two hundred families of the ancient Sinoos,[1] who formerly lived in Arabia Petraea. Neither they nor their ancestors have ever believed the soul to be immortal. They have their five books, as we have our five kings. I have read the translation. Their laws, necessarily similar to those of all other peoples, command them to respect their fathers, not to steal, not to lie, to be neither adulterers nor murderers; but these same laws refer neither to rewards nor to punishments in another life.

KU-SU: If this idea has not yet been developed in that unfortunate people it no doubt will be one day. But what does one wretched little nation signify when the Babylonians, Egyptians, Indians, and all civilized nations have accepted this salutary dogma? If you were ill would you reject a remedy approved by all the Chinese on the pretext that some mountain barbarians wouldn't use it? God has given you reason, it tells you that the soul must be immortal, it is therefore god himself who tells you so.

KOO: But how will it be possible for me to be rewarded or punished when I shall no longer be myself, when I shall no

1. *Note by Voltaire:* These are the Jews of the ten tribes who in their dispersion penetrated as far as China; there they are called *Sinoos*.

longer be anything of that which has constituted my person? It is only by means of my memory that I am always I; I lose my memory in my last illness; wouldn't it require a miracle to return it to me after my death, to make me return into the existence I have lost?

KU-SU: That is to say that if a prince has butchered his family in order to reign, if he has tyrannized over his subjects, he can call it quits by saying to god: 'It is not I, I have lost my memory, you are under a misapprehension, I am no longer the same person.' Do you think god would be satisfied with this sophism?

KOO: Well, so be it, I give in.[1] I wanted to do good on my own, I can do it just as well to please the supreme being. I thought it enough in this life for my soul to be just, I hoped that it would be happy in another. I perceive that this opinion is good for peoples and princes, but I am embarrassed by the worship of god.

1. [*Note added by Voltaire in a 1765 edition:*] Well, wretched enemies of reason and truth, will you still say that this *Dictionary* teaches the mortality of the soul? This passage was printed in all the editions. Then how dare you calumniate it so impertinently? Alas! if your souls keep their character throughout eternity they will eternally be very stupid and very unjust souls. No, the authors of this moderate and useful work do not tell you that the soul dies with the body: they tell you only that you are ignoramuses. Do not blush on that account. All wise men have confessed their ignorance: not one of them has been impertinent enough to know the nature of the soul. Gassendi, summarizing all that antiquity has said about it, speaks to you thus: 'You know that you think, but you who think do not know what kind of substance you are. You resemble a blind man who, feeling the heat of the sun, thinks that he has a distinct notion of this star.' Read the rest of this admirable letter to Descartes. Read Locke. Re-read this *Dictionary* attentively, and you will see that it is impossible for us to have the least notion of the nature of the soul because it is impossible for the creature to know the hidden mechanisms of the creator. You will see that, without knowing the principle of our thought, we must try to think with precision and with justice, that we must be all that you are not: modest, gentle, beneficent, indulgent. Resemble Ku-Su and Koo, and not Thomas Aquinas or Scotus, whose souls were quite obscure, or Calvin and Luther, whose souls were very hard and very choleric. Try to make your souls resemble ours a little, then you will see how ridiculous you are.

FOURTH CONVERSATION

KU-SU: What do you find shocking in our *Chu-king*, that first canonical book so respected by all the Chinese emperors? You cultivate a field with your royal hands to give an example to the people, and you offer its first fruits to Chang-ti, to Tien, to the supreme being. You sacrifice to him four times a year. You are king and pontiff. You promise god to do all the good in your power. Is there something revolting in this?

KOO: I'm far from finding anything objectionable in it. I know that god hasn't the slightest need for our sacrifices or our prayers, but we need to address them to him; his worship was not established for him but for us. I love to say my prayers. Above all I don't want them to be ridiculous; for, when I have exclaimed that 'the mountain of the Chang-ti is a fat mountain, and that we must not look at fat mountains',[1] when I have made the sun flee and have dried up the moon, will this farrago be agreeable to the supreme being, and useful to my subjects and to myself?

Above all I can't suffer the madness of the sects that surround us. On one side I see Lao-Tse, who was conceived by his mother by the union of heaven and earth, and whom she carried for eighty years. I have no more faith in his doctrine of annihilation and universal renunciation than in the white hair with which he was born and the black cow he mounted to go and preach his doctrine.

The god Fo does not impress me either, although his father was a white elephant and he promises an immortal life.

What displeases me most of all is that such fantasies are constantly preached by bonzes who beguile the people in order to govern them. They obtain respect by means of mortifications that terrify nature. Some deprive themselves all their lives of the most healthy food, as if one could please god only by a bad diet. Others put round their necks an iron collar of which they sometimes become very deserving. They drive

---

1. The allusion is to *Psalms* lxviii. 15–16; and in the same way the next words ironize about the miracles of the *Bible*, such as the stopping of the sun.

nails into their thighs as if their thighs were planks. The people follow them in crowds. If a king puts out some edict that displeases them, they tell you coldly that this edict is not mentioned in the commentary of the god Fo, and that it is better to obey god than men. How are we to remedy so extravagant and dangerous a popular malady? You know that toleration is the principle of the government of China and all the countries of Asia; but is this indulgence not very baleful when it exposes an empire to disruption by fanatical views?

KU-SU: May the Chang-ti preserve me from wishing to extinguish in you the spirit of toleration, this virtue so worthy of respect, which is to souls what a permission to eat is to the body! Natural law permits everyone to believe what he pleases, just as he can eat what he pleases. A doctor has no right to kill his patients because they do not observe the diet he prescribed for them. A prince has no right to have those of his subjects hanged who do not think like him; but he has the right to prevent disturbances; and if he is wise it will be very easy for him to uproot superstitions. You know what happened to Daon, sixth king of Chaldea, about 4,000 years ago?

KOO: No, I've no idea; be so kind as to tell me about it.

KU-SU: The Chaldean priests took it into their heads to worship the pikes in the Euphrates. They alleged that a famous pike named Oanness had in times past taught them theology, that this pike was immortal, that he was three feet long and had a little crescent on its tail. It was out of respect for this Oanness that it was forbidden to eat pike. A great dispute arose between the theologians to determine whether the pike Oanness had soft roe or hard roe. The two parties excommunicated one other, and several times came to blows. This is how king Daon managed to put an end to these disorders.

He imposed on both parties a strict fast of three days, after which he asked the partisans of the hard roe pike to dine with him. He sent for a three-foot pike on whose tail a little crescent had been put. 'Is that your god?' said he to the doctors. 'Yes, sire, for it has a crescent on its tail, and he is certainly hard-roed.' The king commanded the pike to be opened, and it had the finest soft roe in the world. 'You can see,' said he, 'that this is not your god since it has soft roe.' And the pike was eaten by the king and his satraps, to the great satisfaction of the hard-roe theologians, who saw that the god of their adversaries had been fried.

The doctors of the opposing party were at once sent for. They were shown a three-foot god which had hard roe and a crescent on its tail, and declared that it was the god Oanness and had soft roe. It was fried like the other, and was seen to be hard-roed. Thus the two parties were equally foolish, and as they had broken their fast they were told by the good king Daon that he had nothing but pike to offer them for their dinner. They ate them voraciously, whether soft-roed or hard-roed. The civil war ended, everybody blessed the good king Daon; and from that time on the citizens served pike for dinner as much as they pleased.

KOO: I like king Daon very much, and I promise faithfully to imitate him at the first opportunity that presents itself. I shall always prevent as far as I can (without doing violence to anyone) the worship of Fos and pikes.

I know that in Pegu and in Tongking there are little gods and little talapoins[1] who make the moon wane, and who foretell the future precisely, that is, they see precisely what is not, for the future is not. So far as I can I shall prevent talapoins from coming into my country to take the future for the present and to make the moon wane.

What a pity that there are sects which go from town to town retailing their fantasies like charlatans who sell their drugs! What a disgrace for the human mind that small nations think that only they have a right to the truth, and that the vast empire of China is given up to error! Could the eternal being merely be the god of the island of Formosa or the island of Borneo? Would he abandon the rest of the universe? My dear Ku-Su, he is the father of all men. He allows them all to eat pike. The worthiest homage we can render him is to be virtuous. A pure heart is the finest of all his temples, as said the great emperor Hiao.

1. This name is given to both priests and monkeys.

FIFTH CONVERSATION

KU-SU: Since you have virtue, how will you practise it when you are king?

KOO: By being unjust neither to my neighbours nor to my peoples.

KU-SU: It is not enough to do no evil, you will do good. You will feed the poor by employing them in useful work, and not by endowing idleness. You will beautify the highways, you will dig canals, you will erect public buildings, you will encourage all the arts. You will reward merit of every kind. You will forgive involuntary misconduct.

KOO: That's what I mean by not being unjust; these are all duties.

KU-SU: You think like a true king; but there is the king and the man, public life and private life. You will soon marry. How many wives do you intend to have?

KOO: Oh, I think a dozen will do; a larger number might rob me of time intended for business. I don't at all like those kings who have their 300 wives and their 700 concubines and their thousands of eunuchs to serve them. Most of all, this mania for eunuchs appears to me to be too great an outrage against human nature. I can go so far as to forgive the caponizing of cocks, it makes them better to eat; but eunuchs have not yet been put on the spit. What use is their mutilation? The dalai lama has fifty of them to sing in his pagoda. I should very much like to know whether the Chang-ti takes great pleasure in listening to the pure voices of these fifty geldings.

I also find it very ridiculous that there are bonzes who don't marry. They boast of being wiser than the other Chinese: well then, let them make wise children. It's a funny way to honour the Chang-ti by depriving him of worshippers! It's a singular way to serve mankind by setting an example of the annihilation of mankind! The good little lama named Stelca ed isant Errepi[1] thought 'that every priest should make as many

1. *Note by Voltaire:* Stelca ed isant Errepie means, in Chinese, the *abbé* Castel de Saint-Pierre. [The former name is an anagram of the latter. Charles Irénée Castel de Saint-Pierre was unfortunately not as reasonable

children as he could'. He practised what he preached and was most useful in his time. As for me, I would marry off all the lamas and bonzes and lamesses and bonzesses who have any vocation for this holy work. They will certainly be better citizens for it, and I think I should thus be doing the kingdom of Loo a great service.

KU-SU: Oh, what a good prince we shall have in you! You make me weep with joy. You will not content yourself with having wives and subjects, for after all one cannot spend the whole day in making edicts and children: you will no doubt have friends?

KOO: I already have some, and good ones, who warn me of my defects. I take the liberty of reproving theirs. They console me, and I console them. Friendship is the balm of life; it is worth more than that of the chemist Erueil and even than the sachets of the great Ranoud.[1] I'm astonished that friendship has not been made a religious precept; I am tempted to insert it into our ritual.

KU-SU: Take care not to. Friendship is sacred enough in itself; never impose it. The heart must be free. Besides, if you made friendship into a precept, a mystery, a rite, a ceremony, there would be a thousand bonzes who would make friendship ridiculous by preaching and by writing down their fantasies. It must not be exposed to this profanation.

But how will you behave to your enemies? Confucius recommends us in twenty texts to love them. Doesn't that seem to you a little difficult?

KOO: Love one's enemies! Great heavens! nothing is more common.

KU-SU: How do you mean?

KOO: I think I mean it as one should. I served my apprenticeship of war under the prince Décon against the prince

as he was well-meaning; Voltaire had a sort of affectionate contempt for him and his *Projet de paix perpétuelle* (1713).]

1. These are anagrams of Lièvre, to whom Voltaire refers in a letter of September 1768 (Best. 14252) as one who sold his 'balm of life' to a lot of people who died of it; and of Arnoud, whose sachets, Voltaire tells us in the same letter, were alleged to cure apoplexy.

of the Vis-Brunck.[1] Whenever one of the enemy was wounded and fell into our hands we took care of him as if he were our brother. We often gave our own beds to our wounded and captured enemies, and we slept next to them on tiger-skins spread on the ground. We waited on them ourselves. What more do you want? that we should love them as one loves one's mistress?

KU-SU: I'm very edified by everything you tell me, and I wish that all the nations could hear you; for I'm assured that there are peoples so impertinent that they dare to say that we don't know true virtue, that our good actions are only splendid sins,[2] that we need the lessons of their talapoins to implant good principles in us. Alas! wretches! it is only since yesterday that they can read and write, and they want to teach their masters!

SIXTH CONVERSATION

KU-SU: I won't repeat to you all the commonplaces about all the virtues retailed among us for five or six thousand years. Some of them are of purely personal application, like prudence for guiding our souls, temperance for governing our bodies: these are precepts of policy and health. The true virtues are those which are useful to society, such as loyalty, magnanimity, beneficence, toleration, etc. Thank heaven, there is no old woman among us who doesn't teach all these virtues to her grandchildren. This is the grounding of our youth in the village as in the town. But to my great regret there is one great virtue which is falling out of fashion.

KOO: Which one is it? Name it at once; I'll try to revive it.

KU-SU: It's hospitality. This virtue so important to a

1. *Note by Voltaire:* It is a remarkable thing that by turning inside out Décon and Vis-Brunck, which are Chinese names, we discover Condé and Brunswick [Louis II de Bourbon, prince de Condé ('the great Condé') and Ferdinand, prince of Brunswick, two 'great' soldiers] so famous throughout the world are these famous names!

2. All this is of course directed against Christian teachings: here in particular Voltaire alludes to saint Augustine, who said that the good actions of pagans could at most be *peccata splendida*.

society, this sacred bond between men has begun to slacken since we have taverns. It is said that this pernicious institution came to us from certain western savages. These wretches apparently have no home in which to welcome travellers. How pleasant to receive in the great city of Loo, in the fine Honchan square, in my house Ki, a generous stranger just arrived from Samarkand, for whom I become from this moment a holy man, and who is obliged by all divine and human laws to entertain me when I travel in Tartary, and to be my intimate friend!

The savages I have in mind entertain strangers only for money, in disgusting shanties. They sell this infamous reception dearly, and what's more I'm told that these poor people regard themselves as our superiors, that they boast of having a purer morality. They allege that their ministers preach better than Confucius, in short, that it is for them to teach us justice because they sell bad wine on the highways, because their women behave madly in the streets, and because they dance while ours cultivate silkworms.

KOO: I think hospitality is an excellent thing; I practise it with pleasure, but I dread its abuse. There are people in the region of the great Tibet who are very badly lodged, who like to travel, and who would voyage for nothing from one end of the world to another; and if you were to go to the great Tibet to enjoy there the obligations of hospitality you would find neither bed nor stock-pot. It's enough to put one off politeness.

KU-SU: The disadvantage is small; it is easy to remedy it by receiving only well-recommended people. There are no virtues free of danger; and this is just why it's noble to embrace them.

How wise and holy is our Confucius! There is no virtue he does not inspire; every one of his sayings tends to the happiness of mankind; this one comes to my mind; it is the fifty-third:

Acknowledge benefits by benefits, and never avenge injuries.[1]

What maxim, what law can western peoples set against so pure a morality? In how many passages does Confucius

---

1. This sentiment is not expressed in the *Analects* in so many words.

recommend humility? There would never be quarrels on earth if this virtue were practised.

KOO: I have read everything Confucius and the sages of earlier centuries have written on humility; but it appears to me that they have never given a precise enough definition of it. There is perhaps little humility in daring to criticize them, but at least I've the humility to admit that I haven't understood them. What do you think?

KU-SU: I will obey humbly. I believe that humility is the modesty of the soul, for external modesty is merely courtesy. Humility cannot consist of denying to oneself the superiority one may have acquired over another. A good doctor cannot conceal from himself that he knows more than his delirious patient. He who teaches astronomy must admit to himself that he is more learned than his disciples. He cannot help but know it, but he should not become conceited. Humility is not abjection, it is the corrective of self-esteem, as modesty is the corrective of pride.

KOO: Good! I want to live in the practice of all these virtues and in the worship of a simple and universal god, far from the chimeras of sophists and the illusions of false prophets. Love of my neighbour will be my virtue on the throne, and the love of god my religion. I will despise the god Fo and Lao Tse and Vishnoo, who has incarnated so often among the Indians, and Sammonocodom[1] who descended from heaven to play at flying kites among the Siamese, and the Camis[2] who arrived in Japan from the moon.

Woe betide the people so stupid and so barbarous as to think that there is a god for its province alone! That is a blasphemy. What! the light of the sun illuminates all eyes, and we are to believe that the light of god illuminates only a small and puny nation in a corner of the globe! What a horror, and what a stupidity! The divinity speaks to the hearts of all men, and the bonds of charity should unite them from one end of the universe to the other.

1. A corruption of Samana-Gotama, one of the names of the Buddha.
2. The Japanese Kami is a supernatural being, god, guardian spirit and the like.

KU-SU: O wise Koo! You have spoken like a man inspired by the very Chang-ti. You will be a worthy prince. I was your teacher, and you have become mine.

Catéchisme du curé: The priest's catechism

ARISTON: Well my dear Théotime, so you're going to be a country priest?

THEOTIME: Yes, they're giving me a small parish, which I like better than a big one. I have only a limited share of intelligence and energy. I certainly wouldn't be able to direct seventy thousand souls, since I have only one; and I've always wondered at the self-confidence of those who are in charge of these immense districts. I don't feel capable of such an administration; a big flock frightens me, but I could do some good for a small one. I have studied enough law to prevent my poor parishioners, so far as possible, from ruining themselves with lawsuits. I know enough medicine to explain simple remedies to them when they're ill. I have enough knowledge of agriculture to give them useful advice occasionally. The lord of the place and his wife are decent people who are not at all devout, and who will help me to do good. I flatter myself that I shall live happily enough, and that I shan't make my parish unhappy.

ARISTON: Aren't you sorry to have no wife? It would be a great comfort. Having preached, chanted, confessed, administered communion, baptized, buried, it would be pleasant to find at home a tender, agreeable and decent wife, who would take care of your linen and your person, who would cheer you up in health, who would care for you in sickness, who would bear you pretty children, who would be useful to the state when well educated. I'm sorry for you, you who serve men, that you are deprived of a comfort so necessary to men.

THEOTIME: The Greek church takes great care to encourage priests to marry; the Anglican church and the Protestants have the same wisdom; the Latin church has a contrary wisdom: I must submit to it. Perhaps, now that the philosophic spirit has made so much progress, a council will make laws more favourable to humanity than those of the council of Trent. In the meanwhile I must conform to existing laws. It is very hard, I know, but so many people who were better than I am submitted to it that I mustn't grumble.

ARISTON: You are learned, and you have a wise eloquence; how do you intend to preach to countrymen?

THEOTIME: As I would preach to kings. I shall always speak of morality and never of controversy. God forbid that I should elaborate on concomitant grace, the efficacious grace we resist, the sufficient grace which does not suffice; or examine whether the angels who ate with Abraham and Lot had bodies or whether they pretended to eat. There are a thousand things my audience would not understand, nor I either. I shall try to make good men and to be good myself, but I shall not create theologians, and I shall be one as little as I can.

ARISTON: Oh! what a good priest! I'd like to buy a country house in your parish. Tell me please how you will conduct confession.

THEOTIME: Confession is an excellent thing, a curb on crimes, invented in the most distant antiquity. People confessed in the celebration of all the ancient mysteries. We have imitated and sanctified this wise practice. It is very good for bringing to forgiveness hearts ulcerated by hate, and for inducing petty thieves to return what they may have stolen from their neighbours. It has some drawbacks. There are many tactless confessors, especially among the monks, who sometimes teach the girls more foolishness than the village lads could do to them. No details in confession: it is not a judicial interrogation, it is the avowal of his wrong-doing made by a sinner to the supreme being through another sinner who will accuse himself in turn. This salutary avowal is not made to satisfy human curiosity.

ARISTON: And excommunications? Will you use them?

THEOTIME: No. There are rituals for the excommunication of grasshoppers, sorcerers and actors. I shall not forbid grasshoppers to go to church, since they never go there. I shall not excommunicate sorcerers because there are no sorcerers. And as for actors, as they are subsidized by the king and authorized by law, I shall take great care not to defame them.[1] I will even admit, as between friends, that I like the theatre when it does not offend morality. I passionately love *Le Misanthrope, Athalie*[2] and other plays which, it seems to me, are schools of virtue and propriety. The lord of my village has some of these plays performed in his manor by young people of talent. These performances inspire virtue by the allurement of pleasure. They form taste, they teach to speak well and to pronounce well. All this appears to me very innocent and even very useful. I certainly hope to attend these performances for my instruction, but in a curtained box so as not to scandalize the weak.

ARISTON: The more you disclose your views, the greater is my wish to become your parishioner. There's one important detail that troubles me. How will you prevent the peasants from getting drunk on feast days? That's the chief way they celebrate. Some of them can be seen overpowered by liquid poison, heads hanging to the knees, hands dangling, seeing nothing, hearing nothing, reduced to a state far below that of beasts, led home, staggering, by their tearful wives, unable to work the next day, often ill, and brutalized for the rest of their lives. Others can be seen, enraged by wine, provoking bloody quarrels, exchanging blows, and sometimes ending with murder these fearful scenes which are the disgrace of mankind. It must be admitted, the state loses more subjects through feasts than through battles. How will you be able to diminish so execrable an abuse in your parish?

THEOTIME: I have decided what to do. I shall allow them, I shall even press them, to cultivate their fields on feast days, after divine service, which I will celebrate very early. It is the idleness of the holiday that leads them to the tavern. Working days are not days of debauchery and murder. Moderate labour contributes to the health of the body and to that of the

1. This is a typical example of Voltaire's exacerbated sense of justice: although the point at issue was a relatively minor one, Voltaire was wellnigh obsessed by the ambivalent attitude of the *ancien régime* to the actor; see, for instance, his *Notebooks*, index *s.v.* 'actor'.
2. The former by Molière, the latter by Racine.

soul. Besides, this labour is necessary to the state. Assume five million men who earn on the average ten *sous* a day, and this is quite a moderate estimate. You make these five million men useless for thirty days a year: thus the state loses thirty times five million ten-*sous* pieces in manpower. Now god has certainly never commanded either this loss or drunkenness.

ARISTON: Thus you will reconcile prayer and work: god commands both. You will save god and your neighbour. But what will be your attitude in ecclesiastic disputes?

THEOTIME: None. Virtue is never argued about because it comes from god. We quarrel about opinions held by men.

ARISTON: Oh! what a good priest! what a good priest!

Catéchisme du japonais: Japanese catechism[1]

THE INDIAN: Is it true that formerly the Japanese couldn't cook, that they had subjected their kingdom to the grand lama, that this grand lama ruled the roost in your country, that he sent you from time to time a little lama who came to collect tribute, and that in exchange he gave you a sign of protection made with the first two fingers and the thumb?

THE JAPANESE: Alas! It's only too true. Imagine that even all the posts of *canusi*,[2] who are the chief cooks of our island, were in the gift of the lama, and were not given for the love of god. What is more, every secular house paid an ounce of silver a year to this chief cook of Tibet. In compensation he granted us only the small and rather evil-tasting dishes called relics. And when some new whim took him, like making war against the peoples of the Tangut, he levied new subsidies on us. Our nation often complained, but fruitlessly, and indeed

1. The allusions in this dialogue, in addition to those explained by Voltaire himself, could hardly be more open. Thus it is scarcely necessary to interpret batistapanes (anabaptists), diestes (deists), quekars. The anagrams are only slightly less self-evident; the pispates are the *papistes* (papists), Terluh is Luther, Vincal is Calvin. More general equivalents are the Japanese themselves, who represent the English, and the emperor, who is Henry VIII. The cooks are the priests, and the grand lama is the pope, Tibet is Rome, *daïri* means king.

2. *Note by Voltaire:* The *canusi* are the ancient priests of Japan.

every complaint led only to our paying a little more. Finally love, which does all for the best, delivered us from this servitude. One of the emperors fell out with the grand lama about a woman. But it must be admitted that those who were most useful to us in this affair were our *canusi*, also called pauxcospie.[1] It is to them that we are obliged for having thrown off the yoke; and this is how it was done.

The grand lama had an agreeable mania: he thought that he was always in the right. Our *daïri* and our *canusi* wanted to be in the right, at least sometimes. The grand lama found this an absurd pretension. Our *canusi* stuck to their positions, and broke with him for good.

THE INDIAN: Splendid! since then you have no doubt been happy and peaceful?

THE JAPANESE: Not at all. We persecuted, tore, devoured one another for nearly two centuries. Our *canusi* in vain wanted to be in the right. They have been reasonable for only a hundred years. But since that time we can confidently consider ourselves to be one of the happiest nations on earth.

THE INDIAN: How can you enjoy such happiness if it is true, as I am told, that you have a dozen kitchen factions in your empire? You must have a dozen civil wars every year.

THE JAPANESE: Why? If there are a dozen caterers each of whom has a different recipe, must we on that account cut each others' throats instead of dining? On the contrary, every man will eat well in his fashion with the cook who pleases him best.

THE INDIAN: It is true that we should not dispute about tastes; but we do dispute, and the quarrel gets heated.

THE JAPANESE: After men have disputed for a very long time, and it has been realized that all these quarrels teach men only to harm one another, they finally decide that mutual toleration is unquestionably best.

THE INDIAN: And who, please, are the caterers who divide your nation in the art of drinking and eating?

1. *Note by Voltaire:* Pauxcospie, anagram of *épiscopaux* [bishops].

THE JAPANESE: First there are the Breuxeh,[1] who will never give you either black pudding or bacon. They are devoted to the ancient cookery. They would sooner die than lard a chicken. Besides, they are very long-headed, and if there is an ounce of silver to be shared between them and the eleven other cooks, they first take half for themselves, and the rest is for those who can count best.

THE INDIAN: I suppose that you don't eat with those people.

THE JAPANESE: No. Then there are the pispates, who, on certain days of every week and even for a considerable part of the year, would a hundred times sooner eat a hundred *écus'* worth of turbot, trout, sole, salmon, sturgeon than feed themselves on a veal stew which wouldn't cost them four *sous*.

We *canusi*, for our part, very much like beef and a certain pastry called *pudding* in Japanese. For the rest, everybody agrees that our cooks are infinitely more learned than those of the pispates. Nobody has studied the *garum*[2] of the Romans more deeply than we have, knows better the onions of ancient Egypt, the locust paste of the earliest Arabs, the horsemeat of the Tartars. And there is always something to learn in the books of the *canusi*, commonly called pauxcospie.

I shall say nothing of those who will eat only in the manner of Terluh, nor of those who hold to the regimen of Vincal, nor of the batistapanes, nor of the others; but the quekars deserve special attention. They are the only table companions whom I've never seen getting drunk and swearing. They are very difficult to cheat; but they will never cheat you. It seems that the law to love one's neighbour as yourself was made only for those people. For, really, how can a good Japanese boast of loving his neighbour as himself, when for the sake of a little money he goes into battle to put a lead bullet into his head or to butcher him with a four-inch kriss? He exposes himself to being butchered and to receive lead bullets. Thus it

1. *Note by Voltaire:* It is easy to see that the Breuxeh are the *Hébreux* [Hebrews], *et sic de ceteris*.
2. A sauce, made principally of fish.

can be said much more truthfully that he hates his neighbour as himself. The quekars have never suffered from this frenzy. They say that poor humans are clay pitchers made to last a very little time, and it isn't worth while for them wantonly to crush themselves against each other.

I must admit that if I were not a *canusi* I wouldn't mind being a quekar. You must agree that it is impossible to quarrel with such pacific cooks.

There are others, who are very numerous, called diestes. These give dinner to everybody without distinction, and at their tables you are free to eat anything you please, larded, barded,[1] without lard, without bard, with eggs, with oil, partridge, salmon, grey wine,[2] red wine. All this is indifferent to them. Provided that you say some prayer to god before or after dinner, or even simply before breakfast, and are decent folk, they will laugh with you at the expense of the grand lama, to whom this will do no harm, and at the expense of Terluh, of Vincal, and of Memnon, etc. We only expect our diestes to admit that our *canusi* are very learned in cookery, and above all never to talk of cutting off our revenues; then we shall live together very peacefully.

THE INDIAN: But still there must be a dominant kitchen, the king's kitchen.

THE JAPANESE: I agree, but when the king of Japan has eaten well, he must be of good cheer, and mustn't prevent his worthy subjects from digesting.

THE INDIAN: But if obstinate people are determined to eat sausages to spite the king who has an aversion for them, if four or five thousand of them assemble, armed with grills to cook their sausages, if they insult those who don't eat them?

THE JAPANESE: Then they must be punished like drunkards who disturb the people's peace. We have provided against this danger. Only those who eat like the king are eligible for the dignities of the state. All the others can dine as the fancy takes them, but they are excluded from office. Public gatherings are absolutely forbidden, and punished on the spot without right of appeal. All quarrels at table are carefully

1. That is, larded with bacon.   2. Now usually called *rosé*.

repressed, according to the precept of our great Japanese cook, SUTI RAHO CUS FLAC, who wrote in the sacred language:

> *Natis in usum laetitia scyphis*
> *Pugnare Thracum est . . .*

which means: 'Dinner was made for quiet and decent joy, and we should not throw glasses at each other.'[1]

With these maxims we live happily in our country. Our liberty is strengthened under our *taicosema*, our wealth increases, we have 200 junks of the line, and we are the terror of our neighbours.

THE INDIAN: Why then did the excellent versifier Recina, son of the Indian poet Recina who is so tender, so precise, so harmonious, so eloquent, say in a rhymed didactic work entitled *Grace* and not *The Graces*:

> '*Le Japon, où jadis brilla tant de lumière,*
> *n'est plus qu'un triste amas de folles visions*' ?[2]

THE JAPANESE: The Recina you mention is himself a great visionary. Doesn't this poor Indian know that we taught him what light is; that if the true movement of the planets is now known in India, it is thanks to us; that we alone taught mankind the basic laws of nature and the infinitesimal calculus; that, to descend to things of more general use, the people of his country learned only from us to make junks on mathematical principles; that they owe us even the woven stockings with which they cover their legs? Having invented so many admirable or useful things is it possible that we are no more than fools, and that a man who has versified other men's fantasies is the only wise man? Let him leave us to do our cooking, and write verse, if he must, on more poetic subjects.[3]

1. Horace, *Odes* I. xxvii. 1–2; the literal meaning is 'It is fit only for Thracians to fight with goblets meant for pleasure.' The name of the Japanese cook is an anagram of Horatius Flaccus.

2. Louis Racine, *La Grâce* (1720), iv: 'Japan, where once shone so much light, is now only a wretched mass of mad visions.' The author was the son of Jean Racine.

3. *Note by Voltaire:* N.B. The Indian Recina, on the faith of his country's dreamers, believed that good sauces could not be made unless

THE INDIAN: What can you expect? He has the prejudices of his country, those of his party, and his own.

THE JAPANESE: Oh! that's too many prejudices.

Catéchisme du jardinier ou entretien du bacha Tuctan et du jardinier Karpos: The Gardener's catechism or conversation between the pasha Tuctan and the gardener Karpos

TUCTAN: Well, friend Karpos, you are selling your vegetables at a high price; but they are good. . . . What is your religion now?

KARPOS: Upon my word, pasha, I find it very difficult to tell you. When our little island of Samos belonged to the Greeks, I remember that they made me say that the *agion pneuma*[1] was produced only by the *tou patrou*,[2] They made me pray to god upright on my two legs, hands crossed. I was forbidden to take milk in lent. The Venetians came, and then my Venetian priest made me say that the *agion pneuma* came from the *tou patrou* and the *tou viou*, allowed me to take milk, and made me pray god on my knees. The Greeks returned and chased away the Venetians. Then we had to renounce the *tou viou* and cream. You finally chased away the Greeks, and I hear you shout with all your might *Allah illa Allah*. I hardly

---

Brahma, of his own accord, himself taught the sauce to his favourites; that there was an infinite number of cooks incapable of making a stew though perfectly determined to succeed, and that Brahma by sheer malice deprived them of the means of doing so. Such nonsense is not believed in Japan, where this maxim is held to be an incontestable truth:

'God never acts by partial will, but by general laws.'

[This line was quoted by Voltaire in English, but very approximately, from Alexander Pope's *Essay on Man* (i. 145–6):

'the first Almighty Cause
Acts not by partial, but by general laws; . . .']

1. The holy spirit. 'Tou patrou' is the father, 'tou viou', the son.

2. *Note by Voltaire:* See the article 'Certitude', *Dictionnaire encyclopédique*.

know any longer what I am. I love god with all my heart, and I sell my vegetables very reasonably.

TUCTAN: You've got some very fine figs there.

KARPOS: Pasha, they are entirely at your disposal.

TUCTAN: I'm told that you also have a pretty daughter.

KARPOS: Yes, pasha; but she is not at your disposal.

TUCTAN: Why not, wretch?

KARPOS: Because I'm an honest man: I'm allowed to sell my figs, but not to sell my daughter.

TUCTAN: And by what law aren't you allowed to sell that fruit?

KARPOS: By the law of all honest gardeners. My daughter's honour belongs to her, not to me. It isn't merchandise.

TUCTAN: So you aren't faithful to your pasha?

KARPOS: Very faithful in all things just, for as long as you are my master.

TUCTAN: But if your Greek *papa* conspired against me, and if, on behalf of the *tou patrou* and the *tou viou*, he ordered you to join his plot, wouldn't you be devout enough to do it?

KARPOS: I? Not at all, I most certainly wouldn't.

TUCTAN: And why would you refuse to obey your Greek *papa* when such a fine opportunity offers?

KARPOS: It's because I have taken an oath of obedience to you, and well know that the *tou patrou* does not order conspiracies.

TUCTAN: I'm very glad to hear it. But if your Greeks were unfortunately to recapture the island and expelled me, would you be faithful to me?

KARPOS: Come! how could I then be faithful to you since you would no longer be my pasha?

TUCTAN: And the oath you took to me? What would become of it?

KARPOS: It would be like my figs, you would no longer dispose of it. Isn't it true (with great respect) that if you were dead at this very moment I should no longer owe you anything?

TUCTAN: The supposition is hardly civil, but you are right.

KARPOS: Well, if you were expelled it would be as if you

were dead, for you would have a successor to whom I would
have to take another oath. Could you exact from me a fidelity
which could be of no use to you? It is as if, not being able to
eat my figs, you wanted to prevent me from selling them to
others.

TUCTAN: How your argue! You have principles then?

KARPOS: Yes, in my fashion. They are few, but they suffice
me; and if I had more they would encumber me.

TUCTAN: I should be curious to know your principles.

KARPOS: They are, for instance, to be a good husband, a
good father, a good neighbour, a good subject, and a good
gardener. I don't go beyond that, and I hope that god will
have mercy on me.

TUCTAN: And do you think that he will have mercy on me,
who am the governor of your island?

KARPOS: And how do you expect me to know that? Is it for
me to guess how god deals with pashas? It's a matter between
you and him; I don't interfere in it in any way. I simply
imagine that, if you are as good a pasha as I am a gardener,
god will treat you very well.

TUCTAN: By Mohammed! I'm delighted with this idolator.
Farewell friend; may Allah have you in his holy keeping!

KARPOS: A thousand thanks. May Theos have pity on you,
pasha!

Certain, certitude: Certain, certainty

'How old is your friend Christopher?'

'Twenty-eight. I have seen his marriage contract and his
baptismal certificate. I have known him since his childhood.
He is twenty-eight; it is a certainty, I'm certain of it.'

Hardly had I heard the reply of this man, so sure of what he
says, and of twenty others who confirmed the same thing,
than I discovered that Christopher's baptismal certificate
had been antedated by a strange trick for hidden reasons.
Those to whom I spoke don't yet know about it. In the meanwhile they're still certain of something false.

If you had asked the entire world before the era of Copernicus: 'Did the sun rise today? did it set?' everybody would have answered you: 'We're absolutely certain of it.' They were certain, and they were mistaken.

Spells, divination, possession were for long the surest things in the world in the eyes of all peoples. What an innumerable crowd of people saw all these fine things and were certain of them! Today this certainty has somewhat diminished.

A young man who was beginning to study geometry called on me. He had not got beyond the definition of triangles. 'Aren't you certain,' I said, 'that the three angles of a triangle are equal to two right angles?' He replied that not only was he not at all certain of it, but that he did not even have a clear idea of this proposition. I demonstrated it to him; he then became very certain of it, and will be so all his life.

That certitude is very different from the others: they were no more than probabilities, and these probabilities, once examined, became errors; but mathematical certitude is immutable and eternal.

I exist, I think, I feel pain. Is all this as certain as a geometric truth? Yes. Why? It is because these truths are proved by the same principle that a thing cannot be and not be at the same time. I cannot at the same time exist and not exist, feel and not feel. A triangle cannot at the same time have and not have 180 degrees, which is the sum of two right angles.

The physical certainty of my existence and of my feelings, and mathematical certainty thus have the same value, although they are of a different kind.

This does not apply to the certainty based on appearances or to the unanimous reports made by men.

'But really!' you tell me, 'aren't you certain that Peking exists? Haven't we got fabrics from Peking? People from different countries, of different opinions, who wrote violently against each other while all preached the truth in Peking, haven't they assured you of the existence of this city?' I answered that it seems to me extremely probable that there was then a city of Peking; but I would not wish to bet my life that this city exists, and I would bet my life at any time that the three angles of a triangle are equal to two right angles.

Something very droll has been published in the *Dictionnaire encyclopédique*. It is maintained there that if all Paris told one that marshal de Saxe had been resurrected, one should be as sure, as certain of it as one would be if told by all Paris that marshal de Saxe had won the battle of Fontenoy. Consider, I beg, how admirable is this reasoning: 'I believe all Paris when they tell me something possible in principle; therefore I must believe all Paris when they tell me something impossible in principle and physically.'

Apparently the author of this article wanted to have a good laugh, and the other author, who goes into raptures at the end of this article and writes against himself, also wanted to have a good laugh. As for me, who have undertaken this little *Dictionary* in order to put questions, I am far from being certain.

Chaîne des êtres créés: Great chain of being [1]

The gradation of beings which ascends from the lightest atom to the supreme being, this ladder of the infinite, strikes one with wonder. But when one looks at it attentively this great phantasm vanishes, as formerly all apparitions fled at the crowing of the cock.

At first the imagination is gratified by the imperceptible passage from brute matter to organized matter, from plants to zoophytes, from these zoophytes to animals, from these to man, from man to spirits, from these spirits, dressed in little aerial bodies, to immaterial substances, and finally a thousand different orders of these substances which ascend from beauty to perfection and finally to god himself. This hierarchy much pleases decent folk, who liken it to the pope and his cardinals followed by the archbishops and the bishops, after whom come rectors, vicars, simple priests, deacons, sub-deacons;

1. The notion of the interdependent continuity of created beings has had a fascinating history, admirably described in A. O. Lovejoy's *The Great Chain of Being* (1936).

then appear the monks, and the march-past ends with the capuchins.[1]

But there is a rather greater distance between god and his most perfect creatures than between the holy father and the dean of the sacred college. This dean can become pope, but the most perfect of the spirits created by the supreme being cannot become god: there is infinity between god and him.

Nor does this chain, this alleged gradation exist among the vegetables and the animals which have been destroyed. There are no longer any murex. The Jews were forbidden[2] to eat the griffin and the ixion. These two species have disappeared from the world, whatever Bochart[3] may say. Where then is the chain?

Even if we had not lost several species, it is obvious that they can be destroyed. The lions, the rhinoceros are getting quite rare.

It is very probable that there have been races of men which are no longer found. But I hope that they have all survived, like the whites, the blacks, the Kaffirs, to whom nature has given a skin apron hanging from the belly half way down the thigh, the Samoyedes, whose wives have one beautifully black breast, etc.

Is there not obviously a gap between monkey and man? Is it not easy to imagine an animal with two feet and no feathers, intelligent without having also the power of speech or our appearance, which we could tame, which would answer our signals and serve us? And between this new species and man, could we not imagine others?

Divine Plato, you place in heaven a succession of celestial substances beyond man. For our part, we believe in a few of these substances, because this is taught by our faith. But you, what reason have you for believing in them? It would seem

1. Voltaire had mixed feelings about the Capuchins, and himself later become an honorary member of the order, frequently signing himself 'unworthy Capuchin'.

2. In the original edition Voltaire had merely 'It was forbidden'.

3. In the context the reference must be to Samuel Bochart's *Hierozoicon* (Londini, 1663), in which the animals of the *Bible* are discussed with minute erudition.

that you have not spoken to Socrates's demon, and good old Er who resuscitated specially to reveal to you the secrets of the other world, taught you nothing about these substances.

The alleged chain is no less interrupted in the physical universe.

What gradation, if you please, between your planets? The moon is forty times smaller than our globe. When you have travelled from the moon through space you come to Venus: it is about as big as the earth. Thence you go to Mercury, which revolves in an ellipse very different from the circle traversed by Venus. It is twenty-seven times smaller than we are, the sun a million times bigger, Mars five times smaller. This last makes its revolution in two years, his neighbour Jupiter in twelve, Saturn in thirty, even though Saturn, the most distant of all, is not as big as Jupiter. Where is the alleged gradation?

And then how can you expect there to be a chain that links everything in the great empty spaces? If there is one it is certainly that which Newton discovered: this is what makes all the globes of the planetary world gravitate towards one another in this immense void.

O Plato, so much admired, I fear that you have told us nothing but fables, and that you have never uttered anything but sophisms!

O Plato! You have done much more evil than you think. I shall be asked how, but I shall not answer.

Chaîne des événements: Chain of events

It is said that the present gives birth to the future. Events are linked to each other by an invisible fate: destiny, which in Homer is superior to Jupiter himself. This master of gods and men declared plainly that he could not prevent his son Sarpedon from dying at the appointed time. Sarpedon was born at the moment at which he had to be born, and could not have been born at any other. He could not die anywhere but before Troy. He could not be buried elsewhere than in Lycia. At the appointed time his body had to produce vegetables which had to be changed into the substance of some Lycians. His heirs had to establish a new order in his states. This new order had to influence neighbouring kingdoms. From this resulted a new disposition of war and peace with the neighbours of the neighbours of Lycia. Thus by degrees the destiny of the whole world depended on the death of Sarpedon, which depended on another event, which was bound up with others back to the origin of all things.

If a single one of these facts had been arranged differently a different universe would have resulted; it was not possible for the actual universe to exist and not to exist; therefore it was not possible for Jupiter to save his son's life, for all he was Jupiter.

This system of necessity and fatality was invented in our times by Leibniz, so he claims, under the name of *sufficient reason*. It is nevertheless very old: it is hardly a discovery that there is no effect without a cause, and that the smallest cause often produces the greatest effects.

Lord Bolingbroke admitted that the petty quarrels of the duchess of Marlborough and lady Masham gave him the opportunity to make the special treaty between queen Anne and Louis XIV. This treaty led to the peace of Utrecht. This peace of Utrecht confirmed Philip V on the throne of Spain. Philip V took Naples and Sicily from the house of Austria. The Spanish prince who is today king of Naples clearly owes his kingdom to lady Masham; and he would not have had it, he would perhaps not even have been born, if the duchess of Marlborough had been more indulgent towards the queen of England. His existence in Naples depended on one foolishness more or less at the court of London. Examine the situations of all the peoples of the universe. They are established in the same way on a succession of facts which appear to be connected with nothing, but which are connected with everything. All is wheels, pulleys, ropes, springs in this immense machine.

So it is in the physical order. A wind that blows from deepest Africa and the southern seas brings part of the African atmosphere, which falls as rain in the valleys of the Alps. These rains fertilize our land. Our north wind in its turn sends our vapours to the blacks. We benefit Guinea, and Guinea benefits us in its turn. The chain extends from one end of the universe to the other.

But it seems to me that the truth of this principle is sadly misused. People conclude from it that there is no atom so small that its movement has not influenced the present arrangement of the entire world; that there is no phenomenon too small, whether among men or among animals, to be an essential link in the great chain of destiny.

Let us be clear about this. Every effect obviously has its cause, which can be retraced from cause to cause into the abyss of eternity; but every cause does not have its effect to the end of time. I admit that all events are produced by one another. If the past gives birth to the present, the present gives birth to the future. All things have fathers, but not all things have children. This is exactly like a genealogical tree: we know that every house goes back to Adam, but plenty of people in the family died without posterity.

There is a genealogical tree of this world's events. It is unquestionable that the inhabitants of Gaul and of Spain are descended from Gomer, and the Russians from Magog, his younger brother: this genealogy is found in so many heavy books.[1] It is undeniable that the grand Turk, who is also descended from Magog, owes it to him that he was thoroughly defeated in 1769 by the empress of Russia, Catherine II. This adventure is clearly connected with other great adventures. But whether Magog spat to the right or to the left near mount Caucasus, whether he made two rings in a well or three, whether he slept on his left side or his right, I do not see that this has much influenced our present affairs.

We must reflect that nature is not a plenum, and that all movement is not communicated from one thing to another until it has gone round the world. Throw a body of similar density into water, and you can easily calculate that at the end of a certain time the movement of this body and that which it communicated to the water will have disappeared. Movement

1. All deriving ultimately from the table of nations in *Genesis* x.

is lost and restored. Therefore the movement Magog may have produced when he spat into a well cannot have had any influence on what is happening today in Moldavia and Walla-chia. Therefore the events of the present are not the children of all past events. They have their direct lines of descent, but a thousand little collateral lines are of no use to them. Once again, every being has its father, but not every being has children.

Chine (de la): On China

We go to China for china-clay as if we had none of our own; for fabrics as if we lack fabrics; for a little herb to absorb water as if we had no simples in our climes. In return, we want to convert the Chinese. This is very praiseworthy zeal, but we should not question their antiquity and tell them that they are idolators. In fact, would we approve a Capuchin who, having been well received in a country-house of the Montmorencies, tried to convince them that they are newly created nobles, like the king's secretaries, and accused them of being idolators because they had found in the house two or three statues of profoundly respected high constables?

The famous Wolff, professor of mathematics in the univer-sity of Halle, delivered one day a very fine discourse in praise of Chinese philosophy. He praised that ancient species of men, who differ from us by their beards, eyes, noses, ears and ways of thinking. As I say, he praised the Chinese for wor-shipping a supreme god and for loving virtue. He did this justice to the emperors of China, to the *kalao*, to the law-courts, to the scholars. The justice done to the bonzes was of a differ-ent kind.

It must be appreciated that this Wolff attracted to Halle 1,000 students from all nations. In the same university there was a professor of theology named Lange, who attracted nobody. This man, desperate because he was freezing to death alone in his auditorium, quite naturally wanted to ruin the professor of mathematics. As was the custom of his kind, he inevitably accused him of not believing in god.

Some European writers, who had never been to China, had alleged that the government of Peking was atheist; Wolff had praised the philosophers of Peking; therefore Wolff was an atheist. Envy and hatred have never made a better syllogism. This argument by Lange, supported by a cabal and a protector, convinced the king[1] of the land, who sent a formal dilemma to the mathematician: this dilemma gave him the choice between leaving Halle within twenty-four hours and being hung. And as Wolff reasoned very judiciously he did not fail to leave. His withdrawal deprived the king of two or three hundred thousand crowns a year, which this philosopher had brought into the kingdom by the multitude of his disciples.

This example ought to make sovereigns realize that one should not always listen to calumny and sacrifice a great man to the fury of a fool. Let us return to China.

What are we thinking of, we inhabitants of the far west, to argue bitterly and with torrents of insults whether or not there had been fourteen princes before Fo-hi, emperor of China, and whether this Fo-hi lived 3,000 or 2,900 years before our common era? I should like to see two Irishmen take it into their heads to quarrel in Dublin about the ownership in the twelfth century of the estate I occupy today. Is it not obvious that they should refer to me, since I have the archives in my hands? It seems to me that this is also true of the first emperor of China: we must refer to the courts of that country.

Argue as much as you like about the fourteen princes who reigned before Fo-hi, your fine dispute will succeed only in proving that China was then highly populated and under the rule of law. Now I ask you whether a unified nation, which has laws and princes, does not imply prodigious antiquity. Consider how much time is needed for a singular convergence of circumstances to lead to the discovery of iron in mines, for it to be used in agriculture, for the discovery of the shuttle and all the other crafts.

Those who make children with a stroke of the pen have invented a very amusing calculation. By an elegant computa-

1. Frederick William, King of Prussia.

tion the Jesuit Pétau[1] bestows on the earth, 285 years after the
flood, a hundred times as many inhabitants as we dare to
assume today. The Cumberlands[2] and the Whistons[3] have
made equally comical calculations. These good people had only
to consult the registers of our colonies in America. They would
have been much astonished: they would have learned how
slowly mankind multiplies, and how often it diminishes
instead of increasing.

Let us then, we who were born yesterday, who are descended from the Celts, who have only just cleared the forests
of our savage regions, let us leave the Chinese and the Indians
peacefully to enjoy their lovely climate and their antiquity.
Above all let us stop calling the emperor of China and the
peshwa of Deccan idolators. We must not be devotees of
Chinese merit. It is true that the constitution of their empire is
the best in the world, the only one entirely based on paternal
authority (which does not prevent the mandarins from beating
their children freely); the only one in which a provincial
governor is punished if he was not applauded by the people
when leaving office; the only one that has established prizes
for virtue, when everywhere else the laws are limited to the
punishment of crime; the only one that has made its conquerors adopt its laws, while we were still subject to the customary
law of the Burgundians, the Franks and the Goths, who subjugated us. But it must be admitted that the common people,
dominated by the bonzes, are as rascally as ours; that they
sell everything at high prices to foreigners, as we do; that in
the sciences the Chinese are still where we were 200 years

1. Denis Pétau, whose chronologies went into numerous editions in the
original Latin; the character of the book is best defined by the title of the
English translation: *The History of the World or an Account of Time* (London, 1659).

2. Richard Cumberland, bishop of Peterborough, in his posthumous
*Origines gentium antiquissimae or attempts for discovering the times of the first
planting of nations* (London, 1724).

3. William Whiston was one of the first who tried to reconcile science
and religion; his most famous book was *Primitive Christianity Reviv'd*
(London 1711–12), but Voltaire is probably alluding here to his *Sacred
History of the Old and New Testaments* (London, 1745–6).

ago; that, like us, they have a thousand ridiculous prejudices; that they believe in talismans, in judicial astrology, as we did for a long time.

Let us also admit that they were amazed by our thermometer, at the way we freeze liquids with saltpetre, and at all the experiments of Torricelli[1] and Otto Guericke,[2] just as we were when we saw these scientific amusements for the first time. I must add that their doctors cure mortal illnesses no better than ours, and that nature by herself cures minor illnesses in China as she does here. But all this does not alter the fact that 4,000 years ago, when we could not read, the Chinese knew all the indispensably useful things of which we boast today.

Once again, the religion of the scholars is admirable. No superstition, no absurd legends, none of those dogmas that insult reason and nature and to which bonzes give a thousand different meanings because they have none. For more than forty centuries the simplest worship has appeared to them the best. They are what we think Seth, Enoch and Noah were. They are content to worship a god with all the wise men of the world, when in Europe men are divided between Thomas and Bonaventura, between Calvin and Luther, between Jansen and Molina.

Christianisme, recherches historiques sur le Christianisme: Christianity, historical researches into Christianity

Several learned men have been surprised not to find the least trace of Jesus Christ in the historian Josephus, for everybody now agrees that the brief passage concerning him in the *History* is an interpolation.[3]

1. Evangelista Torricelli invented the barometer, among other things, in the seventeenth century.

2. Otto von Guericke is best known for the invention of the air-pump, also in the seventeenth century.

3. *Note by Voltaire:* The Christians, by one of those frauds called pious, grossly falsified a passage in Josephus. They attribute to this Jew, so

The father of Flavius Josephus must nevertheless have been one of the witnesses of all Jesus's miracles. Josephus was of the priestly caste, related to queen Mariamne, Herod's wife. He goes into the most minute details about all the actions of this prince. Nevertheless he does not say a word about the life or the death of Jesus. And this historian, who does not dissimulate a single one of Herod's cruelties, says nothing about the massacre of all the children ordered by him when he received the news that a king of the Jews had been born. The Greek calendar numbers 14,000 children who were massacred on that occasion.

It was the most horrible of all the acts of the tyrants. There is no parallel to it in the history of the whole world.

Nevertheless the best writer the Jews ever had, the only one esteemed by the Romans and the Greeks, makes no mention whatever of this event, as extraordinary as it was appalling. He says nothing about the new star which had appeared in the east after the birth of the saviour, a startling phenomenon which would not have escaped the attention of so enlightened a historian as Josephus. He is also silent about the darkness that covered the whole earth for three hours at midday on the death of the saviour; about the great number of tombs that opened at this moment; and about the crowd of just men who resuscitated.

Learned men never cease to express their surprise when they see that no Roman historian spoke of these prodigies, which occurred in the reign of Tiberius, under the eyes of a Roman governor and a Roman garrison, who must have sent the emperor and the senate a detailed report of the most miracu-

---

obstinate in his religion, four ridiculously interpolated lines; and at the end of this passage they added: *He was the Christ.* Come now! if Josephus had heard people talk about so many events against nature, he would not have limited himself to four lines about them in the history of his country! Come now! so this obstinate Jew said: *Jesus was the Christ!* Well, if you thought him Christ, you would have been a Christian. What an absurdity to make Josephus speak as a Christian! How can there still be theologians stupid or insolent enough to try to justify this fraud by the first Christians, who are known to have fabricated impostures a hundred times worse!

lous event of which mankind has ever heard. Rome itself must have been plunged in profound darkness for three hours. This prodigy must have been noted in the Roman annals and in those of all nations. God did not want all these divine things to be written down by profane hands.

The same learned men find further difficulties in the history of the gospels. They notice that in *Saint Matthew* Jesus Christ says to the scribes and the Pharisees that all the innocent blood that has been shed on earth must be on their heads, from the blood of Abel the just to that of Zachariah, son of Barachiah, whom they killed between the temple and the altar.

They say that in the history of the Hebrews no Zachariah was killed in the temple before the coming of the messiah, nor in his time. But in Josephus's history of the siege of Jerusalem can be found a Zachariah, son of Barachiah, killed in the heart of the temple by the sect of the zealots; this is in chapter XIX of book IV. From this they suspect that the gospel according to saint Matthew was written after the conquest of Jerusalem by Titus. But all doubts and objections of this kind vanish as soon as we reflect on the infinite difference there must be between divinely inspired books and the books of mankind. God wanted to envelop his birth, his life and his death in a cloud as worthy of respect as it is obscure. His ways are in all things different from ours.

Learned men have also been much tormented by the differences between the two genealogies of Jesus Christ. Saint Matthew names Jacob as Joseph's father; Matthan as Jacob's; Eleazar as Matthan's.[1] Saint Luke, on the contrary, says that Joseph was the son of Heli; Heli of Matthat; Matthat of Levi; Levi of Jannai, etc.[2] They are unable to reconcile the fifty-six ancestors Luke gives Jesus since Abraham, with the forty-two different ancestors that Matthew gives him since this same Abraham.[3] And they are startled that Matthew,

1. *Matthew* i. 15–16.
2. *Luke* iii. 23–4; Voltaire has skipped a generation: Melchi came between Levi and Jannai.
3. The former of these figures was correctly computed by Voltaire from *Luke* ii. 23–38; the second is specified in *Matthew* i. 17.

though he mentions forty-two generations, nevertheless sets out only forty-one.

They make further difficulties about Jesus being Mary's son but not Joseph's. They also raise some doubts about the miracles of our saviour, quoting saint Augustine, saint Hilary, and others, who have given these miracles a mystical, allegorical sense: as to the fig tree cursed and withered for not bearing figs, when it was not the season for figs; to the demons sent into the bodies of swine, in a country in which swine were not domesticated; to the water changed into wine at the end of a meal, when the guests were already excited. But all these criticisms by the learned are confounded by faith, which thereby becomes all the purer. The object of this article is solely to follow the historical thread, and to give an exact notion of facts disputed by none.

In the first place, Jesus was born under the Mosaic law, he was circumcised in accordance with that law, he performed all its precepts, he observed all its festivals, and he preached only morality. He did not reveal the mystery of his incarnation. He never told the Jews that he was born of a virgin. He received John's blessing in the water of the Jordan, a ceremony to which several Jews submitted, but he never baptized anyone. He did not mention the seven sacraments. He instituted no ecclesiastical hierarchy during his life. He concealed from his contemporaries that he was the son of god, begotten from eternity, consubstantial with god, and that the holy ghost proceeded from the father and the son. He did not say that his person was composed of two natures and two wills. He wanted these great mysteries to be announced to mankind in the course of time by those who were to be enlightened by the light of the holy ghost. As long as he lived he departed in no way from the law of his fathers. He displayed to mankind only a just man pleasing to god, persecuted by those who envied him, and condemned to death by prejudiced magistrates. He wanted his holy church, established by him, to do all the rest.

In chapter XII of his *History* Josephus mentions a sect of rigorous Jews newly established by a certain Judas the

Galilean. 'They despise', he says, 'the world's evils. They triumph over suffering by their steadfastness. They prefer death to life when its cause is honourable. They have undergone sword and flame, and have had their bones broken, rather than pronounce the slightest word against their legislator, or eat forbidden food.'

It appears that this portrait represents the Judaites, and not the Essenes. For here are the words of Josephus: 'Judas was the author of a new sect, entirely different from the other three, that is, the Sadducees, the Pharisees and the Essenes.' He continues by saying: 'They are of Jewish nationality. They live united among themselves, and regard sensual pleasure as a vice.' The normal meaning of these words shows that the author is referring to the Judaites.

Be this as it may, these Judaites were known before the disciples of Christ began to play an appreciable role in the world. Some worthy folk have taken them for heretics who worshipped Judas Iscariot.

· The Therapeutes were a body different from the Essenes and the Judaites. They resembled the Indian gymnosophists and the Brahmans. 'They have', says Philo, 'an impulse of celestial love which precipitates them into the enthusiasm of the bacchantes and the corybants, and which puts them into the state of contemplation to which they aspire. This sect was born in Alexandria, which was quite filled with Jews, and spread widely in Egypt.'

The disciples of John the baptist also spread a little into Egypt, but chiefly into Syria and Arabia and towards the Persian gulf. They are known today as *Saint John's Christians*. There were also some in Asia Minor. It is said in the *Acts of the Apostles* (chapter 19) that Paul came across several in Ephesus. He said to them: 'Have you received the holy ghost?' They replied: 'We have not even heard that there is a holy ghost.' He said to them: 'Then what baptism have you received?' They replied: 'John's baptism.'

During the first years following the death of Jesus there were seven bodies or sects among the Jews: the Pharisees, the Sadducees, the Essenes, the Judaites, the Therapeutes, the disciples of John, and the disciples of Christ, a small flock whom god led on paths unknown to human wisdom.

The man who contributed most to the strengthening of this new-born body was the same Paul who had persecuted it with the greatest cruelty. He was born at Tarsus, in Cilicia, and was brought up by the famous Pharisee doctor Gamaliel, a disciple of Hillel. The Jews allege that he broke with Gamaliel, who refused to give him his daughter in marriage. Some traces of this anecdote can be found in the *Acts of Saint Thecla*. According to these *Acts* he had a high forehead, his head was bald, his eyebrows met, his nose was aquiline, his figure short and heavy, and his legs crooked. In his dialogue *Philopatris* Lucian draws a rather similar portrait of him. It is very doubtful whether he was a Roman citizen, for in those days no Jew was given this title. They had been expelled from Rome by Tiberius, and Tarsus did not become a Roman colony until a hundred years later, under Caracalla, as Cellarius[1] points out in his geography, book III, and Grotius[2] in his *Commentaries on the Acts*, in which alone we should have confidence.

The faithful were called Christians in Antioch about the year 60 of our common era; but they were known by other names in the Roman empire, as we shall see in what follows. Before that they were distinguishable only by the names of brothers, saints or the faithful. God, who descended on earth to give an example of humility and poverty, thus gave his church the feeblest of beginnings, and directed it into the same humble condition in which he had chosen to be born. All the first faithful were obscure men: they all worked with their hands. The apostle Paul testifies that he earned his living by making tents. Saint Peter resurrected the seamstress Dorcas, who made the robes of the brethren. The assembly of the faithful was held at Joppa, in the house of a courrier named Simon, as can be seen in chapter ix of the *Acts of the Apostles*.

1. Christophorus Cellarius the elder, *Notitia orbis antiqui* (1701-6).
2. Hugo Grotius (Huig de Groot) but something seems to have gone wrong here, for I cannot find this work in his immense output.

The faithful spread secretly to Greece, and a few went thence to Rome, among the Jews, whom the Romans allowed to have a synagogue. At first they did not separate themselves from the Jews. They kept circumcision, and as I have already mentioned elsewhere, the first fifteen secret bishops of Jerusalem were all circumcised, or at least belonged to the Jewish nation.

When the apostle Paul took with him Timotheus, who was the son of a gentle father, he himself circumcised him in the little town of Lystra. But Titus, his other disciple, refused to submit to circumcision. The brethren, disciples of Jesus, were at one with the Jews up to the moment when Paul underwent persecution at Jerusalem because he brought strangers into the temple. He was accused by the Jews of wanting to destroy the Mosaic law through Jesus Christ. It was to cleanse himself of this accusation that the apostle James proposed to the apostle Paul to have his head shaved and to purify himself in the temple with four Jews who had taken a vow to shave themselves. Take these men with you, James told him (*Acts of the Apostles* xxi). 'Purify thyself with them, and all shall know that there is no truth in the things whereof they have been informed concerning thee, and that you continue to keep the law of Moses.'[1]

Thus Paul, who at first had been the bloody persecutor of the little company established by Jesus; Paul, who later wanted to govern this new-born company; Paul, a Christian, practised Judaism so that the world might know that he was calumniated when it was said that he was a Christian; Paul did what all Christians today regard as an abominable crime, a crime punished by fire in Spain, in Portugal, in Italy; and he did it at the urging of the apostle James; and he did it after having received the holy ghost, that is, after having been taught by god himself that Christians must renounce all the Jewish rites formerly instituted by god himself.

Paul was none the less accused of impiety and heresy, and his criminal trial lasted a long time. But it is clear from the very

[1]. *Acts* xxi. 23–4 abridged.

accusations brought against him that he had come to Jerusalem to observe the Jewish rites.

He spoke these very words (*Acts* xxv) to Festus: 'Neither against the law of the Jews, nor against the temple, have I sinned at all.'[1]

The apostles proclaimed Jesus Christ a Jew, observer of the Jewish law, sent by god to have it observed.

'Circumcision indeed profiteth,' says the apostle Paul (*Romans* ii), 'if thou be a doer of the law: but if thou be a transgressor of the law, thy circumcision is to become uncircumcision. If therefore the uncircumcision keeps the ordinances of the law, shall not his uncircumcision be reckoned for circumcision? He is a Jew, which is one inwardly.'[2]

When this apostle speaks of Jesus Christ in his *Epistles* he does not reveal the ineffable mystery of his consubstantiality with god. 'We are delivered by him,' says he (*Romans* v), 'from the anger of god. The gift of god has spread over us by the grace given to a single man, who is Jesus Christ. . . . Death reigned through the sin of a single man; the just will reign in life through a single man, who is Jesus Christ.'[3]

And in chapter viii: 'We, heirs of god, and joint-heirs with Christ.'[4] And in chapter xvi: 'To the only wise god, through Jesus Christ, to whom be the glory for ever.'[5] 'Ye are Christ's; and Christ is god's' (*I Corinthians* iii).[6]

And (*I Corinthians* xv. 27): 'All is subject to him, excepting undoubtedly god, who has subjected all things to him.'[7]

Some difficulty has been felt in explaining this passage in the *Epistle to the Philippians*: 'Do nothing through faction or through vainglory, but in lowliness of mind each counting others better than himself. Have this mind in you, which was also in Christ Jesus: who, being in the form of god, counted

1. *Acts* xxv. 8.
2. *Romans* ii. 25–6, 29.
3. *Romans* v. 9–16; an accurate though verbally approximate summary.
4. *Romans* viii. 17.
5. *Romans* xvi. 27.
6. *I Corinthians* iii. 23.
7. This is a highly condensed version of *I Corinthians* xv. 27–8.

it not a prize to be on an equality with god.'[1] This passage appears to have been thoroughly studied and elucidated in a letter written in 117, which has come down to us from the churches of Vienne and Lyon, and which is a precious memorial of antiquity. In this letter the modesty of certain of the faithful is praised: 'They did not wish,' says the letter, 'to claim the great title of martyr [for some tribulations], taking as an example Jesus Christ, who, being in the form of god, counted it not a prize to be on an equality with god.' Origen also says in his *Commentary on John*: the greatness of Jesus was more manifest when he humbled himself 'than if he had made it a prize to be on an equality with god.' In fact, the opposite explanation is obvious nonsense. What would be the meaning of 'Count others better than yourself. Imitate Jesus, who did not think that it was a prize, an usurpation to count himself on an equality with god?' This would clearly be to contradict oneself, it would be to offer an example of pride as one of modesty, it would be to sin against dialectics.

The wisdom of the apostles thus established the new-born church. This wisdom was not corrupted by the dispute which arose between the apostles Peter, James and John on one side, and Paul on the other. This contention came up in Antioch. The apostle Peter, otherwise Cephas or Simon Barjon, ate with the converted gentiles, and did not observe with them the ceremonies of the law nor the distinction of meats. He, Barnabas and other disciples ate indifferently pork, the flesh of animals killed by suffocation, and of animals with cloven hoofs and which did not ruminate. But, several Christian Jews having arrived, saint Peter again abstained with them from forbidden meats, and resumed the practice of the ceremonies of the Mosaic law.

This behaviour appeared very prudent. He did not want to scandalize his companions the Christian Jews, but saint Paul rose up against him with a little harshness. 'I resisted him,' he says, 'to the face, because he stood condemned' (*Galatians*, ii).

This quarrel seems all the more extraordinary in saint Paul's

1. *Philippians* ii. 3-6.

case, for having first of all been a persecutor he should have been more moderate, and because he himself had gone to the temple of Jerusalem to sacrifice, because he had circumcised his disciple Timothy, because he had celebrated the Jewish rites for which he now reproached Cephas. Saint Jerome alleges that this quarrel between Paul and Cephas was feigned. He says in his first *Homily*, volume III, that they behaved like two advocates who get excited and offended in court in order to impress their clients. He says that Peter Cephas, being intended to preach to the Jews, and Paul to the gentiles, they pretended to quarrel, Paul in order to win over the gentiles, and Peter to win over the Jews. But saint Augustine is by no means of this opinion: 'I am angry,' says he in the *Epistle to Jerome*, 'that so great a man should make himself the defender of a lie, *patronum mendacii*.' This dispute between saint Jerome and saint Augustine should not diminish our veneration for them, let alone for saint Paul and for saint Peter.

For the rest, if Peter was intended for the orthodox Jews and Paul for strangers, it is very probable that Peter did not come to Rome. The *Acts of the Apostles* make no reference to Peter's voyage to Italy.

Be this as it may, it was about the year 60 of our era that the Christians began to separate themselves from the Jewish community. This is what involved them in many quarrels with and persecutions by the synagogues in Rome, Greece, Egypt and Asia. They were accused of impiety, of atheism by their Jewish brethren, who excommunicated them in their synagogues three times on the sabbath day. But god always sustained them in the midst of their persecutions.

Little by little several churches were established, and the separation between Jews and Christians was complete before the end of the first century. This separation was unknown to the Roman government. Neither the senate of Rome nor the emperors took any part in these quarrels of a little sect which god had so far conducted in obscurity, and which he was raising up by insensible degrees.

We must consider the state of the religion of the Roman

empire at that time. Mysteries and expiations were sanctioned in nearly the whole world. The emperors, it is true, the great and the philosophers, had no faith in these mysteries; but the people, whose choice is law in matters of religion, imposed on the great an outward conformity to their worship. To fetter the people one must appear to wear the same chains as they do. Cicero himself was initiated into the Eleusinian mysteries. Knowledge of one god was the principal dogma proclaimed in these mysterious and magnificent festivals. It must be admitted that the prayers and hymns which have come down to us from these mysteries constitute the most pious and the most admirable things in paganism.

In this way the Christians, who also worshipped a single god, found it easier to convert some gentiles. Several philosophers of the Platonic sect became Christians. This is why the church fathers of the three first centuries were all Platonists.

The thoughtless zeal of a few did no harm to the fundamental truths. Saint Justin, one of the first fathers, has been reproached for having said, in his *Commentary on Isaiah*, that the saints would enjoy all sensual benefits during a reign of 1,000 years on earth. He has been made out a criminal because he said in his *Apology for Christianity* that god, having made the earth, left it in the care of the angels, who, having fallen in love with the women, engendered on them children which are the demons.

Lactantius and other fathers have been condemned for inventing sybilline oracles. He alleged that the Erythrean sybil had uttered these four Greek verses, of which this is a literal rendering: With five loaves and two fish he will feed 5,000 men in the desert; and he will fill twelve baskets with what remains.

The first Christians were also accused of inventing some verse acrostics by an ancient sybil. They all began with initial letters, in their proper order representing the name of Jesus Christ. They have been accused of forging letters written by Jesus Christ to the king of Edessa when there was no king of Edessa; of having forged letters by Mary, letters from Seneca to Paul, letters and documents by Pilate, false gospels, false miracles, and a thousand other impostures.

We also have the history or gospel of the nativity and the marriage of the virgin Mary, in which it is said that she was led to the temple at the age of three, and climbed the steps by herself. It is related in it that a dove descended from heaven to announce that it was Joseph who was to marry Mary.

We have the proto-gospel of James, brother of Jesus by Joseph's first marriage. It is said in it that when Mary was pregnant in the absence of her husband, and her husband complained of it, the priests made them both drink the water of jealousy, and both were declared innocent.

We have the gospel of the childhood, attributed to saint Thomas. According to this gospel Jesus, at the age of five, amused himself with children of his own age by moulding clay, which he shaped into little birds. They found fault with this, and he then gave life to the birds, who flew away. Another time, when a little boy beat him, he made him die on the spot. We also have another gospel, in Arabic, which is more serious.

We have a gospel of Nicodemus. This one seems to deserve greater attention, because in it are found the names of those who accused Jesus before Pilate. These were the principals of the synagogue, Annas, Caiaphas, Summas, Dotam, Gamaliel, Judah, Nephtalim. In this narrative are incidents which agree pretty well with the accepted gospels, and others found nowhere else. In it we find everything that Jesus did when he descended into hell.

Then we have the two letters supposed to have been written by Pilate to Tiberius about the sufferings of Jesus; but the bad Latin in which they are written easily betrays their falseness.

False zeal was pressed so far that several letters from Jesus Christ were given currency. The letter he wrote to Abgar, king of Edessa, has been preserved; but at that time there was no longer a king in Edessa.

Fifty gospels were fabricated and afterwards declared to be apocryphal. Saint Luke himself tells us that a lot of people had composed them.[1] It was believed that there was one entitled the *Eternal Gospel*, because the *Apocalypse*, chapter xiv, says: 'And I saw another angel flying in mid heaven, having an eternal gospel . . .'[2] In the thirteenth century the Franciscans misused these words, composing an *Eternal Gospel* according to which the reign of the holy ghost was to be substituted for that of Jesus Christ; but no work appeared under that title during the first centuries of the church.

Letters written by the virgin to saint Ignatius the martyr, to the inhabitants of Messina, and to others were also invented.

Abdias, the immediate successor of the apostles, wrote their history, with which he mingled fables so absurd that these tales were entirely discredited in the course of time; but at first they were widely credited. It is Abdias who reports the contest between saint Peter and Simon the magician. There was in fact in Rome a very able mechanic, named Simon, who not only devised flights on the stage, as is done today, but himself renewed the marvel attributed to Daedalus. He constructed wings, flew, and fell like Icarus. This is reported by Pliny and Suetonius.

Abdias, who was in Asia, and who wrote in Hebrew, alleges that saint Peter and Simon met in Rome at the time of Nero. A young man, a close relative of the emperor, died. The whole court begged Simon to resuscitate him. Saint Peter, for his part, offered to perform this operation. Simon applied all the rules of his art, he appeared to succeed, the dead man moved his head. 'That's not enough,' cried saint Peter; 'the dead man must speak. Let Simon leave the bedside and we shall see whether the young man is alive.' Simon moved away, the dead man no longer moved, and Peter gave him back his life with a single word.

Simon went to the emperor to complain that a wretched

1. The opening words of *Luke* are: 'For as much as many are taken in hand to draw up a narrative concerning those matters which have been fulfilled among us . . .'
2. *Revelation* xiv. 6.

Galilean took it on himself to perform greater wonders than he. Peter appeared with Simon, and they competed to show which was the better in their art. 'Tell me what I'm thinking,' Simon cried to Peter. 'Let the emperor,' answered Peter, 'give me a loaf of barley bread, and you'll see whether I know what is in your mind.' He was given the bread. Simon immediately caused two large mastiffs to appear. When they threatened Peter, he threw them the bread; and while they were eating it he said: 'Well, didn't I know what you were thinking? You wanted to have me devoured by your dogs.'

After this first encounter a combat by flight was proposed to Simon and Peter, to see which of them could raise himself higher into the air. Simon began, saint Peter made the sign of the cross, and Simon broke his legs. This story was imitated from the one found in the *Sepher toldos Yeshut*,[1] in which it is said that Jesus himself flew, and that Judah, who also wanted to, was thrown down.

Nero, irritated because Peter had broken the legs of his favourite Simon, had Peter crucified head down; and from this arose the belief in Peter's stay in Rome, of his sufferings, and of his sepulchre.

It is this same Abdias who also established the belief that saint Thomas went to king Gondophares, in India, to preach Christianity, and that he went there in the guise of an architect.

The quantity of books of this kind written in the first centuries of Christianity is prodigious. Saint Jerome and even saint Augustine claim that the letters of Seneca and of saint Paul are quite authentic.[2] In the first letter Seneca hopes that his brother Paul is well: *Bene te valere, frater, cupio*. Paul's Latin is not quite so good as Seneca's. 'I have received your letters,' he says, 'with joy: *Litteras tuas hilaris accepi*; and I would have answered it at once had the young man been present whom I would have sent to you: *si praesentiam juvenis habuissem*.' For the rest, these letters, which one would expect to be instructive, are nothing but compliments.

1. Voltaire dealt with these apocryphal gospels at greater length in his *Collection d'anciens évangiles*.
2. That is, the *Book of the Generations of Jesus*.

So many lies fabricated by badly informed and falsely zealous Christians did not injure the truth of Christianity; they did not hinder its establishment. On the contrary, they show that the Christian fellowship increased day by day, and that every member wanted to help its growth.

The *Acts of the Apostles* do not state that the apostles agreed on a creed. Had they in fact drawn up the creed as we now have it, saint Luke would not have omitted from his history this essential foundation of the Christian religion. The substance of the creed is scattered in the gospels, but the articles were not brought together until long after. In a word, our creed is unquestionably the creation of the apostles, but it is not a single writing composed by them. Rufinus, priest of Aquilea, is the first who refers to it; and a homily attributed to saint Augustine is the first source which speculates on the manner in which this creed came about.

Peter said in an assembly: *I believe in god father almighty.* Andrew said: *and in Jesus Christ.* James added: *who was conceived by the holy ghost*; and so on with the rest. This formula was called *symbolos*[1] in Greek, *collatio* in Latin. It should merely be noted that the Greek has: *I believe in god father almighty, maker of heaven and earth*: Πιστεύω εἰς ἕνα θεὸν πατέρα παντοκράτορα, ποιητὴν οὐρανοῦ καί γῆς. The Latin translates *maker, former*, by *creatorem*. But later, at the first council of Nicaea, *factorem* was substituted.[2]

Christianity first established itself in Greece. The Christians there had to combat a new sect of Jews who had become philosophers by dint of frequenting the Greeks. It was that of the gnosis or gnostics. New Christians mingled with it. All these sects then enjoyed complete freedom to dogmatize, to discuss and to write; but under Domitian the Christian religion began to give some offence to the government.

But this zeal of some Christians, which was not orthodox, did not prevent the church from making the progress ordained by god. At first the Christians celebrated their mysteries at night in secluded houses and in cellars. Hence they were

1. The point being that the creed is still called *symbole* in French.
2. *John* xiv. 28.

given the name of *lucifugaces* (according to Minutius Felix). Philo calls them *gesseans*. During the first four centuries the names most commonly given to them by the gentiles were those of Galileans and Nazarenes; but the name of Christian has prevailed over all others.

Neither the hierarchy nor the practices were established all at once. The apostolic ages were different from those that followed. Saint Paul tells us in his first epistle to the Corinthians that when the brethren, whether circumcised or uncircumcised, were assembled and several prophets wanted to speak, it was possible for only two or three to speak, and if one of them had a revelation when they were doing so, the prophet who was holding forth had to stop.

Some Christian communities who still hold assemblies without hierarchies base themselves on this practice of the primitive church. Everybody was then allowed to speak in church, except women. It is true that in *1 Corinthians* Paul forbids them to speak, but in chapter xi, verse 5, of the same epistle, he also appears to authorize them to preach and to prophesy: 'But every woman praying or prophesying with her head unveiled dishonoureth her head: for it is one and the same thing as if she were shaven.' The women therefore believed that they were allowed to speak provided that they were veiled.

What is today the holy mass, which is celebrated in the morning, was then the communion, held in the evening. These practices changed as the church grew stronger. A more extensive association required more regulations, and the pastors prudently conformed to the time and the place.

Saint Jerome and Eusebius report that, when the churches took shape, little by little five different orders were perceived in them: the superintendents, *episcopoï*, who became the bishops; the elders of the society, *presbyteroï*, the priests; the *diaconoï*, their servants or deacons; the *pistoï*, believers, initiates, that is the baptized, who were admitted to the suppers of the *agapes*; and the catechumens and energumens, who were waiting for baptism. In these five orders none wore clothes different from the others. None was constrained to celibacy, as witness Tertullian's book dedicated to his wife, and the example of the apostles. There was no image, whether in painting or in sculpture, in their assemblies during the first three centuries. The Christians carefully hid their books from the gentiles, and they confided them only to the initiates. Not even the catechumens were allowed to recite the lord's prayer.

What most distinguished the Christians, and what has lasted almost to our time, was the power to expel devils with the sign of the cross. In his *Treatise against Celsus*, number 133, Origen admits that Antinous, deified by the emperor Hadrian, performed miracles in Egypt by means of charms and marvels; but he says that devils left the bodies of the possessed when the mere name of Jesus was pronounced.

Tertullian goes further, and from the heart of Africa, where he lived, he says in his *Apologeticus*, chapter XXIII: 'If your gods do not admit that they are devils when confronted by a true Christian, we consent that you shed this Christian's blood.' Can there be a clearer demonstration?

In fact, Jesus Christ sent his apostles to cast out demons. In his time the Jews also had the gift of expelling them, for when Jesus had freed the possessed and sent the devils into the bodies of a herd of pigs, and had performed other cures of the same kind, the Pharisees said: 'This man doth not cast out devils, but by Beelzebub the prince of the devils.' 'And if I by Beelzebub cast out devils,' answered Jesus, 'by whom do your sons cast them out?'[1] It is undeniable that the Jews prided themselves on this power. They had exorcists and exorcisms. The name of the god of Jacob and Abraham was invoked. Consecrated herbs were put into the noses of demoniacs (Josephus reports part of these ceremonies). This power over devils, which the Jews have lost, was transmitted to the Christians, who also seem to have lost it in recent times.

In the power of casting out demons was included that of destroying the workings of magic, for magic has always been in force among all nations. All the fathers of the church testify

1. *Matthew* xii. 24, 27; cf. *Mark* iii. 22.

to magic. Saint Justin admitted in his *Apologeticus*, in book III, that the souls of the dead were often called up, and draws from this an argument in favour of the immortality of the soul. Lactantius, in book VII of his *Divine Institutions*, says that 'if one dared to deny the existence of souls after death, the magician would soon convince one by causing them to appear.' Irenaeus, Clement of Alexandria, Tertullian, bishop Cyprian, all affirm the same thing. It is true that everything has changed nowadays, and that there are equally no magicians and demoniacs. But god has it in his power to warn mankind by means of prodigies at certain times, and to stop them at others.

When the Christian societies became rather more numerous, and when several denounced the religion of the Roman empire, the magistrates dealt severely with them, and above all the people persecuted them. The Jews were not persecuted; they had special privileges, kept to their synagogues, and were allowed to practise their religion, as they are today in Rome. All the different religions found in the empire were tolerated, although the senate did not adopt them.

But the Christians, proclaiming themselves the enemies of all these religions, and above all that of the empire, were several times exposed to cruel trials. One of the first and most famous martyrs was Ignatius, bishop of Antioch, condemned by the emperor Trajan himself, then in Asia, and sent by his orders to be thrown to the beasts in Rome at a time when the other Christians were not massacred there. It is not known of what he had been accused before this emperor, who was widely known for his clemency. Saint Ignatius must have had very violent enemies. Be that as it may, the history of his martyrdom reports that the name of Jesus Christ was found to be engraved on his heart in golden characters; and this is why in some places the Christians took the name of *theophores*, which Ignatius applied to himself.

A letter[1] from him has come down to us, in which he begs the bishops and the Christians not to oppose his martyr-

1. *Note by Voltaire:* Dupin, in his *Bibliothèque ecclésiastique*, proves that this letter is authentic.

dom, implying either that the Christians were already powerful enough to free him, or that among them were people who had enough influence to obtain his pardon. What is more remarkable is that the Roman Christians were allowed to meet him when he was brought to the capital, which proves clearly that the punishment was inflicted on him in his person and not on account of his sect.

The persecutions were not continued. Origen says in his book III against Celsus: 'It is easy to count the Christians who died for their religion, because few died, and only from time to time, and at intervals.'

God took such good care of his church that, despite its enemies, he enabled it to hold five councils – that is, tolerated councils – in the first century, sixteen in the second, and thirty in the third. These assemblies were sometimes prohibited when the false prudence of the magistrates feared that they might become tumultuous.

Little has come down to us of the records kept by the proconsuls and the praetors who condemned Christians to death. These are the only documents from which it would be possible to establish the charges brought against them, and their punishments. We possess a fragment by Denis of Alexandria in which he transcribes an entry in the register of a proconsul of Egypt under the emperor Valerian; here it is:

Denis, Faustus, Maximus, Marcel and Chaeremon, having been brought into court, the prefect Aemilian said to them: 'You have been able to judge by the conversations I have had with you and by all that I have written to you about them, how much goodness our princes have shown you. I should like to tell you again that they regard your preservation and your salvation as depending on yourselves, and your fate to be in your own hands. They ask you for only one thing, which good sense expects from every reasonable person: it is that you worship the gods who protect their empire, and that you abandon this other worship which is so contrary to nature and good sense.'

Denis replied: 'Everyone doesn't have the same gods, and everyone worships those he believes to be really gods.'

The prefect Aemilian resumed: 'I see that you are ingrates who take advantage of the emperor's indulgence for you. Very well, you will no longer remain in this city, and I am sending you to Cephro, in the interior of Libya. That will be the place of your banishment, in accordance with the orders I have received from our emperors. For the rest, don't contemplate holding your assemblies there, nor saying your prayers in the places you call cemeteries. You are absolutely forbidden to do this, and I shall not permit it to anybody.'

Nothing bears more clearly the stamp of truth than this document. It shows that there were times when the assemblies were prohibited. In the same way we forbid the Calvinists to assemble in Languedoc. Sometimes we have even caused ministers or preachers to be hanged and broken on the wheel for holding assemblies against the law. In the same way Roman Catholics are forbidden to hold assemblies in England and Ireland, and on occasion the offenders have been condemned to death.

Despite these prohibitions imposed by the Roman laws god inspired several emperors with indulgence for the Christians. Even Diocletian, whom the ignorant regard as a persecutor, Diocletian, the first year of whose reign was still in the time of the martyrs, was for more than eighteen years the declared protector of Christianity, so much so that several Christians had important posts near his person. He even tolerated the building of a superb church opposite his palace in Nicomedia, where he lived. Finally, he married a Christian.

Galerius, having unfortunately been prejudiced against the Christians, thinking he had some cause for complaint against them, persuaded Diocletian to have the cathedral of Nicomedia destroyed. A Christian, more zealous than wise, tore the emperor's edict to pieces; and thus was caused that famous persecution in which more than 200 persons were condemned to death throughout the whole extent of the Roman empire, not counting those who may have fallen without legal process to the rage of the common people, always fanatical and always barbarous.

There has been so great a number of martyrs at different

times that we must take care not to weaken the historical truth of these authentic confessors of our holy religion by a dangerous admixture of fables and false martyrs.

For instance, the Benedictine dom Ruinart,[1] otherwise as well informed a man as he is estimable and zealous, should have chosen his *Sincere Acts* with more discretion. An act is not authentic merely because the manuscript was found in the abbey of Saint-Benoît-sur-Loire or in a Celestine monastery in Paris, and corresponds to a Bernardine manuscript. The act must be ancient, written by contemporaries, and must also bear all the marks of truth.

He might have dispensed with reporting the adventure of the youthful Romanus, which occurred in 303. This young Romanus had been pardoned by Diocletian in Antioch. Nevertheless he [Ruinart] says that the judge Asclepiades condemned him to death by fire. Some Jews who were present at the spectacle mocked the young saint Romanus, and made it a reproach against the Christians that their god allowed them to burn, he who had delivered Shadrach, Meshach and Abednego from the furnace. Ruinart goes on that a storm at once came up, in the calmest weather, and put out the fire; that the judge then ordered the young Romanus's tongue to be cut out; that the emperor's chief physician, being present, officiously did the executioner's work and cut the tongue at the roots; that the young man, who had previously stuttered, immediately spoke very freely; that the emperor was astonished that he spoke so well without a tongue; that the physician, to repeat the experiment, at once cut out the tongue of a passer-by, who died of it on the spot.

Eusebius, from whom the Benedictine Ruinart took this story, should have had enough respect for the authentic miracles worked in the *New Testament* (which nobody will ever doubt) not to associate them with narratives so suspect, which could scandalize the weak.

1. Thierry Ruinart; the full title of his book shows why Voltaire called it *Actes sincères: Les Véritables actes des martyrs recueillis, revûs et corrigez sur plusieurs anciens manuscrits sous le titre de Acta primorum martyrum sincera & selecta* (Paris, 1708).

This last persecution did not spread throughout the empire. In England there existed at that time a little Christianity, which soon vanished, to reappear later under the Saxon kings. The southern parts of Gaul, and Spain, were filled with Christians. Caesar Constantius Chlorus gave them much help in all these provinces. He had a Christian concubine. She was the mother of Constantine, known as saint Helena, for there was never any authentic marriage between them, and he even turned her away in the year 292, when he married the daughter of Maximian Herculius. But she had kept great influence over him, and had inspired him with great affection for our holy religion.

Divine providence prepared the triumph of its church by means that seemed human. Constantius Chlorus died in 306 at York, in England, at a time when his children by the daughter of a Caesar were young, and could not claim the empire. Constantius had the assurance to have himself elected at York by five or six thousand soldiers, for the most part Germans, Gauls and English. It hardly seemed likely that this election, held without the consent of Rome, the senate and the armies, could be maintained. But god gave him victory over Maxentius, elected in Rome, and at last freed him from all his colleagues. It cannot be denied that at first he made himself unworthy of the favours of heaven by murdering all his intimates, his wife and his son.

What Zosimus reports about this matter may be doubted. He says that Constantine, troubled by remorse after so many crimes, asked the pontiff of the empire whether they could be expiated in any way, and was told that he knew of none. It is quite true that there had been none for Nero, and that he had not dared to take part in the sacred mysteries in Greece. Nevertheless taurobolia were practised, and it is very difficult to believe that an all-powerful emperor could not find a priest willing to accord him expiatory sacrifices. It is perhaps even less credible that Constantine, busy with war, ambition and projects, and surrounded by flatterers, had time for remorse. Zosimus adds that an Egyptian priest from Spain, who had access to the emperor, promised him expiation for all his crimes in the Christian religion. Ozius,[1] bishop of Cordoba, has been suspected of being this priest.

Be this as it may, god chose to enlighten Constantine and to make him the protector of the church. This prince built his city of Constantinople, which became the centre of the empire and of the Christian religion. Then the church took an august form, and it is likely that, cleaned by his baptism and repentant when dying, he won mercy although he died an Arian. It would have been very hard if all the partisans of the two bishops Eusebius had been damned.

It should be noted that from the year 314, before Constantine lived in his new city, those who persecuted the Christians were punished by them for their cruelties. The Christians threw Maximian's wife into the Orontes, and put to death all his relatives. In Egypt and Palestine they massacred the magistrates who had most strongly opposed Christianity. The widow and the daughter of Diocletian, having taken refuge in Thessalonica, were recognized, and their bodies were thrown into the sea. We cannot but wish that the Christians had paid less heed to the spirit of vengeance; but god, who punishes in accordance with his justice, wanted the hands of the Christians to be tinged with the blood of their persecutors as soon as these Christians were free to act.

Constantine summoned, and assembled at Nicaea, opposite Constantinople, the first oecumenical council, which was presided by Ozius. There they took a decision concerning the divinity of Jesus Christ, the great question which was troubling the church. Some relied on the opinion of Origen, who says in chapter VI against Celsus: 'We offer our prayers to god through Jesus, who stands midway between created beings and uncreated nature, who brings us the grace of his father, and in his capacity as our pontiff presents our prayers to the great god.' They also based themselves on several passages from saint Paul, some of which have been recorded. They relied above all on these words of Jesus Christ: 'the father is greater than I';[2] and they regarded Jesus as the

---

1. See above, the article on 'Arius'.
2. *John* xiv. 28.

first-born of creation, as the purest emanation of the supreme being, but not precisely as god.

The others, who were orthodox, adduced passages more consistent with the eternal divinity of Jesus, such as this one: 'My father and I are the same thing',[1] words which the adversaries interpreted to mean: 'My father and I have the same plan, the same will; I have no desires other than those of my father.' Alexander, bishop of Alexandria, and after him Athanasius, led the orthodox; and Eusebius, bishop of Nicomedia, with seventeen other bishops, the priest Arius, and several other priests, were of the opposite party. The quarrel was at once envenomed, because saint Alexander called his adversaries anti-Christs.

Finally, after many arguments, the holy ghost decided thus in the council, by the mouths of 299 bishops against eighteen: 'Jesus is the only son of god, begotten by the father, that is, of the substance of the father, god of god, light of light, true god of true god, consubstantial with the father. We also believe in the holy ghost, etc.' This was the council's formula. This example shows to what an extent the bishops got the better of the common priests. Two thousand persons of the second order were of the same opinion as Arius, according to two Alexandrian patriarchs who wrote the history of Alexandria in Arabic. Arius was exiled by Constantine; but so was Athanasius also soon after, and Arius was recalled to Constantinople. However, saint Macarius prayed god so fervently to kill Arius before this priest could enter the cathedral that god granted his prayer. Arius died on his way to church in 330. The emperor Constantine's life ended in 337. He confided his will to an Arian priest and died in the arms of the chief of the Arians, Eusebius, bishop of Nicomedia, having had himself baptized only on his death-bed, and leaving the church triumphant, but divided.

The partisans of Athanasius and those of Eusebius fought a cruel war, and what is called Arianism was established for a long time in all the provinces of the empire. Julian the philo-

---

1. Or rather, 'I and the Father are one'; *John* x. 30.

sopher, called the apostate, wanted to stifle these divisions, and failed.

The second general council was held in Constantinople in 381. There was explained what the council of Nicaea had not seen fit to say about the holy ghost, and to the Nicaean formula was added that 'the holy ghost is the life-giving lord who proceeds from the father, and that he is worshipped and glorified with the father and the son'.

It was not until about the ninth century that the Latin church decreed little by little that the holy ghost proceeds from the father and the son.

In 431 the third general council, held at Ephesus, decided that Mary was truly the mother of god, and that Jesus had two natures and one person. Nestorius, bishop of Constantinople, who wanted the holy virgin to be called the mother of Christ, was declared a Judas by the council, and the two natures were again confirmed by the council of Chalcedony.

I shall pass lightly over the following centuries, which are well enough known. Unfortunately not one of these disputes failed to cause wars, and the church was always obliged to fight. In the ninth century, to try the patience of the faithful, god also allowed the Greeks and the Latins to divide for ever. He also permitted twenty-nine bloody schisms in the west over the chair of Rome.

During this time nearly the whole of the Greek church, and the whole of the African church, became slaves under the Arabs, and then under the Turks also built the Mohammedan religion, on the ruins of the Christian. The Roman church survived, but always sullied with the blood of more than 600 years of discord between the western empire and the priesthood. These very quarrels made it exceedingly powerful. In Germany the bishops and the abbots made themselves into princes, and the popes little by little acquired absolute dominion in Rome and a hundred leagues around. Thus god tested his church by humiliations, by disorder, by crimes, and by splendour.

In the sixteenth century this Latin church lost half of Germany, Denmark, Sweden, England, Scotland, Ireland, the better part of Switzerland, Holland. With the Spanish conquests it gained more territory in America than it had lost in Europe; but it has far fewer subjects in a greater territory.

Divine providence apparently intended Japan, Siam, India and China to come under the obedience of the pope, to compensate him for Asia Minor, Syria, Greece, Egypt, Africa, Russia, and the other lost states I have mentioned. Saint Francis Xavier, who carried the holy gospel to India and Japan when the Portuguese went there to search for merchandise, performed a very large number of miracles, all attested by the reverend Jesuit fathers. Some say that he resuscitated nine dead men, but the reverend father Ribadeneira limits himself to saying in his *Flower of the Saints*[1] that he resuscitated four: which is quite enough. It was the will of providence that there should be thousands of Catholics in the isles of Japan in less than a hundred years; but the devil sowed his tares amid the good grain. The Christians formed a conspiracy, followed by a civil war, in which they were all exterminated in 1638. Then the nation closed its ports to all foreigners except the Dutch, who were regarded as merchants and not as Christians, and who were at first obliged to trample on the cross to obtain permission to sell their goods in the prison in which they are locked up when they land at Nagasaki.

The catholic, apostolic and Roman religion was recently proscribed in China, but with less cruelty. It is true that the reverend Jesuit fathers had not resuscitated the dead at the court of Peking. They had contented themselves with teaching astronomy, casting guns, and being mandarins. Their wretched disputes with the Dominicans and others scandalized the great emperor Yong-ching to such a point that this prince, who was justice and goodness personified, was so blind as no longer to permit the teaching of our holy religion, about which our missionaries did not agree. He expelled them with paternal goodness, supplying them with food and carriages to the borders of his empire.

All Asia, all Africa, half of Europe, all that belongs to the

1. Pedro de Ribadeneira first published his *Flos sanctorum* in Spanish (1599–1610).

English and the Dutch in America, all the untamed American hordes, all the lands of the southern hemisphere, which constitute a fifth of the globe, have remained the prey of the demon, to confirm this sacred saying: 'Many are called, but few are chosen.' If there are about 1,600 million men on the earth, as some learned men allege, the holy Roman Catholic universal church possesses about 60 million of them: which is little more than a twenty-sixth part of the inhabitants of the known world.

Ciel des anciens (Le): The Heaven of the ancients

If a silkworm gave the name of heaven to the light down that surrounds its cocoon it would be reasoning as well as did all the ancients, when they gave the name of heaven to the atmosphere, which, as m. de Fontenelle[1] says very well in his *Mondes*, is the down of our cocoon.

The vapours that rise from our seas and our earth, and which form the clouds, the meteors and the thunder, were at first taken for the home of the gods. In Homer the gods always come down in clouds of gold. This is why painters today still paint them seated on a cloud. But, since it is only just that the master of the gods be more comfortable than the others, he was given an eagle to carry him, because the eagle flies higher than the other birds.

The ancient Greeks, seeing that the rulers of towns lived in citadels at the tops of mountains, judged that the gods should also have a citadel, and placed it in Thessaly, on mount Olympus, whose summit is sometimes hidden in the clouds, so that their palace was on the same level as their heaven.

The stars and the planets, which seem to be attached to the blue vault of our atmosphere, afterwards became the homes of the gods. Seven of them had each his own planet, the others lodged where they could. The general council of the gods was held in a great hall which was reached by the milky way, for it

1. Bernard Le Bovier de Fontenelle, who had recently died almost a centenarian, published his *Entretiens sur la pluralité des mondes* in 1687; it was then a very advanced popularization of the new scientific ideas.

was clearly necessary for the gods to have a hall in the air since men had town halls on earth.

When the Titans, animals of a kind between gods and men, declared a pretty just war on these gods to reclaim a part of their heritage on the paternal side, being sons of heaven and earth, they piled up only two or three mountains, assuming that this would be quite enough to make themselves masters of heaven and of the castle of Olympus.

> *Neve foret terris securior arduus aether,*
> *Affectasse ferunt regnum caeleste gigantes,*
> *Altaque congestes struxisse ad sidera montes.*

> Heaven was attacked as well as the earth;
> The giants dared to carry the war to the gods,
> Piled up mountains to the stars of the night.[1]

Yet it is 600 million leagues from those stars, and much further still from some of them, to mount Olympus.

Virgil finds no difficulty in saying: *Sub pedibusque videt nubes et sidera Daphnis.* Daphnis sees the stars and the clouds beneath his feet.[2] But then where was Daphnis?

At the opera, and in more serious writings, the gods are made to descend in the midst of winds, clouds and thunder, that is, god is dragged through the vapours of our little globe. These notions are so proportionate to our insignificance that they appear to us to be vast.

This natural philosophy of children and old women was prodigiously old. Nevertheless it is quite certain that the Chaldeans had notions just the same as ours about what is called heaven. They situated the sun in the centre of our planetary world, at about the distance from our globe we ourselves have determined. They made the earth and all the planets revolve around that star; so Aristarchus of Samos tells

1. Ovid, *Metamorphoses* i. 151–3; these lines are translated from Voltaire's French rendering; a literal version of the original Latin follows: 'So that heaven might be no safer than the earth it is said that the giants attempted the very throne of heaven, piling mountains up to the stars.'

2. Virgil, *Eclogues*, v. 57; Voltaire's version, as here translated, is pretty literal.

us. It is the true system of the world, which Copernicus has since renewed, but the philosophers kept the secret to themselves in order to be more respected by the kings and the people, or rather, not to be persecuted.

The language of error is so familiar to mankind that we still give the name of heaven to our vapours and to the space between the earth and the moon. We say 'ascend to heaven', as we say that the sun revolved, although it is well known that it does not revolve. We are probably heaven for the inhabitants of the moon, and each planet situates its heaven in the neighbouring planet.

If Homer had been asked to which heaven the soul of Sarpedon had gone, and where was that of Hercules, Homer would have been quite perplexed: he would have replied in harmonious verse.

What assurance had they that the aerial soul of Hercules would have felt more at home on Venus or on Saturn than on our globe? How would it have felt on the sun? That furnace does not appear comfortable. In any case, what did the ancients understand by heaven? They knew nothing about it. They always exclaimed 'heaven and earth', as if one cried 'the infinite and an atom'. Strictly speaking, there is no heaven: there is a prodigious quantity of globes which revolve in empty space, and our globe revolves like the others.

The ancients believed that to go to heaven was to ascend, but one does not ascend from one globe to another: the celestial globes are sometimes above our horizon, sometimes below. Thus, had Venus, having come to Paphos, returned to her planet when it had set, the goddess would not then ascend in relation to our horizon: she would descend, and that case one should say 'descend to heaven'. But the ancients were not so pedantic. They had vague, uncertain, contradictory notions about everything relating to natural philosophy. Huge volumes have been written to determine what they thought about all sorts of problems of this kind. Four words would have sufficed: *they did not think.*

A small number of wise men must always be excepted, but they came late. Few explained their ideas, and, when they did, the charlatans of the earth promptly despatched them to heaven.

A writer called, I believe, Pluche,[1] alleges Moses to have been a great scientist. Another[2] had previously conciliated Moses with Descartes, and published the *Cartesius mosaïzans*. According to him it was Moses who first invented the vortices and subtle matter, but it is perfectly well known that god, who made Moses a great legislator, a great prophet, by no means wished to make him a professor of science. He instructed the Jews in their duty, but did not teach them a word of philosophy. Calmet, who has compiled a great deal, but has never thought, speaks of the system of the Hebrews, but this rude people were far from having a system; they did not even have a school of geometry; the very name was unknown to them; their only science was the trade of jobbery and usury.

In their books are found a few ambiguous, incoherent ideas, altogether worthy of a barbarous people, about the structure of heaven. Their first heaven was the air, the sea and the firmament, to which the stars were attached. This firmament was made of solid ice, and contained the upper waters, which escaped at the flood through doors, sluice-gates, waterfalls.

Above this firmament, or these upper waters, was the third heaven or empyrean, to which saint Paul was carried off. The firmament was a kind of half-vault that comprised the earth. The sun did not revolve around a globe, which was unknown to them. When it reached the west, it returned to the east by an unknown way; and when it was not seen it was, as says the baron de Foeneste,[3] because it returned at night.

In any case, the Hebrews had taken these fantasies from other peoples. Most nations, except the school of the Chaldeans, regarded heaven as a solid. The earth, fixed and immobile, was longer by a good third from east and west than

1. Noël Antoine Pluche was a very popular interpreter of the new science in terms of the old religion; one of the characters in his *Spectacle de la nature* is called 'M. le Chevalier'.

2. Joannes Amerpoel, author of *Cartesius mosaïzans* (Leovardiae, 1669).

3. The hero of the *Aventures du baron de Faeneste* (1617) by Théodore Agrippa d'Aubigné.

from south to north: hence the terms longitude and latitude which we have adopted. It is clear that according to this view there could be no antipodes. Consequently saint Augustine calls the notion of the antipodes an absurdity, and Lactantius says expressly: 'Are these people mad enough to believe that there are men whose heads are lower than their feet? . . .'

Saint Chrysostom exclaims in his fourteenth homily: 'Where are those who allege that the heavens are mobile, and their form circular?'

Lactantius also says in book III of his *Institutions*: 'I could prove to you with many arguments that it is impossible that heaven surrounds the earth.'

The author of the *Spectacle de la nature* can tell *m. le chevalier* as often as he pleases that Lactantius and saint Chrysostome were great philosophers. My answer is that they are great saints, and that it is not at all necessary to be a good astronomer in order to be a saint. We can believe that they are in heaven, while admitting that we do not know in exactly what part of heaven.

Circoncision : Circumcision

When Herodotus relates what he was told by the barbarians among whom he travelled, he talks nonsense, and so do most of our travellers. To be sure, he does not expect us to believe him when he talks about the adventure of Gyges and Candaules; about Arion, borne on a dolphin; and about the oracle who, consulted about the doings of Croesus, replied that he was at that moment cooking a tortoise in a covered pot; and about Darius's horse, which, having neighed the first, thus proclaimed his master king; and about a hundred other fables fit to amuse children, and to be compiled by gossips. But when he talks about what he has seen, about the customs of the peoples he has investigated, about their antiquities which he has examined, then he speaks to men.

'It seems,' he says in the book *Euterpe*,[1]

that the inhabitants of Colchis originally came from Egypt. I think so myself, not by hearsay, but because I have found that in

1. That is, the second book of Herodotus's *History*.

Colchis the ancient Egyptians were much better remembered than the ancient customs of Colchis were remembered in Egypt.

These inhabitants of the shores of the Pontus Euxinus[1] claimed to be a colony founded by Sesostris. For myself, I would conjecture this not only because they are swarthy and have curly hair, but because the peoples of Colchis, Egypt and Ethiopia are the only ones on earth who have always had themselves circumcised: for the Phoenicians and the peoples of Palestine admit that they took circumcision from the Egyptians. The Syrians, who today inhabit the banks of the Thermodon and of Parthenia, and their neighbours the Macronians, admit that it is not long since they adopted this Egyptian custom. It is chiefly by this that they are recognized as being of Egyptian origin.

As for Ethiopia and Egypt, as this ceremony is very ancient in these two nations, I cannot say which of them received circumcision from the other. Yet it is probable that the Ethiopians took it from the Egyptians. On the other hand, the Phoenicians abolished the custom of circumcising new-born children when they increased their trade with the Greeks.

It is evident from this passage in Herodotus that several peoples had taken circumcision from Egypt; but no nation has ever claimed to have received circumcision from the Jews. To whom should we then attribute the origin of this custom? To the nation from which five or six other peoples avow having taken it, or to another nation, much less powerful, less mercantile, less warlike, hidden in a corner of Arabia Petraea, which has never transmitted any of its practices to any people?

The Jews say that in former times they were received in Egypt out of charity. Is it not highly probable that the little nation imitated a practice of the great, and that the Jews took some customs from their masters?

Clement of Alexandria reports that Pythagoras, travelling among the Egyptians, was obliged to have himself circumcised in order to be admitted to their mysteries. It was thus absolutely necessary to be circumcised to become one of the Egyptian priests. These priests existed when Joseph arrived in Egypt. The government was very ancient, and the antique

---

1. Now called the Black Sea.

ceremonies of Egypt were observed with the most scrupulous exactitude.

The Jews admit that they remained in Egypt for 205 years. They say that they did not have themselves circumcised during this time. It is thus evident that for 205 years the Egyptians did not adopt circumcision from the Jews. Would they have taken it from them after the Jews had stolen all the vessels the Egyptians had lent them, and fled into the desert with their booty, according to their own testimony? Would a master adopt the principal mark of the religion of his thieving and fugitive slave? It is against human nature.

It is said in the book of *Joshua* that the Jews were circumcised in the desert: 'This day have I rolled away the reproach of Egypt from off you.'[1] Now what could this reproach have been for people who found themselves between the nations of Phoenicia, the Arabs and the Egyptians if it was not that which made them contemptible to these three peoples? How was this reproach removed? By removing a bit of foreskin. Is this not the natural meaning of this passage?[2]

Genesis says that Abraham had been circumcised earlier.[3] But Abraham had travelled in Egypt, which had long been a flourishing kingdom, governed by a powerful king. There is no reason why circumcision should not have been practised in so ancient a kingdom long before the Jewish nation was formed. Besides the circumcision of Abraham had no sequel: his posterity was not circumcised until the time of Joshua.

Now before Joshua the Israelites, by their own admission, took many customs from the Egyptians. They imitated them in several sacrifices, in several ceremonies, as in the fasts which they observed on the eve of the festivals of Isis, in the ablutions, in the custom of shaving the priest's head. The incense,

1. *Joshua* v. 9.

2. It may be difficult to understand why Voltaire felt it necessary to argue the point, since the context leaves no doubt that the reproach was in fact the uncircumcised state of the Israelites. He did so, here and elsewhere, because the *Bible* was very nearly a prohibited book among the devout.

3. *Genesis* xvii. 26.

the candelabra, the sacrifice of the red cow, the purification with hyssop, the abstention from pork, the horror of strangers' kitchen utensils, all attest that the little Hebrew people, despite its aversion for the great Egyptian nation, had kept an infinite number of its former masters' customs. The goat Azazel, which was sent into the desert laden with the sins of the people, was an obvious imitation of an Egyptian practice. The rabbis even agree that the word *Azazel* is not Hebrew. There is therefore no reason why the Hebrews should not have imitated the Egyptians in circumcision, as did the Arabs, their neighbours.

It is not at all extraordinary that god, who sanctified baptism, so ancient among the Asiatics, also sanctified circumcision, no less ancient among the Africans. I have already remarked that he is at liberty to attach his grace to the symbols he deigns to choose.

Anyway, the Jewish people has retained this practice to our day ever since it was circumcised under Joshua. The Arabs too have always been faithful to it. But the Egyptians, who circumcised boys and girls in the earliest times, eventually stopped performing this operation on girls, and finally restricted it to priests, astrologers and prophets. This is what Clement of Alexandria and Origen tell us. In fact it does not appear that the Ptolemies were ever circumcised.

The Latin authors, who treat the Jews with such profound contempt that they call them derisively *curtus Apella, credat Judaeus apella, curti Judaei*,[1] do not apply these epithets to the Egyptians. The whole Egyptian people is circumcised today, but for a different reason, because Mohammedanism adopted the ancient Arabian circumcision.

It is this Arabian circumcision that has passed to the Ethiopians, who still circumcise boys and girls.

It must be admitted that this ceremony of circumcision at first appears very strange; but it should be noted that oriental priests have always consecrated themselves to their divinities by special marks. An ivy leaf was engraved with a point on the priests of Bacchus. Lucian tells us that the votaries of the

1. 'The circumcised Jews', as in Horace, *Satires* I. ix. 70.

goddess Isis impressed characters on their wrists and necks. The priests of Cybele made themselves into eunuchs.

It certainly appears that the Egyptians, who revered the instrument of generation, and who carried its image in pomp in their processions, conceived the idea of offering to Isis and Osiris, through whom everything on earth was engendered, a small part of the member by means of which these gods intended the human race to perpetuate itself. Ancient oriental customs are so prodigiously different from ours that nothing can appear extraordinary to anyone who has some reading. A Parisian is taken aback when he is told that the Hottentots cut off one testicle from their male children. The Hottentots are perhaps surprised that the Parisians keep two.

Conciles: Councils

All councils are undoubtedly infallible: for they are composed of men. It is impossible for passions, intrigues, the lust for dispute, hatred, jealousy, prejudice, ignorance ever to reign in these assemblies.

But why, it will be asked, have so many councils contradicted each other? It is to try our faith. Each was in the right in its turn.

Roman Catholics now believe only in councils approved by the Vatican; and the Greek Catholics believe only in those approved in Constantinople. Protestants deride them both. Thus everybody should be satisfied.

I shall refer here only to the great councils; the small ones are not worth the trouble.

The first one was that of Nicaea. It was assembled in 325 of the common era, after Constantine had written and sent by the hand of Ozius this noble letter to the rather confused clergy of Alexandria: 'You are quarrelling about something very trivial. These subtleties are unworthy of sensible people.' The thing was to determine whether Jesus was created or uncreated. This has nothing to do with morality, which is the essential point. Whether Jesus was in time or before time, we must none the less be good. After many altercations it was finally decided that the son was as old as the father, and consubstantial with the father. This decision is hardly comprehensible, but it is all the more sublime on that account. Seventeen bishops protested against the decree, and an ancient chronicle of Alexandria, preserved at Oxford, says that 2,000 priests also protested; but prelates pay little attention to simple priests, who are usually poor. Be that as it may, there was no question whatever of the trinity in this first council. The formula reads: 'We believe Jesus consubstantial with the father, god of god, light of light, begotten and not made; we also believe in the holy ghost.' The holy ghost, it must be admitted, was treated pretty off-handedly.

It is reported in the supplement of the council of Nicaea that the fathers, being very perplexed to know which were the cryphal[1] or apocryphal books of the Old and New Testaments, put them all pell-mell on an altar, and the books to be rejected fell to the ground. It is a pity that this elegant procedure has not survived.

After the first council of Nicaea, composed of 317 infallible bishops, another was held at Rimini, and this time the number of infallibles was 400, not counting a big detachment of about 200 at Seleucia. These 600 bishops, after four months of quarrels, unanimously deprived Jesus of his consubstantiality. It has since been restored to him, except among the Socinians; so everything is fine.

One of the great councils was that of Ephesus in 431. Nestorius, bishop of Constantinople, great persecutor of heretics, was himself condemned as a heretic for maintaining that in truth Jesus was really god, but that his mother was not absolutely the mother of god, but the mother of Jesus. It was saint Cyril who had Nestorius condemned; but then the partisans of Nestorius had saint Cyril deposed in the same council: which much embarrassed the holy ghost.

Note very carefully here, dear reader, that the gospel has never said a word about the consubstantiality of the word, nor

1. This is not a misprint; Voltaire amused himself by inventing the word 'cryphes', by a false etymology.

about the honour Mary had had to be the mother of god, nor about the other disputes which have caused infallible councils to be assembled.

Eutyches was a monk who had much abused Nestorius, whose heresy did not fall short of alleging that Jesus was two persons: which is appalling. The better to contradict his adversary the monk asserted that Jesus had only one nature. A certain Flavian, bishop of Constantinople, maintained against him that it was absolutely necessary for Jesus to have had two natures. A numerous council was assembled at Ephesus in 449. This one was conducted with the quarter-staff, like the little council of Cirta in 355, and a certain conference at Carthage. Flavian's nature became black and blue, and two natures were assigned to Jesus. At the council of Chalcedon, in 451, Jesus was reduced to one nature.

I pass over councils held on account of minute details, and come to the sixth general council, of Constantinople, assembled to determine precisely whether Jesus, having only one nature, had two wills. It will be realized how important this is in order to please god.

This council was called by Constantine the bearded, just as all the others had been by the preceding emperors. The legates of the bishop of Rome sat on the left, the patriarchs of Constantinople and Antioch on the right. I do not know whether the Roman toadies claim the left to be the place of honour. Be this as it may, Jesus obtained two wills from this affair.

The Mosaic law had prohibited images. Painters and sculptors had never done very well among the Jews. It does not appear that Jesus ever possessed any pictures, except perhaps that of Mary painted by Luke. At any rate, Jesus Christ nowhere enjoins the worship of images. Nevertheless Christians worshipped them towards the end of the fourth century, when they had familiarized themselves with the fine arts. This error went so far in the eighth century that Constantine Copronymus assembled in Constantinople a council of 320 bishops, which anathemized the worship of images and branded it as idolatry.

The empress Irene, the same who later had her son's eyes torn out, assembled the second council of Nicaea in 787. In this the worship of images was restored. Nowadays it is sought to justify this council by saying that this worship was one of *dulia* and not of *latria*.[1]

However, be it *latria* or *dulia*, in 794 Charlemagne called another council, at Frankfurt, which stigmatized the second of Nicaea as idolatrous. Pope Adrian IV sent two legates to it but did not convoke it.

The first great council called by a pope was the first Lateran, in 1139. About a thousand bishops were there, but almost nothing was accomplished in it, except that those who said that the church was too rich were anathemized.

There was another Lateran council in 1179, held by pope Alexander III, in which the cardinals for the first time took precedence over the bishops. Only matters of discipline were discussed.

Another great council was the Lateran of 1215. In it pope Innocent III stripped the count of Toulouse of all his possessions, by virtue of excommunication. This was the first council in which there was any question of transubstantiation.

In 1245 took place the general council of Lyon, then an imperial city, during which pope Innocent IV excommunicated the emperor Frederick II, and in consequence deposed him, and forbade him fire and water. It was in this council that the cardinals were given red hats to remind them that they must bathe in the blood of the emperor's supporters. This council brought about the destruction of the house of Swabia, and led to thirty years of anarchy in Italy and Germany.

In the general council of 1311 at Vienne, in Dauphiné, was abolished the order of the Templars, whose leading members had been condemned to the most horrible tortures on the most unsubstantiated accusations.

In 1414 was held the great council of Constance, which contented itself with deposing pope John XXIII, convicted of a

1. In Romanist theology *dulia* means the veneration of the saints, *hyperdulia* that of the virgin Mary, *latria* that of god; Voltaire often used these technical terms with a sort of wry affection.

thousand crimes, and in which John Huss and Jerome of Prague were burned for being obstinate, since obstinacy is a much greater crime than murder, rape, simony and sodomy.

The great council of Basle in 1431 was not recognized in Rome because it deposed pope Eugene IV, who did not consent to be deposed.

The Romans reckon the fifth Lateran council of 1512 as a general council. It was called by pope Julius II against Louis XII, king of France, but this warrior-pope died, and the council went up in smoke.

Finally we have the great council of Trent, which does not have authority in France in matters of discipline. However, its dogma is unquestionable, since the holy ghost came every week from Rome to Trent in the courier's trunk, according to fra Paolo Sarpi; but fra Paolo Sarpi smelled a little of heresy.[1]

Confession

It is still doubtful whether confession, considered merely as a matter of policy, has done more good than harm.

In the mysteries of Isis, Orpheus and Ceres confession was taken by the hierophant and the initiates; for, these mysteries being expiations, it was obviously necessary to confess that one had crimes to expiate.

The Christians adopted confession in the first centuries of the church, just as they more or less took over the rites of antiquity, such as temples, altars, incense, candles, processions, lustral water, priestly dress, and several formulas of the mysteries: the *sursum corda*, the *ite missa est*, and so many others. The scandal of a public confession by a woman,

---

1. At the end of this essay Voltaire added the words 'by m. Abausit, the younger'. Firmin Abauzit was a local scholar, librarian of the university of Geneva, where he occasionally looked up references for Voltaire; but this attribution was of course part of the 'ostensible' pretence required by the French authorities, part joke, part white lie, as everybody knew who lived in that world of 'as if'.

which took place in Constantinople in the fourth century, caused the abolition of confession.

The secret confession made by one man to another was not allowed in our west until about the seventh century. The abbots began by demanding that their monks come to them twice a year to confess all their faults. It was these abbots who invented this formula: 'I absolve you as much as I can and as much as you need.' It seems to me that it would have been more respectful to the supreme being, and juster, to say: 'May he pardon your faults and mine!'

Confession has been beneficial in that it has sometimes procured restitution from petty thieves. The evil it has done is sometimes to have obliged the penitents, when there has been unrest in a country, to be rebellious and sanguinary with an easy conscience. The Guelph priests refused absolution to the Ghibellines, and the Ghibelline priests took good care not to absolve the Guelphs. The assassins of the Sforzas, the Medicis, the princes of Orange, the kings of France, prepared themselves for parricide by the sacrament of confession.

Louis XI and the Brinvilliers[1] went to confession as soon as they had committed a great crime, and confessed frequently, as a gourmand takes medicine to increase his appetite.

If we could be astonished by anything it would be by the bull of pope Gregory XV, which emanated from his holiness on 30 August 1622, and in which he ordered confessions to be revealed in certain cases.

The reply of the Jesuit Coton[2] to Henry IV will last longer than the Jesuit order: 'Would you reveal the confession of a man determined to assassinate me?' 'No, but I would interpose myself between you and him.'

1. Marie Madeleine Marguerite d'Aubray, marquise de Brinvilliers, executed in 1676 for a series of poisonings in which passion was inextricably mingled with greed for money.

2. Pierre Coton, the king's confessor.

Convulsions

There was dancing at the cemetery of Saint-Médard[1] about the year 1724. Many miracles were performed there. Here is one, reported in a song by the duchess Du Maine:

> *Un décrotteur à la royale,*
> *Du talon gauche estropié,*
> *Obtint pour grâce spéciale*
> *D'être boîteux de l'autre pied.[2]*

Everybody knows that the miraculous convulsions continued until a guard was posted at the cemetery.

> *De par le roi, défense à dieu*
> *De plus fréquenter en ce lieu.[3]*

It is also known that the Jesuits, being no longer able to work such miracles since their Xavier had exhausted the society's grace by resuscitating nine dead men by exact count, took it into their heads, in order to match the reputation of the Jansenists, to publish an engraving of Jesus Christ dressed as a Jesuit. A wit in the Jansenist interest, as is also known, put at the bottom of the print:

> *Admirez l'artifice extrême*
> *De ces moines ingénieux:*
> *Ils vous ont habillé comme eux,*
> *Mon Dieu, de peur qu'on ne vous aime.[4]*

The Jansenists, the better to prove that Jesus Christ could never have taken the habit of a Jesuit, filled Paris with convulsions, and attracted everybody to their fold.

1. The dancing and the miracles were connected with a wave of religious hysteria set off by the death of one Pâris. This was not in 1724, but in 1727, as Voltaire well knew, since he witnessed some of the manifestations.
2. 'A bearded boot-black, crippled in his left heel, was, as a special grace, lamed in the other foot.'
3. 'By order of the king god is forbidden to visit this place.'
4. 'Admire the cunning trick of these ingenious monks: bless me! they have dressed you like themselves lest you be loved.'

The councillor Carré de Montgeron went to the king to present him with a quarto collection[1] of these miracles, attested by a thousand witnesses. He was naturally sent to gaol, where they tried to restore his brains by dieting. But truth always prevails over persecutions: the miracles went on for thirty consecutive years, without intermission. People took sister Rose, sister Illuminée, sister Promise, sister Confite, into their homes. They had themselves whipped without any mark being visible the next day. They were hit with logs on their well protected, well padded stomachs, without being hurt. They were put in front of a big fire, their faces rubbed with ointment, without burning. Finally, as all the arts perfect themselves, they ended up by plunging swords into the women's flesh, and by crucifying them. Even a famous theologian[2] also had the good fortune to be put on the cross: all this to convince the world that a certain papal bull was ridiculous, which could have been proved without going to so much trouble. However, the Jesuits and Jansenists all united against the *Esprit des loix*,[3] and against . . . and against . . . and against. . . . And yet we dare to despise the Laplanders, the Samoyedes and the Negroes!

Corps: Body

Just as we do not know what a spirit is, so we are ignorant of what a body is. We see certain properties, but what is this subject in which these properties reside? There are only bodies, said Democritus and Epicurus. There are no bodies, said the disciple of Zeno of Elea.

1. This is the *Vérité des miracles opérés à l'intercession de m. de Páris* (Paris, 1737), by Louis Basile Carré de Montgeron; the particularly acid tone of Voltaire's comments is perhaps due to a rather curious fact: his own brother was a 'convulsionary' Jansenist, and the *Vérité* includes an account of 'miracles' operated in Voltaire's childhood home in the Palais.
2. Voltaire later changed this word to 'schoolmaster'; Abraham Chaumeix was both.
3. Not only was Montesquieu's book condemned, but also nearly all Voltaire's writings, and indeed the great majority of books which could in any way be regarded as progressive or merely unconventional.

Berkeley, bishop of Cloyne, is the last who claims to have proved, by a hundred captious[1] sophisms, that bodies do not exist. They have, he says, neither colours, nor odours, nor heat. These modalities are in your sensations, and not in the objects. He could have saved himself the trouble of proving this truth: it is well enough known. But from this he goes on to extension and solidity, which are essences of a body, and he thinks he has proved that a piece of green cloth has no extension because this cloth is not really green. The sensation of green is only in oneself: therefore the sensation of extension is also in oneself alone. And he concludes, having thus destroyed extension, that the solidity which is attached to it falls automatically, and that there is thus nothing in the world but our ideas. So that, according to this theologian, 10,000 men killed by 10,000 cannon shots are at bottom nothing but 10,000 apprehensions of our understanding; and when a man begets a child on his wife, it is only an idea that lodges itself in another idea, from which a third idea will be born.

It was up to the bishop of Cloyne not to fall into so ridiculous an excess. He thinks he has shown that there is no extension because a body has appeared to him four times larger through his telescope than to his eyes, and four times smaller by using other glasses. From this he concludes that since a body cannot be at once four feet, sixteen feet and a single foot in extent, this extension does not exist: therefore there is nothing. All he had to do was to take a measure, and say: Whatever the apparent extension of a body, its extension is so many of these measures.

It would have been easy enough for him to realize that extension and solidity are not like sounds, colours, tastes, odours, etc. Clearly there are feelings provoked in us by the configuration of the parts, but extension is not a feeling. If this

---

1. It is fascinating to see that when Voltaire first read Berkeley's *Alciphron* thirty years earlier, his reactions were even verbally identical. In 1733 he wrote in English to Andrew Pitt: 'I have read out the whole book. . . . I must tell you plainly that the doctor's sagacity has pleased me more than convinc'd. . . . In many places he is more captious and acute than solid' (Best. D558).

burning wood goes out, I am no longer warm. If this tune is no longer struck, I hear no more. If this rose fades, I no longer smell it. But this wood, this tune, this rose have extension without me. Berkeley's paradox is not worth the trouble of being refuted.

It is useful to know how he was betrayed into this paradox. Long ago I had several conversations with him. He told me that he had arrived at his opinion because it is impossible to conceive the nature of the subject that receives extension. And in fact he triumphs in his book when he asks Hylas what is this subject, this *substratum*, this substance. 'It is the extended body,' replies Hylas. Then the bishop, under the name of Philonous, laughs at him; and poor Hylas, realizing that he has said that the extension is the subject of the extension, and that he has talked nonsense, is embarrassed, and admits that he does not understand, that there is no body, that the material world does not exist, that there is only an intellectual world.

Hylas had only to say to Philonous: We know nothing about the inner meaning of this subject, of this extended substance, solid, divisible, mobile, formed, etc. I know it no better than the thinking, feeling and willing subject. But this subject exists none the less since it has essential properties of which it cannot be deprived.

We are all like most of the ladies of Paris; they live sumptuously without knowing what goes into the stew. Similarly we enjoy bodies without knowing of what they consist. What is the body made of? Of parts, and these parts resolve themselves into other parts. What are these last parts? Always bodies: you divide endlessly, and never advance.

Finally, a subtle philosopher,[1] noticing that a picture is made up of constituents none of which is a picture, and a house of materials none of which is a house, the idea struck him (in a rather different way) that bodies are constructed with an infinity of little beings which are not bodies, and these are called monads. This system does not fail to have its merits, and if it were revealed I would think quite possible. All these

1. Gottfried Wilhelm Leibniz.

little beings would be mathematical points, kinds of souls only waiting for a dress to put on. It would be a continuous metempsychosis. A monad would now go into a whale, then into a tree, another time into a juggler. This system is as good as another. I like it quite as well as dom Calmet's declination of atoms, substantial forms, versatile grace,[1] and vampires.

Credo

I do not resemble mlle Duclos, the famous actress, to whom somebody said: 'I bet you don't know your *credo*.' 'What!' she replied, 'I don't know my *credo*! I'll recite it to you. *Pater noster qui*. . . . Help me, I don't remember the rest.' As for me, I recite my *pater* and my *credo* every morning. I do not resemble Broussin, of whom Reminiac[2] said:

> *Broussin, dès l'âge le plus tendre,*
> *Posséda la sauce-Robert,*
> *Sans que son précepteur lui pût jamais apprendre*
> *Ni son credo ni son pater.*

Symbol[3] or collation comes from the word *symbolein* and the Latin church adopted this word from the Greek church as it has taken everything. Theologians who have some reading know that this symbol, called 'of the apostles', is not at all of the apostles.

The words, the signs by which the initiates of the mysteries of Ceres, of Cybele, of Mithras, recognized one another were

1. The theologians analysed the far from simple notion of grace into even more incomprehensible forms, such as efficacious grace, sufficient grace, prevenient grace, versatile grace, etc., etc.
2. He is a bit of a mystery; Voltaire also cites him in his *Notebooks* i. 262, 296, and in Best. 9193, but I have not been able to identify this poet, if poet he was; but the lines here quoted are of a common *libertin* type (Littré even quotes a version in his dictionary): 'From the tenderest age Broussin knew how to make *sauce-Robert*, though his tutor could never teach him his *credo* and his *pater*.'
3. This is another term for the creed.

called symbols by the Greeks.[1] In time the Christians had their symbol. Had it existed in the time of the apostles, it must be presumed that saint Luke would have spoken of it.

There is supposed to be a history of the symbol in saint Augustine's sermon 115. He is made to say in this sermon that Peter had begun the symbol by saying: 'I believe in god the all-powerful father'. John added: 'Creator of heaven and earth'. James added: 'I believe in Jesus Christ his only son, our lord'; and so on with the rest. This fable was struck out in the last edition of Augustine. I leave it to the reverend Benedictine fathers to tell me whether or not this little passage, which is very curious, should have been deleted.

The fact is that nobody ever heard of this *credo* for over 400 years. The common people say that Paris was not built in a day. The people's proverbs are often in the right.

The apostles had our symbol in their hearts, but they did not write it down. In the time of saint Irenaeus one was composed which in no way resembles the one we recite. It is agreed that our symbol, as it is today, dates from the fifth century. It is later than that of Nicaea. The clause which says that Jesus descended into hell, and that which refers to the communion of saints, are not found in any of the symbols that preceded ours. And in fact neither the gospels nor the acts of the apostles say that Jesus descended into hell. But it was an accepted opinion by the third century that Jesus descended into Hades, into Tartarus, words we translate as hell. In this sense hell is not the Hebrew word *sheol*, which means the underground, the pit. And this is why saint Athanasius later explained to us how our saviour descended into hell. 'His humanity,' says he, 'was neither entirely in the tomb, nor entirely in hell. It was in the tomb by the flesh, and in hell by the soul.'

Saint Thomas asserts that the saints who resuscitated at the death of Jesus Christ died again in order to resuscitate later with him. This is the most general view. All these opinions

---

1. *Note by Voltaire:* Arnobius V, *Symbola quae rogata sacrorum*, etc. See also Clement of Alexandria, in his protreptic sermon, or *Cohortatio ad gentes*. [A protreptic sermon or cohortation is an exhortation.]

have nothing whatever to do with morals. We must be up-right whether the saints resuscitated twice or whether god resuscitated them only once. I admit that our symbol was composed late; but virtue is eternal.

If it is permissible to quote modern writers in so grave a matter, I will reproduce here, faithfully copied, the *credo* of the *abbé* de Saint-Pierre, as written in his own hand in his book on the purity of religion, which has not been published:[1]

I believe in one god only, and I love him. I believe that he illu-minates every soul that comes into the world, as saint John says. By this I mean every soul that seeks him sincerely.

I believe in one god only, because there can be only one soul of the great all, only one vivifying being, a unique creator.

I believe in god the all-powerful father, because he is the common father of nature and of all men, who are equally his children. I believe that he who causes them all to be born equally, who arranged the springs of our life in the same way, who has given them the same moral principles perceived by them as soon as they reflect, has established no difference between his children other than the differ-ence between crime and virtue.

I believe that the just and beneficent Chinese is more precious to him than a pedantic and arrogant doctor.

I believe that it is our duty to regard all men as our brothers since god is our common father.

I believe that the persecutor is abominable, and that he ranks immediately after the poisoner and the parricide.

I believe that theological disputes are at once the world's most ridiculous farce and most frightful scourge, immediately after war, pestilence, famine and the pox.

I believe that the clergy should be paid, well paid, as servants of the public, teachers of marvels, custodians of the registers of children and deaths; but that they should be given neither the wealth of tax-collectors nor the rank of princes, because the one and the other corrupt the soul, and nothing is more revolting than to see men so rich and so proud make people with wages of only a hundred *écus* preach humility and the love of poverty.

I believe that all priests who serve a parish should be married, not only to have decent women to look after their households,

1. Nor has it been published since.

but to be better citizens, to give good subjects to the state, and to have many well brought up children.

I believe that monks must be absolutely extirpated, that this would render a very great service to the fatherland and to themselves. These are men whom Circe has changed into hogs. The wise Ulysses must restore them to human form.

PARADISE FOR THOSE WHO DO GOOD!

I reproduce this symbol by the *abbé* de Saint-Pierre in a historical spirit, without approving it. I regard it merely as a peculiar oddity, and I adhere, with the most respectful faith, to the true symbol of the church.

Critique: Criticism

I do not propose to say anything here about the criticism of the scholiasts, which ineptly restores in an ancient author a word which was quite well understood before. I shall not touch on those true criticisms which have cleared up all they can of ancient history and philosophy. I have in mind the criticisms that border on satire.

A lover of literature one day read Tasso with me; he came on this stanza:

> *Chiama gli abitator dell' ombre eterne*
> *Il rauco suon della tartarea tromba.*
> *Treman le spaziose atre caverne;*
> *E l'aer cieco a quel rumor rimbomba:*
> *Nè stridendo così dalle superne*
> *Regioni del cielo il fulgor piomba;*
> *Nè si scossa giammai trema la terra*
> *Quando i vapori in sen gravida serra.*[1]

He then read at random several stanzas of similar force and harmony: 'Ah! so this,' he cried out, 'is what your Boileau

1. *Gerusalemme liberata*, IV. iii, not quite accurately: 'Those who dwell in the eternal shade are called by the raucous sound of the hellish trump. The vast and open caverns tremble; and the air reverberates with the sound: thus do the highest regions of heaven resound when the thunder roars; thus the earth labours when vapours seek for release.'

calls flashy? So this is the way he tries to belittle a great man who lived 100 years before him, in order to elevate another great man who lived 1,600 years earlier, and who would himself have done justice to Tasso?' 'Cheer up,' I told him, 'let's have a look at Quinault's operas.'

On opening the book we at once found something to infuriate us against criticism. We fell on that admirable poem *Armide*, and found these words:

SIDONIE
La haine est affreuse et barbare,
L'amour contraint les coeurs dont il s'empare
A souffrir des maux rigoureux.
Si votre sort est en votre puissance,
Faites choix de l'indifférence;
Elle assure un repos heureux.

ARMIDE
Non, non, il ne m'est pas possible
De passer de mon trouble en un état paisible,
Mon cœur ne se peut plus calmer;
Renaud m'offense trop, il n'est que trop aimable,
C'est pour moi désormais un choix indispensable
De le haïr ou de l'aimer.[1]

We read the whole play of Armide, in which the genius of Tasso is given even more charms by the hand of Quinault. 'Well!' I said to my friend, 'it is nevertheless this Quinault whom Boileau always tried to pass off as the most contemptible of writers. He even convinced Louis XIV that this pleasing, touching, pathetic, elegant writer has no merit but that he owes to the musician Lully.' 'I can very easily understand

1. Philippe Quinault, *Armide*, III. iii:

'SIDONIE: Hatred is frightful and barbarous, love compels the hearts it captures to bear extreme hardships. If your fate is in your hands, choose indifference: it ensures a happier fate.

'ARMIDE: No, no, it is impossible for me to pass from my agitation to a peaceful state, my heart can no longer calm itself; Renaud offends me too much, he is only too amiable; henceforth I have to make an inescapable choice, to hate him or to love him.'

that,' replied my friend; 'Boileau was jealous of the poet, not of the musician. What confidence can we have in the judgement of a man who, in order to rhyme with a verse in *aut*, now disparaged Boursault, now Hénault, now Quinault, according to the state of his relations with these gentlemen?

'But, so that your zeal against injustice may not cool, just put your head out of the window, look at the beautiful façade of the Louvre, which has immortalized Perrault.[1] This skilful man was the brother of the very learned academician with whom Boileau had had some dispute, reason enough to be branded an ignorant architect.'

My friend, after a moment's reverie, resumed with a sigh: 'Such is human nature. The duc de Sully says in his *Memoirs* that cardinal d'Ossat and Villeroy, the secretary of state, were bad ministers. Louvois did all he could not to esteem the great Colbert.'

'But they printed nothing against each other,' I replied. The duke of Marlborough published nothing against the earl of Peterborough. This is a folly bound up only with literature, the chicanery of the courts, and theology. It is a pity that the *Economies politiques et royales* are sometimes sullied by this defect.

Lamotte Houdard was a man of merit in more than one kind; he wrote very fine stanzas:

> *Quelquefois au feu qui la charme*
> *Résiste une jeune beauté,*
> *Et contre elle-même elle s'arme*
> *D'une pénible fermeté.*
> *Hélas! cette contrainte extrême*
> *La prive du vice qu'elle aime,*
> *Pour fuir la honte qu'elle hait.*
> *Sa sévérité n'est que faste,*
> *Et l'honneur de passer pour chaste*
> *La résout à l'être en effet.*

1. Claude Perrault was the elder brother of Charles Perrault, now generally remembered only for his fairy tales, but then famous for his defence of the moderns in the 'quarrel of the ancients and the moderns'; this was the dispute to which Voltaire refers.

En vain ce sévère stoïque,
Sous mille défauts abattu,
Se vante d'une âme héroïque
Toute vouée à la vertu:
Ce n'est point la vertu qu'il aime;
Mais son cœur, ivre de lui-même,
Voudrait usurper les autels;
Et par sa sagesse frivole
Il ne veut que parer l'idole
Qu'il offre au culte des mortels.[1]

Les champs de Pharsale et d'Arbelle
Ont vu triompher deux vainqueurs,
L'un et l'autre digne modèle
Que se proposent les grands cœurs.
Mais le succès a fait leur gloire;
Et si le sceau de la victoire
N'eût consacré ces demi-dieux,
Alexandre, aux yeux du vulgaire,
N'aurait été qu'un téméraire,
Et César qu'un séditieux.[2]

This author, he said, was a wise man who more than once lent to philosophy the charm of poetry. Had he always written such stanzas he would be the first of lyric poets.

1. Antoine Houdard de La Motte, *L'Amour propre*, ode to the bishop of Soissons, stanzas, v, ix: 'Sometimes a young beauty resists the charming fire, and with painful firmness arms herself against herself. Alas! this extreme constraint deprives her of the vice she loves in order to flee the shame she hates. Her severity is a mere pretence, and the honour of being supposed chaste resolves her to be so in truth. In vain this severe stoic, cast down by a thousand defects, boasts of an heroic soul wholly devoted to virtue: it is not virtue that she loves, but her heart, drunk with itself, would like to usurp the altars, and with her frivolous virtue seeks only to adorn the idol she offers to the worship of mortals.'

2. *La Sagesse du roi supérieure à tous les événements*, stanza iv: 'The fields of Pharsalos and Arbela saw the triumphs of two conquerors, both worthy models for the great-hearted. But success made their glory; and if the seal of victory had not consecrated these half-gods Alexander would have been no more than a dare-devil and Caesar a rebel in the eyes of the vulgar.'

Nevertheless it was when he was writing these fine things that one of his contemporaries called him:

> *Certain oison, gibier de basse-cour.*[1]

Elsewhere he says of Lamote:

> *De ses discours l'ennuyeuse beauté.*[2]

And in another:

> *. . . Je n'y vois qu'un défaut:*
> *C'est que l'auteur les devait faire en prose.*
> *Ces odes-là sentent bien le Quinault.*[3]

He persecutes him everywhere. Everywhere he reproaches him with coldness and lack of harmony. Would you care to see the odes written some years later by this same critic, who judged Lamotte like a schoolmaster and disparaged him like an enemy? Read:

> *Cette influence souveraine*
> *N'est pour lui qu'une illustre chaîne*
> *Qui l'attache au bonheur d'autrui;*
> *Tous les brillants qui l'embellissent,*
> *Tous les talents qui l'ennoblissent*
> *Sont en lui, mais non pas à lui.*[4]

> *Il n'est rien que le temps n'absorbe et ne dévore*
> *Et les faits qu'on ignore*
> *Sont bien peu différents des faits non avenus.*[5]

1. 'A certain gosling, farmyard fowl'; but the line is a prolonged *double-entente*, and also means 'A certain small-game ninny'. This line, and the two succeeding quotations, are all by Jean Baptiste Rousseau.
2. 'The boring beauty of his discourses.'
3. 'I see only one defect in them: it is that the author ought to have written them in prose. These odes distinctly smell of Quinault.'
4. These are fragments extracted from J. B. Rousseau's *Odes*, selected for their absurdity in language or in content: 'This sovereign influence is for him only an illustrious chain which attaches him to the happiness of others. All the brilliance that beautifies him, all the talents that ennoble him, are in him but are not his.'
5. 'There is nothing that time does not absorb and devour, and the events we do not know are very little different from those that never happened.'

La bonté qui brille en elle
De ses charmes les plus doux,
Est une image de celle
Qu'elle voit briller en vous.
Et par vous seule enrichie,
Sa politesse affranchie
Des moindres obscurités,
Est la lueur réfléchie
De vos sublimes clartés.[1]

Ils ont vu par ta bonne foi
De leurs peuples troublés d'effroi
La crainte heureusement déçue,
Et déracinée à jamais
La haine si souvent reçue
En survivance de la paix.[2]

Dévoile à ma vue empressée
Ces déités d'adoption,
Synonymes de la pensée
Symboles de l'abstraction.
N'est-ce pas une fortune
Quand d'une charge commune
Deux moitiés portent le faix,
Que la moindre le réclame,
Et que du bonheur de l'âme
Le corps seul fasse les frais?[3]

'One ought not,' then said my judicious lover of literature, 'one ought certainly not to offer such detestable works as models to the writer one has criticized with such bitterness.

1. 'The goodness that shines in her, the sweetest of her charms, is an image of the goodness she sees shine in you. And, enriched by you alone, her courtesy, freed from the slightest obscurities, is the reflected light of your sublime effulgence.'

2. 'They have seen the fears of their people, disturbed by terror, happily mastered by your good faith, and uprooted for ever the hatred so often remaining to survive the peace.'

3. 'Unveil to my eager view these adopted deities, synonymous of thought, symbols of abstraction. Is it not fortunate when the weaker of two halves that carry a burden together asks to bear it alone, and the body alone undertakes to make the soul happy?'

It would have been better to let one's adversary enjoy his own merits in peace, and preserve one's own. But that's the way it is. The *genus irritabile vatum*[1] suffers from the same bile as in other days. The public forgives these wretched things in men of talent, because the public looks only for amusement. In an allegory entitled *Pluton* it sees judges condemned to be flayed and to sit in hell on seats covered with their own skins instead of *fleurs de lis*. The reader cares little whether the plaintiff who indicts them before Pluto is right or wrong. He reads these lines solely for his pleasure. If they give him some, he asks for no more. If he does not like them, he forgets the allegory, and would not make the slightest effort to have the sentence confirmed or annulled.

Racine's inimitable tragedies were all criticized, and very badly. This is because these criticisms were by rivals. It is true that it is artists who are competent judges of art, but these competent judges are nearly always corrupt.

An artist with a great deal of knowledge and taste, without prejudices and without envy, would be an excellent critic. That is hard to find.'

David

If a young peasant, searching for she-asses, finds a kingdom, that is not a common occurrence. If another peasant cures his king of an attack of madness by playing the harp, this event is also very unusual. But that this little harp-player becomes a king because of a casual meeting with a village priest who empties a bottle of olive oil on his head, that is a still greater marvel.

When and by whom were these marvels written down? I have no idea, but I am quite sure that it was neither by a Polybius nor by a Tacitus. I much revere the worthy Jew, whoever he was, who wrote the true history of the powerful kingdom of the Hebrews for the instruction of the universe, under the dictation of the god of all the worlds, who inspired this good Jew. But I regret that my friend David began by

1. The 'touchy race of poets'.

collecting a band of thieves to the number of 400, that at the head of this troop of decent folk he came to an understanding with the high priest Abimelech, who armed him with the sword of Goliath and gave him holy bread.[1]

I am rather shocked that David, the anointed of the lord, the man after god's own heart, having rebelled against Saul, another anointed of the lord, went off with 400 bandits to lay the country under contribution and to rob the harmless Nabal, and immediately after Nabal's death married his widow without delay.[2]

I have some reservations about his behaviour to the great king Achish, proprietor, if I am not mistaken, of five or six villages in the canton of Gath. David was then at the head of 600 brigands, and made some expeditions to the allies of his benefactor Achish. He pillaged everything, killed everybody, old men, women, children at the breast. And why did he massacre the children at the breast? 'For fear,' says the divine Jewish author, 'lest the children carry the news to king Achish.'[3]

These bandits got angry with him, and wanted to stone him. What did this Jewish Mandrin[4] do? He consulted the lord, and the lord replied that he must set out to attack the Amalekites, that the bandits would win great spoil there and get rich.[5]

In the meanwhile Saul, the anointed of the lord, lost a battle against the Philistines, and was killed. A Jew brought the news to David. David, who apparently had not the means to

1. *Note by Voltaire:* *1 Kings* xxi and xxii. [Voltaire's references to the *Bible* are to the Latin Vulgate, in which *1 Samuel* is called *1 Kings*; the exact reference here is *1 Samuel* xxi. 1–4. It is an odd thing that Voltaire, usually very accurate, made several mistakes in his Biblical references in this section of the *Dictionnaire*; but he afterwards corrected them as shown here.]

2. *Note by Voltaire:* ibid., chapter xxv.

3. *Note by Voltaire:* ibid., chapter xxvii. [*1 Samuel* xxvii. 11 in fact reads: 'And David saved neither man nor woman alive. to bring them to Gath, saying, lest they should tell on us. . .']

4. Louis Mandrin was a sort of French eighteenth-century Robin Hood.

5. *Note by Voltaire:* *1 Kings* xxx.

give the courier the *buona nuncia*,[1] had him killed as his reward.[2]

Ishbosheth succeeded his father Saul. David was strong enough to make war on him. In the end Ishbosheth was murdered. David seized the whole kingdom. He took the little town or village of Rabbah by surprise, and killed all the inhabitants by means of somewhat extraordinary tortures. They were sawn in two, they were torn apart with iron harrows, they were burned in brick kilns: a most noble and generous method of waging war.[3]

After these fine expeditions there was a three years' famine in the land. I can well believe it, for in view of the manner in which the good David made war, the land must have been badly sown. The lord was consulted, and he was asked why there was a famine. This was easy to answer: it was undoubtedly because few people remain to cultivate the soil, in a land which barely produces wheat, when the landworkers are baked in brick kilns and sawn in two. But the lord replied that it was because Saul had formerly killed some Gibeonites.

On this, what does the good David do? He assembles the Gibeonites; he tells them that Saul had been very wrong to make war on them; that Saul was not after god's own heart like him; that it was right to punish his race; and he gave them seven of Saul's grandsons to hang, who were hanged because there had been a famine.[4]

It is a pleasure to see how that imbecile, dom Calmet, justifies and canonizes all these actions, which would make us shudder with horror were they not incredible.

I shall say nothing here of the abominable murder of Uriah, and of the adultery of Bathsheba. All this is familiar enough, and the ways of god are so different from the ways of men that he allowed Jesus Christ to descend from this infamous Bathsheba, the whole thing being purified by this holy mystery.

1. That is, a reward for bringing good news.
2. *Note by Voltaire:* 2 *Kings* i. [2 *Kings* in the Vulgate is 2 *Samuel*.]
3. *Note by Voltaire:* ibid. xii.
4. *Note by Voltaire:* ibid., chapter xxi.

I shall not now inquire how the preacher Jurieu had the insolence to persecute the virtuous Bayle because he did not approve all the doings of the good king David; but I ask how the molestation of a man like Bayle by a wretch like Jurieu was tolerated.

Délits locaux (des): On local crimes

Go where you will, you will find that theft, murder, adultery, calumny are regarded as crimes condemned and put down by society. But should an action approved in England and condemned in Italy be punished in Italy as one of these outrages against all mankind? This is what I call a local crime. That which is criminal only within the walls of a few mountains or between two rivers, does it not require more indulgence from the judges than those outrages which are held in horror in all countries? Should the judge not say to himself: 'I dare not punish at Ragusa what I punish at Loretto'? Should this reflection not soften in his heart the harshness all too easily acquired in the long practice of his profession?

The carnivals of Flanders are well known. In the last century they were so indecent that they could revolt eyes unaccustomed to these spectacles. This is how the festival of Christmas was celebrated in some towns. First appeared a half naked young man with wings on his back. He recited the *Ave Maria* to a girl who replied *fiat*, and the angel kissed her on the mouth. Then a child inside a big cardboard cock cried out, imitating the song of the cock: *puer natus est nobis*.[1] A great bullock bellowed and said *ubi*,[2] which he pronounced *oubi*. A ewe bleated in crying out *Bethlehem*. A donkey cried out *hihanus*, meaning *eamus*.[3] A long procession, preceded by four fools with rattles and baubles, closed the proceedings. Some traces still remain today of these popular devotions, which would be regarded as profanations among more educated people. An ill-tempered Swiss, perhaps also drunker than those who performed the roles of the bullock and the

---

1. 'A boy is born to us.'   2. 'Where.'   3. 'Let us go.'

donkey, had words with them in Louvain; there were blows; and they tried to hang the Swiss, who barely escaped.

The same man had a violent quarrel at The Hague, in Holland, for having boldly taken the part of Barneveldt against an extreme Gomarist. He was imprisoned in Amsterdam for having said that priests are the scourge of mankind and the source of all our misfortunes. 'Really!' he said, 'if one believes that good works can promote salvation, one finds oneself in gaol. If one makes fun of a cock and a donkey one risks the rope.' This adventure, ludicrous though it is, shows clearly enough that one can deserve reproach in one or two corners of our hemisphere, and be absolutely innocent in the rest of the world.

Destin: Fate

Of all the western books that have come down to us Homer is the oldest. It is there that we find the customs of profane antiquity, gross heroes, gross gods made in the image of man. But it is also there that we find the seeds of philosophy, and above all the notion of fate, which is the master of the gods, as the gods are the masters of the world.

When the magnanimous Hector absolutely insisted on fighting the magnanimous Achilles, and for that purpose fled with all his strength and went three times round the town before fighting in order to increase his vigour; when Homer compares to a sleeping man the light-footed Achilles who pursues him (mme Dacier goes into ecstasies of admiration for the art and deep meaning of this passage); then Jupiter[1] in vain tries to save Hector; he consults the fates; he weighs in the balance the fates of Hector and Achilles,[2] he finds that the Trojan absolutely must be killed by the Greek; he cannot resist; and from that moment Apollo, Hector's guardian

1. In all the editions this passage reads: '. . . pursues him, when mme Dacier goes into ecstasies of admiration for the art and deep meaning of this passage; then Jupiter. . . ' – which is nonsense, for I dare say that Jupiter was indifferent to mme Dacier's future ecstasies.
2. *Note by Voltaire: Iliad* xxii.

genius, is obliged to abandon him. It is true that Homer is often prodigal in his poem with quite contrary ideas, as was permitted in antiquity; but still he is the first in whom the notion of fate is found. It must therefore have been quite current in his time.

The Pharisees, among the little Jewish people, did not adopt fate until several centuries later; for these Pharisees, who were the first literate Jews, were themselves quite new. In Alexandria they mixed part of the dogmas of the Stoics with the ancient Jewish ideas. Saint Jerome even alleges that their sect is not much older than our common era.

Philosophers never needed either Homer or the Pharisees to convince themselves that all events are governed by immutable laws, that all is arranged, that all is a necessary effect.

Either the world subsists by its own nature, by its physical laws, or a supreme being formed it in accordance with his supreme laws. In either case these laws are immutable. In either case all is necessary. Heavy bodies tend towards the centre of the earth, incapable of tending to rest in the air. Pear trees can never bear pineapples. The instinct of a spaniel cannot be the instinct of an ostrich. All is arranged, geared and limited.

Man can have only a certain quantity of teeth, hair and ideas. A time comes when he necessarily loses his teeth, his hair and his ideas.

It is a contradiction to say that what was yesterday was not, that what is today is not. It is also a contradiction to say that what must be does not have to be.

If you could alter the fate of a fly there would be nothing to prevent you from creating the fate of all the other flies, all the other animals, all men, all nature. When all is said and done, you would find yourself more powerful than god.

Idiots say: 'My doctor saved my aunt from a fatal illness, he made her live ten years longer than she should have lived.' Other idiots, who affect to know better, say: The prudent man makes his own fate.

> *Nullum numen abest, si sit prudentia, sed nos*
> *Te facimus, fortuna, deam, coeloque locamus.*

La fortune n'est rien; c'est en vain qu'on l'adore.
La prudence est le dieu qu'on doit seul implorer.[1]

But the prudent man, far from making his own fate, often succumbs to it. Prudent men are made by fate.

Profound statesmen assert that if Cromwell, Ludlow, Ireton and a dozen other parliamentarians had been assassinated a week before Charles I's head was cut off, this king could have gone on living and died in his bed. They are right. They can also claim that if the whole of England had been engulfed in the sea, this monarch would not have died on a scaffold in Whitehall (which in English means a white room). But things were arranged in such way that Charles had to have his neck cut.

Cardinal d'Ossat was no doubt more prudent than a madman in the Petites-maisons; but is it not obvious that the organs of the wise Ossat were not made in the same way as those of the lunatic, just as the fox's organs are different from those of a crane and a lark?

Your doctor saved your aunt; but he certainly did not gainsay the order of nature to do so: he obeyed it. It is obvious that your aunt could not prevent herself from being born in a given town, that she could not prevent herself from having a certain illness at a given time, that the doctor could not be elsewhere than in the town in which he was; that your aunt had to send for him; that he had to prescribe the drugs that cured her.

A peasant thinks that hail fell by chance on his field; but the philosopher knows that there is no chance, and that the world being constituted as it is, it was impossible for the hail not to fall that day on that spot.

There are people who, afraid of this truth, grant half of it, like debtors who offer half to their creditors, and ask to be let off the rest. There are, they say, necessary events, and others

1. Juvenal, *Satires* x. 365–6: 'Fate would have no divinity if we were wise: it is we who make her a goddess and place her in heaven.' Voltaire's French version is so free that it must also be translated: 'Fortune is nothing; it is adored in vain. Prudence is the only god to whom we should pray.'

that are not necessary. It would be laughable for one part of this world to be arranged, and not the other, if one part of what happens had to happen, and another part of what happens did not have to happen. When one examines this closely it is seen that the doctrine opposed to fate is absurd. But there are many people fated to reason badly, others not to reason at all, others to persecute those who reason.

There are people who tell you: 'Don't believe in fatalism; for, everything then appearing to be inevitable, you won't work at anything, you'll wallow in indifference, you'll love neither wealth, nor honours, nor praise; you won't want to acquire anything; you'll believe yourself to be equally without value and power. No talent will be cultivated; everything will perish in apathy.'

Fear not, gentlemen, we shall always have passions and prejudices, since it is our fate to be subject to prejudices and to passions. We would be well aware that it no more depends on us to have much merits and great talents than to have a good growth of hair and a beautiful hand. We would be convinced that vanity is not to be drawn from anything, and yet we shall always be vain.

I necessarily have the passion to write this; and you, you have the passion to condemn me: we are both equally foolish, equally the playthings of fate. Your nature is to do evil, mine is to love the truth and to publish it in spite of you.

The owl, who feeds on mice in his shanty, said to the nightingale: 'Stop singing in your shady trees, come into my hole for me to devour you'; and the nightingale replied: 'I was born to sing here and to laugh at you.'

You ask me what will become of freewill. I don't understand you. I do not know what this freewill is that you speak of. You have been arguing for so long about its nature that you assuredly do not know it. If you want peacefully to examine with me what it is, or rather if you can, turn to the letter L.[1]

1. The French word for freewill is *liberté*.

Dieu: God

In the reign of Arcadius, Logomachos, a theologian from Constantinople, went to Scythia, and stopped at the foot of the Caucasus, in the fertile plains of Zephirim, on the borders of Colchis. Good old Dondindac was in his great hall, between his great sheepfold and his immense barn. He was on his knees with his wife, his five sons and five daughters, his relatives and servants, and all sang the praises of god, after a light meal. 'What are you doing there, idolators?' Logomachos asked him. 'I'm not an idolator,' said Dondindac. 'You must be an idolator,' said Logomachos, 'since you are a Scythian, and not a Greek. Now then, what were you singing in your barbarous Scythian jargon?' 'All languages are alike to the ears of god,' answered the Scythian; 'we were singing his praises.' 'How extraordinary!' rejoined the theologist, 'a Scythian family that prays to god without having been instructed by us!' Soon he opened a conversation with the Scythian Dondindac, for the theologist knew a little Scythian, and the other a little Greek. This conversation has been rediscovered in a manuscript preserved in the library of Constantinople.

LOGOMACHOS: Let's see whether you know your catechism. Why do you pray to god?

DONDINDAC: Because it's proper to worship the supreme being, to whom we owe all things.

LOGOMACHOS: Not bad for a barbarian! And for what do you ask him?

DONDINDAC: I thank him for the good things I enjoy, and even for the evils with which he tries me, but I take great care not to ask him for anything: he knows better than we do what we need, and in any case I'd be afraid to ask him for fine weather when my neighbour might be asking for rain.

LOGOMACHOS: Ah! I quite expected him to say something silly. Let's start again further back. Barbarian, who told you that there is a god?

DONDINDAC: All nature.

LOGOMACHOS: That's not enough. What is your notion of god?

DONDINDAC: The notion of my creator, of my master, who will reward me if I do good and punish me if I do evil.

LOGOMACHOS: Nothing but trifles and commonplaces! Let's come to the essential. Is god infinite *secundum quid* or according to the essence?

DONDINDAC: I don't understand you.

LOGOMACHOS: Stupid brute! Is god a place or outside every place or in every place?

DONDINDAC: I've no idea. Just as you like.

LOGOMACHOS: Ignoramus! Can he cause something that has been not to have been, and a stick not to have two ends? Does he see the future as future or as present? How does he draw being from nothingness, and how annihilate being?

DONDINDAC: I've never bothered about such things.

LOGOMACHOS: What a bumpkin! Well, well, I must stoop lower, come down to his level. Tell me, my good fellow, do you believe that matter can be eternal?

DONDINDAC: What do I care whether or not it exists since all eternity? I, for my part, don't exist since all eternity. God is still my master; he's given me the notion of justice; I must follow it. I've no wish to be a philosopher, I want to be a man.

LOGOMACHOS: These blockheads give one a lot of trouble. Let's go step by step. What is god?

DONDINDAC: My sovereign, my judge, my father.

LOGOMACHOS: That's not what I asked. What is his nature?

DONDINDAC: To be powerful and good.

LOGOMACHOS: But is he corporeal or spiritual?

DONDINDAC: How can you expect me to know that?

LOGOMACHOS: What! you don't know what a spirit is?

DONDINDAC: Not in the least. What use would it be to me? Would it make me juster? Would I be a better husband, better father, better master, better citizen?

LOGOMACHOS: It is absolutely necessary to teach you

what a spirit is. Listen, it's, it's, it's. . . . I'll tell you some other time.

DONDINDAC: I'm very much afraid that you'll tell me what he isn't, and not what he is. Permit me to ask you a question in my turn. I once saw one of your temples: why do you paint god with a big beard?

LOGOMACHOS: This is a very difficult question, which requires preliminary instruction.

DONDINDAC: Before receiving your instruction, I must tell you what happened to me one day. I had just had a closet built at the end of my garden. I heard a mole arguing with a cockchafer: 'Here's a fine structure,' said the mole; 'it must have been a very powerful mole who did this work.' 'You're joking,' said the cockchafer; 'it's a cockchafer full of genius who is the architect of this building.' From that moment I resolved never to argue.

Divinité de Jésus: Divinity of Jesus

The Socinians, who are regarded as blasphemers, do not recognize the divinity of Jesus Christ. They dare to maintain, like the philosophers of antiquity, like the Jews, the Mohammedans, and so many other nations, that the notion of a godman is monstrous, that the distance between a god and a man is infinite, and that is is impossible for the infinite being, immense, eternal, to have been contained in a perishable body.

They have the assurance to cite on their behalf Eusebius, bishop of Caesarea, who in his *Ecclesiastical History*, book I, chapter XI, declares it to be absurd for the unbegotten, immutable nature of all-powerful god to take the shape of a man. They cite the church fathers Justin and Tertullian, who said the same thing: Justin in his dialogue with Tryphon, and Tertullian in his discourse against Praxeas.

They cite saint Paul, who never calls Jesus Christ god, and who very often calls him man. They push audacity to the point of affirming that the Christians spent three whole centuries in constructing little by little the apotheosis of Jesus, and that

they raised this astonishing edifice only in imitation of the
pagans, who had deified some mortals. At first, according to
them, Jesus was regarded merely as a man inspired by god,
then as a creature more perfect than the others. Some time
after he was given a place above the angels, as says saint Paul.
Every day added to his stature. He became an emanation of
god manifested in time. That was not enough: he was held to
be born before time itself. Finally he was made god, consubstantial with god. Crellius, Voquelsius, Natalis Alexander,
Hornebeck supported all these blasphemies with arguments
which astonish the wise and corrupt the weak. It was Faustus
Socinus above all who spread the seed of this doctrine in
Europe; and towards the end of the sixteenth century he very
nearly established a new kind of Christianity: there had already been more than 300 kinds.

Dogmes : Dogmas

It is known that every belief taught by the church is a dogma
we must embrace. It is sad that there are dogmas received by
the Latin church and rejected by the Greek. But if unanimity
is lacking, charity replaces it: a reunion is needed most of all
between hearts.

I believe that in this connection I may be allowed to record
a dream which has already found favour in the eyes of some
peaceful people. On 18 February of the year 1763 of the
common era, the sun entering the sign of the fishes, I was
transported to heaven, as all my friends know. My mount was
not Mohammed's mare Borac. Elijah's flaming chariot was
not my carriage. I was borne neither on the Elephant of
Sammonocodom the Siamese, nor on the horse of saint
George, patron of England, nor on saint Anthony's pig: I
confess ingenuously that I do not know how my journey was
done.

It will readily be believed that I was dazzled; but what will
not be believed is that I saw all the dead judged. And who
were the judges? They were, if you please, all those who have
rendered service to mankind: Confucius, Solon, Socrates,

Titus, the Antonines, Epictetus, all the great men who, having taught and practised the virtues required by god, appeared alone to have the right to pronounce his decrees.

I shall not mention on what thrones they were seated, nor how many million celestial beings were prostrated before the creator of all the globes, nor what a crowd of the inhabitants of these innumerable globes appeared before the judges. I shall give an account here only of some little details of special interest that struck me.

I noticed that every dead man who pleaded his case and displayed his fine feelings had by his side all the witnesses of his doings. For instance, when the cardinal de Lorraine boasted that he had made the council of Trent adopt some of his views, and asked for eternal life as the reward for his orthodoxy, twenty courtesans or ladies of the court immediately appeared around him, each bearing on her forehead the number of her rendezvous with the cardinal. Those who had laid the foundations of the *Ligue* with him were seen, all the accomplices of his perverse plans came around him.

Opposite the cardinal de Lorraine was Calvin, who boasted in his coarse dialect that he had kicked the papal idol after others had thrown it down. 'I have written against painting and sculpture,' said he; 'I have made it evident that good works are good for nothing at all, and I have proved that it is diabolic to dance the minuet. Drive away quickly the cardinal de Lorraine, and put me by the side of saint Paul.'

As he spoke a flaming pyre was seen by his side. A frightful spectre, wearing round its neck a half-burned Spanish ruff, rose from the midst of the flames with fearful cries. 'Monster,' he cried, 'execrable monster, tremble! Recognize Servet whom you put to death with the cruellest of tortures because he had argued against you about the manner in which three persons can make a single substance.' On this all the judges ordered the cardinal de Lorraine to be cast into the abyss, and Calvin to be punished more rigorously.

I saw a prodigious crowd of the dead who said: 'I believed, I believed', but on their foreheads was written 'I have done', and they were condemned.

The Jesuit Le Tellier appeared proudly, the bull *Unigenitus* in his hand. But around him suddenly rose up a heap of two thousand *lettres de cachet*. A Jansenist set fire to it: Le Tellier was burnt to a cinder, and the Jansenist, who had plotted no less than the Jesuit, got his share of the burning.

I saw arriving on all sides troops of fakirs, talapoins, bonzes, white, black and grey monks, who had all imagined that it was necessary to sing or to whip themselves or to go naked in order to pay their court to the supreme being. I heard a terrible voice that asked them: 'What good have you done to mankind?' This voice was followed by a gloomy silence. Nobody dared to answer, and they were all taken to the Colney Hatch of the universe: it is one of the vastest buildings imaginable.

One cried: 'We must believe in the metamorphoses of Xaca', another 'In those of Sammonocodom.' 'Bacchus stopped the sun and the moon,' said this one. 'The gods resuscitated Pelops,' said that. 'Here is the bull *In coena domini*,' said a newcomer. And the clerk of the court cried out: 'To Colney Hatch, to Colney Hatch.'

When all these cases were disposed of, I heard this judgement promulgated: 'BY ORDER OF THE ETERNAL CREATOR CONSERVOR, REWARDER, AVENGER, PARDONER, etc. Be it known to all inhabitants of the hundred thousand million billion worlds we have been pleased to create, that we shall never judge any of the said inhabitants by their futile notions, but solely by their actions; for such is our justice.'

I admit that it was the first time I heard such a decree: all those I had read on the little grain of sand where I was born ended with these words, *For such is our pleasure*.

Egalité: Equality

What does a dog owe to a dog, and a horse to a horse? Nothing, no animal depends on his like; but man having received the ray of divinity called *reason*, what is the result? Slavery throughout almost the whole world.

Were this world what it seems that it should be, that is, if man found everywhere on it easy and assured subsistence and a climate appropriate to his nature, it is clear that it would have been impossible for one man to subjugate another. Let this globe be covered with wholesome fruit; let the air which must contribute to our life no longer give us illness and death; let man require no other lodging and no other bed than those of the deer and the stag: then the Genghis Khans and the Tamerlanes would have no other servants than their children, who would be upright enough to help them in their old age.

In this natural state enjoyed by all quadrupeds, birds and reptiles, man would be as happy as they, domination would then be a chimera, an absurdity which would occur to no-body: for why seek for servitors when you need no service?

If some individual with a tyrannical head and vigorous arm got the idea of subjugating a neighbour less strong than he, the thing would be impossible: the oppressed would be 100 leagues away before the oppressor could take action.

Thus all men would necessarily be equal if they were without needs. The poverty characteristic of our species subordinates one man to another. It is not inequality that is the real evil, but dependence. It matters very little that some man is called his highness, and another his holiness; but it is hard to serve one or the other.

A numerous family has cultivated good land. Two small neighbouring families have barren and obstinate fields. It is obvious enough that the two poor families must serve the opulent family or murder it. One of the two indigent families offers its labour to the rich to get bread; the other attacks it and is beaten. The former family originated servants and labourers, the defeated family slaves.

It is impossible on our wretched globe for men living in society not to be divided into two classes, one of oppressors, the other of the oppressed; and these subdivide into a thousand, and the thousand have further gradations.

All the oppressed are not absolutely unhappy. Most of them are born in that state, and continual work prevents them from feeling their condition too keenly; but when they feel it, then we have wars like that in Rome of the popular party against that of the senate, and those of the peasants in Germany, in England, in France. All these wars end sooner or later by the enslavement of the people because the powerful have the money, and in a state money is the master of everything; I say in a state, because it is not so in every nation. The nation making the best use of the sword will always subjugate that having more gold and less courage.

Every man is born with a powerful enough desire for domination, wealth and pleasure, and with much taste for idleness. Consequently every man would like to have other people's money and wives or women, to be their master, to subjugate them to all his caprices, and to do nothing, or at least to do only very agreeable things. Obviously, having such amiable dispositions, it is as impossible for men to be equal as it is impossible for two preachers or two professors of theology not to be jealous of one another.

Mankind cannot subsist at all unless there is an infinite number of useful men who possess nothing at all. For a prosperous man will certainly not leave his land to cultivate yours; and if you need a pair of shoes it is not a judge who will make them for you. Equality is thus at once the most natural and the most chimerical of things.

As men are extreme in everything whenever possible, this inequality has been exaggerated. In some countries it has been claimed that a citizen is not entitled to leave the country in which he is born by chance. The meaning of this law is obviously: *This country is so bad and so badly governed that we forbid every individual to leave it, for fear that everybody leave it*. Do better: make all your subjects wish to remain at home and strangers to come to you.

Every man has the right to believe himself, at the bottom of his heart, entirely equal to all other men. It does not follow from this that a cardinal's cook should order his master to prepare his dinner; but the cook can say: 'I'm a man like my master, like him I am born in tears; like me he will die with the same sufferings and the same ceremonies. Both of us perform the same animal functions. If the Turks capture Rome, and I am then a cardinal and my master a cook, I will take him into my service.' All this speech is reasonable and just; but until the Grand Turk captures Rome the cook must do his duty, or every human society is perverted.

As for a man who is neither a cardinal's cook nor endowed with any other public office; as for a private person of modest views, but who is annoyed because he is received everywhere with an air of patronage or disdain, who sees clearly that several monsignors have no more knowledge, no more intelligence, no more virtue than he, and who is sometimes wearied to find himself in their waiting rooms, what should he do? He should leave.

Enfer: Hell

As soon as men lived in society they must have noticed that some guilty men eluded the severity of the laws. They punished public crimes. It was necessary to create a check on secret crimes: only religion could be this check. The Persians, the Chaldeans, the Egyptians, the Greeks invented punishments after life; and the Jews alone among all the ancient peoples known to us approved only temporal punishments. It is ridiculous to believe, or to pretend to believe, on the strength of a few very obscure passages, that hell was recognized by the ancient laws of the Jews, by their *Leviticus*, by their decalogue, when the author of these laws does not say a single word that could have the slightest bearing on punishments in the future life. One would be entitled to say to the compiler of the *Pentateuch*: 'You are an irresponsible man, without probity and reason, very unworthy of the name of legislator that you arrogate. What! you know a dogma so repressive, and so necessary to the people, as that of hell, and you do not explicitly proclaim it? And, though it is accepted by all the nations around you, you are content to allow this dogma to be guessed at by some commentators who are to come 4,000 years after you and will torture some of your words to find in them something you have not said. Either you are an ignoramus, who are not aware that this belief was universal in Egypt, in Chaldea, in Persia; or you are very ill-advised, knowing this dogma, not to have made it the basis of your religion.'

The authors of the Jewish laws might at best reply: 'We admit that we are exceedingly ignorant; that we learned to write very late; that our people was a savage and barbaric horde which, as we have shown, wandered for half a century in uninhabitable deserts; that it finally usurped a small country by the most odious rapine and the most detestable cruelties ever recorded in history. We had no intercourse with civilized nations: how can you expect us (the most earthly of men) to have invented a wholly spiritual system?

'We used the word meaning *soul* only in the sense of *life*. We knew our god and his ministers, his angels, only as corporeal beings: the distinction between soul and body, the notion of a life after death, can be the fruit only of long meditation and a very subtle philosophy. Ask the Hottentots and the Negroes, who inhabit a country a hundred times larger than ours, whether they know about a future life. We thought we had done enough in persuading our people that god punishes evil-doers to the fourth generation, whether by leprosy, sudden death, or the loss of what little property it was possible for them to possess.'

One would reply to this defence: 'You have invented a system the absurdity of which is self-evident; for the male-factor who was in good health and whose family prospered would necessarily laugh at you.'

The apologist of the Judaic law would then answer: 'You are mistaken; for there were a hundred criminals who did not reason at all, for every one who thought clearly. The man who, having committed a crime, felt unpunished in himself and in his son, feared for his grandson. Besides, if he did not have some stinking ulcer today, he would get one in the course of a few years, for we were much subject to them. Every family has misfortunes, and it was easy for us to inoculate the belief that these misfortunes were sent by a divine hand, the avenger of secret offences.'

It would be easy to respond to this answer, and to say: 'Your excuse is worthless, for it happens every day that very decent folk lose their health and their goods; and if there is no family that has escaped misfortune, and if these misfortunes are god's punishments, all your families must have been families of rascals.'

The Jewish priest could retort further. He would say that there are misfortunes attached to human nature, and others sent expressly by god. But one would make this argufier see how ridiculous it is to think that fever and hail are now a divine punishment, and now a natural effect.

Finally the Pharisees and the Essenes, among the Jews, accepted a belief in a hell in their manner. This dogma had already passed from the Greeks to the Romans, and was adopted by the Christians.

Several church fathers did not believe in eternal punishment: it appeared to them absurd to burn a poor wretch throughout eternity because he had stolen a goat. Virgil can say in the sixth book of the *Aeneid*:

> ... *Sedet aeternumque sedebit*
> *Infelix Theseus.*[1]

He implies in vain that Theseus is seated forever on a chair, and that this position constitutes his torment. Others believed that Theseus is a hero who is not seated in hell, but that he is in the Elysian fields.

Not long ago a good and decent Protestant minister preached and wrote[2] that the damned would one day be pardoned, that the suffering should be proportionate to the sin, and that the error of a moment cannot deserve infinite punishment. The priests, his colleagues, dismissed this indulgent judge. One said to him: 'My dear fellow, I don't believe any more than you do that hell is eternal; but it's a good thing for your maid, your tailor, and even your lawyer to believe it.'

---

1. *Aeneid* vi. 617–18: 'Wretched Theseus sits and shall for ever sit.'
2. *Apologie de m. Petit-Pierre sur son système de non-éternité des peines à venir* (1761).

Enthousiasme: Enthusiasm

This Greek word means *disturbance of the entrails, internal agitation*. Did the Greeks invent this word to express the shocks felt by the nerves, the dilation and tightening of the bowels, the violent contractions of the heart, the precipitate rush of the fiery spirits that mount from the entrails to the brain when one is deeply moved?

Or was the word *enthusiasm*, from disturbance of the entrails, first given to the contractions of that Pythia who, on the tripod at Delphi, received the spirit of Apollo through a part which seems made only to receive bodies?

What do we understand by enthusiasm? What nuances in our sentiments! Approval, sensibility, emotion, distress, shock, passion, frenzy, madness, fury, rage: these are all the states a wretched human soul can pass through.

A geometrician watches a touching tragedy: he sees only that it is well constructed. A young man by his side is moved and sees nothing. A woman weeps. Another young man is so carried away that, unhappily for him, he also decides to write a tragedy: he has caught the disease of enthusiasm.

The centurion or military tribune who looked on war simply as a trade in which a little fortune could be made, went calmly into battle like a thatcher climbing a roof. Caesar wept when he saw the statue of Alexander.

Ovid always spoke amusingly about love. Sappho expressed the enthusiasm of this passion; and if it is true that it cost her her life it is because in her case enthusiasm became madness.

The spirit of party marvellously encourages enthusiasm: no faction is without its fanatics.

Enthusiasm is above all the lot of misguided piety. The young fakir who sees the tip of his nose when praying gradually works himself up until he believes that if he loads himself with chains weighing fifty pounds the supreme being will be much obliged to him. He goes to sleep with his imagination filled with Brahma, and inevitably sees him in his dreams.

Sometimes sparks even shine from his eyes in the state between sleep and walking: he sees Brahma glittering with light, he has ecstasies, and this disease often becomes incurable.

It is the rarest of things to unite reason with enthusiasm. Reason consists of always seeing things as they are. The drunkard is deprived of his reason when he sees things double. Enthusiasm is precisely like wine: it can excite so much tumult in the blood vessels, and such violent vibrations in the nerves, that the reason is entirely destroyed. It can cause only slight jolts, which merely produce a little more activity in the brain. This is what happens in great outbursts of eloquence, and above all in sublime poetry. Rational enthusiasm is the attribute of great poets. This rational enthusiasm is the perfection of their art. In other times it led to the belief that they were inspired by the gods, a thing that has never been said of the other artists.

How can reason govern enthusiasm? This is because a poet first sketches the structure of his canvas: the reason then holds the brush. But when he proceeds to animate his personages and to endow them with passions, then the imagination kindles, enthusiasm takes over: it is a race horse carried away headlong, but its course has been properly laid out.

Esprit faux: Defective understanding

We have people who are blind, one-eyed, cross-eyed, who squint, who are far-sighted, short-sighted, who see distinctly or confusedly, who are weak or untiring. This is all a pretty faithful use of our understanding. But we hardly know of any false vision. Hardly anyone always take a cock for a horse, or a chamber-pot for a house. Why do we often encounter understandings, otherwise correct enough, that are absolutely defective in important matters? Why does this same Siamese who would never let himself be cheated if it were a question of paying him three rupees, believe firmly in the metamorphoses of Sammonocodom? What strange eccentricity makes sensible people resemble don Quixote, who thought he saw giants where other men saw only windmills? As a matter of fact don Quixote was more excusable than the Siamese who believes that Sammonocodom descended on earth several times, and the Turk who is convinced that Mohammed put half the moon into his sleeve; for don Quixote, obsessed by the idea that he had to fight giants, could have imagined that a giant must have a body as large as a mill, and arms as long as its sails. But from what assumption can a sensible man depart to convince himself that half the moon entered into a sleeve, and that a Sammonocodom came down from heaven to fly kites in Siam, to cut down a forest, to do conjuring tricks?

The greatest geniuses may be in error about a principle they have accepted without scrutiny. Newton's understanding was very false when he commented on the *Apocalypse*.

All that certain tyrants of souls wish for is that the men they teach should have defective understanding. A fakir brings up a most promising child. He employs five or six years to beat into his head that the god Fo appeared to men as a white elephant, and he convinces the child that he will be whipped for 500,000 years after his death if he does not believe these metamorphoses. He adds that at the end of the world the enemy of the god Fo will come to fight him.

The child studies and becomes a prodigy. He argufies about his master's teachings, and finds that Fo could have changed himself only into a white elephant, because that is the most beautiful of animals. 'The kings of Siam and Pegu,' says he, 'fought a war over a white elephant. Obviously, if Fo had not been hidden in that elephant these kings would not have been so insensate as to battle for the possession of a mere animal. The enemy of Fo will come to defy him at the end of the world. Obviously, this enemy will be a rhinoceros, for the rhinoceros fights the elephant.'

So does the learned pupil of the fakir reason at a mature age, and he becomes one of the lights of India. The subtler his mind, the more defective it is. And he will in turn form minds defective like his.

Show all these fanatics a little geometry, and they learn it quite easily. But, strangely enough, their minds are not there-by rectified. They perceive the truths of geometry, but it does not teach them to weigh probabilities. Their minds have set hard. They will reason in a topsy-turvy wall all their lives, and I am sorry for it.

Etats, gouvernements: quel est le meilleur?
States, governments: which is the best?

To this day I have not known anyone who has not governed some state. I am not talking of ministers, who really govern, some for two or three years, others for six months, others for six weeks. I am talking about all the other men who, at a supper or in their studies, display their systems of govern-ments, reforming the armies, the church, the law, and the economy.

The *abbé* de Bourzeis[1] set about governing France about the year 1645, under the name of cardinal de Richelieu, and wrote that *Testament politique* in which he seeks to enrol the nobility for three years in the cavalry, oblige the Audit office and the *parlements* to pay taxes, deprive the king of the yield of the salt-tax. Above all he asserts that for the sake of economy 100,000 men should be raised in order to give battle with 50,000. He affirms that 'Provence alone has many more good sea ports than Spain and Italy together.'

The *abbé* de Bourzeis had not travelled. Naturally his work swarms with anachronisms and mistakes. He makes cardinal de Richelieu sign in a manner he never used, just as he makes him speak as he never spoke. For the rest, it takes him an entire chapter to say that 'reason should be the rule of a state', and to try to prove this discovery. This deed of dark-ness, this bastard of the *abbé* de Bourzeis, was for long taken to be the legitimate son of cardinal de Richelieu; and all the

1. Amable de Bourzeis; the complete truth about the so-called political testament attributed to cardinal de Richelieu will probably never be known, but it now seems likely that the cardinal did have some hand in it. Voltaire was fascinated by the problem throughout his life.

academicians, in their inaugural discourses, did not fail to praise it extravagantly as a masterpiece of politics.[1]

Master Gatien de Courtilz, seeing the success of Richelieu's *Testament politique*, printed at The Hague the *Testament de Colbert*,[2] with a fine letter from m. Colbert to the king. It is evident that if this minister had made such a testament it would have had to be suppressed. Nevertheless some authors have quoted this book.

Another scoundrel, whose name is unknown, promptly produced a *Testament de Louvois*,[3] still worse, if possible, than Colbert's. And an *abbé* de Chèvremont made Charles, duke of Lorraine, also execute a testament.[4] We have had the political testament of cardinal Alberoni,[5] of *maréchal* de Belle-Isle,[6] and finally that of Mandrin.[7]

M. de Bois-Guillebert, author of the *Détail de la France*,[8] printed in 1695, proposed under the name of marshal de Vauban the impracticable project of a royal tithe.

In 1720 a starving madman called La Jonchère composed a financial project in four volumes;[9] and some fools have

1. Until Voltaire himself broke away from it, it was the custom for a new member of the Académie française to devote part of his reception discourse to the praises of Richelieu, the academy's founder.

2. [Gatien de Courtilz de Sandras], *Testament politique de messire Jean Baptiste Colbert* (1693).

3. By the same author: *Testament politique du marquis de Louvois* (1695).

4. *Testament politique de Charles duc de Lorraine et de Bar* (1696) was probably by Theodor Heinrich Strattman, though Jean Baptiste Chèvremont had a hand in it.

5. [Joseph Marie Durey de Morsan], *Testament politique du cardinal Jules Alberoni* (Lausanne, 1753); Voltaire published a scathing *Examen* (1753) of this *Testament*.

6. [François Antoine Chevrier], *Testament politique du maréchal-duc de Belle-Isle* (1761).

7. [Ange de Goudar], *Testament politique de L. Mandrin* (Valence, 1755).

8. The credit for this by no means impracticable project is generally given to Sébastien Le Prestre, marquis de Vauban, but Voltaire is quite correct in giving the authorship of *Le Détail de la France* (1697) to Pierre Le Pesant de Bois-Guillebert.

9. [Etienne Lescuyer] de La Jonchère, *Système d'un nouveau gouvernement en France* (Amsterdam, 1720); he was an engineer of some standing, and Voltaire's language was not influenced by his belief that La Jonchère had once tried to blackmail him (see Best. D5595).

referred to this publication as though it were the work of
La Jonchère,[1] the head of the treasury, under the impression
that a treasurer cannot write a bad book on finance.

But it must be agreed that very wise men, perhaps quite
worthy to govern, have written in France, Spain and England
on the administration of states. Their books have done much
good: not that it corrected the ministers who were in office
when the book appeared, for a minister does not and cannot
correct himself. He has reached his full status. No more instruction, no more advice. He has not the time to listen to
them, the tide of business carries him away. But these good
books form the young men destined for office, they form the
princes, and the second generation is educated.

The strengths and weaknesses of all governments have been
closely investigated in recent times. So tell me, you who have
travelled, who have read and observed, in which state, under
what kind of government, would you have liked to be born?
I imagine that a great French landowner would not object
to being born in Germany: he would be master instead of
being subject. A French peer would be delighted to have the
privileges of the English peerage: he would be a legislator.

The lawyer and the financier would be better off in France
than elsewhere.

But what fatherland would be chosen by a wise man, free,
of modest wealth, and without prejudices? A quite learned
member of the council of Pondicherry returned to Europe
overland with a Brahman who was better educated than
ordinary Brahmans. 'What do you think of the government of
the Grand Mogul?' asked the councillor. 'It's abominable,'
answered the Brahman. 'How can you expect a state to be
successfully governed by Tartars? Our rajahs, our omras,[2]
our nabobs are perfectly satisfied, but the citizens not at all,
and millions of citizens count for something.'

1. Gérard Michel de La Jonchère.
2. Voltaire's use of this word is an interesting and typically accurate
echo of his English reading, for it is unrecorded in French. 'Omra', in Voltaire's spelling, is defined by the *New English Dictionary* as a 'lord or
grandee of a Mohammedan court, esp. that of the great Mogul'.

The councillor and the Brahman traversed all upper Asia, debating all the while. 'It occurs to me,' said the Brahman, 'that there isn't a republic in all this vast part of the world.' 'There used to be that of Tyre,' said the councillor, 'but it didn't last long. There was another near Arabia Petraea, in a little corner called Palestine, if one can honour with the name of republic a horde of thieves and usurers, now governed by judges, now by kings of a sort, now by grand pontiffs, enslaved seven or eight times, and finally driven from the country they had usurped.'

'I imagine,' said the Brahman, 'that very few republics are to be found on earth. Men seldom deserve to govern themselves. This happiness seems to be the lot only of small nations hidden in islands, or between mountains, like rabbits who hide from the carnivorous animals; but in the end they are found and devoured.'

When the two travellers arrived in Asia Minor the councillor said to the Brahman: 'Would you believe that a republic was once established in a corner of Italy that lasted more than 500 years, and that possessed this Asia Minor, Asia, Africa, Greece, Spain and the whole of Italy?' 'So it quickly turned into a monarchy?' said the Brahman. 'You're right,' said the other, 'but that monarchy fell, and every day we publish fine dissertations to discover the causes of its decline and fall.'[1] 'You take too much trouble,' said the Indian; 'this empire fell because it existed. Everything must fall. I certainly hope that the same thing will happen to the empire of the Grand Mogul.'

'By the way,' said the European, 'do you believe that a despotic state needs more honour, and a republic more virtue?'[2] When the Indian had been made to understand what is meant by honour, he replied that honour was more necessary in a republic, and that virtue was much more needed in a monarchy. 'For,' said he, 'a man who wishes to be

1. This is not a reference to Gibbon (not yet published) but to Montesquieu's *Considérations sur les causes de la grandeur et de la décadence des Romains* (Amsterdam, 1734).

2. These passages are also allusions to the theories of Montesquieu.

elected by the people won't be if he is dishonoured; while at court he could easily obtain an office, according to the maxim of a great prince[1] that a courtier to succeed must have neither honour nor humour. As for virtue, a prodigious amount is needed to dare to tell the truth at court. The virtuous man is much more at his ease in a republic: he has nobody to flatter.'

'Do you believe,' said the man from Europe, 'that laws and religions are made to suit climates, just as furs are needed in Moscow and gauze in Delhi?' 'Yes, certainly,' said the Brahman, 'all the physical laws are calculated for the meridian one inhabits: a German needs only one wife, a Persian needs three or four. The same is true of religious rites. If I were a Christian how would you expect me to say mass in my province, where there is neither bread nor wine? As for dogmas, that's different, climate has no influence on them. Didn't your religion begin in Asia, where it was driven out? Doesn't it exist on the Baltic, where it was unknown?'

'In what state, under what domination, would you prefer to live?' asked the councillor. 'Anywhere except at home,' said his companion, 'and I have met many Siamese, Tongkinese, Persians and Turks who said as much.' 'But, once again,' said the European, 'which state would you choose?' The Brahman replied: 'That in which only the laws are obeyed.' 'That's an odd answer,' said the European. 'It's no worse on that account,' said the Brahman. 'Where is that country?' asked the councillor. The Brahman said: 'We must look for it.'[2]

Evangile: Gospel

It is very difficult to know which are the first gospels. It is an established fact, whatever Abbadie[3] may say about it, that

1. Voltaire elsewhere identifies him as the regent Philippe d'Orléans.
2. *Footnote by Voltaire:* See the article Genève in the *Encyclopédie*. [This article is by Alembert, and got him into great trouble in Geneva itself, as did Voltaire's own praise of that republic.]
3. Jacques Abbadie, *Traité de la vérité de la religion chrétienne* (La Haye, 1750).

not one of the first fathers of the church, down to and including Irenaeus, quotes a single passage from the four gospels known to us. On the contrary, the Alogi, the Theodosians consistently rejected the gospel of saint John, and always spoke of it with contempt, as averred by saint Epiphanius in his thirty-fourth homily. Our enemies further point out that not only do the most ancient fathers never quote anything from our gospels, but they reproduce several passages found only in the apocryphal gospels rejected from the canon.

Saint Clement, for instance, reports that our lord, having been questioned about the time when his kingdom would come, answered: 'It will be when two will make only one, when outside will be like inside, and when there will be neither male nor female.' Now it must be admitted that this passage is not in any of our gospels. There are a hundred examples to prove this truth. They can be garnered in the *Examen critique* by m. Fréret,[1] permanent secretary of the Paris Académie des belles lettres.

The learned Fabricius took the trouble to collect all the ancient gospels[2] that have survived. That of James appears to be the first. It is certain that it still has much authority in certain eastern churches. It is called the *first gospel*. There remain the passion and the resurrection, which are alleged to have been written by Nicodemus. This gospel of Nicodemus is quoted by saint Justin and by Tertullian. It is there that are found the names of our saviour's accusers: Annas, Caiaphas, Summas, Dothaim, Gamaliel, Judas, Levi, Nephthalim. The trouble taken to report these names gives the

---

1. The *Examen critique des apologistes de la religion chrétienne* (1766) was published over the name of Nicolas Fréret, in accordance with a practice common at that time when unorthodox books were printed surreptitiously; but Voltaire wrote in his copy of the book: 'I do not believe that this *Examen* is by m. Fréret. It is very dangerous for the faith.' The book was probably by Jean Levesque de Burigny.

2. The relevant works by Johann Albert Fabricius are *Salutaris lux evangelii toti orbi per divinam gratiam exoriens* (Hamburgi, 1731) and *Codex apocryphus Novi testamenti* (Hamburgi, 1703); Fabricius was one of the greatest polymaths of all time.

work an appearance of sincerity. Our adversaries have concluded that since so many false gospels were at first taken to be authentic, though forged, those we believe in nowadays may also have been falsified. They lay much stress on the faith of the first heretics who died for these apocryphal gospels. Thus there were forgers and deceivers, and there were the deceived who died for an error: that martyrs should have died for it is therefore not a proof of the truth of our religion.

They further add that the martyrs were never asked: 'Do you believe in the gospel of John or in the gospel of James?' The pagans could not base interrogations on books unknown to them. Magistrates punished some Christians as disturbers of public peace, but they never interrogated them about our four gospels. It was only under Trajan[1] that these books became known at all to the Romans, and it was only in the last years of Diocletian[2] that they came into the hands of the public. Hence the rigid Socinians take our four gospels to be clandestine works, fabricated about a century after Jesus Christ, and carefully hidden from the gentiles for another century: works, they say, crudely written by coarse men, who for long addressed themselves only to the common people. I do not care to repeat here their other blasphemies. This sect, though fairly widespread, is today as obscure as were the first gospels. It is the more difficult to convert them in that they believe only in their reason. The other Christians fight them only with the sacred voice of the scriptures: so it is impossible for the two parties, being always enemies, ever to be reconciled.[3]

D'Ezéchiel: On Ezekiel

On some singular passages in this prophet, and some ancient practices

It is well enough known nowadays that ancient practices must not be judged by modern ones. Scholars would not welcome an attempt to amend the court of Alcinous in the

1. That is, at the beginning of the second century.
2. That is, about the year 300.
3. Voltaire added the fictitious attribution 'By the *abbé* de Tilladet'.

Odyssey in accordance with that of the Grand Turk or of
Louis XIV. It would be a bad critic who objected that Virgil
represented king Evander dressed in a bear-skin and accompanied by two dogs when receiving ambassadors.

The morals of the ancient Jews are even more different
from ours than those of king Alcinous, his daughter Nausicaa,
and dear old Evander.

Ezekiel, a slave among the Chaldeans, had a vision near the
little river of Chebar which merges into the Euphrates. We
must not be surprised that he saw animals with four faces and
four wings, with calves' feet, and wheels turning by themselves
and having the spirit of life. These symbols even please the
imagination, but several critics have been revolted by the
command the lord gave him to eat for 390 days bread made
of barley, wheat and millet, smeared with shit.

The prophet exclaimed: 'Phew! phew! phew! up to now
my soul has not been polluted'; and the lord replied: 'Well,
I'll give you cow dung instead of human excrement, and you
shall knead your bread with the dung.'

As it is not customary to eat such preserves with one's
bread, most men find these commandments unworthy of the
divine majesty. Nevertheless it must be admitted that cow
dung and all the diamonds of the Grand Mogul are absolutely
equal, not only in the eyes of a divine being, but also in those
of a genuine philosopher. And as for the reasons god may have
had to order such a meal for the prophet, it is not for us
to inquire what they were. It is enough to show that these commandments, which seem strange to us, did not seem so to the
Jews. It is true that in the time of saint Jerome the synagogue
did not permit the reading of Ezekiel before the age of thirty,
but this was because he says in chapter xviii that the son will
no longer bear the iniquities of his father, and that it will no
longer be said: 'The fathers have eaten sour grapes, and the
children's teeth are set on edge.'

In this he expressly contradicted Moses, who asserts in
chapter xviii of *Numbers* that children bear the iniquity of their
fathers to the third and fourth generation.

Ezekiel further makes the lord say, in chapter xx, that he

had given the Jews 'statutes that were not good'. That is why the synagogue forbade the young to read what might cast doubt on the irrefutable nature of the Mosaic law.

The critics of our time are still more astonished by chapter xvi of *Ezekiel*. This is how the prophet makes known the crimes of Jerusalem. He introduces the lord speaking to a girl, and the lord says to the girl:

In the day you were born your navel string was not cut, you were not salted, you were quite naked. I took pity on you. You grew up, your breasts were formed, your hair was grown. I passed, I saw you, I knew that it was the time for lovers. I covered your ignominy. I extended myself over you with my mantle. You became mine. I washed you, perfumed you, dressed you well, shod you well. I gave you a cotton scarf, bracelets, a necklace, I put a ring on your nose, gave you ear-rings, and put a crown on your head, etc. But you trusted in your beauty, you fornicated for your profit with all the passers-by. . . . And you built an evil place . . . , and even prostituted yourself in public places, and you opened your legs to all the passers-by . . . , and you laid with Egyptians . . . , and at last you paid to have lovers and you gave them presents that they might lie with you . . . , and in paying instead of being paid you did the contrary of other harlots. . . . The proverb says, like mother like daughter; and this is what is said of you, etc.[1]

Even greater objections are raised against chapter xxiii. A mother had two daughters who lost their virginity early. The elder was named Oholah and the younger Oholibah. 'Oholah doted on young lords, magistrates, horsemen. She whored with Egyptians from her earliest youth. . . . Oholibah, her sister, fornicated even more with officers, magistrates, and desirable horsemen. She discovered her turpitude; she multiplied her fornications; she sought out with passion the embraces of those who had members like those of asses, and whose seed was like that of horses.'[2]

Yet these descriptions, which startle so many weak spirits,

1. Rather than a direct quotation this is a selective abstract, but perfectly accurate, of *Ezekiel* xvi. 4–34, 44.
2. The same comment applies to this passage from *Ezekiel* xxiii. 4–20.

merely represent the iniquities of Jerusalem and Samaria. The expressions that to us appear broad were not then so regarded. The same simplicity is shown fearlessly in more than one passage of the scriptures. There are frequent allusions in them to opening the vulva. The terms used in them to describe the coupling of Boaz with Ruth, of Judah with his daughter-in-law, are not all at all indecent in Hebrew, but would be in our language.

We do not cover ourselves with a veil unless we are ashamed of our nakedness. How could people in those days have blushed to name the genitals, since they touched the genitals of those to whom they made promises? It was a mark of respect, a symbol of fidelity, as formerly our feudal lords put their hands between those of their paramount lords.

We have translated the genitals by 'thigh'. Eliezer puts his hand under Abraham's thigh. Joseph puts his hand under Jacob's thigh. This custom was very ancient in Egypt. The Egyptians were so far from attaching any depravity to what we dare neither uncover nor name that they carried in procession a large image, named *phallum*, of the virile member, to thank the gods for their goodness in making this member serve for the propagation of mankind.

All this shows well enough that our decency is not the decency of other peoples. When did the Romans have better manners than in the century of Augustus? Yet Horace did not at all hesitate to say in a moral piece

Nec metuo ne, dum futuo, vir rure recurrat.[1]

Augustus uses the same expression in an epigram against Fulvia. In our society a man who spoke the word corresponding to *futuo* would be taken for a drunken picklock. This word, and several more used by Horace and other authors, appear to us even more indecent than Ezekiel's terms. We

1. *Satires* I. ii. 127: 'I do not fear her husband's return from the country while I am fucking her.' The terrible word is also found in Catullus and Martial.

must get rid of all our prejudices when we read ancient authors and travel in distant nations. Nature is the same everywhere and customs are everywhere different.[1]

N.B. One day I met in Amsterdam a rabbi who was full of this chapter. 'Ah! my friend,' said he, 'how deeply we are indebted to you! You have made known all the sublimity of the Mosaic law, Ezekiel's lunch, his fine left-handed attitudes; Oholah and Oholibah are admirable; they are types, brother, types who symbolize the fact that the Jewish people will one day master the whole earth. But why have you left out so many more things that are pretty well as astonishing? Why didn't you show the lord saying to the wise Hosea, in the second line of the first chapter: "Hosea, take unto thee a wife of whoredom, and beget upon her sons of whoredom." These are his very words. Hosea took the young lady, had a boy by her, then a girl, and then another boy. And this was a symbol, and the symbol lasted for three years.

'"That's not all," says the lord in the third chapter, "go and take a woman who is not only debauched, but also an adulteress." Hosea obeyed; but it cost him fifteen crowns and one and a half measures of barley, for you know that there was very little wheat in the promised land. But do you know what all this means?' 'No,' I replied. 'Nor do I,' said the rabbi.

A sober scholar approached and told us that they are ingenious fictions full of charm. 'Ah, sir,' answered a very well-read young man, 'if you want fictions, believe me, prefer those of Homer, Virgil and Ovid. Those who like the prophesies of Ezekiel deserve to lunch with him.'

Fables

Are not the most ancient fables obviously allegorical? According to our method of reckoning the eras is not the oldest fable we know that reported in the ninth chapter of the book of *Judges*? A king of the trees was to be chosen. The olive tree did not want to abandon the care of its oil, nor the fig tree

1. The rest of this section was added in one of the 1765 editions.

that of its figs, nor the vine that of its wine, nor the other trees that of their fruits. The thistle, which was good for nothing, made itself king, because it had thorns and could do harm.

Is not the ancient fable of Venus, in the form reported by Hesiod, an allegory of all nature? The generative parts fell from the ethereal regions on to the shore of the sea. Venus was born from this precious foam. Her first name was that of the lover of generation. Could there be a more obvious image? This Venus is the goddess of beauty; beauty ceases to be lovable if not accompanied by the graces; beauty causes love; love has features that pierce the heart; it wears a blind-fold that hides the defects of the things we love. Wisdom, under the name of Minerva, is conceived in the brain of the master of the gods. The soul of man is a divine fire shown by Minerva to Prometheus, who uses this divine fire to animate man.

It is impossible not to recognize in these fables a vivid picture of all nature. Most other fables are either the corruption of ancient tales or caprices of the imagination. The ancient fables are like our modern stories: there are moral ones, which are charming; others are insipid.

The fables of the ingenious peoples of antiquity were crudely imitated by crude peoples: witness those of Bacchus, Hercules, Prometheus, Pandora, and so many others. They amused the ancient world. The barbarians, who heard them talked about confusedly, merged them into their savage mythology; and then they dared to say: 'It is we who invented them.' Alas! wretched peoples, unknown and un-knowing, who knew not a single art, whether agreeable or useful, to whom not even the name of geometry ever penetrated, can you say that you ever invented anything? You were neither able to discover any truths nor to lie cleverly.

Fanatisme: Fanaticism

Fanaticism is to superstition what delirium is to fever, and what fury is to anger. The man who has ecstasies and visions, who takes dream for realities, and his imaginings for prophecies, is an enthusiast. The man who backs his madness with murder is a fanatic. John Diaz, living in retirement at Nuremberg, was firmly convinced that the pope was the Antichrist of the Apocalypse and bore the sign of the beast. He was only an enthusiast, but his brother Bartholomew Diaz, who departed from Rome piously to assassinate his brother, and who in fact killed him for love of god, was one of the most abominable fanatics superstition has ever succeeded in shaping.[1]

Polyeuctès who went to the temple on a solemn occasion to overthrow and smash the statues and ornaments,[2] was a less horrible fanatic than Diaz, but no less stupid. The assassins of duke François de Guise, of William, prince of Orange, of king Henry III and king Henry IV, and so many others, were energumens suffering from the same madness as Diaz.

The most detestable example of fanaticism is that of the bourgeois of Paris who hastened in saint Bartholomew's night to assassinate, butcher, throw out of the windows, cut in pieces their fellow citizens who did not go to mass.[3]

There are cold-blooded fanatics: these are the judges who condemn to death those guilty of no other crime than that of not thinking like them; and those judges are all the guiltier, all the worthier of the execration of mankind, because it would seem that they could have listened to reason, not being in a state of fury like the Clements, the Châtels, the Ravaillacs, the Gérards, the Damiens.

Once fanaticism has cankered a brain, the disease is almost incurable. I have seen convulsionaries who, talking about the miracles of saint Pâris, gradually became excited despite

1. The name of the man who committed this pious murder on 27 March 1546 was in fact Alfonso Diaz.
2. Voltaire had in mind not so much the martyr himself as Corneille's tragedy *Polyeucte*.
3. Voltaire felt so keenly the horrors of the massacre of Saint Bartholomew (24 August 1572) that he ran a temperature throughout his life on the anniversary of this beastly butchery, as already mentioned.

themselves: their eyes blazed, their limbs trembled, passion disfigured their faces, and they would have killed anyone who contradicted them.

There is no other remedy for this epidemic illness than the spirit of free thought, which, spreading little by little, finally softens men's customs, and prevents the renewal of the disease. For as soon as this evil makes any progress we must flee and wait for the air to become pure again. Laws and religion do not suffice against the pest of the soul. Religion, far from being a beneficial food in such cases, turns into poison in infected brains. These wretches always remember the example of Ehud, who assassinated king Eglon; of Judith, who cut off the head of Holofernes while in bed with him; of Samuel, who chopped king Agag to pieces. They do not realize that these examples, respectable in antiquity, are now abominable. They draw their rage from the very religion that condemns it.

Laws also are quite impotent against these attacks of fury: it is as if you read a cabinet decree to a lunatic. These people are convinced that the saint who possesses them is above the law, that their enthusiasm is the only law to which they need attend.

How can you answer a man who tells you that he would rather obey god than men, and who is therefore sure to deserve heaven in cutting your throat?

Fanatics are usually guided by rascals, who put the dagger into their hands. They resemble that old man of the mountain who, it is said, made imbeciles taste the joys of paradise, and who promised them an eternity of the pleasures of which he had given them a foretaste, on condition that they murdered all those he would name. There is only one religion in the world that has never been sullied by fanaticism, that of the Chinese scholars. The philosophical sects were not only free from this pest, they were its remedy. For the effect of philosophy is to make the soul tranquil, and fanaticism is incompatible with tranquillity. If our holy religion has so often been corrupted by this infernal fury, the folly of mankind must be blamed.

Ainsi du plumage qu'il eut
Icare pervertit l'usage;
Il le reçut pour son salut,
Il s'en servit pour son dommage.[1]

> (Bertaud, bishop of Séez)

Fausseté des vertus humaines:
Falseness of human virtues

When the duke of La Rochefoucauld had written his epi-grams on self-love, and had laid bare this human motive, a monsieur Esprit, of the Oratory, wrote a captious book entitled *De la fausseté des vertus humaines.*[2] This Esprit says that there is no virtue; but by god's grace he ends each chapter by referring to Christian charity. Thus, according to master Esprit neither Cato, nor Aristides, nor Marcus Aurelius, nor Epictetus were men of goodwill, for such men can only be found among the Christians. Among Christians, there is virtue only among the Catholics; among the Catholics, it was necessary to exclude the Jesuits, enemies of the Oratorians; in fact, virtue was to be found only among the enemies of the Jesuits.

This monsieur Esprit begins by saying that prudence is not a virtue, and his reason is that it is often deceived. It is as if one said that Caesar was not a great soldier because he was beaten at Dyrrachium.

Had monsieur Esprit been a philosopher he would not have analysed prudence as a virtue but as a talent, as a useful and agreeable quality: for a scoundrel can be very prudent, and I have known some of that kind. What folly to allege that

> *Nul n'aura de* vertu *que nous et nos amis!*[3]

What is virtue, my friend? It is to do good. Do it, that is

---

1. 'Thus Icarus abused his plumage; he received it for his benefit, he used it to do himself harm.' The author's name is Jean Bertaut.
2. Jacques Esprit's *La Fausseté des vertus humaines* was published in 1693.
3. Adapted from Molière, *Les Femmes savantes*, III. ii: 'None shall be virtuous but we and our friends!'

enough. We shall not worry about your motives. What! according to you there is no difference between the president de Thou[1] and Ravaillac,[2] between Cicero and that Popilius whose life he saved and who cut off his head for money? And you would declare Epictetus and Porphyry to be rogues because they did not follow our dogmas? Such insolence is revolting. I shall say no more about it, for I shall lose my temper.

Fin, causes finales: End, final causes

One would really have to be insane to deny that the purpose of stomachs is to digest, of eyes to see, of ears to hear.

On the other hand a man must have a strange love of final causes to assert that stone has been formed for the building of houses, and that silk-worms are born in China so that we may have satin in Europe.

But, it is said, if god has clearly made one thing by design, he must have made everything by design. It is ridiculous to admit providence in one case, and deny it in another. All that has been made was foreseen, arranged. No arrangement without object, no effect without cause. Therefore everything is equally the result, the product of a final cause. Therefore it is as true to say that noses were made to wear glasses, and fingers to be decorated with diamonds, as it is true to say that ears were formed to hear sounds, and eyes to receive light.

I think that this difficulty can easily be resolved. When the effects are invariably the same, everywhere and always, when these uniform effects are independent of the beings to which they belong, then there is clearly a final cause.

All animals have eyes, and they see; ears, and they hear; a mouth, with which they eat; a stomach, or something similar, with which they digest; an orifice that expels the excrements an instrument of generation; and these gifts of nature operate

1. Voltaire much admired the seventeenth-century statesman and historian Jacques Auguste de Thou.
2. François Ravaillac murdered Henry IV.

in them without the intervention of any skill. Here are clearly established final causes, and to deny so universal a truth is to pervert our ability to think.

But stones do not everywhere and always form buildings; not all noses wear spectacles; not all fingers have rings; not all legs are covered with silk stockings. Therefore a silkworm is not made to cover my legs as your mouth is made to eat and your behind to use the closet. There are thus effects produced by final causes, and a very large number of effects which cannot be so described.

But both are equally in the plan of general providence: certainly nothing happens in spite of it, or even without it. All that belongs to nature is uniform, immutable, the immediate performance of the master. It is he who created the laws by which the moon contributes three quarters and the sun one quarter to the cause of the ebb and flow of the ocean. It is he who gave the sun a movement of rotation, by means of which that heavenly body in five and a half minutes sends rays of light into the eyes of men, crocodiles and cats.

But if after many centuries we took it into our heads to invent shears and spits, to clip with the ones the wool of our sheep and to roast them with the others in order to eat them, what can we infer from this but that god so fashioned us that we would one day necessarily become industrious and carnivorous?

No doubt sheep were not absolutely made to be eaten and roasted, since several nations abstain from this horror. Men were not essentially created to massacre each other, since the Brahmans and the Quakers kill nobody. But the clay from which we are kneaded often produces massacres, as it produces calumnies, futilities, persecutions and impertinences. It is not that the creation of man is precisely the final cause of our furies and our follies: for a final cause is universal and invariable always and everywhere. But the horrors and the absurdities of mankind are no less on that account in the eternal order of things. When we thresh our wheat the flail is the final cause of the separation of the grain. But if this flail crushes a thousand insects in threshing my grain, it is not by my settled will, nor is it by chance: it is because the insects were this time under my flail, and had to be there.

It is a consequence of the nature of things for a man to be ambitious, for him sometimes to enlist other men, for him to win or to be defeated; but it can never be said that man was created by god to be killed in war.

The instruments nature has given us cannot always be final causes in progress towards an inevitable effect. Eyes given to see are not always open. Every sense has its periods of rest. There are even senses that are never used. For instance, a wretched girl, an imbecile shut up in a cloister at fourteen, forever closes the door through which a new generation should have emerged; but the final cause subsists no less on that account: it will operate as soon as it is free.

Foi: Faith

I

One day prince Pico della Mirandola[1] met pope Alexander VI in the house of the countess Emilia while Lucretia, the holy father's daughter, was in labour. It was not known in Rome whether the child's father was the pope or his son the duc de Valentinois or Lucretia's husband, Alphonso of Aragon, who was thought to be impotent. The conversation at once became very vivacious. Cardinal Bembo reports a part of it. 'Little Pico,' said the pope, 'who do you think is the father of my grandson?' 'I think it is your son-in-law.' 'Oh! how can you believe such nonsense?' 'I believe it by faith.' 'But don't you know perfectly well that an impotent man doesn't make children?' 'Faith consists,' replied Pico, 'in believing things because they are impossible; and besides, the honour of your house requires that the son of Lucretia be not regarded as the fruit of incest. You oblige me to believe in even more incomprehensible mysteries. Am I not supposed to be convinced that a serpent spoke, that since then all men have been damned, that Balaam's she-ass also spoke very eloquently,

1. The fifteenth-century count Giovanni Pico della Mirandola was a devout but scientifically minded polymath.

and that the walls of Jericho fell at the sound of trumpets?'
Pico promptly intoned a litany of all the admirable things he
believed. Alexander laughed so hard that he fell back on his
couch. 'I believe all that like you,' he said, 'for I quite realize
that I can be saved only by faith, and I won't be saved by
works.' 'Ah! holy father,' said Pico, 'you need neither works
nor faith. That's all right for the wretched profane like me,
but you, who are vice-god, you can believe and do anything
you please. You have the keys of heaven, and saint Peter will
certainly not shut the door in your face. But as for me, I
assure you that I'd need powerful patronage if I'd gone to
bed with my daughter, and if I'd used steel and poison as
often as your holiness.' Alexander VI could take a joke. 'Let's
be serious,' said he to prince della Mirandola. 'Tell me what
can be the use of saying to god that one is convinced of things
of which in fact one cannot be convinced? What pleasure can
that give god? Between ourselves, to say that one believes
what is impossible to believe is to lie.' Pico della Mirandola
made a great sign of the cross. 'Oh! heavenly father,' he
exclaimed, 'may your holiness forgive me, you are not a
Christian.' 'No, in faith,' said the pope. 'I thought not,'
said Pico della Mirandola.[1]

II

What is faith? Is it to believe what appears evident? No.
It is evident to me that there is a necessary, eternal, supreme,
intelligent being. This is not a matter of faith, but of reason.
I have no merit in thinking that this eternal, infinite being,
who is virtue, goodness itself, wants me to be good and
virtuous. Faith consists in believing, not what appears to be
true, but what appears to our understanding to be false. Only
by faith can Asiatics believe in the voyage of Mohammed to
the seven planets, the incarnations of the god Fo, of Vishnu,
of Xaca, of Brahma, of Sammonocodom, etc. etc. etc. They
subordinate their understanding, they tremble to examine,

1. Voltaire signed this article 'By a descendant of Rabelais'; this is a
pretty plain hint, apart from anything else, that these attributions are
jokes.

they want neither to be impaled nor burned; they say 'I believe'.

There is faith in astonishing things, and faith in contradictory and impossible things.

Vishnu incarnated himself 500 times; this is very astonishing, but after all it is not physically impossible, for if Vishnu
has a soul, he can have put his soul into 500 bodies for fun.
As a matter of fact the Indian's faith is not too lively; he is not
intimately convinced of these metamorphoses; but still he
will say to his bonze: 'I have faith. You allege that Vishnu
passed through 500 incarnations: that's worth 500 rupees a
year to you. So be it. You'll run me down, you'll denounce
me, you'll ruin my trade if I don't have faith. Very well! I have
faith, and what's more, here are ten rupees for you.' The
Indian can swear to this bonze that he believes, without
taking a false oath, for after all it has not been demonstrated
to him that Vishnu did not come to India 500 times.

But if the bonze requires him to believe something self-
contradictory and impossible, that two and two make five, that
the same body can be in a thousand different places,[1] that
being and non-being are exactly the same thing, then the
Indian has lied if he said that he has faith, and perjured himself
if he said that he believes. He therefore says to the bonze:
'Reverend father, I can't assure you that I believe these
absurdities, even if they were worth 10,000 rupees a year to
you instead of 500.'

'My son,' answers the bonze, 'give twenty rupees, and god
will give you the grace to believe everything you don't
believe.'

'How can you expect,' answers the Indian, 'god to perform
in me what he cannot perform in himself? It is impossible
for god to make or to believe the self-contradictory. Otherwise he would no longer be god. To be agreeable to you I'm
giving you ten rupees; here are twenty more; believe in
thirty rupees, be a decent fellow if you can, and stop driving
me crazy.'

1. Voltaire accidentally omitted the essential words 'at the same time'.

Folie: Madness

There is no question of renewing Erasmus's book,[1] which today would be a rather insipid commonplace.

We call madness that disease of the organs of the brain which inevitably prevents a man from thinking and acting like others. Unable to administer his property he is declared incapable; unable to have ideas suitable for society, he is excluded from it; if he is dangerous he is locked up; if he is violent he is tied up. Sometimes he is cured by baths, blood-letting and diet.

What is important to notice is that this man is by no means without ideas. He has them like all other men when he is awake, and often when he is asleep. It may be asked how his spiritual, immortal soul, lodged in his brain, receiving all ideas very clearly and distinctly through the senses, nevertheless never judges sanely. It sees objects as the souls of Aristotle and Plato, Locke and Newton saw them. How then, receiving the perceptions experienced by the wisest, does it make of them an extravagant combination, without being able to help itself?

If this simple and eternal substance has the same instruments of action as have the souls of the wisest brain, it must reason like them. Who could prevent it from so doing? I most readily understand that if my madman saw red and the wise men blue; if, when the wise men hear music, my madman hears the braying of a donkey; if, when they listen to a sermon, my madman thinks that he is at the theatre; if, when they hear yes, he hears no; then his soul must think in a different manner from others. But my madman has the same perceptions as they; there is no apparent reason why his soul, having received all its tools from the senses, cannot use them. It is pure, they say; in itself it is not subject to any infirmity; it is thus provided with all necessary aid; whatever happens in

---

1. *Moriae encomium* (*The Praise of Folly*) was first published in 1511.

its body, nothing can change its essence; nevertheless it is conducted to Colney Hatch in its bodily garment.

This reflection may arouse the suspicion that the faculty of thinking, given by god to man, is subject to derangement like the senses.[1] A lunatic is a sick man whose brain is in bad health, just as the man who has gout is a sick man who has pains in his feet and hands. He thought with his brain as he walked with his feet, without knowing anything about his incomprehensible ability to walk nor of his no less incomprehensible ability to think. People have gout in the brain as in the feet. In short, after a thousand arguments perhaps only faith can convince us that a simple and immaterial substance can be ill.

Learned men or doctors will say to the madman: 'My friend, although you have lost your common sense, your soul is as spiritual, as pure, as immortal as ours. But our souls are well housed, and yours badly, the windows of its house are blocked up, it lacks air, it suffocates.' The madman would reply in his lucid moments: 'My friends, as usual you take for granted the matter at issue. My windows are as open as yours since I see the same objects and hear the same words: it must therefore follow that my soul makes bad use of my senses, or that my soul is itself only a vitiated sense, a depraved quality. In a word, either my soul is mad in itself or I have no soul.'

One of the doctors might reply: 'My dear colleague, god has perhaps created mad souls, as he has created wise souls.' The madman would reply: 'If I believed what you tell me I'd be even madder than I am. For pity's sake, you who know so much about it, tell me why I'm mad.'

If the doctors still have a little sense they would reply: 'We don't know.' They will never understand why a brain has incoherent ideas; they will understand no better why another brain has regulated and consistent ideas. They will believe themselves to be wise, and they will be as mad as the lunatic.

1. All the editions have '*les autres sens*', 'the other senses', but this is clearly a misprint or slip of the pen: Voltaire certainly did not believe that thought was a sense.

Fraude: Fraud

SHOULD PIOUS FRAUDS BE PRACTISED ON THE PEOPLE?

One day the fakir Bambabef met one of the disciples of Confutzee, whom we call Confucius; and this disciple's name was Wang; and Bambabef maintained that the people need to be deceived, and Wang claimed that we should never deceive anybody; and here is an abstract of their debate.

BAMBABEF: We must imitate the supreme being, who does not show us things as they are. He makes the sun appear to us as if it has a diameter of two or three feet, although this star is a million times bigger than the earth. He makes us see the moon and the stars attached to one and the same blue background, whereas they are at different distances. He wants a square tower to look round at a distance. He wants fire to seem hot to us although it is neither hot nor cold. In short, he surrounds us with errors appropriate to our nature.

WANG: What you call an error isn't one. The sun, placed as it is millions of millions of lis[1] beyond our globe, is not the one we see. We really perceive, and we can only perceive, the sun that is painted on our retina at a fixed angle. Our eyes were not given to us to know dimensions and distances: other aids and other operations are needed to know them.

Bambabef appeared to be very surprised by this remark. Wang, who was very patient, explained to him the theory of optics; and Bambabef, who was no fool, yielded to the demonstrations of Confucius's disciple. Then he resumed the debate in these terms:

BAMBABEF: If god does not deceive us by means of our senses, as I believed, you must at least admit that doctors always deceive children for their good: they tell them that they are giving them sugar, and really give them rhubarb. So I, a fakir, may deceive the people, who are as ignorant as children.

WANG: I have two sons, whom I have never deceived.

1. *Note by Voltaire:* 'A li has 124 paces.'

When they were ill I told them: 'Here is a very bitter medicine, you must have the courage to take it. It would harm you if it were sweet.' I have never allowed their governesses and their tutors to make them afraid of spirits, ghosts, goblins, sorcerers: in this way I have made them brave and wise young citizens.

BAMBABEF: The people are not born in such happy circumstances as your family.

WANG: All men resemble each other. They are born with the same dispositions. It is the fakirs who corrupt the nature of men.

BAMBABEF: I admit that we teach them errors, but it is for their own good. We make them believe that if they don't buy our consecrated nails, if they don't expiate their sins by giving us money, they'll become post-horses, dogs or lizards in another life: that frightens them and they become well-behaved.

WANG: Don't you see that you pervert these poor people? Among them are many more rational beings than is realized, who laugh at your nails, your miracles, your superstitions, who know perfectly well that they aren't going to be changed into lizards or post-horses. What happens? They have sense enough to see that you are preaching them an impertinent religion, but they don't have enough to raise themselves to a pure religion free from superstition, like ours. Their passions make them believe that there is no religion because the only one they are taught is ridiculous. You become guilty of all the vices into which they plunge.

BAMBABEF: Not at all, for we teach them only good morals.

WANG: You'd be stoned by the people if you taught them impure morals. Men are so made that they are quite willing to do evil, but they don't want it to be preached to them. A wise morality should simply not be mingled with absurd fables, because your impostures, with which you could dispense, weaken the morality you're obliged to teach.

BAMBABEF: Come! you believe that the people can be taught the truth without sustaining it with fables?

WANG: I believe it firmly. The educated people are of the

same stuff as our tailors, our weavers and our labourers. They adore a god who is creator, remunerator and avenger. They sully their worship neither by absurd systems nor by extravagant ceremonies; and there are far fewer crimes amid the literate than among the people. Why not deign to instruct our workers as we instruct our educated people?

BAMBABEF: You'd be committing a great folly. You might as well wish them to be equally polite, or to be legal experts: it's neither possible nor decent. There must be white bread for the masters and wholemeal bread for servants.

WANG: I admit that all men should not be equally educated, but there are things that all must be. It's necessary for everybody to be just, and the surest way to instill justice in all men is to instil them with religion without superstition.

BAMBABEF: That's a fine project, but it's impracticable. Do you think that it's enough for men to believe in a god who punishes and rewards? You told me that it often happens that the cleverest among the people rise up against my fables. They'll rise up also against your truth. They'll say: 'Who will guarantee that god punishes and rewards? Where's the proof? What's your mission? What miracle have you performed that I should believe you?' They'll laugh at you much more than at me.

WANG: That's where you're wrong. You imagine that men will shake off the yoke of an idea that is honest, convincing, useful to everybody, an idea that is in harmony with human reason, because they reject things that are dishonest, absurd, useless, dangerous, that make good sense shudder. The people are quite disposed to believe their magistrates: when their magistrates offer them only a reasonable belief, they willingly embrace it. We need no prodigies to believe in a just god who reads the heart of man. This idea is too natural to be opposed. It's not necessary to explain exactly how god will punish and reward. It's enough to believe in his justice. I assure you that I've seen entire cities which had practically no other dogmas, and they were those in which I saw the most virtue.

BAMBABEF: Take care, you will find in those cities philosophers who will deny both punishments and rewards.

WANG: You must admit that these philosophers will deny your inventions even more strongly: so that won't be any benefit to you. Should there be any philosophers who don't agree with my principles, they will be good men none the less. They will none the less cultivate virtue, which should be embraced for love, and not out of fear. Moreover I'll maintain that no philosopher will ever be sure that providence doesn't reserve punishments for the wicked and rewards for those who are good. For if they ask me who told me that god punishes, I'll ask them who told them that god doesn't punish. In a word I maintain that the philosophers, far from contradicting me, will help me. Do you want to be a philosopher?

BAMBABEF: Willingly; but don't tell the fakirs.

Genèse: Genesis

I will not anticipate here what I say about Moses in the article about him. I will trace several of the principal features of *Genesis*, one after the other.

In the beginning god created the heaven and the earth.[1]

So has the line been translated, but the translation is not accurate. No man who has a little reading is unaware that the text runs: 'In the beginning, the gods made *or* the god made the heaven and the earth.' Besides, this reading is in conformity with the ancient idea of the Phoenicians, who had conceived the notion that god employed inferior gods to clear up the chaos, the *shotereb*. The Phoenicians had long been a powerful people, who had their own theogony before the Hebrews seized a few villages near their country. It is quite natural to suppose that the Hebrews began to learn the language when they finally had a small settlement near Phoenicia, especially when they were slaves there. Then those who knew how to write copied something of the ancient theology of their masters. So the human spirit advances.

In the times in which Moses is placed, the Phoenician

1. *Genesis* i. 1.

philosophers probably knew enough to regard the earth as a point in comparison with the infinite multitude of globes god has placed in the immensity of space called sky. But the idea, so old and so false, that the heavens were made for the earth, has nearly always prevailed among the ignorant. It is more or less as if one said that god created all the mountains and a grain of sand, and supposed that these mountains were made for this grain of sand. It is scarcely possible that the Phoenicians, excellent navigators, had no good astronomers. But the old prejudices prevailed, and these old prejudices had to be respected by the author of *Genesis*, who wrote to teach the ways of god, and not science.

The earth was tohu-bohu and void; and darkness was upon the face of the deep; and the spirit of God moved upon the face of the waters.[1]

The precise meaning of *tohu-bohu* is chaos, disorder; it is one of those imitative words found in all languages, like *dessus dessous*, *tintamarre*, *trictrac*.[2] The earth was not yet formed as it is now: matter existed, but the divine power had not yet organized it. The spirit of god means the breath, the wind, which agitated the waters. This idea is expressed in the fragments of the Phoenician author Sanchuniathon. The Phoenicians, like all other peoples, believed matter to be eternal. Not a single author in antiquity has ever said that something was drawn from nothingness. Not even in the entire *Bible* is a passage to be found saying that matter was made out of nothing.

Men were always divided on the question of the eternity of the world, but never about the eternity of matter.

Ex nihilo nihil, in nihilum nil posse reverti.[3]

Such was the opinion of all antiquity.

1. *Genesis* i. 2.
2. Upside down, noise, backgammon.
3. Adapted from Persius, *Satires* iii. 83–4: 'Nothing can come from nothing or return to nothing.'

God said, Let there be light: and there was light. And God saw the light, that it was good: and God divided the light from the darkness. And God called the light Day, and the darkness he called Night. And there was evening and there was morning, one day. And God said, Let there be a firmament in the midst of the waters, and let it divide the waters from the waters. And God made the firmament, and divided the waters which were under the firmament from the waters which were above the firmament. And God called the firmament Heaven. And there was evening and there was morning, a second day, . . . And he saw that it was good.[1]

Let us begin by considering whether Huet,[2] bishop of Avranches, and Leclerc[3] are not obviously right, rather than those who maintain that this is a stroke of sublime eloquence.

This eloquence is not affected in any history written by the Jews. Here the style is of the greatest simplicity, as in the rest of the work. If an orator, to convey the power of god, used only this expression: 'He said, let there be light, and there was light,' that would be sublime. Such is the passage in a psalm: '*Dixit, et facta sunt.*'[4] This is a flash which, being unique in this context, and placed there to produce a great image, strikes the spirit and carries it away. But here there is the simplest kind of narrative. The Jewish author speaks of light in no other way than he does of the other objects of creation; he says impartially of each clause: 'and God saw that it was good'. No doubt everything in creation is sublime; but the creation of light is no more sublime than that of the grass of the fields: that which rises above the rest is sublime, but the same style reigns throughout this chapter.

It was also a very ancient opinion that light did not come from the sun. It was seen to be diffused in the air before sunrise and after sunset. It was supposed that the sun served only to impel it more strongly. In fact the author of *Genesis* con-

1. *Genesis* i. 3–8, with a couple of insignificant variants.
2. Pierre Daniel Huet, a converted Roman Catholic, though a profoundly learned man, died in 1721 at the age of 91.
3. Jean Leclerc (1657–1736) was a Genevese Arminian, one of the few theologians who was able to see the *Bible* with open eyes.
4. *Psalms* xxxiii. 9: 'He spoke, and it was done.'

forms to this popular error, and by a singular reversal of the order of things does not have the sun and moon created until four days after the light. It is impossible to conceive how there could have been a morning and an evening before there was a sun. There is a confusion here which it is impossible to clear up. The inspired author conformed to the vague and crude prejudices of the nation. God did not purport to teach philosophy to the Jews. He could elevate their spirit to the truth, but he preferred to descend to their level.

The separation of light and darkness is no more scientific. It seems that night and day were mixed together like different kinds of grains that are separated from one another. It is well known that darkness is nothing but the lack of light, and that there is in effect no light unless our eyes receive that impression. But they were then very far from knowing these truths.

The notion of a firmament is also of the highest antiquity. It was imagined that the heavens were very solid, because the same phenomena were always seen there. The heavens turned above our heads: they were therefore of a very hard material. How compute the amount of water the exhalations of the earth and the seas could furnish to the clouds? There was no Halley to make this calculation, so there were water reservoirs in the sky. These reservoirs could be supported only by a good vault. This vault could be seen through; it was therefore crystal. To enable the higher waters to fall to the earth through this vault it was necessary for it to have doors, locks, cataracts that opened and closed. Such was Jewish astronomy; and since one was writing for the Jews it was necessary to adopt their crude ideas, borrowed from other peoples a little less crude than they.

God made two great lights, one to rule the day, the other the night: he made the stars also.[1]

Still the same ignorance of nature. The Jews did not know that the moon gives only reflected light. The author here speaks of stars as of a bagatelle, although they are so many

1. *Genesis* i. 16, slightly abridged.

suns each of which has worlds turning round it. The holy
spirit regulated itself to the spirit of the times.

And God said, let us make man in our image, and let him have
dominion over the fish, . . .[1]

What did the Jews understand by 'let us make man in our
image'? What all antiquity understands:

Finxit in effigiem moderantum cuncta deorum.[2]

Images are made only out of bodies. No nation has conceived of a god without a body, and it is impossible to picture
him in any other way. We could of course say: 'God is not
anything that we know'; but then[3] one can have no idea
what he is. Like all other peoples the Jews always believed
god to be corporeal. All the first fathers of the church also
believed god to be corporeal, until they embraced Plato's
ideas.

Male and female created he them.[4]

If god or the secondary gods created man male and female
in their likeness, it would seem in that case that the Jews
believed god and the gods to be males and females. Anyway,
it is not known whether the author means that man at first
had both sexes, or whether he considers that god made Adam
and Eve on the same day. The most natural meaning is that
god formed Adam and Eve at the same time; but this meaning
would absolutely contradict the formation of woman from
the rib of man long after the seven days.

And he rested on the seventh day.[5]

The Phoenicians, the Chaldeans, the Indians said that god
had made the world in six periods, which the ancient Zoroaster calls the six *gahambārs*, so famous among the Persians.

1. *Genesis* i. 26, slightly abridged.
2. Ovid, *Metamorphoses*, i. 83: 'Moulded in the form of the masterful
gods.'
3. I have inserted this word, clearly required by the sense, though
lacking in all the editions.
4. *Genesis* i. 27.
5. *Genesis* ii. 2.

It is undeniable that all these peoples had a theology before the Jewish horde inhabited the deserts of Horeb and Sinai, before it could have had writers. It is therefore very highly probable that the story of the six days was imitated from that of the six periods.

From the place of delight[1] flowed a river to water the garden, and from thence it was parted, and became four heads. The name of the first is Pishon: that is it which compasseth the land of Havilah, where there is gold. ... And the name of the second is Gihon: that compasseth Ethiopia. ... The third is the Tigris, and the fourth Euphrates.[2]

According to this version the earthly paradise contained nearly a third of Asia and Africa. The Euphrates and the Tigris have their sources at more than sixty great leagues[3] from one another, in horrible mountains which hardly resemble a garden. The river which borders Ethiopia, and which can only be the Nile or the Niger, rises more than 700 leagues from the sources of the Tigris and the Euphrates; and, if the Pishon is the Phasis, it is rather surprising to place the source of a Scythian river in the same place as that of an African river. It has therefore been necessary to look for another explanation and for other rivers. Each commentator has created his own earthly paradise.

In any case, the garden of Eden was manifestly taken from the garden of Eden at Saana, in Arabia Felix, famous throughout antiquity. The Hebrews, a very recent people, were an Arab horde. They prided themselves on what was finest in the best canton of Arabia. They have always used for their own purposes the ancient traditions of the great nations in whose midst they formed an enclave.

The LORD God took the man, and put him into the garden of delight to dress it.[4]

1. Voltaire here and below uses the word '*volupté*'.
2. *Genesis* ii. 10–14, abridged and slightly modified.
3. Not less than 200 miles.
4. *Genesis* ii. 15.

It is a very good thing to cultivate one's garden, but Adam must have found it difficult to cultivate a garden 700 to 800 leagues long: he was no doubt given some helpers.

Of the tree of the knowledge of good and evil, thou shall not eat of it.[1]

It is difficult to conceive that there has been a tree that taught good and evil, as there are pear trees and apricot trees. Besides, why did not god want man to know good and evil? Would not the contrary have been much more worthy of god, and much more necessary to man? It appears to my poor reason that god should have ordered man to eat a great deal of this fruit; but reason must submit.

For in the day that thou eatest thereof thou shalt surely die.[1]

Nevertheless Adam ate of it, and did not die. Several fathers have regarded all this as an allegory. On the contrary, he is said to have lived another 930 years. In fact, it could be said that the other animals do not know that they are going to die, but that man knows it through his reason. This reason is the tree of knowledge that enables him to foresee his end. Perhaps this explanation is the most reasonable one.

And the LORD God said, It is not good that the man should be alone; I will make him an help meet like him.[2]

One assumes that the lord is going to give him a wife; not at all: the lord brings him all the animals.

And whatsoever Adam called every living creature, that was its true name.[3]

The true name of an animal may be understood to be a name that would designate all the properties of its species,

---

1. *Genesis* ii. 17.
2. *Genesis* ii. 18, but here there is a variant of some importance: for 'like him' ('*semblable à lui*') the English versions have 'for him'.
3. *Genesis* ii. 19, with unimportant modifications; one of these, however, has some bearing on what Voltaire says a little further on: in the English versions Adam is not named, but is still 'the man'.

or at least the principal ones; but this is not the case in any language. In each one there are some imitative words, like *coq* in Celtic, which is rather like the cry of the cock, *loupous*[1] in Latin, etc. But there are very few of these imitative words. Besides, if Adam had thus known all the properties of the animals, either he had already eaten the fruit of knowledge, or god had no need to forbid him this fruit. He already knew more than the Royal Society of London and the Académie des Sciences.

Note that this is the first time Adam is named in *Genesis*. Among the ancient Brahmans, prodigiously older than the Jews, the first man was called Adimo, child of the earth, and his wife Procriti, life. This is said in the *Veidam*,[2] which is perhaps the oldest book in the world. Adam and Eve had the same meanings in the Phoenician language.

While Adam slept, God took one of his ribs, and closed up the flesh instead thereof: and the rib, which the LORD God had taken from Adam, made he a woman, and brought her unto the man.[3]

In the previous chapter the lord had already created the male and the female. So why take a rib from the man to make a female who already existed? Some answer that the author announces in one place what he explains in the other.

Now the serpent was more subtil than any beast of the field, . . .; he said unto the woman, etc.[4]

There is no mention of the devil in this entire passage. Everything in it is normal.[5] The serpent was regarded by all the oriental nations not only as the most cunning of animals, but also as immortal. The Chaldeans had a fable about a quarrel between god and the serpent. This fable has been pre-

1. Voltaire spells *lupus*, wolf, thus to indicate the correct pronunciation.

2. That is, the Vedas.

3. *Genesis* ii. 21–2, abridged; in the English versions Adam is still merely 'the man'.

4. *Genesis* iii. 1.

5. Voltaire here and below uses the word 'physique', a word with many overtones.

served by Pherecydes. Origen quotes it in his book VI against Celsus.[1] A serpent was carried in the feasts of Bacchus. The Egyptians attached a sort of divinity to the serpent, according to Eusebius in his *Evangelical Preparation*, book I, chapter X. In Arabia, in India, even in China, the serpent was regarded as the symbol of life. This is why the emperor of China, before Moses, always bore the image of a serpent on his breast.

Eve was not surprised that the serpent spoke to her. Animals spoke in all the ancient tales, and this is why nobody was surprised when Pilpay and Lokman[2] made the animals speak.

The whole of this adventure is so normal and so devoid of all allegory that it explains why the serpent has since then crawled on his belly, why we always try to crush it, and why it always tries to bite us; precisely as the ancient metamorphoses explain why the crow, who was once white, is today black, why the owl leaves its hole only at night, why the wolf enjoys carnage, etc.

I will greatly multiply thy sorrow and thy conceptions, in sorrow thou shalt bring forth children; and thy desire shall be to thy husband, and he shall rule over thee.[3]

One wonders why the multiplication of pregnancies was a punishment. On the contrary, it was a very great blessing, above all among the Jews. The pains of childbirth are considerable only for delicate women. Those who are used to work are very early delivered, especially in warm climates. Animals sometimes differ a great deal in giving birth, some even die of it. And as for the superiority of man over woman, this is perfectly natural, it is the effect of the strength of body and even of mind. Men in general have organs more capable of sustained attention than those of women, and are better fitted for the labour of head and hand. But when a woman has a stronger arm and mind than her husband, she rules him

1. *Contra Celsum*, VI. xxxiii.
2. The fables of Bidpai derive from the Hindu *Panchatantra*, but those of Luqman are in the Arabian tradition.
3. *Genesis* iii. 16.

in all things: it is then the husband who is subject to the wife. This is true, but it is very possible that there was no subjection and no pain before the first sin.

The lord made them coats of skins.[1]

This passage is proof enough that the Jews believed god to be corporeal, since they have him practise the tailor's craft. A rabbi named Eliezer has written that god covered Adam and Eve with the skin of the very serpent that had tempted them; and Origen alleges that this skin tunic was a new flesh, a new body that god made for man.

And the LORD God said, Behold, Adam is become as one of us.[2]

It would seem that the Jews at first acknowledged several gods. It is more difficult to know what they understood by this word god, *Elohim*. Some commentators have alleged that this term 'one of us' signifies the trinity; but there is certainly no question of the trinity in the *Bible*. The trinity is not a composite of several gods, it is the same triple god; and the Jews never heard anything about a god in three persons. By these words 'like us' it is most probable that the Jews understood the angels, *Elohim*, and that therefore this book was not written until they adopted the belief in these inferior gods.

The LORD God sent him forth from the garden of delight, to till the ground.[3]

But the lord had put him into the garden of delight 'to cultivate that garden'. If Adam the gardener became a labourer, it must be admitted that his condition did not become much worse: a good labourer is certainly as good as a good gardener.

The whole of this story, according to over-bold commentators, is connected with the notion all men had, and still have, that primitive ages were better than recent ones. We always complain of the present and vaunt the past. Men overloaded with work have supposed idleness to be happiness, not reflecting that the worst of conditions is that of a man who

1. *Genesis* iii. 21, condensed.   2. *Genesis* iii. 22.   3. *Genesis* iii. 23.

has nothing to do. Men were seen to be often unhappy, and they built up the notion of a time when everybody had been happy. It is more or less as if one said: 'Once upon time no tree died, no animal was ill or weak or devoured by another.' Hence the notion of a golden age, the egg pierced by Ahriman, the serpent that robbed the ass of the recipe for a happy and immortal life which man had put into its pack-saddle. Hence Typhon's fight with Osiris, Ophion's with the gods; and that famous Pandora's box; and all those old stories, some of which are amusing and none of which is instructive.

And he placed in the garden of delight the Cherubim, and the flame of a sword which he turned every way, to keep the way of the tree of life.[1]

The word *kerub* means 'ox'. An ox armed with a flaming sword makes a strange figure at a door. But later, although they were forbidden to make any images, they manifestly took these oxen and these hawks from the Egyptians, whom they imitated in so many ways. The Egyptians first venerated the ox as the symbol of agriculture, and the hawk as that of the winds; but they never made an ox into a doorman.

The gods, Elohim, saw the daughters of men that they were fair; and they took the wives of all that they chose.[2]

This notion was also common to all peoples. There is no nation, except China, in which some god has not come down to engender children on human girls. These corporeal gods often descended to earth to visit their domains, they saw our girls, and took the prettiest ones for themselves. The children born from the intercourse of these gods and the mortal women had to be superior to other men. Nor does *Genesis* fail to say that these gods who lay with our girls produced giants. It again conformed to popular belief.

I will bring a flood of waters upon the earth.[3]

1. *Genesis* iii. 24.
2. *Genesis* vi. 2; for 'the gods, Elohim' the Revised version has 'the sons of God'.
3. *Genesis* vi. 17, with a minor variation. *Note by Voltaire:* See the article 'Inondation'.

I will only remark here that saint Augustine, in his *City of God*, No. 8, says: *Maximum illud diluvium graeca nec Latina novit historia*. Neither Greek nor Latin history know of this great flood. In fact only those of Deucalion and Oxyges, in Greece, were ever known. They were regarded as universal in the fables collected by Ovid, but were totally unknown in east Asia. Thus saint Augustine is not mistaken when he says that history does not mention it.

God said to Noah:

I establish my covenant with you and with your seed after you; and with every living creature.[1]

God made a covenant with the animals! what a covenant! exclaim the unbelievers. But if he enters into an alliance with man, why not with the animals? They have feelings, and there is something as divine in feelings as in the most metaphysical thoughts. Anyway, animals feel better than most men think. It is apparently by virtue of this pact that Francis of Assisi, founder of the seraphic order, said to the grasshoppers and the hares: 'Sing, my sister grasshopper; browse, my brother leveret.' But what were the terms of the treaty? That all the animals would devour one another; that they would feed on our flesh, and we on theirs; that, after having eaten them, we would furiously exterminate each other, and that it would only remain for us to eat our kindred butchered by our own hands. Had there been such a pact it would have been made with the devil.

The whole passage probably means no more than that god is equally the absolute master of everything that breathes. This pact can only be an order, and the word covenant is used only by extension. We must not be startled by words, but worship the spirit, and hark back to the times in which was written this book which scandalizes the weak and edifies the strong.

I will set my bow in the cloud, and it shall be for a token of a covenant, . . .[2]

1. *Genesis* ix. 9–10.
2. *Genesis* ix. 13; the Vulgate has 'ponam' and the Revised version 'I do set'.

Observe that the author does not say 'I have set my bow in the clouds', he says 'I will set'. This clearly implies that according to general opinion the rainbow had not always existed. It is a phenomenon caused by the rain, and it is represented here as a supernatural sign that the earth will not again be flooded. It is strange to choose the sign of rain to assure us that we shall not be drowned. But one could answer that one is reassured by the rainbow when in danger of inundation.

And the two angels came to Sodom at even.[1]

The whole story of the two angels whom the Sodomites wanted to rape is perhaps the most extraordinary invented by antiquity. But it must be remembered that nearly all Asia believed in demons who were incubi and succubi; and moreover that these two angels were creatures more perfect than men, and must have been more beautiful and have more easily than ordinary men inflamed desire in a corrupt people.

As for Lot, who offered his two daughters to the Sodomites in place of the two angels, and Lot's wife changed into a pillar of salt, and all the rest of the story, what can be said about it? The ancient Arabian fable of Cinyra and Myrrha has some resemblance to the incest of Lot and his daughters; and the adventure of Philemon and Baucis is not unlike that of the two angels, who appeared to Lot and his wife. As for the statue of salt, I do not know what it resembles: is it the story of Orpheus and Eurydice?

There have been a few scholars who considered that all these incredible things, which shock the weak, should be removed from the canonical books. But it is said that these scholars are corrupt in heart, men fit to burn, and that it is impossible to be an upright man if one does not believe that the Sodomites wanted to rape two angels. Thus reason the sort of monsters who want to dominate men's minds.

Some famous fathers of the church had the prudence to convert all these stories into allegories, following the example of the Jews, and above all of Philo. Some sages, still more

1. *Genesis* xix. 1.

prudent, tried to prevent the translation of these books into the vernacular, for fear that men be enabled to judge what they were told to revere.

It must certainly be concluded from all this that those who perfectly understand this book should tolerate those who do not understand it; for if the latter understand nothing of it, that is not their fault; but those who understand nothing of it should also tolerate those who understand it all.

Gloire: Glory

Ben-al-Betif, that worthy chief of the dervishes, said to them one day: 'Brothers, it's a very good thing that you often use this sacred formula of our Koran: "In the name of the most merciful god", for god is merciful, and you learn to be so by often repeating the words which advocate a virtue without which there would be few men left on earth. But brothers take care not to imitate those foolhardy men who boast at every opportunity that they are working for the glory of god. If a young idiot sustains a thesis on the categories, a thesis presided over by a gowned ignoramus, he is sure to write at the head of his thesis, in large characters: *Ek Allah abron doxa: ad majorem dei gloriam*.[1] When a good Muslim has his drawing-room whitewashed he inscribes this nonsense on his door. A *saka* carries water for the greater glory of god. What would you say of an impious little valet who, emptying our sultan's close-stool, exclaimed: "To the greater glory of our invincible monarch"? Yet it is certainly further from the sultan to god than from the sultan to the little valet.

'Wretched earthworms called *men*, what do you have in common with the glory of the infinite being? Can he love glory? can he receive any from you? can he enjoy it? Two-legged, featherless animals, how long will you make god in your image? What! because you are vain, because you love glory, you want god also to love it! If there were several gods, each of them might want to be approved by the others. That would be the glory of a god. If one can compare infinite

1. This is the motto of the Jesuits: 'for the greater glory of god'.

grandeur with the lowest of conditions this god would be like king Alexander or Scanderbeg, who competed only with kings. But you, wretches, what glory can you give to god? Stop profaning his sacred name. An emperor called Octavius Augustus forbade the Roman schools to praise him, lest his name be abased. But you can neither abase nor honour the supreme being. Humble yourselves, adore, and be quiet.'

Thus spoke Ben-al-Betif; and the dervishes cried out: 'Glory to god! Ben-al-Betif has spoken well?'

Grâce: Grace

Sacred lawmakers of modern Rome, illustrious and infallible theologians, nobody has greater respect than I for your divine decisions. But you will admit that if Paulus Aemilius, Scipio, Cato, Cicero, Caesar, Titus, Trajan, Marcus Aurelius returned to the Rome which they formerly made rather famous, they would be a little surprised by your decisions on grace. What would they say if they heard of saint Thomas's grace of health, and medicinal grace according to Cajetan[1]; of exterior and interior grace, gratuitous, sanctifying, actual, habitual, cooperative grace; of efficacious grace, which is sometimes ineffective; of sufficient grace, which is sometimes insufficient; of versatile and congruent grace? Honestly, would they understand better than you and I?

What need would these poor men have of your sublime teaching? I seem to hear them say:

Reverend fathers, you are too clever by half. We foolishly thought that the eternal being never acts by particular laws like vile humans, but by his general laws, eternal like him. None of us ever imagined that god is like a senseless master who gives a tip to one slave and refuses food to another, who orders a one-armed man to knead flour, a mute to read to him, a legless cripple to be his messenger.

All that is god's is grace. He did the globe we inhabit the grace of creating it, the trees the grace of making them grow,

1. Giacomo de Vio, in religion cardinal Tommaso Cajetan, who wrote a commentary on Thomas Aquinas; hence the association here.

the animals that of feeding them. But will it be said, when a wolf finds in his path a lamb for his supper, and another wolf dies of hunger, that god gave an individual grace to the first wolf? Did he busy himself, by a prevenient grace, with making one oak grow in preference to another that lacked sap? If all beings in all nature are subject to general laws, how could a single species of animals not be subject to them?

Why should the absolute master of all have spent more time in directing the interior of one man than in guiding all the rest of nature? What eccentricity would lead him to change something in the heart of a Kurlander or of a Biscayan while he changes nothing in the laws he has imposed on all the heavenly bodies?

How pathetic to assume that he constantly makes, unmakes, remakes our feelings! And what audacity to believe ourselves singled out from all beings! And moreover all these changes have been invented only for those who go to confession. On Monday a Savoyard, a Bergamasque will have the grace to have a mass said for twelve *sous*. On Tuesday he will go to the tavern and lack grace. On Wednesday he will have a co-operative grace which will guide him to confession, but he will lack the efficacious grace of perfect contrition. On Thursday it will be a sufficient grace which will be insufficient, as has already been said. God will be operating continuously in the head of this Bergamasque, now forcibly, now weakly, and he will care nothing for the rest of the world! He will not deign to meddle with the interiors of Indians and Chinese! If you have a grain of reason left, reverend fathers, don't you find this system prodigiously ridiculous?

Wretches, look at this oak that raises its head to the clouds, and this reed that creeps at its feet. You will not pretend that efficacious grace was given to this oak and not to this reed. Raise your eyes to heaven, see the eternal demiurge creating millions of worlds which all gravitate one to the other by general and eternal laws. See the same light being reflected from the sun to Saturn, and from Saturn to us, and in this harmony of so many heavenly bodies hastening in their rapid courses, in the general obedience of all nature, dare to believe, if you can, that god troubles to give a versatile grace to sister Theresa and a concomitant grace to sister Agnes.

Atom, whom a foolish atom has told that the eternal has particular laws for some atoms in your neighbourhood; that he gives his grace to this one and refuses it to that; that one who had no grace yesterday will have it tomorrow; don't repeat this nonsense. God has made the universe and isn't going to create new winds to move some blades of straw in a corner of this universe. Theologians are like the combatants in Homer, who believed that the gods sometimes took arms against them, sometimes for them. If Homer were not esteemed as a poet, he would be regarded as a blasphemer.

This is Marcus Aurelius speaking, not I; for god, who inspires you, has given me the grace to believe everything you say, everything you have said and everything you will say.

Guerre: War

Famine, plague and war are the three most celebrated ingredients of this world of ours. In the category of famine can be included all the bad food to which scarcity obliges us to resort, abridging our life in the hope of sustaining it. In plague are comprised all the contagious diseases, which number two or three thousand. These two gifts come to us from providence. But war, which unites all these benefits, comes to us from the imaginations of three or four hundred persons scattered over the surface of this globe under the names of princes or ministers; and it is perhaps for this reason that in many a dedication they are called the living images of divinity.

The most determined flatterer will readily agree that war always drags plague and famine in its train if he has glimpsed the hospitals of the armies in Germany and has been in certain villages in which some great warlike exploit has been performed.

It is certainly a very fine art that desolates the countryside, destroys dwellings, and brings death to 40,000 out of 100,000 men in an average year.[1] This invention was at first cultivated by nations assembled for their common good. For instance, the Greek diet informed the diet of the Phrygians and neighbouring peoples that it intended to set out in a thousand fishing boats to exterminate them if it could.

The assembled Roman people judged it to be in its interest to go before the harvest to fight the Veians or the Volscians. And a few years later all the Romans, furious against the Carthaginians, long fought on land and sea. That is not the way things happen nowadays.

A genealogist proves to a prince that he is the direct descendant of a count whose relatives had made a family pact three or four hundred years ago with a house whose very name has left no memory. This house had remote pretensions to a province whose last owner had just died of apoplexy. The prince and his council conclude without difficulty that the province belongs to him by divine right. This province, which is some hundreds of leagues distant, protests in vain that it does not know him, that it has no wish to be governed by him, that one must at least have a people's consent before legislating for it. These discourses do not even reach the ears of the prince whose rights are incontestable. He immediately finds a great number of men who have nothing to do nor to lose. He dresses them in heavy blue cloth at 110 *sous* the ell, puts a heavy white cord round their hats, makes them turn right and left, and marches to glory.

The other princes who hear of this escapade take part in it, each according to his means, and occupy a small piece of land with more mercenary murderers than Genghis Khan, Tamerlane, Bajazet ever dragged in their train.

Fairly distant peoples hear that there is going to be fighting, and that five or six *sous* a day can be earned if they care to take part. They at once divide themselves into two troops like harvesters, and go off to sell their services to anyone who

1. This form of words appears in all the editions, but the figures are clearly impossible: a mortality rate of forty per cent in war would long since have extinguished the human race; Voltaire no doubt wrote that 40,000–100,000 men were killed every year in war.

wants to employ them. These multitudes go for one another, not only without having any interest in the proceedings, but even without knowing what they are about.

Five or six belligerent powers can be seen at once, now three against three, now two against four, now one against five, all equally hating each other, uniting and fighting with each other turn and turn about, all agreed on a single point, to do as much harm as possible.

What is marvellous about this infernal undertaking is that each chief of murderers has his banners blessed and solemnly invokes god before he sets off to exterminate his neighbours. If a chief has had the good fortune to have only two or three thousand men butchered, he does not thank god for it. But when about 10,000 have been exterminated by fire and sword, and, by a crowning grace, some town has been destroyed from top to bottom, then they sing a rather long four-part song, composed in a language unknown to all those who fought, besides being crammed with barbarisms. The same song serves for marriages and births, as well as murders: which is unpardonable, especially in the nation most famous for new songs.

Natural religion has a thousand times prevented citizens from committing crimes. A well-bred soul has no wish to commit them. A tender soul is afraid of them, remembering a just and vengeful god. But artificial religion encourages all the cruelties done in association, conspiracies, seditions, robbery, ambushes, attacks on towns, pillages, murders. Each one marches gaily off to crime under the banner of his saint.

A certain number of orators are everywhere paid to celebrate these blood-stained days. Some wear long black jackets, doubled by abridged cloaks; others have shirts over gowns; some wear two slings of motley cloth over their shirts. All talk for a long time. When it is about a battle in Veteravia, they refer to what was done of old in Palestine.

The rest of the year these people declaim against the vices. They prove by three points and by antitheses that ladies who lightly spread a little rouge on their fresh cheeks will be the eternal objects of the eternal vengeance of the eternal; that *Polyeucte* and *Athalie* are the works of the demon; that a man who has 200 crowns' worth of sea-food served at his table in lent infallibly brings about his salvation, and that a poor man who eats two and half *sous*' worth of mutton goes forever to all the devils.

Out of five or six thousand declamations of this kind there are three or four at most, composed by a Gaul called Massillon, that an upright man can read without disgust. But among all these discourses there are hardly two[1] in which the orator dares to protest against this scourge and this crime of war, which comprises all scourges and all crimes. The wretched orators speak ceaselessly against love, which is mankind's only consolation and the only way of perpetuating it. They say nothing about the abominable efforts we make to destroy it.

O Bourdaloue! you have delivered a very bad sermon against impurity, but none on these variegated murders, these rapines, these pillages, this universal fury that desolates the world. The united vices of all the ages and of all places will never equal the evils produced by a single campaign.

Wretched physicians of souls, you declaim for five quarters of an hour about some pinprick, and you say nothing about the disease that tears us into a thousand pieces! Philosophical moralists, burn all your books. So long as the whim of a few men causes thousands of our brothers to be honourably butchered, the portion of mankind devoted to heroism will be the most frightful thing in the whole of nature.

What becomes of and what do I care about humanity, benevolence, modesty, temperance, tenderness, wisdom, piety, when half a pound of lead shot from 600 paces shatters my body, and I die at the age of twenty in agony beyond words, in the midst of five or six thousand dying men, while my eyes, opening for the last time, see the town in which I was born destroyed by sword and fire, and the last

1. Here we have a good example of Voltaire's scrupulous justice: he originally wrote 'not a single one'.

sounds I hear are the cries of women and children expiring under the ruins, all for the alleged benefit of a man I do not know?

What is worst is that war is an inevitable scourge. If we examine the matter we find that all men have worshipped the god Mars. Sabaoth, among the Jews, means the god of arms; but Minerva, in Homer, calls Mars a ferocious, senseless, infernal god.

Histoire des rois juifs et paralipomènes: History of Jewish kings and chronicles

All peoples recorded their history as soon as they could write. The Jews also have written theirs. Before they had kings they lived under a theocracy: they were thought to be governed by god himself.

When the Jews wanted to have a king like the neighbouring peoples, the prophet Samuel told them in god's name that they were rejecting god himself.[1] Thus theocracy finished among the Jews when monarchy began. It could therefore be said without blasphemy that the history of the Jewish kings was recorded like that of the other peoples, and that god did not himself take the trouble to dictate the history of a people he no longer governed.

I advance this view only with the most extreme caution. What may confirm it is the fact that *Chronicles* very often contradicts the book of *Kings* in its facts, just as our profane historians sometimes contradict each other. Besides, if god always wrote the history of the Jews we must take it that he still writes it, for the Jews are still his cherished people. They are to be converted one day, and it would appear that they will then be as much entitled to regard as sacred the history of their dispersal as they are entitled to say that god wrote the history of their kings.

We can also reflect that, god having then been their historian, we should have the most profound respect for all Jews. There is no Jewish old-clothes-man who is not in-

1. *1 Samuel* viii. 7.

finitely superior to Caesar and Alexander. Is it possible not to prostrate ourselves before an old-clothes-man who proves to you that his history was written by the divinity himself, while the Greek and Roman histories were transmitted to us by the merely profane?

Though the style of the history of *Kings* and *Chronicles* is divine, it is nevertheless possible that the actions reported in these histories are not divine. David murders Uriah; Ishbosheth and Mephibosheth are murdered; Absalom murders Ammon; Joab murders Absalom; Solomon murders his brother Adonijah; Bassha murders Madab; Zimri murders Elah; Omri murders Zimri; Ahab murders Naboth; Jehu murders Ahab and Joram; the inhabitants of Jerusalem murder Amaziah, son of Joash; Shallum, son of Jabesh, murders Zachariah, son of Jeroboam; Manahem murders Shallum, son of Jabesh; Pekah, son of Remaliah, assassinates Pekahiah, son of Menahem; Hoshea, son of Elah, murders Pokah, son of Remaliah. I pass over in silence many other trifling assassinations. It must be admitted that if the holy spirit wrote this history he did not choose a very edifying subject.

Idée: Idea

What is an idea?

It's an image that paints itself in my brain.

So all your ideas are images?

Assuredly; for the most abstract ideas are the consequences of all the objects I've perceived. In general I utter the word 'being' only because I've known particular beings. I use the word 'infinite' only because I've seen limits, and because I extend these limits in my understanding as far as I can. I've ideas only because I've images in my head.

And by whom is this picture painted?

It's not I, for I'm not a good enough draughtsman. He who made me makes my ideas.

So you agree with Malebranche, who said that we see everything in god?

I'm quite sure at least that if we don't see things in god himself we see them in his all-powerful action.

And how does this action operate?

I've told you a hundred times in our conversation that I haven't the slightest idea, and that god hasn't told his secret to anyone. I don't know what makes my heart beat, and my blood run in my veins; I don't know the cause of all my movements; and you want me to tell you how I feel and how I think! That's not fair.

But at least you know whether your ability to have ideas is related to extension?

Not in the least. It's certainly true that Tatian, in his *Discourse to the Greeks*, says that the soul is manifestly composed of a body. In his chapter LXII of the second book Irenaeus says that the lord taught that our souls retain the forms of our bodies to preserve their memories. Tertullian asserts in his second book *On the Soul* that it is a body. Arnobius, Lactantius, Hilary, Gregory of Nyssa, Ambrose do not differ from this view. It's alleged that other fathers of the church assert that the soul is without any extension, and that in this they share Plato's opinion: which is very doubtful. As for me, I dare have no opinion. I perceive nothing but incomprehensibility in either system, and after having thought about it all my life I'm no further advanced than on the first day.

Then it wasn't worth thinking about.

That's true. The man who enjoys knows more about it than does the one who reflects about thinking, or at least he knows better, he is happier. But what do you expect? I couldn't determine to accept or to reject in my brain all the ideas that entered it to fight each other and that took my medullary cells for their battlefield. When they have thoroughly battled it out I've gathered nothing from their remains but uncertainty.

It's very sad to have so many ideas and not to know precisely the nature of ideas.

I admit it; but it's much sadder and much more foolish to think we know what we don't know.

Idole, idolâtre, idolâtrie: Idol, idolator, idolatry

Idol comes from the Greek εἶδος, form; εἴδωλον, representation of a form; λατρεύειν, to serve, revere, adore. This word adore is Latin, and has many different meanings: it signifies putting a hand to one's mouth when speaking with respect, bowing, kneeling, saluting, and finally, most generally, offering a supreme worship. Nothing but ambiguities.

It is useful to note here that the *Dictionnaire de Trévoux*[1] begins its article by saying that all pagans were idolators, and that the Indians are still idolatrous peoples. First of all, no one was called a pagan before Theodosius the younger. This name was then given to the inhabitants of the Italian cities, *pagorum incolae, pagani*,[2] who kept to their ancient religion. In the second place, Hindustan is Mohammedan, and the Mohammedans are the implacable enemies of images and idolatry. In the third place, many Indian peoples belong to the ancient religion of the Parsees and should not be called idolators, any more than certain castes which have no idols.

INQUIRY WHETHER THERE HAS EVER BEEN AN IDOLATROUS GOVERNMENT

It would appear that no people on earth has taken this name of idolator. The word is an insult, a term of abuse, like that of *gavaches*, which the Spaniards once applied to the French, and that of *maranes*[3], which the French applied to the Spaniards. Had one asked the Roman senate, the Greek areopagus, the court of the kings of Persia: 'Are you idolators?' they would hardly have understood the question. None would have answered: 'We worship images, idols.' This word 'idolator', 'idolatry', is not found in Homer nor in Hesiod nor in Herodotus nor in any author of the religion of the gentiles. There

---

1. The *Dictionnaire universel* published by the Jesuits at Trévoux.
2. The inhabitants of a village, rustics.
3. The former word means 'cowards', the latter is the French form of *Marranos*, Moors.

has never been any edict, any law that ordered men to worship idols, to serve them as gods, to regard them as gods.

When the Roman and Carthaginian leaders made a treaty, they invoked all their gods. 'It is in their presence,' they said, 'that we swear peace.' Now the statues of all these gods, whose number was very great, were not in the generals' tents. They considered the gods to be present at men's actions as witnesses and judges. And it was certainly not the simulacrum that constituted the divinity.

What view did they then take of the statues of their false divinities in the temples? The same view, if I may say so, that we take of the images of the objects of our veneration. The error was not to worship a piece of wood or marble, but to worship a false divinity represented by this wood or marble. The difference between them and us is not that they had images and we have not: the difference is that their images showed fantastic beings in a religion. The Greeks had the statue of Hercules, and we have that of saint Christopher[1]; they had Aesculapius and his goat, and we have saint Roch and his dog: they had Jupiter armed with thunder, and we saint Anthony of Padua and saint James of Compostella.

When the consul Pliny, in the opening of his panegyric of Trajan, addresses his prayers *to the immortal gods*, he does not address himself to images. These images were not immortal.

Neither the last days of paganism nor the most ancient offer a single fact enabling us to conclude that an idol was worshipped. Homer speaks only of the gods who inhabit high Olympus. The *palladium*, although fallen from heaven, was only a sacred pledge of Pallas's protection: it was she who was venerated in the *palladium*.

But the Romans and the Greeks kneeled down before statues, gave them crowns, incense, flowers, paraded them in triumph in public places. We have sanctified these customs, and we are no idolators.

---

1. Whether by design or by accident Voltaire's antithesis is somewhat damaged by the fact that Christopher was not a historical personage; this has recently been recognized by his expulsion from the company of saints.

In times of drought, women, having fasted, carried the statues of the gods. They walked barefoot, their hair dishevelled, and the rain at once came down in pailfuls, as Petronius says, *et statim urceatim pluebat.*[1] Have we not consecrated this practice, illegal among the gentiles and undoubtedly legitimate with us? In how many villages are the reliquaries of the saints not carried barefoot to obtain the blessings of heaven through their intercession? If a Turk or an educated Chinese were to witness these ceremonies, he could, not knowing better, at first accuse us of putting our trust in the images we thus parade in procession: but a word would undeceive him.

One is surprised by the prodigious number of declamations poured out at all periods against the idolatry of the Romans and the Greeks; and then one is even more surprised when it is realized that they were not idolators.

Some temples were more privileged than others. The great Diana of Ephesus had a higher reputation than a village Diana. More miracles were performed in the temple of Aesculapius at Epidaurus than in some other of his temples. The statue of the Olympian Jupiter attracted more offerings than that of the Paphlagonian Jupiter. But, since here we must always contrast the custom of a true religion with those of a false religion, have we not had for several centuries more devotion at certain altars than at others? Do we not take more offerings to Notre Dame of Loretto than to Notre Dame of the snows? It is for us to determine whether this pretext should be seized on to accuse us of idolatry.

Only a single Diana, a single Apollo, a single Aesculapius had been conceived, not as many Apollos, Dianas and Aesculapiuses as they had temples and statues. It is thus proved, so far as a point of history can be, that the ancients did not believe that a statue was a divinity, that worship could be transferred to this statue, this idol. It follows that the ancients were not idolators.

A coarse and superstitious rabble which did not reason, which did not know how to doubt, to deny, to believe, which ran to the temples because it was idle and because there the

1. Petronius, *Satyricon* xliv.

humble were the equals of the great, which brought its
offerings out of habit, which talked continually of miracles
without having ever investigated one, and which hardly rose
above the victims it brought, this rabble, I repeat, might well
have been struck by religious dread at the sight of the great
Diana and of Jupiter the thunderer, and have unknowingly
worshipped the statue itself. This is what has sometimes
happened to our rough peasants in our temples; and they are
then instructed that it is the intercession of the blessed, the
immortals received into heaven, they must seek, and not that
of wooden and stone images.[1]

The Greeks and Romans increased the number of their
gods by apotheoses. The Greeks deified conquerors like
Bacchus, Hercules, Perseus. Rome erected altars to its
emperors. Our apotheoses are of a different kind: we have
saints instead of their demi-gods, their secondary gods, but we
respect neither rank nor conquests. We have raised temples
to men who were simply virtuous, who for the most part
would be unknown on earth were they not placed in heaven.
The apotheoses of the ancients were procured by flattery, ours
by respect for virtue.

In his philosophical works Cicero offers not the slightest
suspicion that the statues of the gods could be misunderstood
and confounded with the gods themselves. His interlocutors
fulminated against the established religion, but not one of
them took it into his head to accuse the Romans of regarding
marble and brass as divinities. Lucretius does not reproach
anyone with this foolishness, he also reproaches the superstitious with everything. Therefore, once again, this opinion
did not exist, there was no notion of it, there were no idolators.

Horace makes a statue of Priapus say: 'I was once the trunk
of a fig tree. A carpenter, doubtful whether to make me into a
god or a bench, finally decided to make me a god, etc.'[2] What
should we conclude from this pleasantry? Priapus was one of

1. Voltaire originally went on 'and that they should worship only god',
but afterwards deleted these words.
2. *Satires* I. i. 1–3.

those little subordinate divinities, given up to the mockers; and this pleasantry is itself the strongest evidence that the image of Priapus, which was erected in the kitchen garden to frighten the birds, was not highly revered.

Adopting the attitude of a commentator, Dacier did not fail to point out that Baruch had predicted this incident when he said: 'They will be only what the workmen wishes'; but he might also have remarked that as much can be said of all statues. Is it to be supposed that Baruch had a vision about the satires of Horace?[1]

A wash-basin can be just as easily drawn from a block of marble as an image of Alexander or of Jupiter or of something else more respectable. The material from which the cherubim of the holy of holies were formed could have served equally well for the basest functions. Is a throne or an altar less revered because the workman could have made it into a kitchen table?

Instead of concluding that the Romans worshipped the statue of Priapus, and that Baruch had predicted it, Dacier should therefore have concluded that the Romans made fun of it. Consult all the authors who refer to the statues of their gods. You will not find one who talks of idolatry. They say expressly the contrary. In Martial you find:

> *Qui finxit sacros auro vel marmore vultus,*
> *Non facit ille deos; . . .*[2]

> *L'artisan ne fait point les dieux.*
>   *C'est celui qui les prie.*

In Ovid:

> *Colitur pro Jove forma Jovis.*[3]

> *Dans l'image de dieu c'est dieu seul qu'on adore.*

1. Voltaire might have pointed out that Dacier, instead of quoting a non-canonical book, could have pointed to the much more precise parallel in *Isaiah* xliv. 10–17.

2. *Epigrams* VIII. xxiv. 5–6: 'He does not make gods who forms sacred images in gold or marble'; here and below I have translated the Latin, not Voltaire's French.

3. *Ex ponto*, II. viii. 62: 'In the image of Jupiter, Jupiter is worshipped.'

In Statius:

> *Nulla autem effigies, nulli commissa metallo*
> *Forma dei; mentes habitare ac numina gaudet.*[1]

> *Les dieux ne sont jamais dans une arche enfermés:*
> *Ils habitent nos coeurs.*

In Lucan:

> *Estne dei sedes, nisi terra et pontus et aer?*[2]

> *L'univers est de dieu la demeure et l'empire.*

One could make a volume of all the passages which testify that images were merely images.

Only those cases in which statues issued oracles might have given rise to the idea that these statues had something divine in them. But the prevailing opinion certainly was that the gods had chosen certain altars, certain simulacra, in which to dwell occasionally in order to give audience to humans, and to answer them.

In Homer and the choruses of the Greek tragedies we find only prayers to Apollo, who delivers his oracles on the mountains, in this temple, in that city. In all antiquity there is not the slightest trace of a prayer addressed to a statue.

Those who practised magic, who believed it to be a science or pretended to believe it, claimed to know how to make the gods descend into their statues – not the great gods, but the secondary ones, the genii. This is what Mercury Trismegistus called *making gods*, and what saint Augustine refuted in his *City of God*. But this in itself shows clearly that the simulacra had nothing divine in them, since it was necessary for a magician to animate them. And it seems to me that a magician very seldom had the skill to give a statue a soul, to make it speak.

In a word, the images of the gods were not gods. Jupiter, and not his image, hurled the thunder; it was not the statue of

---

1. *Thebaid* xii. 503–4; for '*numina*' read '*pectora*': 'God's form is not fixed by statues or metal, he chooses to live in our minds and hearts.'
2. *Pharsalia* ix. 5–78; 'What is god's home if not earth and sea and air?'

Neptune that raised the seas; nor that of Apollo which gave us light. The Greeks and the Romans were gentiles, polytheists, but not idolators.

WHETHER THE PERSIANS, THE SABAEANS, THE EGYPTIANS, THE TARTARS, THE TURKS WERE IDOLATORS, AND HOW ANCIENT IS THE ORIGIN OF THE SIMULACRA CALLED IDOLS. HISTORY OF THEIR WORSHIP

It is a great mistake to describe as idolators peoples who worshipped the sun and the stars. For a long time these nations had neither simulacra nor temples. If they were in error it was in devoting to the stars what they should have devoted to the creator of the stars. In any case, the dogma of Zoroaster or Zerdust, collected in the *Sadder*, proclaims a supreme being, who avenged and rewarded, which is very far from idolatry. The government of China has never had any idol; it has always preserved the simple worship of the master of heaven, King-tien. Among the Tartars Genghis Khan was not an idolator and had no simulacra. The Moslems who filled Greece, Asia Minor, Syria, Persia, India and Africa, called the Christians idolators, *giaours*, because they believed that the Christians worshipped images. They smashed several statues they found in Constantinople in Santa Sophia, in the church of the holy apostles, and in others which they converted into mosques. Appearances misled them as they always mislead mankind, and led them to believe that temples dedicated to saints who had once been men, images of these saints revered on bended knee, miracles performed in these temples, were invincible proof of the most complete idolatry. Nothing of the kind. Christians in fact worship only one god, and revere in the blessed only the quality of god itself operating in his saints. Iconoclasts and Protestants have levelled the same reproach of idolatry against the church, and have been given the same answer.

As men have very seldom had precise ideas, and have even more rarely expressed their ideas in precise and unequivocal words, we applied the name of idolators to the gentiles, and above all to polytheists. Huge volumes have been written, varied notions have been retailed about the origin of this worship of god or of several gods in visible form. This multitude of books and opinions proves only ignorance.

We do not know who invented clothes and footwear, and we want to know who first invented idols. What does a passage in Sanchuniathon matter? He lived before the Trojan war. What does he tell us when he says that chaos, spirit, that is breath, in love with its principles, derived the primal clay from it and made the air luminous, that the wind Colp and his wife Bau begot Eon, that Eon begot Genos, that Chronos, their descendant, had two eyes at the back of his head as well as in front, that he became god, and gave Egypt to his son Thaut? Such is one of the most respectable monuments of antiquity.

Orpheus, earlier than Sanchuniathon, teaches us no more in his *Theogony*, preserved for us by Damascius. He presents the principle of the world in the shape of a dragon with two heads, one a bull's, the other a lion's, with a face in the middle which he calls *god-face*, and gilded wings at the shoulders.

But two great truths can be drawn from these bizarre ideas: one, that visible images and hieroglyphs date from the greatest antiquity; the other, that all the ancient philosophers recognized a first principle.

As for polytheism, good sense will tell you that ever since there have been men, that is, weak animals, capable of reason and folly, subject to every accident, to illness and to death, these men have felt their weakness and their dependence. They have readily recognized that there is something more powerful than they. They have felt a power in the earth that supplies their nourishment, one in the air that often destroys them, one in the fire that consumes and in the water that submerges. What more natural than for ignorant men to imagine beings who preside over these elements? What more natural than to revere the invisible power that makes the sun and the stars shine in our eyes? And, as soon as man sought to form an idea of these powers superior to him, what even more natural than to represent them in a visible manner? Could they ever have done otherwise? The Jewish religion, which preceded ours, and which was given by god himself, was filled with these images by which god is represented. He deigned to speak human language in a bush; he appeared on a mountain; the celestial spirits he sent all came in human shape; finally, the sanctuary is filled with cherubim, which are human bodies with the wings and the heads of animals. This is what led Plutarch, Tacitus, Appian and so many more wrongly to reproach the Jews for worshipping the head of an ass. Although he forbade the painting or carving of any image, god thus deigned to adapt himself to human weakness, which required images to speak to the senses.

Isaiah, in chapter vi, sees the lord seated on a throne, the train of his robe filling the temple. The lord extended his hand and touched Jeremiah's mouth in this prophet's first chapter. Ezekiel, in chapter iii, saw a sapphire throne, and god appeared to him as a man seated on this throne. These images did not corrupt the purity of the Jewish religion, which never used pictures, statues, idols to represent god to the eyes of the people.

The educated Chinese, the Parsees, the ancient Egyptians had no idols, but images of Isis and Osiris soon appeared, soon Bel became a great colossus in Babylon. Brahma was a bizarre monster in the Indian archipelago. Above all the Greeks multiplied the names of the gods, the statues and the temples, but always attributing the supreme power to their Zeus, called Jupiter by the Latins, master of the gods and of men. The Romans imitated the Greeks. These peoples always placed all the gods in the sky, without knowing what they meant by sky.

The Romans had their twelve great gods, six male and six female, whom they named *dii maiorum gentium*: Jupiter, Neptune, Apollo, Vulcan, Mars, Mercury, Juno, Vesta, Minerva, Ceres, Venus, Diana. Pluto was then forgotten. Vesta took his place.

Then came the gods *minorum gentium*: the local deities, the heroes, like Bacchus, Hercules, Aesculapius; the infernal gods, Pluto, Proserpine; those of the sea, like Thetis, Amphitrite, the Nereids, Glaucus; then the Dryads, the Naiads; the gods of the garden, those of the shepherds. There was a god for every profession, for every activity, for children, for nubile girls, for married women, for women in childbed. They had the god Fart. Finally they deified the emperors. But in fact neither these emperors, nor the god Fart, nor the goddess Pertunda, nor Priapus, nor Rumilia the goddess of tits, nor Stercutius the god of the privy, were regarded as the masters of heaven and earth. The emperors sometimes had temples, the minor household gods had none; but all had their images, their idols. These were little figurines with which a man decorated his study. They were the amusements of old women and children, not authorized by any public worship. The superstition of every private person was indulged. These little idols are still found in the ruins of ancient cities.

Though nobody knows when men started to make idols, we know that they are of the highest antiquity. Terah, Abraham's father, made them at Ur in Chaldea. Rachel stole and carried off the idols of her father-in-law Laban. It is impossible to go further back than that.

But what precise notion did the ancient nations have of all these simulacra? What virtue, what power, was attributed to them? Was it believed that the gods descended from heaven to hide themselves in these statues, or that they communicated to them a part of the divine spirit, or that they communicated nothing at all to them? This too has been the subject of much useless writing. It is obvious that each man judged it according to the degree of his reason or his credulity or his fanaticism. It is evident that the priests attached as much divinity as they could to their statues in order to attract more offerings to themselves. We know that the philosophers condemned these superstitions, that the warriors made fun of them, that the magistrates tolerated them, and the people, always absurd, did not know what it was doing. This, in a few words, is the history of all the nations to whom god has not made himself known.

One can gather the same notion about the worship all Egypt gave to an ox, and that several cities gave to a dog, to a monkey, to a cat, to onions. It would seem that these were at first emblems. Then a certain ox Apis, a certain dog called Anubis, were worshipped. They still ate beef, and onions, but it is hard to know what the old women of Egypt thought of sacred onions and oxen.

The idols spoke quite often. The elegant words spoken by the statue of Cybele when it was removed from the palace of king Attalus were commemorated in Rome on the feast day of that goddess.

> *Ipsa peti volui; ne sit mora, mitte volentem:*
> *Dignus Roma locus quo deus omnis eat.*[1]

> I wanted to be carried off, take me quickly away;
> Rome is worthy to be the home of every god.

The statue of Fortune had spoken. It is true that the Scipios, the Ciceros, the Caesars did not believe this, but the old woman to whom Encolpius gave a crown to buy geese and gods[2] may well have believed it.

The idols also uttered oracles, and the priests, hidden in the hollow statues, spoke in the name of the divinity.

In the midst of so many gods and so many different theogonies and individual cults, why is it that there was never any war of religion among the peoples called idolators? This peace was a good born of an evil, of error itself. For each nation, recognizing several inferior gods, thought it right that neighbouring peoples should also have theirs. Except Cambyses, who is reproached for having killed the ox Apis, we do not find in profane history any conqueror who maltreated the gods of a vanquished people. The gentiles had not a single exclusive religion, and the priests thought only of multiplying the offerings and the sacrifices.

The first offerings were fruits. Soon after, animals were needed for the priests' table; they slaughtered them themselves; they became butchers, and cruel; finally they introduced the horrible practice of sacrificing human victims, and above all children and virgins. Neither the Chinese nor the

---

1. Ovid, *Fasti* iv. 269–70.   2. Petronius, *Satyricon* cxxxvii.

Parsees nor the Indians were ever guilty of these abominations, but according to Porphyry men were immolated at Hieropolis, in Egypt.

In Tauris foreigners were sacrificed. Fortunately the priests of Tauris could not have much practice. The first Greeks, the Cypriots, the Phoenicians, the Tyrians, the Carthaginians had this abominable superstition. The Romans themselves fell into this religious crime, and Plutarch reports that they immolated two Greeks, and two Gauls to expiate the love affairs of three vestals. Procopius, contemporary of the king of the Franks Theodobert, tells us that the Franks immolated men when they entered Italy with this prince. The Gauls, the Germans commonly made these frightful sacrifices. It is hardly possible to read history without conceiving a horror of mankind.

It is true that, among the Jews, Jephtah sacrificed his daughter, and Saul was prepared to immolate his son. It is true that those who were dedicated to the lord by anathema could not be bought back as animals were bought back, and had to perish.[1] Samuel, a Jewish priest, chopped into pieces with a sacred hatchet king Agag, a prisoner of war whom Saul had pardoned, and Saul was condemned for observing the law of nations with this king. But god, master of men, can take their lives when he pleases, how he pleases, and by the hand of whom he pleases; and it is not for men to put themselves in the place of the master of life and death, and to usurp the rights of the supreme being.

To console mankind for this horrible spectacle, these pious sacrileges, it is important to know that among nearly all the nations called idolators there was sacred theology and popular error, the secret cult and public ceremonies, the religion of the wise and that of the vulgar. Only one god was taught in the mysteries to the initiates. One has only to glance at the hymn, attributed to the ancient Orpheus, which was sung in the mysteries of Ceres Eleusinus, so famous in Europe and Asia: 'Contemplate divine nature, illuminate your spirit,

1. The rest of this paragraph has been suppressed in the standard editions of Voltaire's works.

govern your heart, walk in the path of justice. May the god of heaven and earth be always present to your eyes. He is unique, he exists in himself alone. All beings derive their existence from him. He sustains them all. He has never been seen by mortals, and he sees all things.'

Read also this passage from the philosopher Maximus of Madaurus in his *Letter to Saint Augustine*: 'What man is gross and stupid enough to doubt that there is a supreme, eternal, infinite god who has begotten nothing like himself, and who is the common father of all things.'

A thousand passages testify that wise men abhorred not only idolatry, but also polytheism.

Epictetus, this model of resignation and patience, this man who was so great in so low a condition, never speaks of anything but a single god. Here is one of his maxims: 'God has created me, god is within me, I bear him everywhere. Could I soil him by obscene thoughts, unjust actions, infamous desires? My duty is to thank god for all, to praise him for all, and to cease from blessing him only when I cease to live.' All the ideas of Epictetus turn on this principle. Is he an idolator?

Marcus Aurelius, perhaps as great on the throne of the Roman empire as Epictetus in slavery, often speaks, it is true, of the gods, whether to conform to accepted language, or to refer to beings intermediate between the supreme being and men. But in how many places does he not show that he recognizes only one eternal, infinite god! 'Our soul,' he says, 'is an emanation of the divinity. My children, my body, my wits come to me from god.'

The Stoics, the Platonists acknowledged a divine and universal nature. The Epicureans denied it. The pontiff spoke of only one god in the mysteries. Where then were the idolators? All our phrase-mongers proclaim idolatry as little dogs yap when they hear a big dog bark.

For the rest, it is one of the great mistakes of Moréri's dictionary to say that at the time of Theodosius idolators were left only in the distant countries of Asia and Africa. Even in the seventh century there were still many gentile peoples in Italy. North Germany, beyond the Weser, was not Christian in Charlemagne's time. Poland and all the north remained long after him in what is called idolatry. Half of Africa, all the kingdoms beyond the Ganges, Japan, the common people of China, a hundred hordes of Tartars preserved their ancient cult. In Europe only a few Laplanders, Samoyedes, Tartars have persevered in the religion of their .ancestors.

I conclude by noting that in the times we name the middle ages, we called the country of the Mohammedans heathendom. We qualified as idolators, image-worshippers, a people who have a horror of images. We must admit once more that the Turks would be more pardonable to take us for idolators when they see our altars loaded with images and statues.

Inondation: Flood

Has there ever been a time when the globe was entirely flooded? This is physically impossible.

It may be that the sea covered all parts of the earth one after the other, but that could have happened only by slow stages in a prodigious multitude of centuries. In a period of 500 years the sea has withdrawn from Aigues-Mortes, from Fréjus, from Ravenna, which were great ports, and has left about two leagues of dry ground. At this rate it is evident that it would take the sea 2,500,000 years to move round our globe. What is very remarkable is that this period is very near that taken by the axis of the earth to right itself and coincide with the equator. This movement, which is very probable, has been suspected for fifty years, and can only be completed in a period of more than 2,300,000 years.

The beds, the layers of shells which have been discovered on all sides, at several leagues from the sea, are incontrovertible proof that it has deposited its maritime products little by little on land that once formed the ocean shore. But that water once covered the entire globe at the same time is a chimera absurd in natural science, demonstrated impossible by the laws of gravitation, by the laws of fluids, by the insufficient quantity of water. I do not claim to undermine in any way the great truth of the universal flood reported in the Pentateuch. On the contrary, it was a miracle, therefore it must be believed; it was a miracle therefore it was not performed by physical laws.

Everything is miraculous in the story of the flood. It was a miracle that forty days of rain inundated the four quarters of the earth, and that the water should have risen fifteen cubits above all the highest mountains. It was a miracle that there were cataracts, doors, openings in the sky. It was a miracle that all the animals should have proceeded to the ark from every part of the world. It was a miracle that Noah found enough to feed them for ten months. It was a miracle that all the animals found room in the ark with their provisions. It was a miracle that most of them did not die in the ark. It was a miracle that they found food on leaving the ark. It was also a miracle, but of another kind, that a certain Le Pelletier[1] thought that he had explained naturally how all the animals fitted into the ark and fed themselves.

Now the story of the flood being the most miraculous thing we have ever heard of, it would be senseless to explain it. It is one of the mysteries we believe by faith, and faith consists in believing what the reason does not believe, which is another miracle in itself.

Thus the story of the universal flood is like that of the tower of Babel, Balaam's she-ass, the fall of Jericho by the sound of trumpets, water changed into blood, the passage of the Red Sea, and all the prodigies god deigned to perform for the benefit of his people's elect. These are profundities beyond human comprehension.

Inquisition

It is well known that the inquisition is an admirable and thoroughly Christian invention to make the pope and the monks more powerful and a whole kingdom hypocritical.

1. Jean Le Pelletier was the author of a *Dissertation sur l'arche de Noë* (1704).

Saint Dominic is usually regarded as the first to whom we owe this holy institution. And in fact there still exists the patent given by this great saint and expressed in these very words:

I, brother Dominic, reconcile with the church one Roger, bearer of these presents, on condition that, on three consecutive Sundays, he will have himself whipped by a priest from the city gate to the door of the church; that he will abstain from meat all his life; that he will fast three lents a year; that he will never drink wine; that he will wear the *san benito*[1] with crosses; that he will recite the breviary every day, ten *paters* during the day and twenty at midnight; that he will henceforth be continent; and that he will present himself every month to his parish priest, etc.; the whole on pain of being treated as a heretic, perjurer and impenitent.

Although Dominic is the true founder of the inquisition, yet Ludovicus de Paramo, one of the most respectable authors and most brilliant luminaries of the holy office,[2] reports in the second section of his second book, that it was god who first instituted the holy office, and that he exercised the power of the preaching brothers against Adam. Adam was first summoned to the tribunal: *Adam, ubi es?*[3] and in fact, he adds, had he not been summoned god's procedure would have been null and void.

The clothing of skin god made for Adam and Eve was the model for the *san benito* the holy office obliges heretics to wear. It is true that this assertion proves god to have been the first tailor, but it is no less evident that he was the first inquisitor.

Adam was deprived of all the real estate he possessed in the earthly paradise: this is why the holy office confiscates the possessions of all those it has condemned.

Ludovicus de Paramo remarks that the inhabitants of

---

1. A penitential garment
2. It is perhaps necessary to explain that all this is ironic: Paramo was a thoroughly obscure compiler, known only for his grotesque history *De origine et progressu sanctae inquisitionis eiusque dignitate et utilitate* (Matriti, 1598).
3. 'Adam, where art thou?'

Sodom were burned as heretics because sodomy is a positive heresy. Thence he moves on to the history of the Jews, in which he finds the holy office everywhere.

Jesus Christ is the first inquisitor of the new law. The popes were inquisitors by divine right, and they finally transmitted their power to saint Dominic.

He then counts all those put to death by the inquisition, and finds that they numbered many more than 100,000.

His book was printed in 1598, in Madrid, with the approval of the theologians, the praise of the bishop and by royal licence. It is impossible for us nowadays to conceive horrors at once so extravagant and so abominable, but then nothing seemed more natural and more edifying. All men are like Ludovicus de Paramo when they are fanatics.

This Paramo was a plain man, very exact in his dates, omitting no interesting fact, and calculating scrupulously the number of human victims immolated by the holy office in all countries. With the greatest simplicity he describes the establishment of the inquisition in Portugal, and he entirely agrees with four other historians who say the same things. This is what they report unanimously.

For a long time pope Boniface IX, at the beginning of the fifteenth century, had delegated preaching friars who went from town to town in Portugal, to burn the heretics, the Moslems and the Jews. But they were itinerant, and even the kings sometimes complained that they were vexatious. Pope Clement VII wanted to give them a settled home in Portugal, like those they had in Aragon and Castile. There were difficulties between the courts of Rome and of Lisbon, feelings were embittered, the inquisition suffered from this and was not fully established.

In 1539 a papal legate appeared at Lisbon. He had come, he said, to establish the holy inquisition on unshakable foundations. He brought king John III letters from pope Paul III. He had other letters from Rome for the principal officers of the court; his patents of legation were duly sealed and signed; he displayed the most ample authorizations to create a grand inquisitor and all the judges of the holy office.

He was a swindler named Saavedra, who could forge every handwriting and fabricate and attach false seals and stamps. He had learned this trade in Rome and had perfected himself in it at Seville, whence he had come with two other rascals. He lived in great style, his suite being composed of more than 120 servants. To sustain this enormous expense, he and his two confidants borrowed enormous sums at Seville in the name of the apostolic chamber of Rome. The whole thing was planned with the most dazzling skill.

At first the king of Portugal was surprised that the pope should send him a legate *a latere* without letting him know in advance. The legate replied haughtily that in so urgent a matter as the firm establishment of the inquisition, his holiness could tolerate no delays, and that the king had been sufficiently honoured by learning the news for the first time from a legate of the holy father. The king dared not answer. That very day the legate established a grand inquisition, sent everywhere to collect tithes, and before the court could receive a reply from Rome, he had already had 200 people burned and collected more than 200,000 crowns.

In the meanwhile the marquis de Villanova, a Spanish noble from whom the legate had borrowed a large sum of money at Seville by means of forged promissory notes, thought it fitting to repay himself by direct action instead of getting involved with the swindler in Lisbon. The legate was then making his rounds on the Spanish frontier; Villanova marched there with fifty men, and carried him off to Madrid.

The imposture was soon exposed in Lisbon, the council of Madrid condemned the legate Saavedra to be whipped and to ten years in the galleys. But what is wonderful is that pope Paul IV later confirmed all that the rascal had established. By the plenitude of his divine power he rectified all the little irregularities of procedure, and sanctified what had been purely human.

Qu'importe de quel bras dieu daigne se servir?[1]

1. Voltaire is here quoting himself, *Zaire* II. i: 'What does it matter what arm god deigns to use?'

Thus did the inquisition establish itself in Lisbon, and the whole kingdom wondered at providence.

For the rest, the procedures of this tribunal are familiar enough. We know the extent to which they differ from the false equity and blind reason of all the other tribunals in the universe. People are imprisoned on the mere denunciation of the most infamous individuals. A son can denounce his father, a wife her husband. One is never confronted by one's accusers. Property is confiscated for the benefit of the judges. At least, this is how the inquisition has behaved until now. There is something divine here, for it is incomprehensible that men should have patiently borne this yoke.

At last count Aranda has been blessed by the whole of Europe for paring the monster's nails and filing his teeth: but it still breathes.

Jephté ou des sacrifices de sang humain: Jephthah or human blood sacrifices

It is evident from the text of the book of *Judges* that Jephthah promised to sacrifice the first person who came out of his house to congratulate him on his victory over the Ammonites. His only daughter came to meet him. He tore his clothes and immolated her after allowing her to go up to the mountains to weep her misfortune in dying a virgin. Jewish girls long commemorated this adventure by weeping for Jephthah's daughter for four days.[1]

I am not investigating in what times this story was written, whether it was imitated from the Greek story of Agamemnon and Idomeneus or the other way about, whether it was earlier or later than similar Assyrian stories. I stick to the text: Jephthah dedicated his daughter as a burnt offering and accomplished his vow.

The Jewish law expressly ordered the immolation of men

1. *Note by Voltaire:* See chapter xii of *Judges.* [The correct reference is xi. 30–40.]

dedicated to the lord. 'None devoted, which shall be devoted of men, shall be ransomed; he shall surely be put to death.' The Vulgate translates: *Non redimetur, sed morte morietur.* (*Leviticus* xxvii. 29).

It is by virtue of this law that king Agag, whom Saul had forgiven, was cut to pieces by Samuel. It was indeed because he had spared Agag that Saul was condemned by the lord and lost his kingdom.

Human blood sacrifices were thus clearly established. No historical detail is better attested. A nation can be judged only by its archives and by what it tells about itself.

Job

Good morning, friend Job. You are one of the most ancient characters mentioned in books. You were not a Jew. We know that the book which bears your name is older than the *Pentateuch.* Genuine scholars have no doubt that although the Hebrew used the word Jehovah to designate god, they borrowed this word from the Phoenicians and the Egyptians, and translated it from the Arabic. The word Satan was not Hebrew but Chaldean. This is well known.

You lived on the borders of Chaldea. Commentators, worthy of their profession, allege that you believed in the resurrection because, lying on your dung-heaps, you said in your nineteenth chapter, 'that you would rise from it'[1] one day. A sick man who hopes to be cured does not on that account hope to be resurrected. But I want to talk about other things.

You must admit that you were a great chatterbox; but your friends surpassed you. It is said that you possessed 7,000 sheep, 3,000 camels, 1,000 oxen, and 500 she-asses. I should like to draw up your balance-sheet.

---

1. This is merely an abstract of *Job*, ixx 26–7.

> 'And after my skin hath been thus destroyed,
> Yet from my flesh shall I see God:
> Whom I shall see for myself,
> And mine eyes shall behold, and not another.'

7,000 sheep, at three *livres*[1], ten *sous* each,
make twenty-two thousand, five hundred
　livres tournois, that is　　　　　　　　　　22,500 l.
I value the 3,000 camels at 50 crowns each　450,000
　1,000 oxen cannot be valued, one with
　another, at less than　　　　　　　　　　　80,000
And 500 she-asses, at 20 *francs* the she-ass　10,000
　　　　　　　　　　　　　　　　　　　　　―――――
The whole amounts to　　　　　　　　　　562,500
without counting your furniture and personal trinkets.[2]

I have been much richer than you; and although I have
lost a large part of my property, and am ill like you, I have
not grumbled against god, as your friends appear to reproach you with doing.

I am not at all pleased with Satan, who asked for permission
to take away your property and to give you the itch in order
to tempt you into sin and to make you forget god. It is in
these conditions that men always have recourse to god: it is
happy people who forget him. Satan was not worldly-wise
enough. He has made up for it since, and when he wants to
make sure of someone he makes him a farmer-general or
something better, if possible. My friend Pope has shown this
clearly in his story of the knight Balaam.

Your wife was a saucy creature, but your so-called friends,
Eliphaz, a native of Teman in Arabia, Bildad of Shuha, and
Zophar of Naamath, were even more insupportable than she.
They exhorted you to patience in a manner fit to make the
gentlest of men impatient. They addressed you in long sermons more boring than those preached by the V . . ., and the
scoundrel V . . . e in Amsterdam, and the . . . etc.[3]

1. The *livre tournois* or franc was worth about one U.S.A. dollar
around the middle of the eighteenth century, or five new French francs in
1970.

2. Voltaire loved these imaginary statistics; he once worked out a
balance-sheet for a man who tried to blackmail him, concluding that he
was not asking nearly enough.

3. These abbreviations, however tempting they may appear, are not
allusions to Voltaire himself.

It is true that you did not know what you were saying when you exclaimed: 'My god! am I a sea or a whale to have been shut up by you as in a prison?'[1] But your friends were no better informed when they answered 'that the day cannot become green again without moisture, and that the grass of the fields cannot grow without water'.[2] Nothing is less consoling than this axiom.

Zophar of Naamath reproaches you for being a babbler, but none of these good friends offers you a crown. I would not have treated you like that. People who give advice are very common, nothing is rarer than those who help. It is hardly worth while having three friends if you cannot get a drop of soup from them when you are ill. I imagine that when god gave you back your wealth and your health, these eloquent personages did not dare to show themselves to you. Anyway 'Job's comforters' have become proverbial.

God was very displeased with them, and told them plainly, in chapter xlii, that they 'were boring and imprudent',[3] and he condemned them to a fine of seven bulls and seven rams for having talked nonsense. I would have condemned them for not helping their friend.

Please tell me whether it is true that you lived 140 years after this adventure. I like to see decent folk live long; but the men of today have such short lives that they must be great rascals.

Apart from all this, the book of *Job* is one of the most precious of all antiquity. It is evident that this book was written by an Arab who lived before the times in which we place Moses. It is said that Eliphaz, one of the interlocutors, is

1. *Job* vii. 12:

> 'Am I a sea, or a sea-monster
> That thou settest a watch over me?'

2. *Job* viii. 11:

> 'Can the rush grow up without mire?
> Can the flags grow without water?'

3. The lord merely told Eliphaz and Bildad that they had not spoken of him 'the thing that is right' (*Job* xlii. 7–8), but unfortunately we do not know what he said to Zophar.

from Teman, which is an ancient town in Arabia. Bildad was from Shuha, another Arabian town. Zophar was from Naamath, a still more easterly Arabian region.

But what is much more noteworthy, and proves that this fable cannot be by a Jew, is the fact that it mentions the three constellations today named the Bear, Orion, and the Hyades. The Hebrews never had the slightest knowledge of astronomy; they did not even have a name to designate this science. All that relates to knowledge[1] was unknown to them, even to the word geometry. The Arabs, on the contrary, living in tents, being constantly able to observe the heavenly bodies, were perhaps the first who regulated their years by inspecting the heavens.

A more important observation is that only a single god is mentioned in this book. It is an absurd error to have imagined that the Jews were the only ones who recognized a single god. This was the doctrine of nearly the whole orient, and in this, as in everything, the Jews were only plagiarists.

In the thirty-eighth chapter god himself speaks to Job from the midst of a whirlwind, and this was later imitated in *Genesis*. It cannot be too often repeated that the Jewish books are very recent. Ignorance and fanaticism proclaim that the *Pentateuch* is the oldest book in the world. It is evident that those of Sanchionathon, those of Thoth, 800 years older than those of Sanchionathon, those of the first Zoroaster, the *Shasta*; the *Vedas* of the Indians – which we still have, the five *Kings* of the Chinese, finally the book of *Job* are of an antiquity much more distant than any Jewish book. It has been established that this little nation could not have had any annals until it had a stable government, that it had such a government only under its kings, that its jargon was formed only in the course of time out of a mixture of Phoenician and Arabic. There is incontestable evidence that the Phoenicians cultivated the written word a very long time before them. The profession of the Jews was that of brigands and brokers. They were writers only by chance. The books of the Egyptians and the

1. Voltaire's term is '*les arts de l'esprit*', the exact meaning of which is arguable.

Phoenicians have been lost, the Chinese, Brahmans, Parsees, Jews have preserved theirs. All these monuments are curious, but they are only monuments of human imagination, in which we cannot learn a single truth, whether scientific or historical. Any little book on natural philosophy is nowadays more useful than all the books of antiquity.

The good Calmet or dom Calmet (for the Benedictines want to be called dom), this naïve compiler of so many day-dreams and imbecilities, this man whose simplicity had made him so useful to whoever wants to laugh at ancient follies, faithfully reports the opinions of those who tried to guess at the illness by which Job was attacked, as if Job had been a real person. He does not hesitate to say that Job had syphilis, and in his usual way he piles passage on passage to prove what is not. He had not read Astruc's history of syphilis, for Astruc, not being a father of the church, nor a theologian from Salamanca, but a very learned doctor, dear old Calmet did not even know that he existed. Monkish compilers are wretched folk![1]

Joseph

The story of Joseph, considered merely as a curiosity and as literature, is one of the most precious monuments of antiquity to have come down to us. It appears to be the model for all oriental writers. It is more affecting than Homer's *Odyssey*, for a hero who pardons is more touching than one who avenges himself.

We regard the Arabs as the first authors of those ingenious fictions that have passed into all languages; but I see in them no adventure comparable to Joseph's. Nearly everything in it is marvellous, and the end brings a lump to the throat. Here we have a young man of sixteen whose brothers are jealous. They sell him to a caravan of Ishmaelite merchants, he is taken to Egypt, and bought by one of the king's eunuchs. This eunuch had a wife, which is not at all surprising. The

1. Voltaire added one of his jesting signatures: 'By an invalid at the waters of Aix-la-Chapelle.'

Kislar-aga, a complete eunuch, who has had everything cut off, has a harem today in Constantinople.[1] He was left his eyes and his hands, and nature has not lost its rights in his heart. The other eunuchs, who have had cut off only the two accompaniments of the organ of generation, still use that organ frequently, and Potiphar, to whom Joseph was sold, may very well have been one of those eunuchs.

The wife of Potiphar fell in love with the young Joseph, who, faithful to his master and benefactor, rejected the woman's attentions. This irritated her, and she accused Joseph of trying to seduce her. It is the story of Hippolytus and Phaedra, Bellerophon and Stheneboea, Hebrus and Damasippa, Tanis and Peribea, Myrtil and Hippodamia, Peleus and Demenette.[2]

It is difficult to know which of all these stories is the original. But in the ancient Arabic authors the adventure of Joseph and Potiphar's wife contains a very ingenious touch. The author imagines that Potiphar, undecided between his wife and Joseph, did not consider Joseph's tunic, which his wife had torn, to be proof of the young man's attack. There was a child in a cradle in the woman's room. Joseph said that she had torn and removed his tunic in the child's presence. Potiphar consulted the child, whose intelligence was very developed for its age. The child said to Potiphar: 'See whether the tunic is torn in front or behind: if in front this is evidence that Joseph tried to violate your wife, who defended herself; if behind it is evidence that your wife was running after him.' Thanks to this child's genius, Potiphar recognized the innocence of his slave. This is how the adventure is recounted in the *Koran* after the ancient Arabic author. He is not concerned to tell us to whom belonged the child who judged with so much intelligence. If it was the son of Potiphar's wife, Joseph was not the first she had pursued.

Be that as it may, according to *Genesis* Joseph was im-

1. Voltaire misunderstood his informant: *kislar aghasi* is the title of the chief of the harem eunuchs.
2. O, rather, Astydamia.

prisoned, and found himself in company with the Egyptian king's cup-bearer and baker. These two prisoners of state dreamed during the night. Joseph explained their dreams, predicting that in three days the cup-bearer would be restored to favour, and the baker hung: which is what came to pass.

Two years later the king of Egypt also dreamed. His cup-bearer told him that there was a young Jew in prison who understood dreams better than anyone else in the world. The king sent for the young man, who predicted seven years of plenty and seven years of want.

Let us here briefly interrupt the thread of the story to consider how prodigiously ancient is the interpretation of dreams. Jacob had seen in a dream the mysterious ladder that led to god himself. He learned in a dream a way to multiply his flocks, a way that succeeded only for him. Joseph himself had learned in a dream that he would one day dominate his brothers. Long before, Abimelech had been warned in a dream that Sarah was the wife of Abraham.[1]

Let us return to Joseph. As soon as he had explained Pharaoh's dream, he became prime minister on the spot. We may doubt whether a king could be found nowadays, even in Asia, who would bestow such an office for the explanation of a dream. Pharaoh made Joseph marry one of Potiphar's daughters. It is said that this Potiphar was the high priest of Heliopolis. So this was not his first master the eunuch, or if it was he, he was certainly entitled to be called something else in addition to high priest, and his wife had been a mother more than once.

In the meanwhile famine came as Joseph had predicted, and Joseph, to deserve the marked favour of his king, obliged everybody to sell their land to Pharaoh, and the entire nation enslaved itself to get grain. This was apparently the origin of despotic power. It must be admitted that never had a king made a better bargain, but the people can hardly have blessed the prime minister.

Finally Joseph's father and brothers also needed grain, for

1. *Note by Voltaire:* See the article 'Songes'.

'the famine was sore in all the earth'.[1] It is hardly necessary to relate here how Joseph received his brothers, how he forgave and enriched them. All that constitutes an interesting epic poem is found in this story: exposition, crux, recognition, vicissitudes and marvels. Nothing bears more clearly the hallmark of oriental genius.

What old Jacob, father of Joseph, replied to Pharaoh, must strongly impress anyone who can read. 'How many are the days of the years of thy life?' asked the king. 'The days of the years of my pilgrimage are 130 years, and I have not yet had one happy day in this short pilgrimage.'[2]

Judée: Judea

I have not been to Judea, thank God, and will never go. I have met people of all nationalities who have come back from it. They have all told me that the site of Jerusalem is horrible, that all the surrounding country is stony, that the mountains are naked, that the famous river Jordan is only forty-five feet wide, that the only good province in this country is Jericho. In short, they all repeat saint Jerome, who lived for so long in Bethlehem, and who depicts this land as the scrap-heap of nature. He says that in the summer there is not even water to drink. Nevertheless this country must have appeared to the Jews a delightful spot in comparison with the deserts they had come from. Wretches who had left the Landes to live on the mountains of the Lampourdan[3] would praise their new home, and if they hoped to penetrate into the good parts of the Languedoc these would strike them as the promised land.

This is precisely the history of the Jews. Jericho and Jerusalem are Toulouse and Montpellier, and the Sinai desert is the country between Bordeaux and Bayonne. But if the god who conducted the Jews wanted to give them good land, and

1. *Genesis* xli. 57.
2. *Genesis* xlvii. 8–9; but Jacob in fact concludes 'few and evil have been the days of the years of my life'.
3. This is the now obsolete name of the Basque province around Bayonne.

if these unfortunates had in fact lived in Egypt, why did he not leave them there? The only answers given to this question are theological phrases. Judea, it is said, was the promised land. God said to Abraham: 'I will give you all this land from the river of Egypt unto the Euphrates.'[1]

Alas! my friends, you have never seen these fertile banks of the Euphrates and the Nile. They fooled you. The masters of the Nile and the Euphrates were, each in his turn, your masters. You have nearly always been slaves. To promise and to perform are two things, my poor Jews. You had an old rabbi who, reading the wise prophecies that foretell for you a land of milk and honey, exclaimed that you had been promised more butter than bread. Do you realize that if the Grand Turk offered me today the lordship of Jerusalem I would spurn it?

On seeing this detestable country Frederick II said publicly that Moses was very ill-advised to lead his company of lepers to it: 'Why didn't he go to Naples?' said Frederick. Good-bye my dear Jews; I am sorry that the promised land should be waste land.[2]

Julien le philosophe, empereur romain: The philosopher Julian, Roman emperor[3]

Justice is sometimes done very late. Two or three authors, either mercenaries or fanatics, talk about the barbarian and effeminate Constantine as of a god, and call the just, the wise, the great Julian a scoundrel. All the others, who copied the first, repeat the flattery and the calumny. These almost become an article of faith. Finally the time for sound criticism arrives, and, after 1,400 years, enlightened men review the cause that

1. *Note by Voltaire: Genesis*, chapter xv, verse 18.
2. Voltaire signed: 'By the Baron of Broukana'.
3. Shortly after publishing this essay in the *Dictionnaire philosophique* Voltaire used it, with changes and additions, as a 'portrait' of Julian prefixed to the *Discours de l'empereur Julien contre les Chrétiens*, which is dated 1768, but was in fact published in the following year; this is the text I have used.

ignorance had judged. Constantine is seen as a man, successful in his ambitions, who laughed at god and at mankind. He had the insolence to pretend that god sent him a heavenly sign which ensured his victory. He soaked himself in the blood of all his family, and went to sleep in sloth; but he was a Christian, and was canonized.

Julian was sober, chaste, disinterested, brave, merciful; but he was not a Christian, and was for long regarded as a monster.

Today, having compared the facts, the documents, Julian's writings and those of his enemies, we are compelled to recognize that although he did not like Christianity it was pardonable for him to hate a sect sullied by the blood of all his family; that having been persecuted, imprisoned, exiled, threatened with death by the Galileans in the reign of the barbarous Constantine, he never persecuted them, that on the contrary he pardoned ten Christian soldiers who had conspired against his life.

We read his letters, and we admire him. 'The Galileans,' he says, 'suffered exile and imprisonment under my predecessor. Those who called each other heretics turn and turn about, massacred each other. I have recalled those they exiled, and freed their prisoners. I have returned their property to the outlawed. I have compelled them to live in peace. But such is the restless rage of the Galileans that they complain because they can no longer devour one another.'[1] What a letter! what a verdict pronounced by philosophy against persecuting fanaticism!

In short, everyone who has studied the facts impartially recognizes that Julian had all the qualities of Trajan, except the inclination for which the Greeks and the Romans have so long been forgiven; all the virtues of Cato, but not his obstinacy and his bad temper; all that we admire in Julius Caesar, and none of his vices; he was as chaste as Scipio. In a word, he was in all things the equal of Marcus Aurelius, the greatest of men.

Nowadays we no longer dare to repeat, after the calumni-

1. Letter 41, to the citizens of Bostra.

ator Theodoret, that Julian immolated a woman in the temple
of Carrhae to propitiate the gods. We no longer repeat that in
dying he threw with his hand some drops of his blood towards
heaven, saying to Jesus Christ: 'You have vanquished,
Galilean!' as if he had fought against Jesus in warring against
the Persians; as if this philosopher, who died with so much
resignation, had acknowledged Jesus; as if he had believed
that Jesus was in the air, and that the air was heaven! These
inaptitudes of people who are called fathers of the church are
no longer repeated nowadays.

They were finally reduced to ridiculing him, as did the
frivolous citizens of Antioch. They reproached him his un-
kempt beard and the way he walked. But master La Bletterie,[1]
you have not seen him walk, and you have read his letters
and his laws, monuments of his virtues. What does it matter
whether his beard was dirty and his walk hurried, so long as
his heart was magnanimous and all his steps tended towards
virtue?

One important fact today remains to be examined. Julian is
reproached with wanting to falsify Jesus Christ's prophecy by
rebuilding the temple of Jerusalem. It is said that fires came
out of the ground which prevented the work. It is said that
this was a miracle, and that this miracle converted neither
Julian, nor Alypius, manager of the enterprise, nor any
member of the court. Whereupon the *abbé* de La Bletterie
says this: 'He and the philosophers of his court no doubt
had recourse to their knowledge of natural philosophy to
deprive the divinity of so striking a prodigy. Nature has
always been the refuge of the incredulous, but she serves
religion so aptly that they ought at least to suspect her of
collusion.'

First, it is not true that the gospels say that the Jewish
temple would never be rebuilt. It is true that the gospel of
Matthew, obviously written after the destruction of Jerusalem
by Titus, prophesies that not one stone would be left upon

1. The references here and elsewhere in this essay are to the Oratorian
Jean Philippe René de La Blèterie's *Histoire de l'empereur Julien l'apostat*
(1735), one of Voltaire's favourite butts.

another[1] of this temple of the Idumaean Herod. But no evangelist says that it will never be rebuilt. It is quite false that not one stone remained upon another after Titus had it pulled down. He preserved all the foundations, an entire wall, and the Antonia tower.

Secondly, what does it matter to the divinity whether there is a Jewish temple or a powder magazine or a mosque on the spot where the Jews slaughtered oxen and cows?

Thirdly, it is not known whether these alleged fires, which according to some burned the workmen, emanated from the walled enclosure of the city or from that of the temple. But it is difficult to understand why Jesus should have burned the emperor Julian's workmen when he did not burn those of the caliph Omar who, long after, built a mosque on the ruins of the temple, nor those of the great Saladin, who restored this same mosque. Did Jesus have so great a predilection for the mosques of the Moslems?

Fourthly, Jesus, having predicted that not one stone would remain on another in Jerusalem, did not forbid that it be rebuilt.

Fiftly, Jesus predicted several things the accomplishment of which has not been permitted by god. He predicted the end of the world and his advent in the clouds with great power and great majesty at the end of the generation then living. Nevertheless the world still lasts and apparently will last for some time.[2]

Sixthly, if Julian had described this miracle I would have said that he had been deceived by a false and ridiculous report, I would believe that his enemies the Christians spared no effort to oppose his enterprise, that they killed the workmen and made people believe that those workmen had been killed by a miracle. But Julian does not say a word about it. He was busy then with the war against the Persians. He deferred for a time the building of the temple, and died before he could begin it.

Seventhly, this prodigy is reported by Ammianus Marcellinus, who was a pagan. It is very possible that it was inter-

1. *Matthew* xxiv. 2.   2. *Note by Voltaire: Luke,* xxi.

polated by the Christians: they have been authentically accused of so many others.

But it is no less likely that at a time when people talked of nothing but prodigies and stories of witchcraft, Ammianus Marcellinus should have reported this fable on the word of some credulous mind. Since Titus Livius down to Thou inclusively all histories are tainted by prodigies.

Eighthly, contemporary writers report that at this time there was a great earthquake in Syria, that fire broke out in several places, and that several towns were swallowed up. Thus no miracle remains.

Ninthly, if Jesus worked miracles, would it be to prevent the rebuilding of a temple in which he himself had offered up sacrifices and had been circumcised? Would he not work miracles to Christianize so many nations which jeer at Christianity, or rather to make his Christians gentler and more humane, they who, from Arius and Athanasius to Roland and Cavalier[1] in the Cévennes, have poured out torrents of blood and behaved like cannibals?

From this I conclude that nature is not in *collusion with Christianity*, as La Bletterie says, but that La Bletterie is in collusion with old wives' tales, as Julian says: *Quibus cum stolidis aniculis negotium erat*.

After doing justice to some of Julian's virtues La Bletterie nevertheless ends the history of this great man by saying that his death was a consequence of 'divine vengeance'. If that was so, all heroes who died young were punished by god, from Alexander to Gustavus Adolphus. Julian died the finest of deaths, pursuing his enemies after several victories. Jovian, who succeeded him, reigned a much shorter time than he, and reigned shamefully. I detect no divine vengeance, and I see no more in La Bletterie than a dishonest ranter. But where are the men who dare to speak the truth? The stoic Libanius was one of these rare men. He praised the brave and merciful Julian to Theodosius, the murderer of the Thessalonians, but

1. Jean Cavalier was the leader of the Camisards in the religious uprisings in the Cévennes in the first years of the eighteenth century.

master Le Beau[1] and master La Bletterie are afraid to praise him to faithful parishioners.

Julian has been reproached because he gave up Christianity, as soon as he could do so without risking his life. This is to reproach a man, taken by thieves and enrolled in their gang with a knife to his throat, for escaping from these brigands. The emperor Constant, no less barbarous than his father Constantine, had soaked himself in the blood of Julian's entire family. He had just killed this great man's blood brother. The empress Eusabia had great difficulty in persuading Constant to allow the young Julian to live. In order not to be murdered this unfortunate prince had to accept a monk's tonsure to ensure and receive what are called the four minor orders. He imitated Junius Brutus, who pretended to be mad in order to outwit Tarquin's fury. He was senseless until the moment when, finding himself in Gaul at the head of an army, he became a man and a great man. This is what is called apostasy by the apostates of reason, if such a term can be applied to those who have never known it.

Montesquieu says: 'Woe to the reputation of any prince who is survived by an enemy faction.'[2] Let us imagine that Julian had completed his victory over the Persians, and that, during a long and peaceful old age, he had seen his ancient religion restored, and Christianity annihilated with the sects of the Pharisees, Sadducees, Rechabites, Essenians, Therapeutes, with the worship of the Syrian goddess, and so many more of which no trace remains – then what praises would all the historians have lavished on Julian! Instead of the epithet of apostate he would have been given that of restorer, and the title of divine would not have seemed exaggerated.

Look at the way all our unworthy compilers of Roman history are on their knees to Constantine and Theodosius, with what baseness they palliate their crimes! Nero certainly

---

1. Charles Le Beau, the pietistic compiler of a vast *Histoire du bas-empire* (1757–76).

2. In the first chapter of the *Grandeur et décadence des Romains*. Voltaire has abridged Montesquieu's phrase.

never did anything comparable to the massacre of the Thessalonians. The Cantabrian Theodosius pretended to pardon
the Thessalonians, and six months later he invited them to
games in the municipal circus. This circus had room for at
least 15,000 persons, and it is certain that it was full. The
people's passion for spectacles is notorious. Fathers and
mothers brought children who could hardly walk. As soon
as the crowd had arrived, the Christian emperor sent Christian
soldiers, who massacred old men, youngsters, women, girls,
children, without sparing a single one. And this monster is
exalted by all our compiling plagiarists because, they say, he
did penance. Good god, what penance! He did not give an
obol to the families of the dead. But he did not go to mass.
It must be admitted that one suffers horribly when one does
not go to mass, that god is infinitely grateful to you for it,
that it redeems all crimes.

The infamous continuator of Laurent Echard[1] calls the
massacre ordered by Theodosius a vivacity.

The same wretches who scribble Roman history in a
bombastic style full of solecisms, tell you that Theodosius,
before engaging battle with his rival Eugene, saw saint John
and saint Philip dressed in white, who promised him
victory. Let such writers sing hymns to John and to Philip,
but let them not write history.

Reader, examine your conscience. You admire, you love
Henry IV. But if he had fallen at the battle of Arques, where
his enemies were ten to one against him, and where he was
victorious only because he was a hero in the fullest sense of the
word, you would not know him: he would only be the
Bearnese, a guerilla, a relapsed heretic, an apostate. The duc
de Mayenne would be a man sent by god, the pope would
have canonized saint Philip, riddled though he was by the
pox, and saint John would have appeared to him more than
once. And you, Daniel the Jesuit, how you would have

---

1. Laurence Eachard's *The Roman history* was first published in 1698,
the French translation *Histoire romaine* in 1728, and its continuation by
C. M. Guyon in 1736–42; in French the author's name became Laurent
Echard.

flattered Mayenne in your poor and arid history![1] how he would have 'pushed after him', how he would always have 'beaten' the Bearnese 'hollow'! how the church would have 'triumphed'![2]

> *Careat successibus opto*
> *Quisquis ab eventu facta notanda putaat.*[3]

Juste (du) et de l'injuste:
On right and wrong

Who gave us the feeling of right and wrong? God, who gave us a brain and a heart. But when does your reason tell you that there is vice and virtue? When she tells us that two and two make four. There is no innate knowledge for the same reason that there is no tree that bears leaves and fruit on emerging from the earth. Nothing is what is called innate, that is, born developed; but, let me repeat again, god caused us to be born with organs which, as they grow, make us feel all that our species must feel in order to preserve this species.

How does this continuous mystery operate? Answer me, yellow inhabitants of the Sunda isles, black Africans, beardless Canadians, and you, Plato, Cicero, Epictetus. You all feel equally that it is better to give away what remains of your bread, your rice and your manioc to the poor man who humbly asks you for it, than to kill him or to put out his two eyes. It is obvious to the whole world that a service is better than an injury, that gentleness is preferable to anger.

It only remains therefore to use our reason to discern the shades of goodness and badness. Good and evil are often allied. Our passions fail to distinguish between them. Who

1. G[abriel] Daniel, *Histoire de France*, first published in 1715, grew to immense proportions.

2. *Note by Voltaire:* Expressions used by father Daniel.

3. Ovid, *Heroides* ii. 85: 'I beg that he come to naught who thinks that the deed should be judged by its result.' At the end of the original version of this essay appears another of Voltaire's imaginary attributions: 'Drawn from M. Boulanger.'

will enlighten us? We ourselves, when we are calm. Whoever has written about our duties has written well in every country of the world, because he wrote only with his reason. They have all said the same thing: Socrates and Epicurus, Confucius and Cicero, Marcus Antoninus[1] and Amurath II had the same morality.

Let us repeat every day to all men: 'Morality is one, it comes from god. Dogmas differ, they are ours.'

Jesus taught no metaphysical dogma at all. He wrote no theological exercises. He did not say: 'I am consubstantial, I have two wills and two natures with one sole person.' He abandoned to the Franciscans and the Dominicans, who were to come 1,200 years after him, the trouble of arguing whether his mother had been conceived in original sin. He never said that marriage is the visible sign of an invisible thing. He did not say a word about concomitant grace. He instituted neither monks nor inquisitors. He commanded nothing of what we see today.

God had given knowledge of right and wrong in all the ages that preceded Christianity. God has not changed and cannot change. The essential of our souls and of our principles of reason and morality will eternally be the same. Of what use to virtue are theological distinctions, dogmas based on these distinctions, persecutions based on these dogmas? Nature, frightened and aroused with horror against all these barbarous inventions, cries out to all men: 'Be just, and not sophistical persecutors.'

In the *Sadder*, which is the abridgement of the laws of Zoroaster, you can read this wise maxim: 'When it is uncertain whether an action you are asked to take is right or wrong, abstain.' Who has ever proposed a more admirable rule? what legislator has spoken better? This is not the system of probable opinions invented by people who call themselves the Society of Jesus.

1. That is, Marcus Aurelius Antoninus.

Lettres, gens de lettres ou lettrés:
Literature and writers

Schools and universities were instituted in our barbaric past, when the Franks, Germans, Bretons, Lombards, Spanish, Mozarabs could neither read nor write. They nearly all consisted of ecclesiastics, who, knowing only their jargon, taught this jargon to those who were willing to learn it. Academies came only much later. They despised the nonsense of the schools, but did not always dare to protest against them, because some nonsense is respected, since it is connected with respectable things.

The men of letters who have rendered most services to the small number of thinking beings scattered throughout the world are the isolated writers, the true scholars shut up in their studies, who have neither argufied on the benches of the universities nor said things by halves in the academies; and these have nearly all been persecuted. Our wretched species is so made that those who walk in the beaten path always throw stones at those who teach a new path.

Montesquieu says that the Scythians put out the eyes of their slaves so that they be less distracted when churning their butter. This is the practice of the inquisition, and nearly everybody is blind in the countries in which this monster reigns. In England everybody has had two eyes for over a hundred years. The French begin to open an eye, but sometimes there are men in office who will not even permit men to be one-eyed. These poor people in office are like doctor Lumpish in Italian comedy, who wants to be served only by the stupid Harlequin and is afraid to have too penetrating a valet.

Compose odes in praise of his royal highness, Superbus Fadus, and madrigals for his mistress. Dedicate a book on geography to his porter, and you will be well received. Enlighten men, and you will be crushed.

Descartes was obliged to leave his country, Gassendi was calumniated, Arnauld dragged out his days in exile. Every freethinker is treated as were the prophets by the Jews. Who would believe that in the eighteenth century a philosopher[1] has been dragged before the secular courts, and called impious by the ecclesiastical tribunals, for having said that men could not practise their skills if they had no hands? I am not unhopeful that the first man who has the insolence to say that a man would not think if he had no head will promptly be condemned to the galleys. 'For,' a bachelor will tell him, 'the soul is a pure spirit, the head is only matter. God can place the soul in the heel as easily as in the head. Consequently I denounce you as impious.'

The greatest misfortune of a writer is not perhaps to be the object of his colleagues' jealousy, the victim of intrigue, to be despised by the powerful of this world – it is to be judged by fools. Fools sometimes go far, especially when ineptitude is added to fanaticism, and vengefulness to ineptitude. It is also the great misfortune of writers that they usually stand alone. A bourgeois buys a minor post, and obtains with it the support of his colleagues. If he is the victim of an injustice, he at once has defenders. The man of letters is helpless. He is like a flying fish: if he rises a little, the birds devour him; if he dives, the fish eat him.

Every man in the public eye pays tribute to malignity, but he is compensated by cash and honours. The writer pays the same tribute without receiving anything; he has descended into the arena for his pleasure, he has condemned himself to the beasts.

Liberté (de la): On freewill

A: Here is a battery of guns shot off within our hearing. Are you free to hear it or not to hear it?

B: Clearly I can't prevent myself from hearing it.

A: Do you want this gun to carry off your head and the heads of your wife and daughter, who are taking a walk with you?

1. Voltaire's *protégé* Claude Adrien Helvétius, because of his book *De l'esprit*.

B: What an idea! So long as I'm in my right mind I can't want such a thing; I'm incapable of it.

A: Good. You necessarily hear this gun, and you and your family necessarily don't want to die from a cannon ball while taking a walk. You're unable not to hear it, and unable to stay here.

B: Obviously.[1]

A: Consequently you took a score of steps to shelter from the gun. You had the power to walk these few steps with me?

B: This is still obvious.

A: And if you had been a paralytic you wouldn't have been able to avoid being exposed to this battery; you wouldn't have had the power to be where you are; you would necessarily have heard and received a cannon ball; and you would necessarily be dead?

B: Nothing is truer.

A: What then does your freewill consist of if it is not in the power your self has exercised to do what your will required of it as an absolute necessity?

B: You perplex me. So freewill is nothing but the power to do what I want to do?

A: Think it over, and see if freewill can be understood in any other way.

B: In that case my hunting dog is as free as I am. He necessarily has the will to run when he sees a hare, and the power to run if he has not hurt his legs. So I have no advantage over my dog: you reduce me to the condition of the animals.

1. *Note by Voltaire, added in the second edition:* A dull-witted fellow, in an honourable, polite and, above all, well-reasoned little work objects that if the prince ordered B to remain exposed to the gun, he would remain. Yes, no doubt, if he has more courage, or rather more fear of shame than love of life, as very often happens. First, this is quite a different case. Secondly, when the instinct of the fear of shame triumphs over the instinct of self-preservation, the man is under as much of a necessity to remain exposed to the gun as he is obliged to flee when it is not shameful to flee. The dull-witted fellow was under a necessity to make ridiculous objections and to utter insults, and freethinkers feel under a necessity to make a little fun of him, and to forgive him.

A: Such are the wretched sophisms of the wretched sophists who taught you. Here you're upset because you're as free as your dog! Come! don't you resemble your dog in a thousand ways? Don't you have hunger, thirst, wakefulness, sleep, the five senses in common with him? Would you like to smell otherwise than with the nose? Why do you want to have a freewill different from his?

B: But I've a soul that reasons a great deal and my dog hardly reasons at all. He has little more than simple ideas, and I've a thousand metaphysical ideas.

A: Very well, you're a thousand times freer than he is, that is, you have a thousand times greater power of thought than he has, but you don't have a different kind of freewill.

B: What! I'm not free to want what I want?

A: What do you mean by that?

B: I mean what everybody means. Isn't it said every day: 'We are free to will'?

A: A proverb is not a reason. Explain yourself better.

B: I mean that I'm free to want as I please.

A: By your leave, that makes no sense. Don't you see that it is ridiculous to say: 'I want to want'? You want necessarily, in consequence of the ideas that have come to you. Do you want to get married, yes or no?

B: But if I told you that I want neither one nor the other?

A: You'd reply like the man who said: 'Some believe cardinal Mazarin to be dead, others believe him to be alive, and I believe neither one nor the other.'

B: Very well, I want to get married.

A: Now that's answering! Why do you want to get married?

B: Because I'm in love with a girl who is beautiful, tender, well bred, rich enough, who sings very well, whose parents are very decent people, and because I flatter myself that she loves me and that I'm very acceptable to her family.

A: There's a reason! You see that you can't want without a reason. I declare to you that you're free to marry, that is, that you have the power to sign the contract.

B: Really! I can't want without a reason? Then what will

become of this other proverb: *Sit pro ratione voluntas*: my will is my reason, I want because I want?

A: That's absurd, my dear fellow: you would have in you an effect without a cause.

B: What! when I play odd or even, I have a reason to choose even rather than odd?

A: Yes, certainly.

B: Please, what is this reason?

A: It is that the notion of even presented itself to your mind rather than the contrary notion. It would be strange if there were cases in which you want because there is a cause for wanting, and other cases in which you want without cause. When you want to marry, you obviously feel the dominant reason. You don't feel it when you play at odd and even, and nevertheless there must be one.

B: But, once again, I therefore do not possess freewill?

A: Your will is not free, but your actions are. You are free to act when you have the power to act.

B: But all the books I have read on indifferent free-will[1] . . .

A: Are nonsense. There is no indifferent freewill. This is a term without sense invented by people who had little.

Liberté de pensée: Freedom of thought

About 1707, at the time when the English won the battle of Saragossa,[2] protected Portugal, and for a while gave Spain a king, lord Boldmind, a field officer who had been wounded, was taking the waters at Barèges. There he met count Medroso who was also taking the waters, having fallen from his horse in the rear of the baggage, a league and a half from the battlefield. He was a familiar of the inquisition; lord Boldmind was familiar only in conversation. One day, after drinking, he had this conversation with Medroso:

1. Voltaire later added a passage in which he explains that this term denotes decisions of no significance, as whether to spit to the right or to the left.

2. To be precise, this was in 1710.

BOLDMIND: So you are a tipstaff of the Dominicans? What a shabby trade!

MEDROSO: That's true, but I would sooner be their valet than their victim, and I have preferred the misfortune of burning my neighbour to that of being roasted myself.

BOLDMIND: What a horrible alternative! You were a hundred times happier under the yoke of the Moors, who left you to wallow freely in all your superstitions, and who, for all that they were conquerors, didn't arrogate to themselves the unheard-of right of keeping the mind in chains.

MEDROSO: What do you expect? We aren't allowed to write, nor to talk, not even to think. If we speak it is easy to interpret our words, let alone our writings. Finally, as they can't condemn us in an auto-da-fe for our secret thoughts, they threaten to burn us in eternity by order of god himself if we don't think like the Dominicans. They have convinced the government that if we had common sense the whole state would be in ferment and the nation would become the unhappiest on earth.

BOLDMIND: Does it seem to you that we are so unhappy, we English who cover the seas with ships and who have just won battles for you at the other end of Europe? Do you find that the Dutch, who have robbed you of nearly all your discoveries in the Indies, and who today are among your protectors, are cursed by god for having given the press complete freedom and for trading in men's thoughts? Was the Roman empire less powerful because Tullius Cicero wrote freely?

MEDROSO: Who is this Tullius Cicero? I've never heard this name spoken at the holy Hermandad.

BOLDMIND: He was a bachelor of the university of Rome, who wrote what he thought, like Julius Caesar, Marcus Aurelius, Titus Lucretius Carus, Plinius, Seneca and other learned men.

MEDROSO: I don't know them; but I have been told that the Catholic religion, Basque and Roman, would be lost if men began to think.

BOLDMIND: It's not for you to believe it, for you're sure

that your religion is divine, and that the gate of hell cannot prevail against it. If that's so, nothing can ever destroy it.

MEDROSO: No, but it can be reduced to little, and it's because they thought so that Sweden, Denmark, the whole of your island, half of Germany groan under the appalling misfortune of no longer being subjects of the pope. It's even said that if men continue to follow their false lights they will soon stop at the single adoration of god and virtue. If the gates of hell ever prevail to that extent what will become of the holy office?

BOLDMIND: Isn't it true that there would have been no Christianity if the first Christians hadn't had freedom of thought?

MEDROSO: What do you mean? I don't understand you.

BOLDMIND: No doubt. I mean that if Tiberius and the first emperors had had Dominicans, who would have prevented the first Christians from having pens and ink, had free thought not long been permitted in the Roman empire, it would have been impossible for the Christians to establish their dogmas. So, since Christianity constituted itself only by means of freedom of thought, by what contradiction, by what injustice does it now wish to annihilate the freedom on which alone it is founded?

When some business matter is proposed to you, don't you consider it at length before taking a decision? What greater business is there in the world than that of our eternal happiness and misery? There are a hundred religions in England all of which damn you if you believe in your dogmas, which they call absurd and impious. You should therefore examine these dogmas.

MEDROSO: How can I examine them? I'm not a Dominican.

BOLDMIND: You are a man, and that's enough.

MEDROSO: Alas, you're much more a man than I am.

BOLDMIND: It's up to you to learn to think. You were born with intelligence. You're a bird in the cage of the inquisition. The holy office has clipped your wings, but they can grow again. He who knows no geometry can learn it. Every man can educate himself. It's shameful to put one's mind into the hands of those whom you wouldn't entrust with your money. Dare to think for yourself.

MEDROSO: It's said that if every man thought for himself there would be utter confusion.

BOLDMIND: Quite the contrary. When people go to see a play, each one freely expresses his opinion of it, and peace is not troubled. But if some insolent protector of a bad poet tried to compel all people of taste to find good what appears to them to be bad, then hisses would be heard, and the two parties might throw apples at each other, as once happened in London. It is these tyrants of the mind who have caused part of the misfortunes of the world. We are happy in England only since every one freely enjoys the right to say what he thinks.

MEDROSO: We are also very peaceful in Lisbon, where nobody does.

BOLDMIND: You're peaceful, but you're not happy: it is the peace of galley slaves, who row uniformly and in silence.

MEDROSO: So you believe that my mind is a galley slave?

BOLDMIND: Yes, and I should like to free it.

MEDROSO: But if I'm satisfied in the galleys?

BOLDMIND: In that case you deserve to be there.

Lois (des): On laws

I

In the time of Vespasian and Titus, while the Romans were disembowelling the Jews, a very rich Israelite who did not want to be disembowelled fled, with all the gold he had made at his trade of usurer, to Eziongaber with all his family, which consisted of his old wife, a son and a daughter. He had two eunuchs in his suite, one of whom served as cook, the other being a farm labourer and vine-grower. A good Essenian, who knew the *Pentateuch* by heart, served as his almoner. All these people embarked at the port of Eziongaber, crossed the sea called Red, which it is not, and entered the Persian gulf to look for the land of Ophir, not knowing where it was. As you can imagine, a horrible storm came up which drove the Hebraic family towards the coast of India. The ship was wrecked on one of the Maldive islands, now called Padrabranca, which was then uninhabited.

The old money-bags and his wife were drowned, the son, the daughter, the two eunuchs and the almoner were saved. Some provisions were dragged from the ship as best they could, little huts were built on the island, and they lived there comfortably enough. You know that the island of Padrabranca is five degrees from the line, and that the biggest coconuts and the best pineapples in the world grow there. It was very pleasant to live there when the rest of the chosen people was being butchered elsewhere, but the Essenian wept when he reflected that they were perhaps the only Jews who remained on earth, and that the seed of Abraham was about to be extinguished.

'You can resuscitate it if you want to,' said the young Jew; 'marry my sister.'

'I'd like to,' said the almoner, 'but it's against the law. I'm an Essenian, I've taken a vow never to marry. By law vows must be observed. The Jewish race can expire for all I care but I shall certainly not marry your sister, even though she's very pretty.'

'My two eunuchs can't give her children,' rejoined the Jew, 'so I'll do it if you please and you'll celebrate the marriage.'

'I would a hundred times sooner be disembowelled by the Roman soldiers,' said the almoner, 'than to be the means of your committing incest. If she were your sister by your father, that might do, the law allows it; but she is your sister through your mother, that's abominable.'

After fourteen years the mother died. The father said to the almoner: 'Have you at last got rid of your old prejudices? Will you marry my daughter?' 'God forbid!' said the Essenian. 'Very well then, I'll marry her myself,' said the father. 'Come what may I don't want the seed of Abraham to be brought to nothing.' The Essenian, appalled by this horrible utterance, would no longer live with a man who disobeyed the law, and fled. The bridegroom shouted after him in vain: 'Stay, my friend, I obey the natural law, I serve the nation,

don't abandon your friends.' The other let him shout, his
head being always full of the law, and fled by swimming to the
neighbouring island.

This was the big island of Attole, thickly populated and
highly civilized. As soon as he landed he was enslaved. He
learned to mumble the language of Attole. He complained
very bitterly of the inhospitable way in which he had been
received. He was told that it was the law, and that since the
island had nearly been surprised by the inhabitants of the
island of Ada, it had been wisely laid down that all foreigners
landing on Attole would be enslaved. 'This cannot be a law,'
said the Essenian, 'for it is not in the *Pentateuch*.' They replied
that it was in the country's law-books, and he remained a
slave. Happily he had a very good and very rich master who
treated him well, and to whom he became very attached.

Some murderers came one day to kill the master and to steal
his treasures. They asked the slaves whether he was at home,
and whether he had a lot of money. 'We swear to you,' said
the slaves, 'that he has no money, and that he's not at home.'
But the Essenian said: 'The law does not permit me to lie;
I swear to you that he's at home, and that he's got a lot of
money.' So the master was robbed and killed. The slaves
accused the Essenian before the judges of betraying his
employer. The Essenian said that he did not want to lie, and
that he would not lie for anything in the world; and he was
hanged.

I was told this story, and many others like it, during my last
voyage from India to France. When I arrived I went to
Versailles on business. I saw a beautiful woman go by attended
by several beautiful women. 'Who is this beautiful woman?' I
asked my lawyer, who had come with me, for I had a lawsuit
on my hands in the courts about the clothes made for me in
India, and I wanted to have my lawyer always by my side.
'It's the king's daughter,' he said; 'she's charming and
benevolent. It's a great pity that in no circumstances can she
ever be queen of France.' 'What!' I said to him, 'if we had
the misfortune to lose all the king's relations and the princes
of the blood (which god forbid!) she couldn't inherit her

father's kingdom?' 'No,' said the advocate, 'the Salic law expressly forbids it.' 'And who made this Salic law?' I asked the advocate. 'I've no idea,' he said, 'but it is alleged that an ancient people called the Salians, who could neither read nor write, had a written law which declared that on Salic territory a girl could not inherit a freehold; and this law has been adopted in non-Salic countries.' 'As for me,' I said, 'I set it aside. You've assured me that this princess is charming and benevolent: therefore she has an unquestionable right to the crown, if she should have the misfortune to be the only surviver of royal blood. My mother inherited from her father, and I want this princess to inherit from hers.'

On the following day my lawsuit was heard in one of the courts, and I lost everything by one vote. My advocate told me that I would have won it by one vote in another court. 'That's very funny,' I told him; 'so each court has its own law.' 'Yes,' he said, 'there are twenty-five commentaries on the customary law of Paris; that is, it's been proved twenty-five times that the customary law of Paris is equivocal, and if there were twenty-five judicial chambers, there would be twenty-five different jurisprudences. We have,' he went on, 'fifteen leagues from Paris, a province called Normandy, where you would have been judged quite differently.' This made me want to see Normandy. I went there with one of my brothers. At the first inn we met a young man in despair. I asked him why he was in trouble. He replied that it was because he had an elder brother. 'Why is it such a great misfortune to have a brother?' I asked him. 'My brother is the elder, and we get on very well.' 'Alas, sir,' he told me, 'the law here gives everything to the eldest and nothing to the younger ones.' 'You're right to be angry,' I told him, 'in our province we share equally, and sometimes brothers don't like each any better on that account.'

These little adventures led me to make fine and profound reflections about the laws, and I saw that they are like our clothes: I had to wear a dolman in Constantinople and a jacket in Paris.

If all human laws are conventions, I said, we must make the

best of them. The citizens of Delhi and Agra say that they made a very bad bargain with Tamerlane. The burghers of London congratulate themselves on having made a very good bargain with king William of Orange. A citizen of London once said to me: 'It is necessity that makes the laws, and they are kept by force.' I asked him whether force did not also make laws sometimes, and whether William the bastard and the conqueror had not given them orders without striking a bargain with them. 'Yes,' he said, 'we were cattle then. William yoked us, and made us walk by pricking us. Since then we have changed into men, but we've kept the horns, and we use them to strike anyone who wants to make us work for him, and not for ourselves.'

Filled with all these reflections I flattered myself with the thought that there is a natural law, independent of all human conventions: the fruit of my labour must be mine, I must honour my father and my mother, I have no rights over the life of my neighbour, and my neighbour has none over mine, etc. But I was very distressed when I reflected that from Chodorlahomor[1] to Menzel,[2] colonel of hussars, everyone has loyally killed and plundered his neighbour, letters patent in his pocket.

I was told that there are laws among thieves, and also in war. I inquired about these laws of war. 'If a brave officer,' I was told, 'were to hold out in a bad position, without guns, against a royal army, these laws would cause him to be hanged. The law is to hang a prisoner if the others have hung one of yours. The law is to put to fire and sword the villages which failed to bring you all their provisions on the day appointed by the orders of the gracious sovereign of the neighbour-hood.' 'Splendid,' I said, 'here we have the *Spirit of the laws*.'[3]

Having been thoroughly instructed, I discovered that there

1. Chedorlaomer smote the Rephaim, the Zuzim, the Emim, the Hor-ites, the Amalekites, the Amorites, the Sodomites and others, and was himself smitten by Abraham (*Genesis* xiv. 5–15).

2. Baron Johann David von Menzel, notorious partisan leader, who captured Munich in February 1742.

3. An ironic reference to the title of Montesquieu's book.

are wise laws by which a shepherd is condemned to nine years in the galleys for having given a little foreign salt to his sheep. My neighbour was ruined by a lawsuit about two oaks which belonged to him and which he had cut down in his wood, because he had been unable to observe a formality he could not have known about. His wife died in misery, and his son drags out a life unhappier than death. I admit that these laws are just, although their execution is a little hard, but I am annoyed about laws that authorize a hundred thousand men loyally to go and slaughter a hundred thousand neighbours. It appeared to me that most men have received enough common sense from nature to pass laws, but that not everybody has enough justice to make good laws.

Assemble simple and quiet farmers from every corner of the world, and they will all readily agree that they should be permitted to sell the surplus of their grain to their neighbours, and that the law to the contrary is inhuman and absurd; that the currency representing produce should no more be debased than the fruits of the earth; that the father of a family should be the master at home; that religion should bring men together in order to unite them, and not to make them into fanatics and persecutors; that those who work should not deprive themselves of the fruit of their labours to endow superstition and idleness. In an hour they would make thirty laws of this kind, all useful to mankind.

But let Tamerlane arrive in India to subjugate it, and then you will see only arbitrary laws. One will oppress a province to enrich one of Tamerlane's tax-collectors; another will make it a crime of *lèse-majesté* to have spoken ill of the mistress of the first valet of a rajah; a third will lay hands on half the farmer's crop, and dispute his right to the rest; and finally there will be laws by which a Tartar beadle will come to seize your children in the cradle, make the most robust one into a soldier, and the weakest a eunuch, and will leave the father and mother without resource and consolation.

Now which would be better, to be Tamerlane's dog or his subject? It is obvious that his dog is much better off.

II

Sheep live very quietly in society. They are supposed to have very mild characters, because we do not see the prodigious quantity of animals they devour. It may even be assumed that they eat them innocently and unknowingly, as when we eat a Sassenage cheese. The republic of sheep is the faithful image of the golden age.

A hen-roost is manifestly the most perfect monarchical state. No king can compare to a cock. It is not by vanity that he walks proudly in the midst of his people. If the enemy approaches he does not order his subjects to get themselves killed for him by virtue of his sure knowledge and absolute power: he advances himself, keeps his hens behind him, and fights to the death. If he is the victor it is he who sings the *Te deum*. In private life there is nothing so courteous, so upright, so disinterested. He has all the virtues. If he has a grain of wheat or a worm in his royal beak, he gives it to the first of his subjects who presents herself. In short, Solomon in his harem did not compare to a farmyard cock.

If it is true that bees are governed by a queen with whom all her subjects make love, then that is a still more perfect government.

The ants are regarded as an excellent democracy. It is the best of all states, since everybody in it is equal, and each individual works in it for the happiness of all.

The beaver republic is still better than that of the ants, at least if we judge it by its buildings.

Monkeys resemble mountebanks rather than a civilized people, and they do not appear to be united by fixed and fundamental laws like the species just mentioned. We resemble monkeys more than any other animal in the gift of imitation, the triviality of our ideas, and our inconstancy, which has never enabled us to have uniform and durable laws.

When nature formed our species she gave us a few instincts: self-esteem for our preservation, benevolence for the preservation of others, the love which is common to all species, and the inexplicable gift of being able to combine more ideas than all animals put together. After thus giving us our portion she said to us: 'Do what you can.'

There is not a single good code in any country. The reason for this is evident: laws have been made by degrees, according to times, places, needs, etc. When needs have changed the laws that remained became ridiculous. Thus the law that forbade the eating of pork and the drinking of wine was very sensible in Arabia, where pork and wine are pernicious. It is absurd in Constantinople.

The law that gives the whole property to the eldest son is very good in a time of anarchy and pillage. Then the eldest son is the captain of the castle which will sooner or later be assailed by brigands. The younger sons are his chief officers, the labourers his soldiers. The only thing to fear is that the younger brother murder or poison the Salic lord, his elder brother, in order to become in his turn the master of the shanty, but these cases are rare because nature has so combined our instincts and our passions that we have a greater horror of murdering an elder brother than we have envy of taking his place. Now this law, appropriate to owners of dungeons at the time of Chilperic, is detestable when it is a question of dividing income in a city.

To men's shame, it is well known that the laws of gambling are the only ones that are everywhere just, clear, inviolable and kept. Why is the Indian who laid down the rules of chess cheerfully obeyed throughout the world, while, for instance, the decretals of the popes are today an object of horror and contempt? It is because the inventor of chess arranged everything with precision to satisfy the players, while the popes in their decretals had only their own benefit in view. The Indian wanted equally to exercise men's mind and give them pleasure. The popes wanted to bestialize men's minds. So the basis of chess has remained the same for 5,000 years, and is common to all the inhabitants of the earth; and the decretals are recognized only at Spoleto, Orvieto and Loretto, where the meanest of jurists secretly hates and despises them.

Lois civiles et ecclésiastiques: Civil and ecclesiastical laws

These notes were found among the papers of a jurist, and perhaps deserve some attention.

That no ecclesiastical law should ever have authority unless it has been expresssly sanctioned by the government. This is why Athens and Rome never had religious quarrels. These quarrels are the lot of barbarous nations, or those become barbarous.

That only the magistrate should be able to permit or prohibit work on feast days, because it is unbecoming for priests to forbid men to cultivate their fields.

That anything concerning marriage should depend solely on the magistrate, and that priests should restrict themselves to the august function of blessing them.

That lending at interest should be the business purely of the civil law, because it alone watches over commerce.

That all ecclesiastics should be subjected to the government in everything because they are subjects of the state.

That one should never suffer the shameful ridicule of paying to a foreign priest the first year of the income of an estate given by citizens to a priest who is a fellow citizen.

That no priest should ever deprive a citizen of the least prerogative on the pretext that this citizen is a sinner, because the priestly sinner should pray for other sinners, and not judge them.

That magistrates, labourers and priests should equally pay the expenses of the state, because all belong equally to the state.

There should be only one weight, one measure, one law.

That the punishment of criminals should be useful. A hanged man is good for nothing, and a man condemned to public labour still serves the fatherland and is a living lesson.

That the whole of the law should be clear, uniform and precise: to interpret it is nearly always to corrupt it.

That only vice should be infamous.

That taxes should never be anything but proportional.

That law should never conflict with custom; for if the custom is good the law is superfluous.[1]

Luxe: Luxury

For 2,000 years people have declaimed in verse and prose against luxury, and have always loved it.

What has not been said about the earliest Romans, these brigands who ravaged and pillaged the harvests of their neighbours, who destroyed the poor villages of the Volscians and the Samnites in order to aggrandize their own poor village? They were disinterested and virtuous men! They had not yet been able to steal either gold or silver or precious stones, because there was none in the places they sacked. Neither their woods nor their marshes produced partridges or pheasants, and their temperance is praised!

When little by little they had pillaged everything, stolen everything from the far end of the Adriatic to the Euphrates, and had had enough sense to enjoy the fruit of their rapines for seven or eight hundred years, when they cultivated all the arts, tasted every pleasure, and made even the vanquished taste them, then, it is said, they ceased to be wise and upright.

All these declamations come down to proving that a thief must never eat the dinner he has stolen nor wear the clothes he has purloined nor adorn himself with the ring he has taken. All this, it is said, should have been thrown into the river if the thieves wanted to live as honest men. Say rather that one should not steal. Condemn the brigands when they pillage, but do not call them lunatics when they enjoy what they have taken. Honestly,[2] when a large number of English sailors

1. *Note by Voltaire:* See the poem on the *Loi naturelle* [by Voltaire himself].

2. *Note by Voltaire:* The witless fellow I have already quoted, having read this passage in a bad edition in which there was a full stop after this word honestly, thought that the author meant that thieves enjoy honestly. I know of course that this witless fellow is malicious, but, honestly, he cannot be dangerous.

enriched themselves on taking Pondicherry and Havana, were they wrong to enjoy themselves later in London in return for the pains they had taken at the extremities of Asia and Africa?

Do the windbags want the wealth amassed by the fortunes of war, agriculture, trade and industry to be buried? They instance Lacedaemon. Why do they not cite also the republic of San Marino? Of what benefit was Sparta to Greece? Did she ever have a Demosthenes, Sophocles, Apelles or Phidias? The luxury of Athens produced great men of every kind. Sparta had a few captains, and even those in smaller numbers than the other cities. But so be it! Let a little republic like Lacedaemon preserve its poverty. We attain death just as surely lacking everything as enjoying whatever makes life agreeable. The Canadian savage survives and reaches old age just like the English citizen who has an income of 50,000 guineas. But who will ever compare the country of the Iroquois with England?

Let the republic of Ragusa and the canton of Zug make sumptuary laws. They are right, it is necessary for the poor man not to spend beyond his means, but I have read somewhere:

> *Sachez surtout que le luxe enrichit*
> *Un grand état, s'il en perd un petit.*[1]

If by luxury you mean excess, everybody knows that excess of every kind is pernicious, in abstinence as in gluttony, in economy as in liberality. I do not know how it has come about that in my villages, in which the land is barren, the taxes heavy, the prohibition against exporting the wheat we have sowed intolerable, there is nevertheless hardly a husbandman without clothes made of good cloth and who is not well shod and well fed. If this farmer cultivates the land in his fine clothes, white linen, curled and powdered hair, that would certainly be the greatest luxury, and the most impertinent. But if a bourgeois of Paris or London appeared in the theatre

1. Voltaire, *Défense du mondain*, lines 53–4: 'Know above all that luxury enriches a great state, though it ruins a small one.'

dressed like this peasant, that would be the crudest and most ridiculous niggardliness.

> *Est modus in rebus, sunt certi denique fines,*
> *Quos ultra citraque nequit consistere rectum.*[1]

Scissors are certainly not of the greatest antiquity. When they were invented what was not said against the first who pared their nails and cut part of the hair that fell over their noses? They were no doubt called dandies and prodigals, who bought at a high price a tool of vanity to spoil the work of the creator. What an enormous sin to shorten the horn that god causes to grow at the ends of our fingers! It was an insult to divinity.[2] It was much worse when shirts and socks were invented. We know how furiously the old councillors, who had never worn them, cried out against the young magistrates who yielded to this fatal luxury.

Maître: Master

How was it possible for a man to become another man's master, and by what kind of incomprehensible magic could he become the master of several other men? A large number of good volumes has been written about this phenomenon; but I give the preference to an Indian fable, because it is short, and because fables have said everything.

Adimo, father of all Indians, had two sons and two daughters by his wife Procriti. The elder son was a vigorous giant, the younger a little hunchback. The two daughters were pretty. As soon as the giant felt his strength, he went to bed with his two sisters, and made the hunchback his servant. One of his two sisters became his cook, the other his gardener. When the giant wanted to sleep he began by chaining his little brother the hunchback to a tree; and when he ran away the giant

1. Horace, *Satires* I. i. 106–7: 'There is a measure in all things, fixed limits which virtue must neither overstep nor fail to attain.'

2. It is impossible to point out the significance of all Voltaire's allusions, but here for once I may be allowed to mention that this is not a wild invention. It is in fact a personal reminiscence: Voltaire long before had got into trouble because of an unkind reference in the *Mondain* to Adam's fingernails.

caught up with him in four strides and gave him twenty blows with a bull whip.

The hunchback submitted, and became the best subject in the world. The giant, content to see him fulfill his duties as a subject, allowed him to lie with one of his sisters of whom he had had enough. The children who came from this marriage were not precisely hunchbacked, but their shape was rather deformed. They were brought up in the fear of god and the giant. They received an excellent education. They were taught that their great-uncle was a giant by divine right, that he could do as he pleased with all his family, that if he had some pretty niece or grand-niece she was evidently for him alone, and that nobody could lie with her when he no longer wanted her.

When the giant died, his son, who was not nearly so strong or so big as he, nevertheless believed that he was a giant by divine right like his father. He claimed the right to make all the men work for him, and to lie with all the girls. The family united against him, he was done to death, and they formed themselves into a republic.

The Siamese, on the contrary, claimed that the family began by being republican, and that the giant came along only after a great many years and dissensions. But all the authors of Benares and Siam agree that men lived an infinity of centuries before they had the intelligence to make laws; and they prove this by an unanswerable argument, that even today when every man prides himself on his intelligence, it has not yet been found possible to make a score of tolerably good laws.

Again, it is still an insoluble question in India whether republics were established before or after monarchies, whether disorder would have appeared more horrible to mankind than despotism. I do not know the chronological sequence of events; but in that of nature it must be agreed that, all men being born equal, violence and ability made the first masters, and laws the most recent.

Martyr

We can only guffaw at all the humbug we are told about martyrs. Such men as Titus, Trajan, Marcus Aurelius, these models of virtue, are depicted as monsters of cruelty. Fleury,[1] *abbé* of the Loc-Dieu, dishonoured his ecclesiastical history with stories a sensible woman would not tell to little children.

Can it be seriously repeated that the Romans condemned each of seven virgins of seventy to pass through the hands of all the young men of the city of Ancyra, the same Romans who punished vestals with death for the slightest love-affair? It was apparently to give pleasure to inn-keepers that the story was invented of a Christian inn-keeper called Theodotus, who prayed to god to kill these seven virgins rather than to expose them to the loss of the oldest virginities. God gave ear to the prudish inn-keeper, and the proconsul had the seven misses drowned in a lake. As soon as they were drowned they went to Theodotus to complain of the trick he had played on them, and begged him earnestly to prevent the fishes from eating them. Theodotus took with him three topers from his tavern, marched to the lake with them, preceded by a celestial torch and a celestial horseman, fished up the seven old ladies, buried them, and finished by being hanged.

Diocletian met a little boy called saint Roman, who stuttered. He wanted to have him burnt because he was a Christian. Three Jews who happened to be there started to laugh because Jesus Christ allowed a little boy who belonged to him to be burnt. They exclaimed that their religion was superior to the Christian since god delivered Shadrach, Meshach and Abednego from the fiery furnace. The flames which enveloped the young Roman without hurting him at once divided and burned the three Jews. The emperor, very astonished, said that he wanted to have no quarrel with god, but a village judge, less scrupulous, condemned the little stutterer to have his tongue cut out. The emperor's chief physician had the decency to perform the operation himself. As soon as he had cut out the little Roman's tongue, the child started to chatter with a volubility that transported the whole assembly with admiration.

A hundred stories of this kind are to be found in the martyr-

1. Claude Fleury, author of a vast *Histoire ecclésiastique* that dragged on through the eighteenth century.

ologies. Thinking to make the ancient Romans odious they made themselves ridiculous. Do you want good, well-attested barbarities; good, well-authenticated massacres; rivers of blood that really ran; fathers, mothers, husbands, women, children at the breast really butchered and piled up on each other? Persecuting monsters, seek these truths only in your annals: you will find them in the crusades against the Albigensians, in the massacres of Mérindol and Cabrières, in the appalling day of saint Bartholomew, in the Irish massacres, in the valleys of the Waldenses. It well becomes you, barbarians that you are, to impute extravagant cruelties to the best of emperors, you who have inundated Europe with blood, and covered it with dying bodies, to prove that it is possible to be in a thousand places at once, and that the pope can sell indulgences! Stop slandering the Romans, who gave you your laws, and ask god's forgiveness for the abominations of your fathers.

It is not the suffering, you say, that makes the martyr; it is the cause. Well, I grant that your victims should not be given the name of martyr, which means witness. But what name shall we give your executioners? Phalaris and Busiris were the gentlest of men compared with you. Does not your inquisition, which still survives, make reason, nature, religion shudder? Good god! if this infernal tribunal were reduced to ashes, would your vengeful gaze be displeased?

Matière: Matter

Wise men who are asked about the soul answer that they have no idea what it is. If they are asked what matter is, they give the same reply. It is true that some professors, and above all some schoolboys, know it all perfectly; and when they have repeated that matter is extended and divisible, they think they have settled everything; but if they are asked to say what this extended thing is, they find themselves in difficulty. 'It is composed of parts,' they say. And these parts, what are they composed of? Are the elements of these parts divisible? Then they are dumb or talk a lot, which is equally suspect. This nearly unknown being called matter, is it eternal? All antiquity thought so. Does it possess inherent active power? Several philosophers have thought so. Are those who have denied it entitled to do so? It is inconceivable that matter can be anything in itself. But how can you assert that it does not possess in itself all the properties necessary to it? You do not know what its nature is, and you deny its modes, which are nevertheless in its nature. For after all, given that it exists, it must do so in a certain way, it must have form; and given that it necessarily has form, is it impossible that other modes relate to its configuration? Matter exists; you know it only by your sensations. Alas! what is the use of all the intellectual subtleties devised since man reasons? Geometry has taught us many truths, metaphysics very few. We weigh matter, we measure it, we decompose it; and if we want to take a step beyond these coarse operations we find impotence within us and an abyss before us.

Pray forgive the entire universe, which has made the mistake of believing that matter exists in itself. Could it do anything else? How is one to imagine that what is without succession has not always been? Were it not necessary for matter to exist, why does it exist? And if it had to be, why should it not always have been? No axiom has ever been more universally accepted than this: *Nothing is made out of nothing.* The contrary is in fact incomprehensible. Among all peoples chaos preceded the organization of the world by a divine hand. In no people has the eternity of matter prejudiced the cult of divinity. Religion was never shocked by the recognition of an eternal god as the master of an eternal matter. We now have the good fortune to know by faith that god drew matter from the void, but no nation had been informed of this dogma, even the Jews did not know of it. The first verse of *Genesis* says that the gods, Elohim not Elohi,[1] made the heaven and the earth. It does not say that heaven and earth were created out of nothing.

Philo, who lived at the only epoch in which the Jews had some erudition, says in his chapter on creation: 'God, being

1. *Elohim* is the plural of the Hebrew *Elohi*.

good by nature, did not envy substance, matter, which had nothing good in itself, which in its nature has nothing but inertia, confusion, disorder.'

The notion of a chaos cleared up by a god is found in all the ancient theogonies. Hesiod respected what the east thought when he said in his *Theogony*: 'Chaos is the first thing that existed.' Ovid was the interpreter of the whole Roman empire when he said:

> *Sic ubi dispositam, quisquis fuit ille deorum*
> *Congeriem secuit* [1] . . . .

Thus matter in the hands of god was thought to be like the clay on the potter's wheel, if it is permissible to use such feeble images to express the divine power.

Matter, being eternal, must have had eternal properties, such as configuration, the power of inertia, movement and divisibility. But this divisibility is only the consequence of movement; for without movement nothing divides, separates or organizes itself. Movement was thus regarded as essential to matter. Chaos had been a confused movement, and the arrangement of the universe a regular movement imprinted on all bodies by the master of the world. But how could matter have a movement in itself as it has, according to all the ancients, extension and impenetrability? But it cannot be conceived without extension, and it can be conceived without movement. To which they answered: 'It is impossible for matter not to be permeable; so, being permeable, something must continually pass into its pores. What is the use of passages if nothing passes through them?'

We shall never finish by piling retort on retort. The system of eternal matter has very great difficulties, like all systems. That of matter made from nothing is no less incomprehensible. We must admit this, and not flatter ourselves that we have mastered the problem: philosophy does not explain everything. How many incomprehensible things are we not obliged to admit, even in geometry? Can we conceive of

1. *Metamorphoses* i. 32–3; 'When whichever of the gods it was, ordered that chaotic mass . . .'

two lines that always approach one another and will never meet?

Of course the geometers will tell us: 'The properties of the asymptotes have been demonstrated; you cannot help but accept them. But creation has not; why do you accept it? What is your difficulty in believing, like all antiquity, that matter is eternal?' Elsewhere the theologians will press you, saying: 'Since you believe matter to be eternal you must recognize two principles, god and matter: you fall into the error of Zoroaster, of Manes[1].'

We will not answer the geometricians, because people of that sort understand only their lines, their surfaces and their solids. But we could say to the theologian: 'In what respect am I a Manichean? Here are some stones not made by an architect. He has raised them into an immense building. I don't recognize two architects. The crude stones obeyed power and genius.'

Happily, whatever system we adopt, none harms morality: for what difference does it make whether matter is made or organized? In either case god is our absolute master. We must be as virtuous in a settled chaos as in a chaos created out of nothing. Hardly any of these metaphysical questions influence the conduct of one's life. These disputes are like idle table conversation: each one forgets after dinner what he has said, and goes where his interests and his taste call him.

Méchant: Wicked

We are told loudly that human nature is essentially perverse, that man is born the child of the devil, and wicked. Nothing is more ill-considered. For, old friend, you who preach that the whole world is born perverse, you warn me that you were born thus, that I must distrust you like a fox or a crocodile. 'Not at all!' you tell me, 'I'm regenerated, I'm neither heretical nor infidel, you can trust me.' 'But the rest of mankind, which is either heretical or what you call infidel, is nothing but an assembly of monsters; and every time you

1. The founder of Manicheism.

talk to a Lutheran or to a Turk you must feel sure that they will rob and murder you, for they are children of the devil, born wicked, one unregenerated, the other degenerated. It would be much more rational, much more elegant to say to men: *You are all born good; consider how awful it would be to corrupt the purity of your being.* We ought to have behaved to mankind as we behave to every individual man. If a monk leads a scandalous life, we say to him: 'Would you really dishonour the dignity of a monk?' A lawyer is reminded that he has the honour to be a royal councillor, and should give an example. In order to encourage a soldier he is told: 'Remember that you belong to the regiment of Champagne.' Every individual should be told: 'Remember your human dignity.'

And in fact, whatever is said about it, we always come back to that; for what is the meaning of the saying, so often used in all nations, *search your heart*?[1] If you were born a child of the devil, if your origin were criminal, if your blood were composed of an infernal liquid, this phrase *search your heart* would mean: consult, follow your diabolic nature, be an impostor, a thief, a murderer, it is the law of your father.

Man is not born wicked; he becomes wicked, as he falls ill. Doctors come along and say: 'You were born ill.' It is quite certain that these doctors, whatever they say and do, will not cure him if his sickness is inherent in his nature; and these thinkers are very ill themselves.

Collect all the children of the universe, and you will see in them only innocence, gentleness and fear. If they were born wicked, evil-doing, cruel, they would show some sign of it, just as small serpents try to bite and little tigers to claw. But nature, not having given more offensive arms to men than to pigeons and rabbits, could not give them an instinct of destruction.

So man is not born evil. Then why are some of them infected by this plague of wickedness? It is because their leaders, being infected by the disease, communicate it to the rest of mankind, just as a woman attacked by the malady brought back from America by Columbus spread this poison

1. Or 'examine your conscience', that is, '*rentrez en vous-même*'.

from one end of Europe to the other. The first ambitious man corrupted the earth.

You are going to say that this first monster brought out the germ of pride, rapine, fraud, cruelty that is in all men. I admit, generally speaking, that most of our brothers can acquire these qualities; but does everybody have putrid fever, the stone and the gravel because everybody is exposed to them?

There are whole nations that are not wicked: the Philadelphians, the Banians,[1] have never killed anyone; the Chinese, the peoples of Tongking, Laos, Siam, even Japan, have had no war for more than a hundred years. One of the great crimes that shock human nature is hardly seen once in ten years in the cities of Rome, Venice, Paris, London, Amsterdam, although in these cities cupidity, the mother of all crimes, is extreme.

If men were essentially wicked, if they were all born subject to a being as malevolent as he is unhappy, who inspired them with all his rage to avenge himself for his own suffering, we would see every morning husbands murdered by their wives, and fathers by their children, as we find at daybreak chickens strangled by a weasel who came to suck their blood.

If there are a billion men on earth, it is a lot. That would make about 500 million women who sew, spin, feed their little ones, clean their houses or huts, and gossip a little about their neighbours. I do not see what great harm these innocents do on earth. Out of this number of inhabitants of the globe, there are at least 200 million children, who certainly neither kill nor plunder, and about as many old or sick people who are not able to do so. At most there remain 100 million young people, robust and capable of crime. Of these 100 million ninety million are regularly occupied in prodigious labour to force the earth to yield them food and clothing: these hardly have time to do wrong.

Among the ten million who remain are included the idle and the gregarious, who only want to enjoy themselves; men of talent, busy with their professions; magistrates, priests,

1. That is, roughly, the Hindus.

obviously concerned to live pure lives, at least in appearance.
So the only really wicked men who remain are a few politic
individuals, whether secular or religious, who always want to
create trouble, and a few thousand vagabonds who hire out
their services to these intriguers. In fact, there are never a
million of these ferocious beasts employed at one time; and
in this number I include highwaymen. So there is at most on
earth, in the stormiest times, one man in a thousand who can
be called wicked, and even he is not so all the time.

There is thus infinitely less evil on the earth than is said and
believed. No doubt there is still too much. Horrible misfortunes and crimes are seen, but the pleasure of complaining
and exaggerating is so great that at the slightest scratch you
exclaim that the earth overflows with blood. If you have been
cheated all men are perjurers. A melancholic who has suffered
an injustice sees the universe covered with the damned, just
as a young voluptuary, supping with his lady after the opera,
cannot imagine that unfortunates exist.

Messie: Messiah

In Hebrew *messiah* or *meshia*; in Greek *christos* or *eleimmenos*,[1] in
Latin *unctus*; anointed.

We see in the *Old Testament* that the name *messiah* was
often given to idolatrous or infidel princes. It is said[2] that
god sent a prophet to anoint Jehu, king of Israel. He announced
the sacred unction to Hazael, king of Damascus and Syria,
these two princes being the *messiahs* of the most high to
punish the house of Ahab.

In the forty-fifth chapter of *Isaiah* the name of *messiah* is
expressly given to Cyrus. 'Thus saith the eternal to Cyrus, his
anointed, his *messiah*, whose right hand I have taken, to sub-
due nations before him[3] . . .'

Ezekiel, in the twenty-eighth chapter of his revelations,

1. A persistent misprint for *eleimennos*.
2. *Note by Voltaire: 3 Kings*, chapter xix, verses 15 and 16. [*3 Kings* in the
Vulgate is *1 Kings* in the English *Bible*.]
3. *Isaiah* xlv. 1, slightly modified.

gives the name of *messiah* to the king of Tyre, whom he also calls *cherub*. 'Son of man,' said the eternal to the prophet, 'utter loudly a lamentation for the king of Tyre, and say to him: "Thus saith the lord, the eternal: Thou wast the seal of the resemblance of god, full of wisdom and perfect in beauty. Thou wast in Eden the garden of the lord (or, according to other versions), Thou wast all the delight of the lord. Thy clothes were of sardius, topaz, jasper, chrysolite, onyx, beryl, sapphire, carbuncle, emerald and gold. The workmanship of thy tabrets and of thy pipes was in thee; in the day that thou wast created they were prepared. Thou wast a cherub, a Messiah." '[1]

This name of *messiah*, *christ*, was given to the kings, to the prophets and to the high priests to the Hebrews. We read in *I Kings* xii. 5: 'The lord and his *messiah* are witnesses', that is to say: 'The lord and the king that he has established.'[2] And elsewhere: 'Do not touch my anointed and do no harm to my prophets.' David, filled with the spirit of god, in more than one place gives his reprobate father-in-law Saul, who was persecuting him, the name and quality of the anointed, the *messiah* of the lord. 'God preserve me,' says he frequently, 'from raising my hand against the anointed of the lord, the *messiah* of god.'

Herod, being anointed, was called *messiah* by the Herodians, who formed a little short-lived sect.

If the name *messiah*, the anointed of the eternal, was given to idolatrous kings, to reprobates, it was very often used in our ancient oracles to designate the true anointed of the lord, pre-eminently the *Messiah*, the Christ, son of god, in short, god himself.

If one compares all the various oracles usually applied to the *messiah*, there could emerge some apparent difficulties, which the Jews used to justify their obstinacy if they could. Several eminent theologians grant them that in the state of oppression in which the Jewish people groaned, and after all the promises

---

1. *Ezekiel* xxviii. 12–13, much modified, but correct in essentials.
2. *I Samuel* xii. 5, condensed; *I Samuel* is *I Kings* in the Vulgate.

the eternal had so often made them, they could sigh for the coming of a victorious and liberating *messiah*, and that they were therefore in a sense excusable for not having at once recognized this liberator in the person of Jesus, especially as there is not a single passage in the Old Testament that says: 'Believe in the *messiah*.'

It was in the plan of the eternal wisdom that the spiritual ideas of the true *messiah* should be unknown to the blind multitude. So unknown were they that Jewish scholars have thought fit to deny that the passages I have adduced apply to the *messiah*. Several say that the *messiah* had already appeared in the person of Hezekiah. This was the view of the famous Hillel. Others, in great number, allege that belief in the coming of a *messiah* is not a fundamental article of faith, and that this dogma, being neither in the decalogue nor in *Leviticus*, it is no more than a consoling hope.

Several rabbis will tell you that they have no doubt the *messiah* came at the time appointed by the ancient oracles, but that he does not age, that he remains hidden on this earth, and that he waits for Israel to keep the sabbath properly before manifesting himself.

The famous rabbi Solomon Izhaqi or Rashi, who lived at the beginning of the twelfth century, says in his *Talmudics* that the ancient Hebrews believed that the *messiah* was born on the day of the last destruction of Jerusalem by the Roman armies: this is, as they say, to send for the doctor after the patient's death.

Rabbi Kimchi, who also lived in the twelfth century, announced that the *messiah*, whose coming he believed to be very near, would drive out of Judea the Christians who then possessed it. It is true that the Christians lost the holy land, but it was Saladin who vanquished them. If only that conqueror had protected the Jews and taken their part, in their enthusiasm they would probably have made him their *messiah*.

The sacred authors, and our lord Jesus himself, often compare the reign of the *messiah* and eternal bliss to wedding days, to feasts, but the talmudists strangely deformed these parables.

According to them the *messiah* will give to his people, assembled in the land of Canaan, a meal at which the wine will
be that made by Adam himself in the terrestrial paradise, and
which is preserved in the vast cellars dug by angels in the
centre of the earth.

For the entrée will be served the famous fish called the great
Leviathan who cannot be less than 300 leagues long, and
swallows in one gulp a fish smaller than himself. The whole
mass of the waters is borne by Leviathan. In the beginning
god created one male and one female, but for fear lest they
overturned the earth and filled the universe with their like,
god killed the female and salted her for the feast of the
messiah.

The rabbis add that the bull Behemoth would be killed for
this meal. He is so large that he eats every day the hay of
1,000 mountains. The female of this bull was killed at the
beginning of the world in order to prevent so prodigious a
species to multiply, which could only have harmed the other
creatures. But they assure us that the eternal did not salt her,
because cow is not so good salted as she-Leviathan. The Jews
still have such faith in these rabbinical reveries that they
often swear by their share of the bull Behemoth.

After such gross notions about the coming of the *messiah*
and his reign, can we wonder that the Jews, both ancient and
modern, and even a number of the first Christians, could not
elevate themselves to the idea of the divine nature of the
lord's anointed, and did not attribute to the *messiah* the
quality of god? See how the Jews express themselves about it
in the work entitled *Judaei lusitani quæstiones ad Christianos*.[1]
'To acknowledge,' they say, 'a man-god is to delude oneself,
to fabricate a monster, a centaur, the bizarre compound of
two natures that cannot unite.' They add that the prophets do
not teach the *messiah* to be man-god, that they expressly distinguish between god and David, that they declare the first
to be master, and the second servant, etc.

It is well known that the Jews, great literalists, have never
penetrated, like us, the meaning of the scriptures.

1. *Note by Voltaire:* Questions 1, 2, 4, 23, etc.

When the saviour appeared, Jewish prejudices rose up against him. Jesus Christ himself appears extremely reserved in the matter of his divinity, so as not to shock their blind spirits: 'He wanted,' says saint Chrysostom, 'to accustom his listeners insensibly to believe a mystery so far above reason.' When he assumed the authority of a god in forgiving sins, this action aroused all those who are its witnesses. His most obvious miracles could not convince of his divinity even those on whose behalf he operated them. When he admitted before the tribunal of the sacrificing sovereign, with modest circumlocution, that he was the son of god, the high priest tore his robe and talked of blasphemy. Before the coming of the holy ghost the apostles did not even suspect the divinity of their master. He asked them what the people thought of him. They answered that some took him for Elijah, others for Jeremiah, or for some other prophet. Saint Peter required a personal revelation to recognize that Jesus was the Christ, the son of the living god.

The Jews, rebellious against the divinity of Jesus Christ, had recourse to all sorts of methods to destroy this great mystery. They distorted the meaning of their own oracles, or did not apply them to the *messiah*. They alleged that the name of god, *Elohi*, was not peculiar to the divinity, and was even applied by the sacred authors to judges, to magistrates, in general to those raised up in authority. They cite, in fact, a very large number of passages in the holy scriptures which justify this observation, but which in no way derogate from the express terms of the ancient oracles concerning the *messiah*.

Finally they claim that if the saviour, and after him the evangelists, the apostles and the first Christians, called Jesus the son of god, this august term meant in apostolic times no more than the opposite of son of Belial, that is, a good man, a servant of god, in opposition to a wicked man, a man who does not fear god.

The Jews not only contested Jesus Christ's status as the *messiah* and his divinity, they also neglected nothing to make him contemptible, to heap on his birth, his life and his death all the ridicule and all the opprobrium their criminal tenacity could invent.

Of all the works produced by the blindness of the Jews, there is none more odious and more extravagant than the old book entitled *Sepher toldos Jeschut*,[1] saved from the dust by m. Wagenseil in the second volume of his work entitled *Tela ignea*, etc.

It is in this *Sepher toldos Jeschut* that we read a monstrous history of the life of our saviour, fabricated with all possible animus and bad faith. For instance, they dared write that one Panther or Pandera, an inhabitant of Bethlehem, fell in love with a young woman married to Iochanan. From this impure intercourse came a son who was named Jesua or Jesu. The father of this child was obliged to flee, and went to Babylon. As for the young Jesu, he was sent to school; but, adds the author, he had the insolence to raise his head and to uncover it before the sacrificers, instead of appearing before them with lowered head and covered face, as was the custom: a boldness for which he was sharply scolded. This led to an investigation into his birth, which was found to be impure, and soon exposed him to ignominy.

This detestable book *Sepher toldos Jeschut* has been known since the second century. Celsus quotes it with confidence and Origen refutes it in his ninth chapter.

There is another book, also entitled *Toldos Jeschut*,[2] edited in 1705 by m. Huldrich, which follows more closely the gospel of the infancy, but which is filled with the grossest anachronisms and mistakes. It records Jesus Christ as born and dying in the reign of Herod the great. It alleges that it was to this prince that were made the complaints about the adultery of Panther and Mary, mother of Jesus. The author, who takes the name of Jonathan, describes himself as a contemporary of

---

1. This anonymous life of Jesus was first published by Johann Christoph Wagenseil in a book pleasantly entitled *Tela ignea satanae. Hoc est: arcani, & horribilis Judaeorum adversus Christum deum, & christianam religionem libri* 'ανεκδοτοι (Altdorfi Noricorum, 1681).

2. J. J. Haldricus [Huldrich], ed., *Historia Jeschuae Nazareni, a Judæis blaspheme corrupta* (Lugd[uni] Bat[avorum], 1705).

Jesus Christ living in Jerusalem, and asserts that Herod submitted the case of Jesus Christ to the senators of a town in the province of Caesarea. I shall leave there an author so absurd in all his contradictions.

Nevertheless it is by means of all these calumnies that the Jews sustain their implacable hatred of Christians and the gospel. They have neglected no opportunity to garble the chronology of the *Old Testament*, and to spread doubts and difficulties about the coming of our saviour.

Ahmad ibn Kasim, the Andalusian, a Moor from Granada, who lived towards the end of the sixteenth century, cites an ancient Arabic manuscript found in a cave near Granada with sixteen strips of lead engraved with Arabic characters. Dom Pedro y Quinones, archbishop of Granada, testified to it. These leaden strips from Granada, as they are called, were later taken to Rome, where, after an examination lasting several years, they were finally condemned during the pontificate of Alexander VII as apocryphal. They contain only fabulous stories about the life of Mary and her son.

The name of *messiah*, accompanied by the epithet *false*, is still given to the impostors who at various times tried to deceive the Jewish nation. Some of these false messiahs appeared even before the coming of the true anointed god. The wise Gamaliel speaks[1] of one Theudas, whose history can be read in the *Jewish antiquities* of Josephus, book XX, Chapter II. He boasted of crossing the Jordan with dry feet. He drew many people to follow him, but the Romans happening on his little flock, dispersed it, cut off the head of the wretched leader, and exposed it in Jerusalem.

Gamaliel also speaks of Judas, the Galilean, who is no doubt the same one to whom Josephus refers in the twelfth chapter of the second book of the *Jewish Wars*. He says that this false prophet had assembled nearly 30,000 men; but hyperbole characterizes the Jewish historian.

By apostolic times was seen Simon, called the magician,[2]

1. *Note by Voltaire: Acts of the Apostles*, chapter v, verses 34, 35, 36.
2. *Note by Voltaire: Acts of the Apostles*, chapter viii, verse 9.

who had succeeded in beguiling the inhabitants of Samaria to such a point that they regarded him as the power of god.

In the following century, in the years 178 and 179 of the Christian era, in the reign of Hadrian, the false messiah Barcochebas appeared at the head of an army. The emperor sent Julius Severus, who, after several encounters, confined him to the town of Bether, which was taken after a stubborn siege. Barcochebas was captured there and put to death. Hadrian thought that he could best forestall the constant rebellions of the Jews by forbidding them by edict to go to Jerusalem. He even posted guards at the gates of the city to prevent access to it by the remnants of the people of Israel.

In Socrates, ecclesiastical historian,[1] we can read that in the year 434 there appeared in the island of Candia a false messiah whose name was Moses. He said that he was the ancient liberator of the Hebrews, resuscitated to free them again.

A century later, in 530, there was a false messiah in Palestine called Julian. He proclaimed himself a great conqueror who, at the head of his nation, would destroy the whole of the Christian people by force of arms. Beguiled by his promises the Jewish armies massacred a number of Christians. The emperor Justinian sent troops against him, the false christ was engaged in battle, he was taken and condemned to the extreme penalty.

At the beginning of the eighth century Serenus, a Spanish Jew, pretended to be the messiah, preached, had disciples, and died wretchedly like them.

Several false messiahs arose in the twelfth century. One appeared in France under Louis the young. He and his adherents were hanged, without the names of the master and the disciples ever becoming known.

The thirteenth century was fertile in false messiahs. We can count seven or eight who appeared in Arabia, Persia, Spain, Moravia. One of them, whose name was David el Re, is thought to have been a very great magician. He beguiled the

1. *Note by Voltaire:* Socrates, *Histoire ecclésiastique*, book II, chapter XXXVIII. [This writer is usually called Socrates Scholasticus.]

Jews, and found himself at the head of a considerable party.
But this messiah was murdered.

Jacques Ziegler, of Moravia, who lived in the middle of the
sixteenth century, announced the manifestation at an early date
of the messiah who had been born, he asserted, fourteen
years earlier. He had seen him, he said, at Strasbourg, and he
carefully guarded a sword and a sceptre to put into his hands
as soon as he was old enough to teach.

In the year 1624 another Ziegler confirmed the prediction
of the first.

In the year 1666 Sabbatai Zebi, born in Aleppo, claimed to
be the messiah foretold by the Zieglers. He started by preaching on the highways in the heart of the country. The Turks
laughed at him, while his disciples admired him. It would
appear that at first he failed to win over the greater part of the
Jewish nation, since the leaders of the synagogue at Smyrna
sentenced him to death. But he was let off with a fight and
banishment.

He contracted three marriages, and it is alleged that he
consummated none, saying that this was beneath him. He
took one Nathan Levi as an associate. This man took the role
of the prophet Elijah, who was expected to precede the
messiah. They went to Jerusalem, and there Nathan announced Sabbatai Zebi as the liberator of the nation. The
Jewish populace accepted them; but those who had something to lose anathematized them.

To flee the storm Zebi retired to Constantinople, and thence
to Smyrna. Nathan Levi sent him four ambassadors, who
acknowledged and publicly saluted him as the messiah. This
embassy impressed the people and even some scholars, who
declared Sabbatai Zebi messiah and king of the Hebrews. But
the synagogue of Smyrna condemned its king to be impaled.

Sabbatai placed himself under the protection of the cadi of
Smyrna, and soon had the whole of the Jewish people behind
him. He had two thrones erected, one for him, and the other
for his favourite spouse. He took the name of king of kings,
and gave Joseph Zebi, his brother, that of king of Judah. He
promised the Jews the conquest of the Ottoman empire as a

certainty. He pressed his insolence so far as to have the name of the emperor removed from the Jewish liturgy, and to have his own substituted.

He was imprisoned at the Dardanelles. The Jews gave out that his life was spared only because the Turks well knew that he was immortal. The governor of the Dardanelles grew rich on the presents the Jews lavished on him to visit their king, their imprisoned messiah, who conserved all his dignity in irons, and made them kiss his feet.

Nevertheless the sultan, who held court at Adrinople, wanted to end this comedy. He sent for Zebi and told him that if he was a messiah he must be invulnerable. Zebi agreed. The grand signior put him up as a target for the arrows of his icoglans. The messiah admitted that he was not invulnerable, and protested that god had sent him only to testify to the holy Moslem religion. Thrashed by the minions of the law, he turned Mohammedan, and lived and died despised alike by Jews and Moslems: which so much discredited the profession of false messiah that Zebi was the last to appear.[1]

Métamorphose, métempsychose: Metamorphosis, metempsychosis

Is it not quite natural that all the metamorphoses seen on earth led in the east, where everything has been imagined, to the notion that our souls pass from one body to another? A nearly imperceptible speck becomes a worm; this worm becomes a butterfly. An acorn is transformed into an oak, an egg into a bird. Water becomes cloud and thunder. Wood changes into fire and ashes. In short, everything in nature appears to be metamorphosed. What was physically seen in the crudest bodies was soon extended to souls, which were regarded as light forms. The idea of metempsychosis is perhaps the most ancient dogma of the known universe, and it still reigns in a large part of India and China.

It is also very natural that all the metamorphoses we witness

1. Voltaire attributed this essay to Polier de Bottens.

should have produced those ancient fables which Ovid collected in his admirable works. Even the Jews had their metamorphoses. If Niobe was changed to marble, Edith, wife of Loth, was changed into a statue of salt. If Eurydice remained in hell because she looked behind her, it is for the same indiscretion that the wife of Loth was deprived of human nature. The little town in which lived Baucis and Philemon was changed into a lake; the same thing happened to Sodom. The daughters of Anius changed water to oil; in the scriptures we have almost the same metamorphosis, but truer and more sacred. Cadmus was changed into a serpent; Aarod's rod also became a serpent.

The gods very often changed themselves into men. The Jews never saw the angels in any but human form: the angels ate with Abraham. In his *Epistle to the Corinthians* Paul says that the angel of Satan slapped him: *Angelos Satana me colaphiset*.[1]

Miracles

A miracle, in the full meaning of the word, is an admirable thing. In this sense everything is miraculous. The prodigious order of nature, the rotation of 100 million globes around a million suns, the activity of light, the life of animals are perpetual miracles.

By conventional usage we call miracle the violation of these divine and eternal laws. If there is an eclipse of the sun at full moon, if a dead man walks two leagues carrying his head in his arms, we call that a miracle.

Several natural philosophers maintain that in this sense there are no miracles; and here are their arguments.

A miracle is the violation of the divine, immutable, eternal laws of mathematics. By this very definition a miracle is a contradiction in terms. A law cannot be at once immutable and violated. But, they are asked, cannot god suspend a law established by himself? They have the hardihood to answer that it cannot, that it is impossible for a being infinitely wise

1. *2 Corinthians* xii. 7.

to have made laws in order to violate them. He could disturb his machine, they say, only to make it function better. Now it is clear that this immense machine is as good as he; being god, he could make it: if he saw that there would be imperfection because of the nature of the material, he dealt with it from the beginning; therefore he will never change anything in it.

Besides, god cannot do anything without a reason; and what reason could lead him to disfigure his own work for a time? They will be told that it is for the benefit of mankind. They reply that it must then be for the benefit of all men, for it is impossible to conceive that the divine nature would work for a few individual men, and not for the entire human species. In any case, the human species is not up to much: it is much less than a small ant-hill in comparison with all the beings that fill immensity. Now is it not the most absurd of follies to imagine that the infinite being would invert the eternal play of the immense engines which move the entire universe for the sake of three or four hundred ants on this little heap of mud?

But let us suppose that god wanted to distinguish a small number of men by particular favours: would he have to change what he established for ever and for everywhere? He certainly has not the least need for such a change, for such inconstancy, to favour his creatures: his favours are in his very laws. He has foreseen everything, arranged everything for them: all obey irrevocably the power he has impressed for ever on nature.

Why should god perform a miracle? To accomplish a given plan for a few living beings? He would then be saying: 'I have been unable to accomplish a certain plan by the manufacture of the universe, by my divine decrees, my eternal laws. I am going to change my eternal ideas, my immutable laws to try to perform what I could not accomplish with them.' It would be a confession of his weakness, and not of his power. It would seem to be the most inconceivable contradiction in him. Hence it is really to insult him (if men can insult god) to dare to attribute miracles to him, it is to say to him: 'You are a weak and inconsistent being.' It is therefore absurd to believe in miracles, it is as it were to dishonour the divinity.

These philosophers are pressed, they are told: 'You exalt in vain the immutability of the supreme being, the eternity of his laws, the regularity of his infinite worlds. Our little mud heap has seen an abundance of miracles, history is as full of prodigies as of natural events. The daughters of the high priest Anius changed whatever they chose into wheat, wine or oil. Athalida, daughter of Mercury, resuscitated several times. Aesculapius resuscitated Hippolytus. Hercules dragged Alcestis back from death. Heres returned to the world after passing a fortnight in hell. The parents of Romulus and Remus were a god and a vestal virgin. The Palladium fell from heaven in the city of Troy. The hair of Berenice became a constellation. The hut of Baucis and Philemon was changed into a superb temple. The head of Orpheus rendered oracles after his death. The walls of Thebes were built by the sound of a flute alone, in the presence of the Greeks. The cures performed in the temple of Aesculapius were innummerable, and we still have monuments covered with the names of the eye-witnesses of the miracles of Aesculapius.'

Give me the name of one people among whom incredible prodigies were not performed, especially when few knew how to read and write.

Freethinkers answer these objections only by laughing and shrugging their shoulders. But Christian philosophers say: 'We believe in the miracles operated in our holy religion. We believe them by faith and not by reason, to which we take great care not to listen, for it is well known that the reason must not utter a single word when faith speaks. We have a firm and entire belief in the miracles of Jesus Christ and the apostles, but you must permit us to doubt a little about some others. Permit us, for instance, to suspend our judgement about the story told by a simple man to whom the name of great has been given. He asserts that a little monk was so much accustomed to perform miracles that the prior finally forbade him to exercise his talent. The little monk obeyed; but, having seen a poor tiler falling from the top of a roof, he hesitated between the wish to save his life and holy obedience. He simply ordered the tiler to remain in the air until further notice, and ran to tell his prior how things stood. The prior gave him absolution of the sin he had committed in beginning a miracle without permission, and allowed him to finish it, provided that he stopped there and did not do it again. We agree with freethinkers that this story must be distrusted a little.'

But how do you dare to deny, they will be asked, that saint Gervase and saint Protasius appeared in a dream to saint Ambrose, and told him where their relics were to be found? that saint Ambrose unearthed them, and that they cured a blind man? Saint Augustine was then in Milan. It is he who reports this miracle. *Immenso populo teste*, says he in the *City of God*, Chapter XXII. This is one of the best attested miracles. Freethinkers say that they do not believe a word of it, that Gervase and Protasius appeared to nobody, that it matters very little to mankind whether the whereabouts of the remnants of their carcasses be known or not, that they have no more faith in this blind man than in Vespasian's, that it is a useless miracle, that god does nothing useless; and they hold firmly to their principles. My respect for saint Gervase and saint Protasius does not permit me to share the opinion of these freethinkers. I merely report their incredulity. They make much of the passages in Lucian, in his *Death of Peregrinus*: 'When a deft juggler becomes a Christian he is bound to make his way.' But as Lucian is a profane author he should have no authority for us.

These freethinkers cannot bring themselves to believe the miracles operated in the second century. It is in vain that eye-witnesses write that saint Polycarp, bishop of Smyrna, having been condemned to be burned and thrown into the flames, they heard a heavenly voice crying out: 'Courage, Polycarp! be strong, show yourself a man'; that the flames of the pyre then parted from the body and formed a tent of fire above his head, and a dove came out of the midst of the pyre. At last they had to cut off Polycarp's head. 'What was the good of this miracle?' ask the incredulous. 'Why did the flames lose their nature, and not the executioner's axe? Why is it that so many martyrs have emerged safe and sound from boiling oil, and could not resist the edge of the sword?' They answer that it is the will of god. But the freethinkers would have liked to see all this with their own eyes before believing it.

Those who fortify their arguments with knowledge will tell you that the fathers of the church themselves have often admitted that no more miracles were performed in their times. Saint Chrysostom says expressly: 'The extraordinary gifts of the spirit were given even to the unworthy because the church then needed miracles; but today they are no longer given even to the worthy, because the church no longer needs them.' Then he admits that there is no longer anyone who resuscitates the dead, or even who cures the sick.

Saint Augustine himself, despite the miracle of Gervase and Protasius, says in his *City of God*: 'Why are the miracles that used to be performed no longer performed today?' And he gives the same reason: '*Cur, inquiunt, nunc illa miracula quae praedicatis facta esse non fiunt? Possem quidem dicere necessaria prius fuisse quam crederet mundus, ad hoc ut crederet mundus.*'[1]

It is objected to the freethinkers that saint Augustine, in spite of this admission, nevertheless mentions an old cobbler of Hippo who, having lost his clothes, went to pray in the chapel *of the twenty martyrs*. When he returned he found a fish in whose body was a gold ring, and the cook who prepared the fish said to the cobbler: 'This is what the twenty martyrs give you.'

To this the freethinkers answer that nothing in this story contradicts the laws of nature, that natural laws are not in the least offended by a fish who swallows a gold ring, and a cook who gives this ring to a cobbler, that this is no miracle.

If these freethinkers are reminded that according to saint Jerome, in his *Life of the Hermit Paul*, this hermit had several

1. 'Why', they ask, 'are the miracles that used to be done, as you boast, not now done? I could say that they were necessary before the world believed, so that the world should believe.'

conversations with satyrs and fauns, that a raven brought him every day for thirty years half a loaf for his dinner, and a whole loaf on the day saint Anthony called on him, they could again reply that all this is not absolutely against nature, that satyrs and fauns may have existed, and that in any case since this story is puerile, it has nothing in common with the true miracles of the saviour and of his apostles. Several good Christians have objected to the story by Theodoret about saint Simon Stylites. Many miracles that pass for authentic in the Greek church have been called in question by several Latin ones, just as some Latin miracles have been doubted in the Greek church. Then came the Protestants, who have much ill-treated the miracles of both churches.

A learned Jesuit[1] who preached a long time in the Indies complains that neither his colleagues nor he could ever perform a miracle. Xavier laments in several of his letters that he does not have the gift of tongues. He says that he is nothing but a dumb statue among the Japanese. Nevertheless the Jesuits have written that he resuscitated eight dead people: that's a lot, and we must also take into account that he resuscitated them 5,000 leagues from here. Since then some people have been known to say that the abolition of the Jesuits in France is a much greater miracle than those of Xavier and Ignatius.

Be that as it may, all Christians agree that the miracles of Jesus Christ and the apostles are incontestably veridical, but that we are entitled to doubt with all our strength some miracles done in recent times and which have not been positively authenticated.

For a miracle to be well established one would wish it to be performed in the presence of the Académie des Sciences of Paris, or the Royal Society of London, and the faculty of medicine, supported by a detachment of the regiment of guards to control the crowd of people whose indiscretion might prevent the operation of the miracle.

One day a freethinker was asked what he would say if he saw the sun stop, that is, if the movement of the earth round

1. *Note by Voltaire:* Ospiniam, p. 230.

this body stopped, if all the dead resuscitated, and if the mountains in unison fell into the ocean, the whole to prove some important truth, such as versatile grace. 'What I would say?' answered the freethinker. 'I would turn Manichean; I would say that there is one principle which undoes what the other has done.'

Moïse: Moses

Several learned men have held that the *Pentateuch* cannot have been written by Moses.[1] They say that scripture itself proves that the first known copy was found in the time of king Josiah, and that this unique copy was brought to the king by the secretary Shaphan. Now by Hebrew computation there

1. *Note by Voltaire:* Was there really a Moses? If a man who gave orders to the whole of nature had really existed among the Egyptians, would not such prodigious events have played a leading part in the history of Egypt? Would not Sanchoniathon, Manetho, Megasthenes, Herodotus have spoken of him? The historian Josephus collected all possible evidence in favour of the Jews. He dared not say that any of the authors whom he cited had said a single word about the miracles of Moses. Really! the Nile was changed to blood, an angel slaughtered all the first-born in Egypt, the sea parted, its waters were suspended on the right and the left, and no author mentioned it! and the nations forgot these prodigies! and only a little nation of barbaric slaves told us these stories, thousands of years after the event!

Who then was this Moses who was unknown to the whole world until the moment a Ptolemy had the curiosity to have the writings of the Jews translated into Greek? For a great many centuries oriental fables attributed to Bacchus everything the Jews have said about Moses. Bacchus had crossed the Red Sea on dry feet, Bacchus had changed the waters into blood, Bacchus had every day worked miracles with his rod. All these events were sung in the Bacchic orgies before there was the slightest intercourse with the Jews, before it was so much as known whether this wretched people had books. Is it not probable in the highest degree that this people, so new, wandering for so long, so recently known, established so late in Palestine, took over the Phoenician fables with the Phoenician language, and embroidered them still further, as do all crude imitators? So poor a people, so ignorant, so unaware of all the arts, could it do anything but copy its neighbours? Is it not well known that everything was Phoenician, even to the name of *Adonai, Ihaho, Elohi* or *Eloa,* which means god in the Jewish nation?

were 1,167[1] years between Moses and this incident of the
secretary Shaphan, for god appeared to Moses in the burning
bush in the year of the world 2213 and the secretary Shaphan
published the book of the law in the year of the world 3380.
This book found in the reign of Josiah was unknown until
the return from the Babylonian captivity; and it is said that it
was Ezra, inspired by god, who brought all the sacred
scriptures to light.

But whether it was Ezra or another who composed this
book is absolutely indifferent since the book is inspired. It is
not said in the *Pentateuch* that Moses is its author. It would
therefore have been permissible to suppose that the divine
spirit had dictated it to some other man had the church not
decided that the book is by Moses.

Some adversaries add that no prophet has quoted the books
of the *Pentateuch*, and there is no question of them in the
psalms, nor in the book attributed to Solomon, nor in *Jeremiah*, nor in *Isaiah*, nor, in short, in any of the canonical
books of the Jews. The words corresponding to *Genesis*,
Exodus, *Numbers*, *Leviticus*, *Deuteronomy*, are not found in any
other work accepted by them as authentic.

Others, still more daring, have put the following questions:

1. In what language would Moses have written in a savage
desert? It could only have been in Egyptian, for from this
very book it can be seen that Moses and all his people were
born in Egypt. It is probable that they spoke no other
language. The Egyptians did not yet use papyrus: they engraved hieroglyphs on marble or wood. It is even said that
the tables of the commandments were engraved on stone.
Five volumes must therefore have been engraved on polished
stones, which required prodigious effort and time.

2. Is it likely that men skilled enough to engrave the five
books of the *Pentateuch* on marble or wood would have been
available in a desert in which the Jewish people had neither
shoemaker nor tailor, and in which the god of the universe
was obliged to work a continual miracle to preserve the Jews'

---

1. The first edition has 867, which may well have been Voltaire's mistake, for his arithmetic was always erratic.

old clothes and old shoes? It will be said that there were craftsmen enough to make a golden calf in one night, and then to reduce the gold to powder, an operation impossible in ordinary chemistry, which had not yet been invented; to build the tabernacle, which they embellished with thirty-four columns of brass with capitals of silver; to weave and embroider linen veils, hyacinth, purple and scarlet; but all this in itself reinforces the view of the adversaries. They reply that it would have been impossible to do such elaborate work in a desert, where everything was lacking; that they should have begun by making shoes and tunics, that those who lack necessities do not indulge in luxuries; and that it is a self-evident contradiction to say that there were metal-founders, engravers, embroiderers when they had neither clothes nor bread.

3. If Moses had written the first chapter of *Genesis* would all young people have been forbidden to read this first chapter? Would so little respect have been shown to the legislator? If it was Moses who had said that god punishes the iniquity of the fathers to the fourth generation, would Ezekiel have dared to say the contrary?

4. If Moses had written *Leviticus* could he have contradicted himself in *Deuteronomy*? *Leviticus* forbids a man to marry his brother's wife. *Deuteronomy* orders him to do so.

5. Would Moses have spoken in his book of towns which did not exist in his time? Would he have said that towns were west of the Jordan when from his point of view they were east of it?

6. Would he have assigned forty-eight towns to the Levites in a country in which there have never been ten towns, and in a desert in which he had always wandered without having a house?

7. Would he have prescribed rules for Jewish kings when not only did this people have no kings but held them in horror, and it was not probable that they would ever have any? Come! Moses gave precepts for the conduct of the kings who did not reign until 800 years after him, and said nothing for the benefit of the judges and pontiffs who succeeded him.

Does not this reflection lead us to believe that the *Pentateuch* was composed in the times of the kings, and that the cere- monies instituted by Moses had been merely a tradition?

8. Could he really have said to the Jews: 'I have made you leave the land of Egypt to the number of 600,000 warriors under the protection of your god'? Would the Jews not have answered him: 'You must have been very timid not to have led us against the Pharaoh of Egypt; he could not oppose us an army of 200,000 men. Egypt has never had that many soldiers in the ranks. We would easily have vanquished them, we would have been the masters of this country. What! the god who speaks to you butchered for our pleasure all the first-born of Egypt, which makes, to avenge us, 300,000 men dead in one night if there were 300,000 families in that country, and you didn't help your god! and you didn't give us this fertile country which couldn't be defended! you made us leave Egypt like thieves and cowards to perish in the desert, between the precipices and the mountains! You could at least have led us by the direct route to this land of Canaan to which we have no right, which you promised us, and which we haven't yet been able to enter.

'It would have been reasonable for us to travel from the land of Goshen along the Mediterranean to Tyre and Sidon. But you made us cross almost the whole of the isthmus of Suez, you made us re-enter Egypt, go up beyond Memphis, and we are now at Baal-Zephon, or the shore of the Red Sea, turning our backs to the land of Canaan, having walked eighty leagues in this Egypt we wanted to avoid, and finally close to perishing between the sea and Pharaoh's army!

'Had you wanted to deliver us to our enemies would you have taken another route and other measures? You say that god saved us by a miracle, the sea parted to let us pass, but after such a favour should we have been made to die of hunger and weariness in the horrible deserts of Etam, Kadesh- barnea, Marah, Elim, Horeb and Sinai? All our fathers perish in these frightful solitudes, and forty years later you tell us that god took particular care of our fathers!'

That is what these grumbling Jews, these unjust children

of Jewish vagabonds who died in the desert, could have said to Moses, if he had read them *Exodus* and *Genesis*. And what would they not have done and said when he came to the golden calf? 'What! you dare to tell us that your brother made a golden calf for our fathers when you were with god on the mountain, you who tell us once that you spoke with god face to face, and then that you saw him only from behind! Still, you were with this god, and your brother moulded a golden calf in a single day and gave him to us to worship; and, instead of punishing your unworthy brother, you make him our pontiff, and you order your Levites to butcher 23,000 men of your people! Would our fathers have tolerated this? Would they have let themselves be slaughtered like victims by bloodthirsty priests? You tell us that, not satisfied with this incredible butchery, you had another 24,000 of your wretched followers massacred because one of them had gone to bed with a Midianite, although you yourself married a Midianite. And you add that you're the kindest of men! A few more examples of this kindness and nobody would have been left!

'No, had you been capable of such cruelty, had you been able to practise it, you would have been the most barbarous of all men, and no suffering would have sufficed to expiate so strange a crime.'

These, more or less, are the objections made by scholars to those who think that Moses is the author of the *Pentateuch*. But they are answered that the ways of god are not those of men; that god tested, led and abandoned his people out of a wisdom unknown to us; that the Jews themselves have believed for more than 2,000 years that Moses is the author of these books; that the church which succeeded the synagogue, and which is also infallible, has settled this point of controversy, and that learned men should be silent when the church speaks.

Morale: Morality

I have just read these words in a fourteen-volume harangue
entitled *Histoire du Bas-Empire*:[1]

The Christians had morals; but the Pagans had none.

Ah! monsieur Le Beau, author of these fourteen volumes,
where did you find this nonsense? If so, what about the morals
of Socrates, Zaleucus, Charondas, Cicero, Epictetus, Marcus
Aurelius?

There is only one morality, monsieur Le Beau, just as there
is only one geometry. But, I shall be told, most men know
nothing of geometry. Yes, but everybody agrees as soon as it
is studied a little. Farmers, artisans, artists have not taken a
course in morality. They have read neither Cicero's *De finibus*
nor Aristotle's *Ethics*, but as soon as they reflect they are un-
wittingly Cicero's disciples: the Indian dyer, the Tartar
shepherd and the English sailor know justice and injustice.
Confucius did not invent a system of morality as one constructs a system in natural philosophy. He found it in the
hearts of all men.

This morality was in the heart of the praetor Festus when
the Jews urged him to condemn Paul to death because he had
brought strangers into their temple. 'Know,' he told them,
'that the Romans never condemn anyone without giving
him a hearing.' If the Jews lacked morality or failed to
observe it, the Romans knew it and honoured it.

There is no morality in superstition, it is not in ceremonies,
it has nothing in common with dogmas. It cannot be too
often repeated that all dogmas are different, and that morality
is the same among all men who use their reason. Therefore
morality comes from god like light. Our superstitions are
nothing but darkness. Reader, reflect, spread this truth, draw
your conclusions.

1. [Charles] Le Beau's *Histoire du Bas-Empire* (Paris, 1757–1817) eventually achieved twenty-nine volumes.

Nécessaire: Necessary

OSMIN: Aren't you saying that everything is necessary?

SELIM: If everything weren't necessary it would follow that god had made useless things.

OSMIN: That is, it was necessary for the divine nature to have made everything it made?

SELIM: I believe so, or at least I suspect it. There are people who think otherwise. I don't understand them. Perhaps they are right. I'm afraid of disputes about it.

OSMIN: Anyway I want to talk to you about another necessity.

SELIM: Which? Of what is necessary to an upright man to live? Of the wretchedness to which one is reduced when one lacks necessities?

OSMIN: No, for what is necessary for one isn't always necessary for another. It's necessary for an Indian to have rice, for an Englishman to have meat, a Russian needs furs, an African gauze materials. One man believes that he needs twelve coach horses, another limits himself to a pair of shoes, a third gaily walks barefoot. I want to talk to you about what is necessary for all men.

SELIM: It appears to me that god gave our species all it needed: eyes to see, feet to walk, a mouth to eat, an oesophagus to swallow, a stomach to digest, a brain to reason, organs to produce their kind.

OSMIN: How then does it happen that some men are born deprived of a part of these necessary things?

SELIM: It's because the general laws of nature have produced accidents, which have caused monsters to be born; but in general man is provided with all he needs to live in society.

OSMIN: Are there notions common to all men that help them to live in society?

SELIM: Yes. I have travelled with Paul Lucas,[1] and wherever I went I saw that people respected their fathers and mothers, felt it necessary to keep their promises, pitied the

1. He wrote books about his travels chiefly in the Near East.

oppressed innocent, hated persecution, looked upon liberty of thought as a natural right, and the enemies of this liberty as the enemies of mankind. Those who think differently appeared to me to be ill-balanced creatures, monsters like those born without eyes and hands.

OSMIN: Are these necessary things necessary always and everywhere?

SELIM: Yes, otherwise they wouldn't be necessary to mankind.

OSMIN: So a new belief was not necessary to our species. Men could live very well in society and accomplish their duties to god before they believed that Mohammed had frequent conversations with the angel Gabriel.

SELIM: Nothing is more obvious. It would be ridiculous to think that one couldn't have carried out one's duties as a man before Mohammed came into the world. It was not at all necessary for the human species to believe in the *Koran*. The world wagged before Mohammed just as it does today. If Mohammedanism had been necessary for the world it would have existed since the beginning of the world, it would have existed everywhere. God, who gave us all eyes to see his sun, would have given us all intelligence to see the truth of the Moslem religion. Therefore this sect is merely like practical laws that change according to time and place, like fashions, like the opinions of doctors, which succeed each other. So the Moslem sect cannot be essentially necessary to man.

OSMIN: But as it exists, god permitted it?

SELIM: Yes, as he permits the world to be filled with nonsense, errors and calamities. This doesn't mean that men are all essentially made to be stupid and unhappy.

OSMIN: What do you mean when you say: 'God permits?' Can nothing occur without his orders? To permit, to want and to do are they not for him the same thing?

SELIM: He permits crime, but doesn't commit it.

OSMIN: To commit a crime is to act against divine justice, to disobey god. Now god can't disobey himself, he can't commit a crime; but he so made man that he commits many. How does that come about?

SELIM: There are people who know that, but I'm not one of them. All I'm convinced of is that the *Koran* is ridiculous, although it contains some pretty good things here and there. The *Koran* is certainly not necessary to man. That's enough for me. I see clearly what is false, and I know very little what is true.

OSMIN: I thought you were going to instruct me, and you teach me nothing.

SELIM: Isn't it a lot to know the people who deceive you, and the gross and dangerous errors they utter?

OSMIN: I'd have reason to complain of a doctor who explained to me which plants are harmful, but never showed me a beneficial one.

SELIM: I'm not a doctor and you're not ill, but it seems to me that I should be giving you a very good prescription if I said to you: 'Beware of all the inventions of charlatans, worship god, be upright, and believe that two and two make four.'

Orgueil: Pride

In one of his letters Cicero says familiarly to his friend: 'Let me know to whom you would like me to give Gaul.' In another he complains that he is tired of the letters of various princes who thank him for having had their provinces elevated into kingdoms, and he adds that he does not even know where these kingdoms are.

It may be that Cicero, who of course had often been applauded and obeyed by the Roman people, a people that was sovereign, and who was thanked by kings he did not know, had some impulses of pride and vanity.

Although this feeling is not at all suitable for so puny an animal as man, we might nevertheless pardon it in a Cicero, a Caesar, a Scipio, but that at the far end of one of our semi-barbarous provinces a man who has bought a minor office and printed some mediocre verse, should take it into his head to be proud, that is enough to make us laugh loud and long.

Papisme (sur le): Dialogue, le papiste et le trésorier
On popery: Dialogue, the papist and the treasurer

THE PAPIST: His royal highness has Lutherans, Calvinists, Quakers, Anabaptists, and even Jews in his princedom; and you want him to admit also Unitarians!

THE TREASURER: If these Unitarians bring you their industry and their money, what harm can they do us? Your wages will be all the safer.

THE PAPIST: I admit that the withdrawal of my pay would be more painful to me than the admission of these gentlemen; but after all they don't believe that Jesus Christ was the son of god.

THE TREASURER: What does it matter, so long as you are permitted to believe it, and that you are well fed, well clothed, well housed? The Jews are far from believing that he is the son of god, and nevertheless you are quite happy to find Jews here with whom you invest your money at six per cent. Saint Paul himself never spoke of the divinity of Jesus Christ; he openly called him a *man*: 'Death,' he said, 'reigned through the sin of one *man*, the just will reign through one *man* who is Jesus. ... You belong to Jesus, and Jesus belonged to god.'[1] All your first fathers of the church thought like saint Paul. It is obvious that for three centuries Jesus contented himself with his humanity. Imagine that you're a Christian of the first three centuries.

THE PAPIST: But, sir, they don't believe in eternal punishment.

THE TREASURER: Neither do I. Be damned for ever if you like; as for me I don't in the least expect to be.

THE PAPIST: Well, sir, it's very hard not to be able to damn at will all the heretics in the world! But the mania of the Unitarians to make all souls happy one day is not the only thing that troubles me. You know that these monsters don't

1. *Romans* v. 12 and 17, much fragmented, the last words not being part of the text.

believe in the resurrection of the body any more than the Sadducees. They say that we are all cannibals, that the particles composing your grandfather and your great-grandfather, having necessarily been dispersed in the atmosphere, have become carrots and asparagus, and that it is impossible for you not to have eaten a few little bits of your ancestors.

THE TREASURER: So be it: my grandchildren will make the same use of me; it will be tit for tat, and the papists will do as much. That's no reason why you should be driven from his royal highness's state, nor is it a reason why he should drive the Unitarians from it. Resuscitate as you can. I care very little whether the Unitarians resuscitate or not, so long as they're useful to us when they're alive.

THE PAPIST: And what do you say, sir, of original sin, which they brazenly deny? Aren't you completely scandalized when they assert that the *Pentateuch* doesn't say a word about it, that the bishop of Hippo, saint Augustine, was the first who positively taught this dogma, although it was clearly indicated by saint Paul?

THE TREASURER: Upon my word, it isn't my fault if the *Pentateuch* doesn't speak of it. Why don't you add a little reference to original sin to the *Old Testament*, since you have added to it, it is said, so many other things? I understand nothing of these subtleties. My business is to pay your wages regularly when I have money . . .

Patrie: Fatherland

A fatherland is a composite of several families; and as we usually stand by our family out of self-love when we have no conflicting interest, so because of the same self-love we support our town or village, which we call our fatherland. The bigger the fatherland the less we love it, because divided love is weaker. It is impossible to love tenderly too numerous a family which we hardly know.

He who burns with ambition to become aedile, tribune, praetor, consul, dictator, cries out that he loves his country, and he loves only himself. Every man wants to be sure that he can sleep at home without another man arrogating to himself the power to make him sleep elsewhere. Every man wants to be sure of his fortune and his life. Thus, all having the same wishes, it turns out that private interest becomes the general interest: when we express our hopes for ourselves we are expressing them for the republic.

There cannot be a state on earth which was not first governed as a republic: it is the normal course of human nature. A few families first assembled against the bears and the wolves. The family which had grain exchanged it with that which had only wood.

When we discovered America we found all the tribes divided into republics. There were only two kingdoms in all this part of the world. Only two out of 1,000 nations were found to be subjugated.

So it was in the ancient world. All was republican in Europe before the petty kings of Etruria and Rome. Republics are still seen today in Africa. Tripoli, Tunis, Algeria, towards the north, still live as men are said to have lived in the first ages of the world, free, equal among themselves, without masters, without subjects, without money, and almost without needs. The flesh of their sheep feeds them, their skins clothe them, huts of wood and earth are their shelters. They stink worse than any other men, but do not know it. They live and die more calmly than we do.

Eight republics without monarchs remain in our Europe: Venice, Holland, Switzerland, Genoa, Lucca, Ragusa, Geneva and San Marino.[1] Poland, Sweden, England can be regarded as republics under a king; but Poland is the only one that takes the name.

Is it better today for one's country to be a monarchical or a republican state? This question has been debated for 4,000 years. Apply for a solution to the rich, they all prefer an aristocracy. Question the people, they want democracy. Only kings prefer a monarchy. How then is it possible that nearly the whole world is governed by monarchs? Ask the rats who

1. *Note by Voltaire:* Written in 1764.

proposed to hang a bell round the cat's neck.[1] But in truth the real reason is, as I have said,[2] that men are very seldom worthy to govern themselves.

It is sad that, to be a good patriot, one is often the enemy of the rest of humanity. The elder Cato, that good citizen, when speaking in the senate, always said: 'Such are my views, and let Carthage be destroyed.' To be a good patriot is to want one's city to be enriched by commerce and powerful in arms. It is obvious that a country cannot gain unless another loses, and that it cannot vanquish without causing unhappiness.

So it is the human condition that to wish for the greatness of one's fatherland is to wish evil to one's neighbours. The citizen of the universe would be the man who wishes his country never to be either greater or smaller, richer or poorer.

Paul: questions sur Paul:
Paul: questions about Paul

Was Paul a Roman citizen, as he boasts? If he was from Tarsus in Cilicia, Tarsus only became a Roman colony 100 years after him; all antiquaries are agreed about this. If he came from the little town or village of Gishala, as saint Jerome believed, that town was in Galilee, and the Galileans were certainly not Roman citizens.

Is it true that Paul entered the new-born society of Christians, who were then half-Jews, only because Gamaliel, whose disciple he had been, refused his daughter in marriage? It seems to me that this accusation is found only in the *Acts of the Apostles* acknowledged by the Ebionites, acts preserved and refuted by bishop Epiphanius in his thirtieth chapter.

Is it true that saint Thecla visited saint Paul dressed as a man? and are the *Acts* of saint Thecla admissible? Tertullian, in his book on baptism, chapter XVI, holds that his history

---

1. See Jean de La Fontaine, *Conseil tenu par les rats* (*Fables* II. ii).
2. *Essai sur les mœurs*, lxvii.

was written by a priest attached to Paul. Jerome and Cyprian, while refuting the fable of the lion baptized by saint Thecla, affirm the truth of these *Acts*. It is there that a rather strange portrait of Paul is found: 'He was fat, short, broad-shouldered; his black eyebrows met over his aquiline nose, his legs were crooked, his head bald, and he was filled with the grace of the lord.'

This is more or less as he is depicted in Lucian's *Philopatris*, waiving the grace of the lord, of which Lucian unfortunately had no knowledge.

Can Paul be excused for reproaching Peter for judaizing when he himself went judaizing in the temple of Jerusalem?

When Paul was arraigned by the Jews before the governor of Judea because he had brought strangers into the temple, was it right for him to tell this governor: 'Touching the resurrection of the dead I am called in question before you this day', when the resurrection of the dead was not the point at issue?[1]

Was it right for Paul to circumcise his disciple Timothy after he had written to the Galatians: 'If ye receive circumcision, Christ will profit you nothing.'[2]

Was it right for him to write to the Corinthians, chapter ix: 'Have we not the right to live at your expense and to bring a wife with us? ...'[3] Was it right for him to write to the Corinthians in his second epistle: 'I do say ... to them that I have sinned heretofore, and to all the rest, that ... I will not spare?'[4] What would be thought today of a man who claimed the right to live at our expense, he and his wife, to judge us, to punish us, and to confound the guilty and the innocent?

What is understood by the ravishment of Paul to the third heaven? What is a third heaven?

---

1. *Note by Voltaire: Acts of the Apostles*, chapter xxv [xxv. 21].
2. *Galatians* v. 2.
3. *1 Corinthians* ix. 4–5; Voltaire has reproduced the meaning rather than the actual words.
4. *2 Corinthians* xiii. 2.

Finally, which is the more probable (humanly speaking), that Paul become a Christian because he was thrown from his horse by a great light at midday, and because a celestial voice cried: 'Saul, Saul, why persecutest thou me?'[1]; or else that Paul was irritated against the Pharisees, either because of the refusal of Gamaliel to give him his daughter, or for some other reason? In any other story would not the refusal of Gamaliel appear more natural than a celestial voice, were we not obliged for other reasons to believe this miracle?

Every one of these questions is asked only for my instruction, and I insist that anyone who wishes to instruct me should speak rationally.

Péché original: Original sin

This is the alleged triumph of the Socinians and Unitarians. They call this foundation of the Christian religion its original sin. It is to offend god, they say, it is to accuse him of the most absurd barbarity, to dare to say that he made all the generations of men in order to torment them by eternal sufferings on the pretext that their first father ate some fruit in a garden. This sacrilegious imputation is all the more inexcusable in Christians because there is not a single word about this invention of original sin in the *Pentateuch* or the prophets or the gospels whether apocryphal or canonical, or in any of the writers who are called the first fathers of the church.

It is not even said in *Genesis* that god condemned Adam to death because he swallowed an apple. He did tell him: 'in the day that thou eatest thereof thou shalt surely die';[2] but this same *Genesis* makes Adam live 930 years after this criminal meal. The animals and plants which did not eat this fruit died in the time prescribed by nature. Man is born to die, like all the rest.

Besides the punishment of Adam formed no part of the Jewish law. Adam was no more a Jew than a Persian or a Chaldean. The first chapters of *Genesis* (whatever the period of their composition) were regarded by all Jewish scholars

1. *Acts* ix. 4, xxii. 7, xxvi. 14.   2. *Genesis* ii. 17.

as an allegory, and even as a very dangerous fable, since the reading of it was forbidden before the age of twenty-five.

In a word, the Jews knew original sin no better than Chinese ceremonies, and although theologians find whatever they want in the scriptures, *totidem verbis* or *totidem litteris*, it can be asserted that no reasonable theologian will ever find this surprising mystery in it.

Let us admit that saint Augustine was the first to authorize this strange idea, worthy of the fiery and romantic head of a debauched and repentant African, Manichean and Christian, indulgent and persecuted, who spent his life contradicting himself.

'Ho whorrible,' exclaim the strict Unitarians, 'to calumniate the author of nature to the point of imputing to him continual miracles in order to damn for ever men whom he has given life for so little time! Either he created souls from all eternity, and by this system, being infinitely older than Adam's sin, they have no connection with him. Or these souls are formed every time a man lies with a woman, and in that case god is continually on the watch for all the assignations in the universe in order to create the spirits whom he will make eternally unhappy. Or god is himself the soul of all men, and in that case he damns himself. Which of these three suppositions is the most horrible and most senseless? There is not a fourth, for the view that god waits for six weeks to create a damned soul in a foetus is equivalent to that which holds it to be created at the moment of copulation: what matter six weeks more or less?'

I have reported the view of the Unitarians, and men have attained to such profound superstition that I shuddered in reporting it.[1]

Persécution: Persecution

It is not Diocletian whom I would call a persecutor, for he protected the Christians for eighteen whole years; and if, in

1. *Terminal note by Voltaire:* This article is by the late m. Boulanger. [This, once again, is just Voltaire's fun.]

the last part of his reign, he did not rescue them from the resentment of Galerius, he was in that merely a prince, like so many others, seduced and drawn away by conspiracies from his true character.

Still less would I give the name of persecutors to Trajan and to Marcus Aurelius: I would feel like a blasphemer.

Who is a persecutor? It is he whose wounded pride and furious fanaticism irritate the prince or the magistrate against innocent men guilty only of the crime of holding different opinions. 'Impudent fellow, you worship a god; you preach virtue, and practise it; you have served mankind, and consoled it; you have found the orphan girl a home; you have helped the poor; you have changed the deserts in which a few slaves dragged out a wretched existence into a fertile countryside peopled with happy families. But I have discovered that you despise me, and that you have never read my published disputation; you know that I am a rascal; that I have forged the handwriting of G—; that I have stolen —; you might well say so; I must forestall you.[1] So I shall go to the prime minister's confessor, or the podesta. I'll demonstrate to them, inclining my head and twisting my mouth, that you had erroneous views about the cells in which the seventy[2] were locked up; that ten years ago you even talked about Tobias's dog in a manner by no means respectful, maintaining that it was a spaniel although I proved that it was a greyhound; I'll denounce you as the enemy of god and men.' Such is the language of the persecutor; and if these words don't exactly leave his mouth, they're engraved in his heart with the burin of fanaticism dipped in the gall of envy.

Thus did the Jesuit Le Tellier persecute cardinal de Noailles, and Jurieu persecute Bayle.

When the persecution of the Protestants began in France, it was not Francis I nor Henry II nor Francis II who spied on these unfortunates, who took arms against them with deliberate fury, and who consigned them to the flames to wreak their vengeance on them. Francis I was too busy with the

1. This picture of the persecuted man is a fragment of autobiography.
2. That is, the translators of the *Septuagint*.

duchesse d'Etampes, Henry II with his old Diana, and Francis II was too young. Who started these persecutions? Jealous priests, who armed the prejudices of the magistrates and the politic manoeuvres of the ministers.

Had the kings not been deceived, had they foreseen that the persecution would cause fifty years of civil war, and that half the nation would be exterminated by the other half, their tears would have quenched the first pyres they allowed to be lit.

O god of mercy! if any man can resemble this malignant being who is depicted as ceaselessly busy in destroying your works, is it not the persecutor?

Philosophe: Philosopher

Philosopher, *lover of wisdom*, that is, *of truth*. All philosophers have had this double character: there is none in antiquity who has not given men examples of virtue and lessons in moral truth. They may all have been wrong about natural philosophy, but this is so little needed for the conduct of life that the philosophers could dispense with it. Centuries were needed to know a part of the laws of nature. A day is enough for a wise man to know the duties of man.

The philosopher is not an enthusiast, he does not set himself up as a prophet, he does not claim to be inspired by the gods. So I would not include among the philosophers the ancient Zoroaster, nor Hermes, nor the ancient Orpheus, nor any of the legislators boasted by the nations of Chaldea, Persia, Syria, Egypt and Greece. Those who called themselves children of the gods were the fathers of imposture, and if they used lies to teach truths they were unworthy to teach them, they were not philosophers: they were at most very careful liars.

By what fatality, perhaps shameful for western nations, is it necessary to go to the extreme east to find a simple sage, without ostentation, without imposture, who taught men to live happily 600 years before our common era, at a time when the entire north knew nothing of the alphabet, and the Greeks had hardly begun to distinguish themselves by wisdom? This sage was Confucius, who, alone among the ancient legislators, never sought to deceive mankind. What finer rules of conduct have ever been given on earth?

'Regulate a state as you regulate a family; a man can govern his family well only by setting an example.'

'Virtue must be common to the labourer and the monarch.'

'Make it your business to forestall crime in order to diminish the need to punish it.'

'Under the good kings Yao and Xu the Chinese were good; under the bad kings Kye and Chu they were wicked.'

'Do to others as to yourself.'

'Love men in general, but cherish those who are good. Forget wrongs, never kindnesses.'

'I have seen men incapable of learning, I have never seen any incapable of virtue.'[1]

We must admit that no legislator has enunciated truths more useful to mankind.

A crowd of Greek philosophers later taught an equally pure morality. Had they limited themselves to their unreal systems of nature their names would be spoken today with mockery. If they are still respected it is because they were just, and taught men to be just.

One cannot read certain passages in Plato, and above all the admirable exordium of the laws of Zaleucus, without feeling in one's heart the love of upright and generous actions. The Romans have their Cicero, who alone is perhaps worth all the philosophers of Greece. After him came men still more worthy of respect, but whom we almost despair to imitate: the slave Epictetus, Marcus Aurelius and Julian on the throne.

What citizen in our midst would deprive himself, like Julian, Antoninus and Marcus Aurelius, of all the delicacies of our soft and effeminate life? Who, like them, would sleep hard? Who would impose their frugality on himself? Who would march like them on foot and bareheaded at the head of

1. Again these exact words are not found; this is not surprising when it is considered that these texts are here given in English through French, Latin and Chinese successively.

the armies, now exposed to the heat of the sun, now to the cold of winter? Who like them would master all his passions? There are pious men among us; but where are the wise ones? where are the unflinching, just and tolerant souls?

There have been closet philosophers in France; and all, except Montaigne, were persecuted. It seems to me that it is the final degree of the malignity of our nature that we seek to oppress the very philosophers who want to correct it.

I can readily understand that the fanatics of one sect should slaughter the enthusiasts of another, that the Franciscans hate the Dominicans, and that a bad artist conspires to ruin one who surpasses him. But that the life of the wise Charron should have been threatened, that the learned and generous Ramus should have been assassinated, that Descartes should have been obliged to flee to Holland to escape the fury of the ignorant, that Gassendi should several times have been forced to retire to Digne, far from the calumnies of Paris: that is the eternal obloquy of a nation.

One of the most persecuted philosophers was the immortal Bayle, the honour of the human race. I shall be told that the name of Jurieu, his calumniator and persecutor, has become execrable; I admit it. So has that of the Jesuit Le Tellier; but have the great men whom he oppressed any the less ended their days in exile and want?

One of the pretexts used to crush Bayle and to reduce him to poverty was his article on 'David' in his useful dictionary. He was reproached for not having praised actions which in themselves were unjust, bloody, atrocious, or dishonourable, or which make modesty blush.

In fact Bayle did not praise David for having assembled, according to the Hebrew books, 600 vagabonds ruined by debts and crimes, for having plundered his compatriots at the head of these bandits; for having planned to butcher Nabal and all his family because he refused to pay David's exactions; for having betrayed this king Achish; for having massacred even the children at the breast in these villages, for fear lest one day someone might make his depredations known, as if a child at the breast could have revealed his crime; for having made to perish all the inhabitants of some other villages with saws, iron harrows, iron hatchets, and in brick kilns; for having ravished his throne from Ishbosheth, son of Saul, by perfidious means; for having despoiled and put to death Mephibosheth, the grandson of Saul and the son of his friend and protector Jonathan; for having delivered up to the Gibeonites two of Saul's other children, and five of his grandchildren, who died on the gallows.

I say nothing of David's prodigious incontinence, of his concubines, of his adultery with Bathsheba, and of the murder of Uriah.

So then would Bayle's enemies have wished him to praise all these cruelties and all these crimes? Should he have said: 'Princes of the world, imitate the man who was after god's heart; massacre without pity your benefactor's allies; slaughter all your king's family, or have it slaughtered; lie with all the women while you cause the blood of the men to be shed; and you will be a model of virtue when some psalms are attributed to you.'

Was not Bayle perfectly right to say that if David was after god's heart it was because of his penitence and not his crimes? Did not Bayle render mankind a service in saying that god, who no doubt dictated the whole Jewish history, has not endorsed all the crimes reported in that history?

Yet Bayle was persecuted, and by whom? By men persecuted elsewhere, by fugitives who would have been consigned to the flames in their own country; and these fugitives were combated by other fugitives called Jansenists, driven from their country by the Jesuits, who were finally expelled in their turn.

Thus all the persecutors declared mortal war on each other, while the philosopher, oppressed by them all, contented himself with pitying them.

It is not well enough known that in 1713 Fontenelle was on the point of losing his pensions, his office, his freedom because twenty years earlier he had edited in France the *Traité des oracles* of the learned van Dale, from which he had carefully eliminated everything that might alarm fanaticism. A Jesuit had written against Fontenelle; he did not deign to reply; and that was enough to induce the Jesuit Le Tellier, the confessor of Louis XIV, to accuse Fontenelle to the king of atheism. But for monsieur d'Argenson it would have come about that Corneille's nephew would have been outlawed in his old age by the worthy son of a forger, an attorney at Vire, himself known to be a forger.

It is so easy for a confessor to seduce his penitent that we should bless god that Le Tellier did not do greater harm. There are two refuges in the world where seduction and calumny cannot be resisted: the bed and the confessional.

We know that philosophers have always been persecuted by fanatics; but is it possible that writers should dabble in this, and themselves sharpen against their brethren the arms that pierce them one after another?

Wretched writers! is it for you to become informers? Consider whether the Romans ever had a Garasse, a Chaumeix, a Hayer, who accused a Lucretius, a Posidonius, a Varro, a Pliny.

To be a hypocrite, how vile! but to be a hypocrite and wicked, how horrible! There were never any hypocrites in ancient Rome, which regarded us as a small section of its subjects. There were scoundrels, I admit, but not religious hypocrites, who are the most cowardly and the most cruel of all. Why is there none in England, and how is it that there are still some in France? Freethinkers, it will be easy for you to resolve this problem.[1]

Pierre: Peter

In Italian, Piero or Pietro; in Spanish, Pedro; in Latin, Petrus; in Greek, Petros; in Hebrew, Cepha.

Why have the successors of Peter had so much power in the west and none in the east? This is like asking why the bishops

1. Voltaire begins this essay with philosophers, and finishes with *philosophes* in the specialized sense, that is, with freethinkers. François Garasse, Abraham Joseph de Chaumeix and Jean Nicolas Hayer were prominent ecclesiastics in anti-freethought polemics.

of Wurzburg and Salzburg assumed regalian rights in times of anarchy, while the Greek bishops have always remained subjects. Time, opportunity, the ambition of some and the weakness of others have done and will do everything in this world.

The common opinion was added to this anarchy, and opinion is the queen of men: not that in reality they have clearly defined opinions, but words take their place.

It is reported in the gospel that Jesus said to Peter: 'I will give unto thee the keys of the kingdom of heaven.'[1] The partisans of the bishop of Rome maintained about the eleventh century that he who gives the greater gives also the lesser, that the heavens envelop the earth, and that, Peter having the keys of the container, had also the keys of the content. If by the heavens be understood all the stars and all the planets, it is evident according to Thomasius, that the keys given to Simon Bar-Jona, called Peter, formed a master-key. If by the heavens be understood the clouds, the atmosphere, the ether, the space in which revolve the planets, there are no locksmiths, according to Meursius, who can make a key for such doors as those.

In Palestine keys were wooden pegs tied with a strap. Jesus said to Bar-Jona: 'Whatsoever thou shalt bind on earth shall be bound in heaven.'[1] The pope's theologians have concluded from this that the popes had received the right to bind people to the oath of fidelity made to their kings, and to unbind them from it, and to dispose as they please of all the kingdoms. It is a magnificent conclusion. In the estates general of France of 1302 the communes said in their petition to the king, that 'Boniface VIII is a b— who believed that god binds and imprisons in heaven what this Boniface binds on earth.' A famous Lutheran in Germany (I think it was Melanchthon) had great difficulty in swallowing that Jesus said to Simon Bar-Jona, Cepha or Cephas: 'Thou art Peter, and upon this rock I will build my assembly, my church.'[2] He

1. *Matthew* xvi. 19.
2. *Matthew* xvi. 18; the English versions have lost the pun of the Greek and Romance texts: in French Pierre is Peter and *pierre* means stone.

could not believe that god could have used such a play on words, so extraordinary a jest, and that the power of the pope should be based on a pun.

Peter was thought to have been bishop of Rome, but it is well known that at that time and for long after there was no individual see. Christian society only took shape at about the end of the second century.

It is possible that Peter made the journey to Rome; it is even possible that he was crucified head down, although that was not the practice; but there is no proof of all that. We have a letter under his name in which he says that he is in Babylon: judicious canonists have maintained that by Babylon we should understand Rome. Hence if he had dated the letter from Rome we could have concluded that it had been written in Babylon. Such inferences have long been drawn, and so has the world been regulated.

There was a saintly man who had been made to pay dearly for a benefice in Rome. This is called simony. He was asked whether he believed that Simon Peter had been in Rome. He answered: 'I don't know about Peter, but Simon certainly has.'

As for Peter personally, it must be admitted that Paul was not the only one who was shocked by his behaviour. He and his successors have often and openly been resisted. Paul bitterly reproached him for eating forbidden flesh, that is, pork, black pudding, hare, eel, ixion and griffin. Peter defended himself by saying that he had seen the heavens open about the sixth hour, and a great cloth descend from the four corners of the sky, filled with eels, quadrupeds and birds, and that the voice of an angel had cried out: 'Kill and eat.' This is apparently the same voice, says Wollaston, that has cried to so many pontiffs: 'Kill everything, and eat the substance of the people.'

Casaubon could not approve the way in which Peter treated the good Ananias and his wife Sapphira. By what right, asks Casaubon, did a Jew, slave of the Romans, order or allow all those who believed in Jesus to sell their inheritance and put the proceeds at his feet? If some Anabaptist in London made his brethren lay all their money at his feet, would he not be arrested as a traitorous seducer, a robber who would infallibly be sent to Tyburn? Was it not horrible to put Ananias to death because, without saying anything, he held back a few crowns for his necessities and those of his wife when he sold his property and gave the money to Peter? His wife arrived when Ananias had only just died. Peter, instead of warning her mercifully that he had just caused her husband to die of an apoplexy for keeping a few oboles, and telling her to take care of herself, made her fall into the trap. He asked whether her husband had given all his money to the saints. The good woman answered yes, and died on the spot. What harshness!

Coringius[1] asks why Peter, who thus killed those who gave him alms, did not rather kill all the theologians who had caused the death of Jesus Christ, and had him scourged more than once. O Peter! you kill two Christians who gave you alms, and you allow to live those who crucified your god!

Coringius evidently was not living in any of the homes of the inquisition when he put these daring questions. Erasmus noticed a very peculiar thing in connection with Peter: it is that the head of the Christian religion began his apostolate by denying Jesus Christ, and that the first pontiff of the Jews had begun his ministry by making a golden calf, and worshipping it.

Be that as it may, Peter is depicted as a poor man who catechized the poor. He is like those founders of orders who lived in indigence, and whose successors have become great lords.

The pope, Peter's successor, now won, now lost; but apart from his immediate subjects, about 50 million men on earth remain to him, subject in various ways to his laws.

To acknowledge a master three or four hundred leagues away; to wait before you think until that man has seemed to think; dare to give a final verdict only through commissioners appointed by this foreigner in a law-suit between your own fellow citizens; not dare to take possession of the

1. Hermann Conring, a seventeenth-century German polymath.

fields and vineyards secured from one's own king without paying considerable sums to this foreign master; violate the laws of one's country, which prohibit a man from marrying his niece, yet does so legitimately by giving his foreign master a still greater sum; not dare to cultivate one's field on whatever day this foreigner requires one to celebrate the memory of an unknown whom he has sent to heaven by his private authority: this is part of what it means to acknowledge a pope, these are the liberties of the Gallican church.

Some other peoples carry their submission further. In our own day we have seen a sovereign[1] ask the pope's permission to have some monks accused of parricide tried by his royal tribunal, failing to obtain this permission, and not daring to judge them.

It is well known that formerly the rights of the popes went further. They were far above the gods of antiquity, for these gods were merely said to dispose of empires, and the popes really did dispose of them.

Sturbinus[2] says that those who doubt the pope's divinity and infallibility can be forgiven when it is considered:

that forty schisms have profaned the seat of saint Peter, and that twenty-seven have steeped it in blood;

that Stephen VII, son of a priest, disintered the body of his predecessor Formosus, and had the corpse's head cut off;

that Sergius III, convicted of murders, had a son, by Marozia, who inherited the papacy;

that John X, the lover of Theodora, was strangled in his bed;

that John XI, son of Sergius III, was known only as a debauchee;

that John XII was murdered in his mistress's house;

that Benedict IX bought and resold the pontificate;

that Gregory VII was the initiator of 500 years of civil war sustained by his successors;

that finally, among so many ambitious, bloody and de-

1. Joseph II, king of Portugal.
2. Voltaire maintained a high level of accuracy in his references; here the printer has probably deformed Sturmius (Joannes).

bauched popes, there was an Alexander VI, whose name is spoken with the same horror as that of Nero and Caligula.

It is said that it is evidence of the divine nature of the papacy that it has survived so many crimes; but then the caliphs would have been even more divine had they behaved even more atrociously. This is the reasoning of Dermius,[1] but the Jesuits have answered him.

Préjugés: Prejudices

A prejudice is an irrational opinion. Thus throughout the world all sorts of opinions are instilled into children before they are able to use judgement.

There are universal and necessary prejudices, which constitute virtue itself. In all countries children are taught to acknowledge a god who rewards and avenges; to respect and love their fathers and mothers; to regard theft as a crime, selfish lying as a vice, before they can imagine what is a vice and a virtue.

There are therefore very good prejudices: they are those ratified by the judgement when one is able to reason.

Feeling is not mere prejudice, it is something much stronger. A mother does not love her son because she has been told that she must love him: she happily cherishes him despite herself. It is not out of prejudice that you run to help an unknown child about to fall into a precipice or to be devoured by an animal.

But it is out of prejudice that you respect a man dressed in a certain way, who behaves solemnly and talks in the same way. Your parents told you that you should bow to this man. You respect him before you know whether he deserves your respect. You grow in age and knowledge. You perceive that this man is a charlatan eaten up with pride, selfishness and guile. You despise what you revered, and prejudice yields to judgement. Out of prejudice you believed the fables with which your childhood was deluded. You were told that the Titans made war on the gods and that Venus was in love with

1. He appears to be unknown to fame.

Adonis. When one is twelve one takes these fables for truths, at twenty-one regards them as ingenious allegories.

Let us examine in a few words the different kinds of prejudices, so as to put our affairs into order. We shall perhaps be like those who, at the time of Law's system, realized that they had been counting on imaginary wealth.

PREJUDICES OF THE SENSES

Is it not an odd thing that our eyes always deceive us, even when we see very well, but that on the contrary our ears do not deceive us? If your ear is in good order and hears: 'You're beautiful, I love you', it is quite certain that you were not told: 'I hate you, you're ugly.' But you see a smooth mirror, and it has been proved that you are mistaken, that in fact it has a very uneven face. The sun has a diameter of about two feet to your eyes. It has been proved to be a million times bigger than the earth.

It seems that god has put the truth into your ears and error into your eyes; but study optics and you will see that god has not deceived you, and that in the present state of things it is impossible for objects to appear to you otherwise than they do.

PHYSICAL PREJUDICES

The sun rises, so does the moon, the earth is immobile: these are natural prejudices concerning the physical world. But that crayfish are good for the blood because they too are red when boiled; that eels cure paralysis because they quiver; that the moon influences illnesses because it was once observed that a patient's fever increased during the waning of the moon: these notions, and a thousand more, were the errors of ancient charlatans, who concluded without reasoning, and who, being deceived, deceived others.

HISTORICAL PREJUDICES

Most histories have been believed without investigation, and this credulity is a prejudice. Fabius Pictor tells us that several centuries before his time a vestal going to draw water in her pitcher, in the town of Elba, was raped, that she gave birth to Romulus and Remus, that they were suckled by a she-wolf, etc. The Roman people believed this fable. They did not inquire whether there had been vestals in Latium at that time, whether it was credible that the daughter of a king should leave her convent with her pitcher, whether it was probable that a she-wolf should suckle two children instead of eating them. The prejudice established itself.

A monk wrote that Clovis, being in great danger at the battle of Tolbiac, vowed to become a Christian if he got through it safely. But is it natural to address oneself to an alien god at such a time? Is it not then that the religion in which one was born acts most powerfully? What Christian, in a battle against the Turks, would not address himself to the holy virgin rather than to Mohammed? It is also said that a pigeon brought the holy ampulla in its beak for the anointment of Clovis, and that an angel brought the oriflamme to guide him. Prejudice believed all the anecdotes of this kind. Those who know human nature are well aware that the usurper Clovis and the usurper Rolon or Rol became Christians in order more easily to control the Christians, just as the Turkish usurpers became Moslems more easily to control the Moslems.

RELIGIOUS PREJUDICES

If your nurse told you that Ceres presides over corn, or that Vishnu and Xaca have several times taken human form, or that Sammonocodom came to cut down a forest, or that Odin is waiting for you in his hall somewhere in Jutland, or that Mohammed or somebody else made a journey into heaven; if then your tutor drove into your brain what your nurse engraved there, you will keep hold of it for life. Should your

judgement seek to rise above these prejudices, your neighbours, above all the women, scream impiety and frighten
you. Your dervish, fearing to see his income diminish,
accuses you to the cadi, and his cadi has you impaled if he
can, because he wants to command fools, and believes that
fools obey better than others. And that will last until your
neighbours and the dervish and the cadi begin to understand
that folly is worthless and that persecution is abominable.

Prêtre: Priest

Priests are in a state more or less what tutors are in the
homes of its citizens: employed to teach, pray, and set an
example. They can have no authority over the masters of the
house unless it can be proved that he who pays the wages must
obey him who receives them.

The religion of Jesus is unquestionably that which most
positively excludes priests from all civil authority: 'Render
unto Caesar the things that are Caesar's.'[1] 'Among you there
is neither first nor last.'[2] 'My kingdom is not of this world.'[3]

The quarrels between empire and priesthood which have
bloodied Europe for more than six centuries have therefore
been no more on the part of the priests than rebellions against
god and men, and a continual sin against the holy ghost.

From Calchas, who murdered the daughter of Agamemnon,
down to Gregory XIII[4] and Sixtus V, two bishops of Rome
who tried to deprive the great Henry IV of the kingdom of
France, sacerdotal power has been disastrous to the world.

Prayer is not domination, exhortation is not despotism. A
good priest should be the physician of souls. Had Hippocrates ordered his patients to take hellebore on penalty of
being hanged, Hippocrates would have been madder and
more barbarous than Phalaris, and he would not often have
been consulted. When a priest says: 'Worship god, be just,

1. *Matthew* xxii. 21; *Mark* xxii. 17; *Luke* xx. 25.
2. *Mark* ix. 35, etc.
3. *John* xxiii. 36.
4. This should be XII.

indulgent, compassionate', then he is a very good doctor. When he says: 'Believe me or you will be burned', he is a murderer.

The magistrate should sustain and restrain the priests, as the head of the household should respect the tutor of his children and prevent him from taking advantage of that respect. The accord of priesthood and empire is the most monstrous of systems: the search for this accord necessarily implies a division. We should say: the protection given by the empire to the priesthood.

But what should be done in countries in which the priesthood has become the empire, as in Salem, where Melchisedek was priest and king, as in Japan, where the *dairo* was for so long the emperor? I reply that the successors of Melchisedek and the *dairos* were dispossessed.

The Turks are wise in this respect. It is true that they journey to Mecca; but they do not allow the sherif of Mecca to excommunicate the sultan. They do not go to Mecca to buy permission not to observe *ramadan*, and to marry their cousins or their nieces. They are not judged by imans delegated by the sherif. They do not pay the last year of their revenues to the sherif. What things could be said about all this! Reader, it is for you to say them to yourself.

Prophètes: Prophets

The prophet Jurieu was hissed, the prophets of the Cévennes were hanged or broken on the wheel, the prophets who came to London from the Languedoc and the Dauphiné were pilloried, the Anabaptist prophets were condemned to various punishments, the prophet Savonarola was roasted in Florence, the prophet John the baptizer or baptist had his throat cut.

It is alleged that Zacharias was murdered, but happily this has not been proved. The prophet Jeddo or Addo, who was sent to Bethel on condition that he would neither eat nor drink, having unfortunately eaten a piece of bread, was eaten in his turn by a lion; and his bones were found on the highway, between this lion and his ass. Jonah was swallowed by a fish. It is true that he remained in its belly for only three days and three nights, but still it was a very uncomfortable seventy-two hours.

Habakkuk was carried by the hair to Babylon by air. It is true that this is not a great misfortune, but it is a very inconvenient form of transport. It must be very painful to hang by one's hair for 300 miles. I should have preferred a pair of wings, the mare Borak, or the hippogriff.

Micaiah, son of Imlah, saw the lord seated on his throne with the army of heaven to right and left, and, the lord having asked for somebody to go to cheat king Ahab, the devil presented himself to the lord and undertook the commission. Micaiah reported this celestial incident to king Ahab on behalf of the lord. It is true that his reward was to receive a swingeing slap from the hands of the prophet Zedekiah. It is true that he was thrown into a dungeon only for a few days. But still it is disagreeable for a man inspired to be smacked and crammed into an oubliette.

It is thought that king Amaziah had the prophet Amos's teeth drawn to prevent him from talking. In fact it is not absolutely impossible to speak without teeth. Very talkative old and toothless ladies have been known. But a prophecy must be pronounced distinctly, and a toothless prophet is not listened to with the respect that is his due.[1]

Baruch suffered much persecution. Ezekiel was stoned by his companions in slavery. It is not known whether Jeremiah was stoned or sawed in two. As for Isaiah, it is generally accepted that he was sawed by order of Manasseh, a kinglet of Judah.

It must be agreed that the prophet's craft is a wretched one. For an odd one who, like Elijah, rides about from planet to planet in a fine chariot of light drawn by four white horses, a hundred go on foot and are obliged to seek their dinner from door to door. They somewhat resemble Homer, who was obliged, it is said, to beg in the seven towns which have since disputed for the honour of witnessing his birth. His

[1]. Voltaire could never resist a good joke: by this time he had lost his teeth.

commentators have attributed to him endless allegories he never thought of. The same honour has often been done to the prophets. I do not gainsay that there have been people fully informed about the future. One need only give one's soul a certain degree of exaltation, as has been admirably conceived by the honest philosopher[1] or fool in our days who wanted to pierce a hole to the antipodes, and wanted to smear the sick with resin. The Jews exalted their souls so well that they very clearly saw all futurity: but it is difficult to make out precisely whether by Jerusalem the prophets always understood eternal life; whether Babylon means London or Paris; whether when they talk about a stately dinner it should be interpreted a fast; whether red wine means blood; whether a red cloak means faith, and a white cloak charity. It is the grand effort of human intelligence to understand the prophets. That is why I shall say no more about it.

Religion

FIRST QUESTION

The bishop of Worcester, Warburton, author of one of the most learned works[2] ever written, says this on page 8 of the first volume: 'Whatsoever religion and society have no future state for their support, must be supported by an extraordinary Providence. The Jewish religion and society had no future state for their support; therefore the Jewish religion and society were supported by an extraordinary Providence.'

Several theologians objected, and as all arguments can be twisted, his was turned against him; he was told: 'Every religion which is not founded on the immortality of the soul and on eternal punishments and rewards is necessarily false; now Judaism did not know these dogmas; therefore Judaism, far from being supported by providence, was, on your

---

1. Maupertuis, who, if he was not so great a philosopher as he thought himself, was by no means so great a fool as Voltaire thought him.

2. *The Divine Legation of Moses*; Voltaire possessed the 1738–41, 1755 and 1758 editions; his translation is very accurate, and I have therefore reproduced Warburton's original text.

principles, a false and barbarous religion which attacked providence.'

This bishop had some other adversaries who maintained against him that the immortality of the soul was known among the Jews, even in Moses's time. But he proved to them quite positively that neither the decalogue nor *Leviticus* nor *Deuteronomy* said a single word about this belief, and that it is ridiculous to try to twist and corrupt some passages in the other books to extract from them a truth which is not announced in the book of the law.

His lordship the bishop, having written four volumes to prove that the Judaic law offered neither punishments nor rewards after death, could never answer his adversaries in a quite satisfactory way. They told him: 'Either Moses knew this dogma, and in that case he deceived the Jews by not proclaiming it; or he did not know it, and in that case he was too ignorant to found a good religion. In fact, had the religion been good why should it have been abolished? A true religion must be for ever and for everywhere. It must be like the light of the sun, which illuminates all peoples and all generations.'

This prelate, enlightened as he was, had a lot of trouble getting out of these difficulties; but what system is exempt from them?

SECOND QUESTION

Another much more philosophical scholar, who is one of the most profound metaphysicians of our times, gives powerful reasons to prove that polytheism was mankind's first religion, and that several gods were first believed in before reason was enlightened enough not to recognize more than one supreme being.

I venture to think, on the contrary, that men first acknowledged a single god, and that human weakness later adopted several; and this is how I see it.

It is indubitable that there were hamlets before big towns were built, and that all mankind was divided into little republics before these were assembled into great empires. It is perfectly natural that a little township, frightened of thunder, afflicted by the loss of its harvests, ill-treated by the neighbouring hamlet, feeling its weakness every day, sensing an invisible power everywhere, should soon have said: 'There is some being over us who brings us good and evil.'

It seems to me impossible that it said: 'There are two powers.' For why several? One always begins with the simple, then comes the complex, and by superior enlightenment one often reverts in the end to the simple. Such is the course of human intelligence.

What is this being that was first invoked? Would it have been the sun? would it have been the moon? I think not. Let us consider what happens in children: they are more or less the same as ignorant men. They are struck neither by the beauty nor the usefulness of the star that animates nature, nor by the help the moon gives us, nor by the regular variations of its path: they give no thought to these things, for they are too used to them. We worship, we invoke, we try to appease only what we fear. All children see the sky with indifference, but they tremble and hide themselves when it thunders. The first men undoubtedly behaved in the same way. Only philosophers of a sort noticed the movements of the stars, and caused them to be admired and worshipped. But simple and unenlightened husbandmen were too ignorant to embrace so noble an error.

Therefore a village would have been content to say: 'There is a power that thunders, that makes hail fall on us, that kills our children. We must appease it, but how? We see that we can calm the anger of irritated folk by means of little presents. Let us therefore give presents to this power. And of course we must also give it a name. The first that suggests itself is *chief*, *master*, *lord*; this power is therefore called *my lord*. This is probably why the first Egyptians called their god Knef, the Syrians Adonai, the neighbouring peoples Baal or Bel or Melch or Moloch, the Scythians Papee: all words meaning lord, master.

This is why nearly the whole of America was found to be divided into a multitude of little clans, each of which had its protective god. Not even the Mexicans or the Peruvians, who were great nations, had more than one god: the one worshipped Manko Kapac, the other the god of war. The Mexicans gave the name Vitzliputzli to their warrior god, just as the Hebrews had called their lord Sabaoth.

It is not because of superior and cultivated intelligence that all people began in this way by acknowledging a single divinity. Had they been philosophers, they would have worshipped the god of all nature, and not the god of a village. They would have studied the infinite relations between beings, which prove a creative and preservative being, but they studied nothing, they felt. That is the progress of our feeble understanding: each township felt its weakness and its need of a powerful protector. It conceived this tutelary and terrible being as living in the near-by forest or on the mountain or in a cloud. It conceived only one because the hamlet had only one war-chief. It imagined him to be corporeal because it was impossible for it to conceive him otherwise. It could not believe that the neighbouring settlement did not also have its god. That is why Jephtah said to the Moabites: 'You legitimately possess what your god Chemosh has made you conquer; you should let us enjoy what our god has given us by his victories.'[1]

This discourse addressed by one foreigner to other foreigners is very remarkable. The Jews and the Moabites had dispossessed the country's natives; both of them had no right but that of force, and one says to the other: 'Your god has protected you in your usurpation, permit my god to protect me in mine.'

Jeremiah and Amos both ask by what right the god Melchom seized the country of Gad. It appears to be clear from these passages that antiquity attributed a protective god to each country. Traces of this theology can still be found in Homer.

It is quite natural that, men's imaginations having become heated and their minds having acquired confused knowledge, they should soon have multiplied their gods, and assigned

1. *Judges* xi. 24, a very free version.

protectors to the elements, the seas, the forests, the fountains, the countryside. The more they scrutinized the stars the more they would have been struck with admiration. How can one help but worship the sun when one worships the divinity of a stream? Once the first step was taken the earth was soon filled with gods; and finally men came down from heavenly bodies to cats and onions.

Nevertheless reason was bound to improve. Time at last produced philosophers who saw that neither onions nor cats nor even the heavenly bodies had organized nature. All these Babylonian, Persian, Egyptian, Scythian, Greek and Roman philosophers acknowledged one supreme god, rewarder and avenger.

They did not immediately tell the people, for anyone who spoke badly about onions and cats in front of old women and priests would have been stoned. Anyone who reproached certain Egyptians for eating their gods would have been eaten himself, as in fact Juvenal reports that an Egyptian was killed and eaten raw during a doctrinal dispute.[1]

But what was done? Orpheus and others established mysteries, which the initiates swore with execrable oaths not to reveal, and the main point of these mysteries was the worship of a single god. This great truth spread over half the earth; the number of initiates became immense. It is true that the ancient religion survived; but as it was not contrary to the dogma of the uniqueness of god, it was allowed to survive. And why should it have been abolished? The Romans acknowledged *Deus optimus maximus*; the Greeks had their Zeus, their supreme god. All the other divinities were only intermediary beings. Heroes and emperors were placed amid the gods, that is, the blessed; but it is certain that Claudius, Octavius, Tiberius and Caligula were not regarded as the creators of heaven and earth.

In a word, it appears to be proved that in the time of Augustus all those who had a religion acknowledged one god, superior and eternal, and several orders of secondary gods, whose worship was later called idolatry.

1. Juvenal xv. 78–83.

The laws of the Jews never favoured idolatry; for, although they admitted *malakkim*, angels, celestial beings of an inferior order, they did not command that these secondary divinities be worshipped. They worshipped the angels, it is true, that is, they prostrated themselves when they saw them; but as that did not happen often no ceremonial nor legal cult was established for them. The cherubim of the ark received no homage. It is definite that the Jews openly worshipped a single god, as the innumerable crowd of initiates secretly worshipped him in their mysteries.

THIRD QUESTION

It was at this time, when the worship of one supreme god was universally established among all wise men in Asia, Europe and Africa, that the Christian religion was born. Platonism greatly helped in the understanding of its dogmas. The *Logos* which in Plato signified wisdom, the intelligence of the supreme being, became for us the word and a second person of god. A profound metaphysic beyond human comprehension was an inaccessible sanctuary in which religion was hidden.

I shall not repeat here how Mary was later declared to be the mother of god, how the consubstantiality of the father and the word was established, together with the procession of the *pneuma*, divine organ of the divine *logos*, two natures and two wills resulting from hypostasis, and finally the superior manducation, the soul as well as the body nourished by the parts and the blood of the man-god worshipped and eaten in the form of bread, present to the eyes, perceptible to the taste, and nevertheless annihilated. All the mysteries were sublime.

The casting out of demons in the name of Jesus started by the second century. Previously they were expelled in the name of Jehovah or Ihaho, for saint Matthew tells us that the enemies of Jesus having said that he cast out demons in the name of the prince of the demons, he replied: 'If I by Beelzebub cast out devils, by whom do your sons cast them out?'[1]

1. *Matthew* xii. 27.

It is not known when it was that the Jews acknowledged Beelzebub, who was a foreign god, as the prince of demons; but it is known (and it is Josephus who tells us) that in Jerusalem there were exorcists appointed to expel the demons from the bodies of the possessed, that is, men attacked by peculiar maladies, which were then attributed, in a large part of the world, to maleficent genii.

So these demons were expelled by the correct pronunciation, now lost, of Jehovah, with other now forgotten ceremonies. This exorcism by Jehovah or by the other names of god was still in use in the first centuries of the church. Origen, disputing with Celsus, tells him, number[1] 262: 'If in invoking god or in swearing by him you name him the god of Abraham, of Isaac and of Jacob, you will operate certain things by these names, whose nature and power are such that the demons submit to those who pronounce them. But if you name him by another name, such as god of the noisy sea or supplanter, these names will have no virtue. The name Israel translated into Greek can achieve nothing, but pronounce it in Hebrew, with the other words required, and you will operate the conjuration.'

The same Origen has these remarkable words at number[2] 19: 'There are names which by nature have virtue, such as those used by the Egyptian sages, the Persian magi, the Brahmans in India. What is called magic is not a vain and chimerical art as alleged by the Stoics and the Epicureans. The names Sabaoth and Adonai were neither of them made for created beings: they form part of a mysterious theology connected with the creator, hence the efficacy of these names when they are arranged and pronounced in the proper manner' etc.

In speaking thus Origen is not expressing his personal opinion, he merely reports the universal view. All the religions then known acknowledged a kind of magic, and

1. Or rather, page; although Voltaire possessed only a French translation of 1700, the reference here is to Ὠριγενης κατα κολσου (Cantabrigiae, 1677), lib. 5; Voltaire's translations are not literal.
2. Or rather, page 19; as in the previous note, lib. 1.

celestial and infernal magic, necromancy and theurgy were distinguished. Everything was prodigy, divination, oracle. The Persians did not deny the miracles of the Egyptians, nor the Egyptians those of the Persians. God permitted the first Christians to believe in the oracles attributed to the sybils, and left them a few other errors of little importance, which did not corrupt the basis of the religion.

Another very remarkable thing is that the Christians of the first two centuries loathed temples, altars and images. Origen admits this, number[1] 374. All this changed later, when discipline came in, when the church received its permanent form.

FOURTH QUESTION

Once a religion is legally established in a state, the tribunals are all busy to prevent the renewal of most of the things that were done in that religion before it was accepted publicly. The founders had met in secret despite the magistrates; now only public assemblies under law are permitted, and all association in secret is forbidden.

The ancient maxim was that it is better to obey god than men; the contrary maxim is now accepted, that to follow the laws of the state is to obey god. There was talk about nothing but obsessions and possessions: the devil was then unloosed on earth. Today the devil no longer leaves his dwelling-place. Prodigies and predictions were then necessary: they are no longer admitted. A man who publicly predicted calamities would be sent to Colney Hatch. The founders secretly received money from the faithful: a man who now collected money and disposed of it without being authorized by the law would be arrested. Thus no part of the scaffolding that served to build the edifice is any longer used.

FIFTH QUESTION

After our holy religion, which is undoubtedly the only good one, which would be the least bad?

1. Or rather, page; as in note 5, lib. 7.

Would it not be the simplest? Would it not be that which taught much morality and very little dogma? that which tended to make men just without making them absurd? that which did not order one to believe in things that are impossible, contradictory, injurious to divinity, and pernicious to mankind, and which dared not menace with eternal punishment anyone possessing common sense? Would it not be that which did not uphold its belief with executioners, and did not inundate the earth with blood on account of unintelligible sophisms? that in which an ambiguity, a play on words and two or three forged charters would not make a sovereign and a god, out of an often incestuous, murderous and poisoning priest? that which did not subject kings to this priest? which taught only the worship of one god, justice, tolerance and humanity?

SIXTH QUESTION

It has been said that the religion of the gentiles was absurd in several respects, contradictory, pernicious; but has not more evil been imputed to it than it ever did and more folly than it preached?

> *Car de voir Jupiter taureau,*
> *Serpent, cygne, ou quelque autre chose,*
> *Je ne trouve point cela beau,*
> *Et ne m'étonne pas si parfois on en cause.*[1]

That is no doubt very impertinent, but show me in all antiquity a temple dedicated to Leda lying with a swan or a bull. Was a sermon ever preached in Athens or Rome to encourage girls to have children with their farmyard swans? Do the fables collected and adorned by Ovid form a religion? Do they not resemble our *Golden legend*, our *Flower of the saints*? If some Brahman or some dervish protested against our story of saint Mary the Egyptian, who, when she could

---

1. Molière, *Amphitryon*, prologue: 'For to see Jupiter as a bull, snake, swan, or something else, I don't find that very nice, and I'm not surprised that it is sometimes gossiped about.'

not pay the sailors who had brought her to Egypt, gave each one what are called favours instead of money, we would say to the Brahman: 'Reverend father, you are making a mistake, our religion is not the *Golden legend*.'

We reproach the ancients for their oracles, their prodigies. If they returned to earth and it were possible to count the miracles of our lady of Loretto and those of our lady of Ephesus, to whose advantage would the balance be struck?

Human sacrifice was established among nearly all peoples, but was very seldom practised. Only Jephthah's daughter and king Agag were immolated by the Jews, for Isaac and Jonathan were spared. Among the Greeks the story of Iphigenia is not well authenticated. Human sacrifice is very rare among the ancient Romans. In a word, very little blood was shed by the pagan religion, and ours has covered the earth with it. Ours is no doubt the only good, the only true one; but we have done so much evil by means of it that we should be modest when we talk about other religions.

SEVENTH QUESTION

If a man wants to convert foreigners or compatriots to his religion, should he not go about it with the most insinuating gentleness and the most winning moderation? If he begins by saying that what he asserts has been proved, he will encounter a crowd of the incredulous. If he dares to tell them that they reject his doctrine only in so far as it condemns their passions, that their hearts have corrupted their minds, that their intelligence is no more than false and proud, he revolts them, arouses them against him, and himself ruins what he wants to establish.

If the religion he announces is true, will transports of rage and insolence make it any truer? Should one lose one's temper while saying that people should be gentle, patient, beneficent, just, and fulfil all the duties of society? No, because everybody agrees with you. Why then do you insult your brother when you preach a mysterious metaphysic to him? It is because his good sense irritates your vanity. Your pride requires your brother to subject his intelligence to yours. Humiliated pride produces anger, it has no other source. A man wounded by twenty musket-shots in a battle does not lose his temper. But a theologian wounded by a refusal to assent becomes enraged and implacable.

EIGHTH QUESTION

Should not state religion and theological religion be carefully distinguished? The former requires imans to maintain registers of the circumcised, and priests or ministers registers of the baptized; that there be mosques, churches, temples, days devoted to worship and rest, rites established by law; that the ministers of these rites be given respect without power; that they teach good behaviour to the people, and that the ministers of the law watch over the behaviour of the ministers of the temples. Such a state religion can never make trouble.

This is not true of theological religion. This is the source of all imaginable follies and disorders; it is the mother of fanaticism and civil discord; it is the enemy of mankind. A bonze asserts that Fo is a god; that he was predicted by fakirs; that he was born to a white elephant; that every bonze can create a Fo by making faces. A talapoin says that Fo was a holy man whose doctrine has been corrupted by the bonzes, and that it is Sammonocodom who is the true god. After a hundred assertions and a hundred denials, the two factions agree to refer the matter to the dalai lama, who lives 300 leagues away, and who is immortal and even infallible. The two factions send him a solemn deputation.

The dalai lama begins, as is his divine custom, by sharing out his close-stool. At first the two rival sects receive it with equal respect, dry it in the sun, and enshrine it in little rosaries which they kiss devoutly. But as soon as the dalai lama and his council pronounce the name of Fo, the condemned party throws the rosaries in the vice-god's face, and tries to give him a hundred strokes of the whip. The other party defends its lama, from whom it has received handsome estates. The two fight for a long time, and when they are tired of exterminating, murdering, poisoning each other, they still hurl insults at each other. The dalai lama laughs at all this, and continues to distribute his close-stool to anyone who is agreeable to receiving the good father lama's excrement.

Résurrection: Resurrection

I

It is said that the Egyptians built their pyramids only to use them as tombs; and that their bodies, embalmed inside and outside, waited for their souls to revive them after a thousand years. But if their bodies were to resuscitate why was the perfumers' first operation to pierce the skull with a small hook and to extract the brain? The idea of resuscitating without a brain makes one suspect (if this word may be used) that the Egyptians had none when they lived; but we must consider that most of the ancients believed that the soul is in the chest. And why is the soul in the chest rather than elsewhere? It is because, when undergoing any violent emotion, we do in fact experience a dilation or constriction in the region of the heart, that people came to think that the soul's lodging-place was there. This soul was an airy thing; it was a light figure that wandered where it could until it rediscovered its body.

The belief in resurrection goes back far beyond history. Athalida, daughter of Mercury, could die and resuscitate at will; Aesculapius brought Hippolytus back to life; Hercules revived Alcestis; Pelops, having been hacked to pieces by his father, was resuscitated by the gods; Plato tells us that Heres resuscitated for only a fortnight.

The Pharisees, among the Jews, did not adopt the dogma of resurrection until very long after Plato.

In the *Acts of the Apostles* is recorded a very odd incident, most worthy of attention. Saint James and several of his companions advised saint Paul, Christian though he was, to go to the temple of Jerusalem to observe the ceremonies of the ancient law, 'so that all may know', they said, 'that all that is said of you is false, and that you continue to keep the law of Moses'. This was to say quite clearly: 'Go and lie, go and perjure yourself, go and disown publicly the religion you teach.'

So saint Paul went to the temple for seven days, but on the seventh day he was recognized. He was accused of coming there with strangers and of having profaned it. This is how he got out of trouble.

'But when Paul perceived that the one part were Sadducees, and the other Pharisees, he cried out in the council, Brethren, I am a Pharisee, a son of Pharisees: touching the hope and resurrection of the dead I am called in question.'[1] There had been no question whatever in all this affair of the resurrection of the dead; Paul said this only to animate the Pharisees and the Sadducees against each other.

v. 7. And when he had so said, there arose a dissension between the Pharisees and the Sadducees: and the assembly was divided.

v. 8. For the Sadducees say that there is no resurrection, neither angel, nor spirit: but the Pharisees confess both.

It has been alleged that Job, whose story is very ancient, knew the dogma of the resurrection. These words are cited:

> But I know that my redeemer liveth,
> And that he shall stand up at last upon the earth:
> And after my skin hath been thus destroyed,
> Yet from my flesh shall I see God.[2]

But several commentators understand by these words that Job hopes that he will soon recover from illness, and that he will not always remain lying on the earth. What follows shows conclusively that this explanation is correct, for a moment later he exclaims to his false and hard-hearted friends: 'Why then do you say: let us persecute him' or 'Because you will say: Because we have persecuted him'?[3] Does this not

---

1. *Note by Voltaire: Acts of the Apostles,* chapter xxiii, verses 6, 7, 8.
2. *Job* xix. 25–6.
3. *Job* xix. 28; the Revised version reads: 'If ye say, How we will persecute him!'

obviously mean: 'You will regret having offended me when you see me once again well and opulent'? A sick man who says: 'I will get up', does not say: 'I will resuscitate.' To give clear passages arbitrary meanings is the surest way of preventing people from understanding each other, or rather of being regarded by honest people as people of bad faith.

Saint Jerome situates the birth of the sect of Pharisees a very short time before Jesus Christ. Rabbi Hillel is taken to be the founder of the Pharisaic sect, and this Hillel was the contemporary of Gamaliel, the teacher of saint Paul.

Some of these Pharisees believed that only the Jews would resuscitate, and that the rest of mankind was not worthy of it. Others maintained that resuscitation would take place only in Palestine and that the bodies of those who were buried elsewhere would be secretly transported to Jerusalem to be reunited with their souls. But saint Paul, writing to the inhabitants of Thessalonia, told them that 'the second coming of Jesus Christ is for them and for him, that they will be witnesses of it'.

v. 16. For the Lord himself shall descend from heaven, with a shout, with the voice of the archangel, and with the trumps of God: and the dead in Christ shall rise first.

v. 17. Then we that are alive, that are left, shall together with them be caught up in the clouds, to meet the Lord in the air: and so shall we ever be with the Lord.[1]

Does not this important passage prove clearly that the first Christians expected to see the end of the world, as is in fact foretold in saint Luke for the very time in which saint Luke lived? If they did not see this ending of the world, if nobody was resuscitated at that moment, what is deferred is not lost.

Saint Augustine thought that children, even still-born children, would resuscitate as adults. Origen, Jerome,

1. *Note by Voltaire:* Epistle to the Thessalonians, chapter iv. [*1 The salonians* iv. 16–17; the preceding passage is not a direct quotation.]

Athanasius, Basil did not believe that women would keep their sex when they resuscitated.

In short, what we were, what we are, and what we will be has always been a matter of dispute.

II

Father Malebranche proves the resurrection by caterpillars that become butterflies. It can be seen that this proof has as little weight as the wings of the insects from which he takes it. Thoughtful calculators advance arithmetical objections against this amply demonstrated truth. They say that men and other animals are really nourished by the substance of their predecessors, and get their growth from it. The body of a man, reduced to dust, scattered in the air, and falling back on the surface of the earth becomes a vegetable wheat. Thus Cain ate a part of Adam; Enoch fed on Cain; Irad on Enoch; Mahalaleel on Irad; Methuselah on Mahalaleel; and so it happens that not one of us but has swallowed a small portion of our first father. This is why it has been said that we are all anthropophagous. Nothing strikes one more forcibly after a battle. Not only do we kill our brothers, but after two or three years, when the field of battle has been harvested, we eat them all. Nobody will make any difficulty about eating us in our turn. How then, when we have to resuscitate, shall we return to each the body that belonged to him without losing some of our own?

That is what is said by those who have doubts about resurrection; but the resurrectors have answered them very pertinently.

A rabbi named Samai proves resurrection by this passage from *Exodus*: 'I appeared to Abraham, Isaac and Jacob; and I promised them under oath to give them the land of Canaan.' And despite this oath, says this great rabbi, god did not give them this land; therefore they will resuscitate in order to enjoy it, so that the oath be accomplished.

The profound philosopher dom Calmet finds a much more conclusive proof in vampires. He has seen some of these vampires leaving cemeteries to suck the blood of sleeping people; it is obvious that they could not suck the blood of the living if they were still dead; they were therefore resuscitated. The argument is peremptory.

Another certainty is that on the day of judgement all the dead will walk under the earth like moles, according to the *Talmud*, to appear in the valley of Jehoshaphat, which is between the city of Jerusalem and the mount of olives. We shall be very crowded in this valley; but it will suffice to reduce the bodies proportionately, like Milton's devils in the hall of pandemonium.

Saint Paul says that resurrection will be performed to the sound of the trumpet. There will obviously have to be several trumpets, for thunder itself is hardly heard for more than three or four leagues around. One wonders how many trumpets there will be. The theologians have not yet made the calculation: but they will.

The Jews say that queen Cleopatra, who no doubt believed in resurrection like all the ladies of her time, asked a Pharisee whether we shall resuscitate in the nude. The theologian answered that we shall be handsomely clothed, because the seed we sow, being dead in the earth, resuscitates with a robe and tassels. This rabbi was an excellent theologian: he reasoned like dom Calmet.

Salomon: Solomon[1]

The name of Solomon has always been revered in the east. The works believed to be by him, the annals of the Jews, the fables of the Arabs, have carried his fame as far as India. His reign was the great epoch of the Hebrews.

He was the third king of Palestine. The first book of *Kings* says that his mother Bathsheba persuaded David to have her son Solomon crowned instead of his elder brother Adonijah.[2] It is not surprising that a woman involved in the murder of her first husband should have been cunning enough to

1. This article was revised by Voltaire in a more detailed fashion than any other; the text here given is an eclectic one.
2. *1 Kings* i.

deprive the legitimate son, who was also older, of his inheritance in favour of the fruit of her adultery.

It is a very remarkable thing that the prophet Nathan, who
reproached David with his adultery, with the murder of Uriah,
and with the marriage that followed this murder, was the
same one who later backed Bathsheba in placing Solomon on
the throne, born as he was from this bloody and infamous
marriage. This conduct, even considered only by *the flesh*,
proves that Nathan had two weights and two measures
according to the circumstances. The book itself does not say
that Nathan received a special mission from god to have
Adonijah disinherited. If he had one, we must respect it;
but we can accept only what we find written.

Adonijah, excluded from the throne of Solomon, asked
him for only one favour, permission to marry Abishag, the
girl who had been given to David to warm him in his old
age. Scripture does not say whether Solomon contended with
Adonijah for his father's concubine, but it does say that
Solomon had him assassinated for making this request.
Apparently god, who gave him a wise mind, refused him the
principles of justice and humanity, as he afterwards refused
him the gift of continence.

It is said in the same book of *Kings* that he was master of a
great kingdom extending from the Euphrates to the Red
Sea and the Mediterranean; but unfortunately it is said at the
same time that the king of Egypt had conquered the land of
Gezer in Canaan, and that he gave the town of Gezer as a
dowry to his daughter, whom Solomon is alleged to have
married. It is said that there was a king in Damascus. The
kingdoms of Sidon and Tyre flourished. Surrounded by
powerful states he certainly displayed his intelligence in
remaining at peace with them all. The extreme abundance
which enriched his country could have been the fruit only of
this profound wisdom, since in Saul's time there was not a
single iron-worker in his country, and only two swords were
found when Saul was obliged to go to war against the
Philistines, to whom the Jews were subjected.

Saul, who at first possessed only two swords in his state,

soon had an army of 330,000 men. The sultan of the Turks never had so great an army, which was enough to conquer the world. These extraordinary contradictions appear to make all discussion impossible; but those who want to investigate find it very hard to understand that David, who succeeded Saul (vanquished by the Philistines), should have been able to found a vast empire during his administration.

The wealth he left to Solomon is even more incredible. He gave him 103,000 gold talents in cash, and 1,013,000 silver talents. The gold talent of the Hebrews is worth about 6,000 pounds sterling, the silver talent about 500 pounds sterling. The total value of the bequest in ready cash, without the jewellery and other effects, and without the income, no doubt proportional to this treasure, amounted to 119,500 million pounds sterling, or to 597,000 million French francs. So much specie did not then circulate in the entire world.

In view of this one wonders why Solomon took so much trouble to send his fleets to the land of Ophir to fetch gold. It is still harder to understand how it was that this powerful monarch did not have in his vast territories a single man who knew how to cut timber in the forest of Lebanon. He was obliged to ask Hiram, king of Tyre, to lend him woodcutters and labourers for this work. It must be admitted that these contradictions make demands on the genius of the commentators.

Fifty oxen and 100 sheep, with poultry and game in proportion, were served every day in his house for dinner and supper. This would amount to 60,000 pounds of meat each day: a good household.

It is added that he had 40,000 stables and as many coach-horses for war-chariots, but only 12,000 stables for his cavalry. That is a lot of chariots for a mountainous country, and a great display for a king whose predecessor had had only a mule at his coronation, and in a terrain that can feed only donkeys.

It was not thought proper that a prince who had so many chariots should limit himself to a small number of wives.

They gave him 700 who were called *queens*, and the strange thing is that he had only 300 concubines, contrary to the custom of kings, who usually have more mistresses than wives. If these stories were dictated by the holy ghost we must admit that he loved marvels.

He kept 412,000 horses, no doubt to go for a ride along the lake of Gennesaret, or to that of Sodom, or to the torrent of Kidron, which would be one of the most delicious spots on earth if this torrent were not dry nine months of the year, and if the terrain were not rather stony.

As for the temple he built, and which the Jews believed to be the finest structure in the universe, if Bramante, Michelangelo and Palladio had seen it they would not have admired it. It was a sort of small, square fortress enclosing a court. In this court stood a building forty cubits long, and another of twenty. The second building, which was the temple proper, the oracle, the holy of holies, is simply said to have been twenty cubits in width and length, and twenty high. M. Soufflot[1] would not have been pleased with the proportions.

The books attributed to Solomon have lasted longer than his temple. This is perhaps one of the outstanding proofs of the strength of prejudices and the weakness of the human understanding. Only the name of the author has caused these books to be respected: they have been thought good because they were thought to be by a king, and because this king was taken to be the wisest of men.

The first work attributed to him is the book of *Proverbs*. It is a collection of trivial, low, incoherent maxims, made without taste, without selection and without plan. Can it be believed that an enlightened king compiled a collection of sayings among which there is not one about government, politics, the morals of courtiers, the customs of the court? Entire chapters are about nothing but trollops who invite passersby in the streets to go to bed with them.

Let us take a few of these proverbs at random:

1. Jacques Germain Soufflot is best known as the architect of the Panthéon, but the Lyons theatre is perhaps his finest work.

There are three things that are never satisfied,
Yea, four that say not, Enough:
The grave; and the barren womb;
The earth that is not satisfied with water;
And the fire that saith not, Enough.[1]

There are three things which are too wonderful for me,
Yea, four which I know not:
The way of an eagle in the air;
The way of a serpent upon a rock;
The way of a ship in the midst of the sea;
And the way of a man with a maid.[2]

There be four things which are little upon the earth;
But they are exceeding wise:
The ants are a people not strong,
Yet they provide their meat in the summer;
The conies are but a feeble folk,
Yet make their houses in the rocks;
The locusts have no king,
Yet go they forth all of them by bands;
The lizard taketh hold with her hands,
Yet is she in the kings' palaces.[3]

Is it to a great king, to the wisest of mortals, that we dare to impute inanities so low and so absurd?[4] Those who make him the author of such flat puerilities, and who say they admire them, are certainly not the wisest of men.

Proverbs has been attributed to Isaiah, to Elijah, to Shebnah, to Eliakim, to Joah, and to several others. But whoever it was that compiled this collection of oriental sayings, there is

---

1. *Proverbs* xxx. 15–16.
2. *Proverbs* xxx. 18–19.
3. *Proverbs* xxx. 24–8.
4. Before condemning Voltaire the reader should ask himself how much of his love of such passages as these is due to their content and how much to the language of the old English versions; for comparison here is Voltaire's rendering (from the Vulgate) of *Proverbs* xxx. 15–16: '*Il y a trois choses insatiables, et une quatrième qui ne dit jamais,* C'est assez; *le sépulcre, la matrice, la terre qui n'est jamais rassasiée d'eau; et le feu, qui est la quatrième,* ne dit jamais, C'est assez.'

no likelihood that it was a king who took the trouble to do so. Would he have said that 'the terror of a king is as the roaring of a lion'?[1] That is the language of a subject or a slave who trembles before the anger of his master. Would Solomon have talked so much about unchaste women? Would he have said:

> Look not thou upon the wine when it is red,
> When it giveth its colour in the cup.[2]

I very much doubt whether there were any drinking glasses in Solomon's time. They are a very recent invention. All antiquity drank from wood or metal cups, and this passage alone shows that the work was done by an Alexandrian Jew, long after Alexander.[3]

Ecclesiastes, for which Solomon is made responsible, is a work of an entirely different kind and taste. The man who speaks in this work is undeceived by illusions of grandeur, weary of pleasures, and disgusted with knowledge. He is an Epicurean philosopher who repeats on every page that the just and the impious are subject to the same mishaps, that man is no more than an animal, that it is better not to have been born than to exist, that there is no other life, and that the only good and sensible thing is to enjoy the fruits of one's labour in peace with the woman one loves.

The whole work is by a materialist who is at once sensual and satiated. It would appear that an edifying word about god was inserted into the last verse to diminish the scandal that such a book would be expected to cause.

Critics have difficulty in convincing themselves that this book is by Solomon; and Grotius claims that it was written

1. *Proverbs* xx. 2.
2. *Proverbs* xxiii. 31.
3. *Note by Voltaire:* A pedant thinks that he has found a mistake in this passage; he alleges that I have wrongly translated by the word *glass* the goblet which, he says, was made of wood or metal: but how could the wine have sparkled in a goblet of metal or wood? Anyway, what does it matter? [Voltaire disdained to add that his '*dans le verre*' correctly translated the Vulgate's '*in vitro*'.]

under Zorobabel. It is not natural for him to have said: 'Woe to thee, O land, when thy king is a child!'[1] The Jews had not yet had such kings.

It is not natural for him to have said: 'I observe the face of the king.'[2] It is much more likely that the author wanted to make it appear that Solomon was speaking, and that by the absent-mindedness with which the writings of the Jews are filled, he often forgot in the body of the work that it was a king who was supposed to be speaking.

What is still surprising is that this impious work should have been consecrated among the canonical books. If we had to establish the canon of the *Bible* today *Ecclesiastes* would certainly not be included; but it was included at a time when books were very rare and when they were more admired than read. All that can be done today is to palliate as far as possible the Epicureanism that reigns in this work. *Ecclesiastes* has been treated like so many other things that are excessively revolting. They were established in times of ignorance, and to the shame of reason we are obliged to maintain them in enlightened times, and to disguise by allegories their absurdity or their horror.

The *Song of Songs* is also attributed to Solomon because the king's name appears in it two or three times, because the beloved is made to say that she is beautiful 'as the skins of Solomon',[3] because the beloved says that she is black,[4] and because it was thought that Solomon so described his Egyptian wife.

These three reasons are equally ridiculous:

1. When the beloved, speaking to her lover, says: 'The king hath brought me into his cellars',[5] she is obviously referring

---

1. *Ecclesiastes* x. 16.

2. These exact words are not in *Ecclesiastes*.

3. *Song of Songs* i. 5; the explanation is quite simple: the Vulgate has '*pelles*' which Voltaire correctly translated '*peaux*', while the English versions, in substituting 'curtains', have rendered the meaning rather than the word.

4. *Song of Songs* i. 5.

5. *Song of Songs* i. 4; here again the English reader will be puzzled by the text, for the English versions have 'chambers', but the Vulgate word

to one who is not her lover. Therefore the king was not that lover: she means the king of the feast, the paranymph, the major-domo; and this Jewess is so far from being the mistress of a king that throughout the work it is a shepherdess, a country girl, who searches for her lover in the country and in the city streets, and who is stopped at the gates by the guards, who steal her dress.

2. 'I am comely as the skins of Solomon' is the expression of a village girl who means: 'I am as beautiful as the king's tapestries.' And it is precisely because the name of Solomon is found in this work that it cannot be by him. What monarch would make so ridiculous a comparison? 'Behold,' says the beloved in the third chapter, 'behold king Solomon, with the crown wherewith his mother hath crowned him in the day of his espousals'.[1] Who does not recognize in these expressions the comparison usually made by girls of the people when talking about their lovers? They say: 'He is as handsome as a prince', 'He has the air of a king', etc.

3. It is true that the shepherdess who is made to speak in this amorous hymn says that she is sun-burned, that she is 'brown'. In fact, were she the daughter of the king of Egypt she would not have been all that sun-burned. Girls of quality in Egypt are white. Cleopatra was, and in a word this personage could not have been at once a village girl and a queen.

A monarch who had a thousand wives might well have said to one of them: 'Let her kiss me with a kiss from her mouth, for your tits are better than wine.'[2] A king and a shepherd can use the same expressions about a kiss on the mouth. But it is certainly strange that the girl should have been supposed to be speaking here, eulogizing the tits of her lover.

---

is '*cellaria*', which Voltaire correctly rendered as '*cellier*'; hence his conclusion is justified. However, the English translators were again right in giving the real meaning rather than the word: for it is not likely that there were cellars below the tents.

1. *Song of Songs* iii. 11.
2. This is a complex conflation of several passages in the *Song of Songs*.

Nor will I deny that a gallant king might have made his mistress say:

> My beloved is unto me as a bundle of myrrh,
> That lieth betwixt my breasts.[1]

I do not understand too well what is a bundle of myrrh; however, when the beloved requests her lover to put his left hand on her neck, and to embrace her with his right hand, I understand her very well.

The author of the *Song* might also be asked for some explanations when he says:

> Thy navel is like a round goblet,
> Wherein no mingled wine is wanting:
> Thy belly is like a heap of wheat;
> Thy two breasts are like two fawns
> That are twins of a roe.
> Thy nose is like the tower of Lebanon.[2]

I must admit the Virgil's eclogues are in a different style; but each has his own, and a Jew is not obliged to write like Virgil.

It is apparently another example of oriental eloquence to say: 'Our sister is still small, she has no tits. What shall we do with our sister? If she is a wall, let us build on her; if she is a door, let us close it.'[3]

Capital! Solomon, the wisest of men, may well have spoken thus when on a spree, but several rabbis have maintained that this little eclogue is not by king Solomon, and is not even authentic. Theodore of Mopsuestia was of this opinion, and the famous Grotius called the *Song of Songs* a libertine work, *flagitiosus*. Nevertheless it is sacred, and it is regarded as a perpetual allegory of the marriage of Jesus Christ with his church. It must be admitted that the allegory is a bit strong, and that we do not know what the church means when the author says that his little sister has no tits.

---

1. *Song of Songs* i. 13.
2. *Song of Songs* vii. 2–4, incompletely.
3. *Song of Songs* viii. 8–9, much modified.

Still, this hymn is a precious fragment of antiquity: it is the only Hebrew book of love that has come down to us. It is true that it is an inept rhapsody, but it contains much sensuality. It is about nothing but kisses on the mouth, tits better than wine, cheeks the colour of turtle-doves. There is much about sexual pleasure. It is a Jewish eclogue. The style is like that of the Jewish works of eloquence, incoherent, without continuity, full of repetitions, confused, ridiculously metaphorical; but there are passages that breathe artlessness and love.

The book of *Wisdom*[1] is of a more serious kind; but it is no more by Solomon than the *Song of songs*. It is usually attributed to Jesus, son of Sirach, by others to Philo of Byblos. But whoever was the author it seems that in his time the *Pentateuch* did not yet exist, for he says in chapter x that Abraham wanted to immolate Isaac at the time of the flood, and elsewhere he refers to the patriarch Joseph as if he were a king of Egypt.

It seems very likely that Solomon was rich and learned for his time and his people. Exaggeration, the inseparable companion of vulgarity, attributed to him wealth he could not have possessed and books he could not have written. Respect for antiquity has since consecrated these errors.

But what does it matter to us if these books were written by a Jew? Our Christian religion is based on the Jewish one, but not on all the books written by Jews. Why should the *Song of songs* be more sacred to us than the fables of the *Talmud*? It is, they say, because we have included it in the canon of the Hebrews. And what is this canon? It is a collection of authentic works. Very well! but is a work divine because it is authentic? For instance, is a story about the kinglets of Judah and Shechem anything but a story? What a strange prejudice! We have a horror of the Jews, and we want everything that they wrote and that we collected to bear the imprint of divinity. There has never been so palpable an inconsistency.

1. The book of *Wisdom* (*Ecclesiasticus* in the Vulgate) has been excluded from the Protestant English versions of the *Bible*.

· Secte: Sect

Every sect of whatever kind is the rallying point for doubt and error. Scotists, Thomists, realists, nominalists, papists, Calvinists, Molinists, Jansenists are nothing but pseudonyms.

There is no sect in geometry; one does not refer to a Euclidean or Archimedean.

When the truth is evident, it is impossible for parties and factions to arise. There has never been a dispute whether daylight could be seen at noon.

Since that part of astronomy which determines the course of the stars and the recurrence of the eclipses has been known, astronomers have no longer disputed about it.

In England nobody says: 'I am a Newtonian, a Lockean, a Halleyan.' Why? Because nobody who has read them can withhold his assent to the truths taught by these three great men. The more one reveres Newton, the less one calls oneself a Newtonian. This word would assume that there are anti-Newtonians in England. We perhaps still have some Cartesians in France. This is solely because Descartes's system is a tissue of erroneous and ridiculous fancies.

So it is with the small number of well-authenticated factual truths. The documents in the Tower of London have been authentically published by Rymer.[1] There are no Rymerians, because no one takes it into his head to combat this collection.[2] It contains no ambiguities, no absurdities, no prodigies, nothing that revolts the reason, consequently nothing that sectaries could try to maintain or overthrow by means of absurd argumentation. So everybody agreed that Rymer's documents are worthy of confidence.

You are a Mohammedan, there are people who are not, so you may well be wrong.

Which would be the true religion if Christianity did not

1. Thomas Rymer, *Foedera* (Londini, 1704–32).
2. Not in the sense Voltaire here implies, but in fact some pages were suppressed by order of parliament.

exist? That in which there are no sects, that in which all minds would necessarily be in accord.

Now on what dogma are all minds in accord? On the worship of a god and on probity, All the philosophers on earth who had a religion said at all times: 'There is a god, and we must be just.' So here we have the universal religion established in all times and among all men.

The point on which they all agree is therefore true, and the systems about which they differ are therefore false.

'My sect is the best,' a Brahman told me. But, my friend, if your sect is good, it is necessary; for if it were not absolutely necessary, you must agree that it would be useless; if it is absolutely necessary, it is so to all men. How then can it be that all men do not have what is absolutely necessary? How can it be that the rest of the world laughs at you and your Brahma?

When Zoroaster, Hermes, Orpheus, Minos and all great men say: 'Let us worship god and be just', nobody laughs; but the whole world hisses the man who claims that we can please god only by holding a cow's tail when we die, and the one who wants us to have a bit of foreskin cut off, and the one who consecrates crocodiles and onions, and the one who connects eternal salvation with bones of the dead worn under our shirts or with a plenary indulgence that can be bought in Rome for two and a half sous.

What is the cause of this universal scorn and hissing from one end of the universe to the other? Things at which everybody laughs can hardly be obvious truths. What verdict would we pronounce on a secretary of Sejanus who dedicated to Petronius a bombastically written book entitled *The Truths of the Sybilline oracles proved by the facts*?

This secretary first proves to you that it was necessary for god to send several sybils on earth one after the other, for he had no other way of instructing mankind. It has been demonstrated that god spoke to the sybils, for the word *sybil* means god's council. They must have had long lives, for it is only to be expected that people to whom god speaks should have this privilege. There were twelve of them, for this number is sacred. They had certainly foretold all the events of the world, for Tarquin the superb bought three of their books from an old woman for 100 crowns. What unbeliever, adds the secretary, would dare to deny all these factual events which occurred in a corner in the sight of the whole world? Who could deny the accomplishment of their prophecies? Did not Virgil himself quote the sybil's predictions? If we do not possess the original texts of the sibylline books, written at a time when neither writing nor reading was known, do we not have authentic copies? Such proofs must silence impiety. Thus spoke Houttevillus to Sejanus. He hoped to be appointed an augur, which would have brought him 50,000 francs a year, and got nothing.[1]

'What my sect teaches is obscure, I admit,' said a fanatic[2]; 'and it is by virtue of this obscurity that it must be believed; for it says itself that it's full of obscurities. My sect is extravagant, therefore it is divine; for how could what appears so mad have been embraced by so many peoples if there were not something divine in it? It's just like the Koran which, according to the Sunnites, has the face of an angel and the face of a beast; do not be shocked by the snout of the beast, and reverence the face of the angel!' So spoke this lunatic; but a fanatic of another sect answered this fanatic: 'You're the beast, and I'm the angel'.

And who will judge this cause? Who will decide between two demoniacs? The rational man, impartial, learned in a science which is not that of words; the man liberated from prejudice and loving truth and justice; in a word the man who is not a beast and does not think he is an angel.

Sens commun: Common sense

Popular phrases sometimes reflect what goes on deep in the hearts of all men. Among the Romans *sensus communis* meant not only common sense, but humanity, sensibility. Since we

1. All this is a barely veiled satire on Claude François Houtteville's *La Religion chrétienne prouvée par les faits* (Paris, 1722).

2. Pascal; see Theodore Besterman, *Voltaire* (1969), pp. 540–41.

are not up to the Romans this word means only half as much to us as it did to them. It means only good sense, crude reason, the beginnings of reason, the first notion of ordinary things, a state midway between stupidity and intelligence. 'This man has no common sense', is a great insult. 'This man has common sense', is also an insult; it means that he is not exactly stupid, but that he lacks what is called mother wit. But where does this expression *common sense* come from if not from the senses? When they invented this word men admitted that nothing enters the mind but by the senses. Otherwise would they have used the word 'sense' to denote ordinary reasoning?

It is sometimes said: 'Common sense is very rare.' What does this phrase mean? That in some men the beginnings of reason are halted in their progress by various prejudices, that a given man who judges very sensibly in one affair, will always grossly err in another. An Arab, who may well be a good calculator or a learned chemist or a precise astronomer, will nevertheless believe that Mohammed put half the moon into his sleeve.

Why will he surpass common sense in the three sciences I have mentioned, and fall below common sense when this half moon is in question? It is because in the first cases he saw with his own eyes, he has practised his intelligence; and in the last he saw with the eyes of others, closed his own, and perverted his innate common sense.

How can this strange mental disorder come about? How can ideas, which advance with so regular and firm a step in the brain in a great many subjects, limp so miserably in others a thousand times more palpable and easier to understand? This man always has the same principles of intelligence within him. There must therefore be a defective organ, just as it happens sometimes that the most refined gourmet can have a depraved taste for a certain kind of food.

How was the organ of this Arab, who sees half the moon in Mohammed's sleeve, vitiated? It was by fear. He had been told that if he did not believe in this sleeve his soul, when crossing the steep bridge immediately after his death, would fall for ever into the abyss. He had been told what is even worse: 'If you ever doubt that sleeve a dervish will accuse you of impiety; another will prove to you that you are a madman who, having every possible reason to believe, yet refuse to submit your haughty reason to the evidence; a third will denounce you to the little divan of a little province, and you will be legally impaled.'

All this puts the good Arab, his wife, his sister, and all his little family into a state of terrified panic. They are sensible about all the rest, but here their imagination is wounded like Pascal's, who constantly saw a precipice beside his armchair. But does our Arab really believe in Mohammed's sleeve? No; he tries hard to believe; he says: 'It is impossible, but it is true; I believe what I do not believe.' A chaos of ideas, which he is afraid to resolve, forms in his head around this sleeve; and that is what lack of common sense really means.

Sensation

It is said that oysters have two senses, moles four, the other animals five, like men. Some people recognize a sixth, but it is obvious that the voluptuous sensation they have in mind comes down to the feeling of touch, and that five senses are our share. It is impossible for us to imagine or to want any more.

It may be that on other globes they have senses of which we have no idea. It may be that the number of senses increases from globe to globe, and that a being who has innummerable and perfect senses is the ultimate goal of all beings.

But as for us, with our five organs, of what are we capable? We always feel in spite of ourselves, and never because we want to. It is impossible for us not to have the sensation nature intends us to have when the object strikes us. The sensation is within us, but it cannot depend on us. We receive it; and how do we receive it? It is well known that there is no connection between the throbbing given to the air by the words sung to me, and the impression that these words make in my brain.

We are astonished by thought, but sensation is just as marvellous. A divine power is manifested in the sensations of the lowest of insects as in those of Newton's brain. Yet if a thousand animals die before our eyes we do not worry about the fate of their sensory faculties, although these faculties are the work of the being of beings. One looks on them as natural machines, born to perish and to make room for others.

Why and how could their sensations subsist when they themselves no longer exist? What need could the author of all that is have to preserve the properties the subject of which has been destroyed? One might as well say that the ability of the plant called sensitive[1] to draw in its leaves to its branches still subsists when the plant is no more. You will no doubt ask how it is possible that men's thoughts should not die when the sensations of the animals die with them. I cannot answer this question, I do not know enough to resolve it. Only the eternal author of sensation and thought knows how he gives it and how he conserves it.

All antiquity maintained that there is nothing in our understanding that has not been in our senses. Descartes declared in his romances[2] that we had metaphysical ideas before knowing our nurse's breast. A theological faculty[3] proscribed this dogma, not because it was an error, but because it was a novelty; then it adopted this error because it had been destroyed by Locke, an English philosopher, and because an Englishman must necessarily be wrong. Finally, after having changed its mind so often, it again pointed the ancient truth that the senses are the doors of the understanding. It has acted like encumbered governments which first circulate certain bank-notes, and then cry them down; but for a long time nobody has wanted any of this faculty's notes.

All the faculties in the world will never prevent philosophers from realizing that we begin by sensing, and that our memory is only a prolonged sensation. If a man born without

1. *Mimosa pudica.*
2. Elsewhere (Best. D 1666) Voltaire calls Descartes's theories 'bad fairy tales'.
3. The Sorbonne.

his five senses could live, he would be without any idea. Metaphysical notions come only through the senses, for how can one measure a circle or triangle if one has never seen or touched a circle or a triangle? How can one arrive at an imperfect idea of infinity but by pressing back limits? and how can limits be expanded if one has never seen or felt them?

Sensation envelops all our faculties, says a great philosopher.[1]

What are we to conclude from all this? You who read and think, conclude.

Songes: Dreams

Somnia, quae ludunt animos volitantibus umbris,
Non delubra deum nec ab aethere numina mittunt,
Sed sua quisque facit.[2]

But all the senses being dead during sleep, how can there be an internal one that is alive? When our eyes no longer see and our ears hear nothing, how do we nevertheless see and hear in our dreams? The dog hunts in his dream, he barks, follows his prey, he is at the death. The poet writes verse when asleep; the mathematician sees figures; the metaphysician reasons well or ill. We have striking examples of all this.

Are these the only active organs of the machine? Is it the pure soul that, free from the empire of the senses, enjoys its nights in freedom?

If the organs alone produce the dreams of the night, why do they not produce alone the ideas of the day? If the pure soul, calm in the repose of the senses, acting by itself, is the unique cause, the unique subject of all the ideas we have when we sleep, why are these ideas nearly always irregular, irrational, incoherent? Strange! it is just when this soul is

---

1. *Note by Voltaire:* Condillac, *Traité des sensations*, volume 2, p. 128. [The reference is to the 1754 edition.]

2. Petronius civ. 1–3, not quite accurately: 'Dreams, which tease the mind with flying shades, do not come by divine command from etherial sanctuaries, but each makes his own.'

least disturbed that all its imaginings are most disturbed! It is free, and it is mad. If it were born with metaphysical ideas, as has been said by so many writers who dream with their eyes open, its pure and luminous ideas of being, of infinity, of all the basic principles, should awaken in it with the greatest energy when its body is asleep: we would never be good philosophers but in our dreams.

Whatever system we may embrace, whatever vain efforts we may make to prove to ourselves that memory stimulates our brains, and that our brains stimulate our souls, we must all agree that all our ideas come to us in sleep without and in spite of ourselves: the will has no part in it. So it is certain that we can think for seven or eight hours at a stretch without having the slightest wish to think and even without being sure that we are thinking. Weigh that up, and try to divine how the animal is compounded.

Dreams have always been a great object of superstition: nothing was more natural. A man keenly affected by his mistress's illness dreams that he sees her dying, she dies the next day, therefore the gods have foretold her death to him. A general in the army dreams of winning a battle, he really wins it, the gods informed him that he would be the victor.

We take account only of dreams that have come true and forget the others. Dreams, together with oracles, constitute a large part of ancient history.

The Vulgate translates thus the end of verse 26 of chapter xix of *Leviticus*: 'You shall not observe dreams.'[1] But the word 'dream' is not in the Hebrew, and it would be rather strange if the observation of dreams were condemned in the same book in which it is related that Joseph became the benefactor of Egypt and of his family because he had explained three dreams.

The interpretation of dreams was so commonplace that people did not limit themselves to this ability: it was sometimes necessary to divine what another man had dreamed.

1. The end of *Leviticus* xix. 26 in fact reads in the Vulgate '*Non augura-bimini, nec observabitis somnia*', that is, 'neither shall ye use enchantments, nor practise augury' [i.e. divination by dreams].

Nebuchadnezzar, having forgotten one of his dreams, ordered his magi to divine it, and threatened them with death if they failed; but the Jew Daniel, who had been to school with the magi, saved their lives by divining and interpreting the king's dream. This story and many others could serve to prove that the law of the Jews did not prohibit oneiromancy, that is, the science of dreams.

Superstition

I

CHAPTER TAKEN FROM CICERO, SENECA AND PLUTARCH

Nearly all is superstition that goes beyond the worship of a supreme being and the submission of the heart to his eternal commands. A very dangerous one is to associate pardon for crimes with certain ceremonies.

> *Et nigras mactant pecudes, et manibu divis*
> *Inferias mittunt.*[1]

> *Oh! faciles nimium qui tristia crimina caedis,*
> *Fluminea tolli posse putatis aqua!* [2]

You think that god will forget your homicide if you bathe in a stream, if you immolate a black sheep, and if words are spoken over you. So you will be forgiven a second homicide at the same price, then a third, and 100 murders will cost you only 100 black sheep and 100 ablutions! Do better, wretched men: no murders and no black sheep.

What an infamous idea to imagine that a priest of Isis and of Cybele could reconcile you with divinity by playing cymbals and castanets! And what is this priest of Cybele, this wandering eunuch who lives on your weaknesses, to establish himself as a mediator between heaven and you? What patents has he

---

1. Lucretius, *De rerum natura*, iii. 52–3: 'And they slaughter black cattle and send oblations to the ghosts of the dead.'

2. Ovid, *Fasti*, ii. 45–6: 'Ah! easy-going men who think that the wretched crime of murder can easily be laved by the river's water!'

received from god? He receives money from you for mutter-ing some words, and you think that the being of beings ratifies the words of this charlatan?

There are innocent superstitions. On feast days you dance in honour of Diana or Pomona or one of the secondary gods with whom your calendar is filled. Capital! Dancing is very agreeable, it is useful to the body, it rejoices the soul, it does nobody any harm; but do not conclude that Pomona and Vertumnus are much obliged to you for having leaped in their honour, and that they will punish you for failing to do so. There is no other Pomona nor other Vertumnus than the gardener's spade and mattock. Do not be so idiotic as to believe that your garden will be damaged by hail if you fail to dance the Pyrrhic or the Cordaxian.

There is one superstition that is perhaps pardonable and even encouraging to virtue: that of placing among the gods the great men who have been the benefactors of mankind. It would no doubt be better to content ourselves with regard-ing them simply as venerable men, and above all to try to imitate them. Venerate a Solon, a Thales, a Pythagoras with-out making it into a cult, but do not worship Hercules be-cause he cleaned the Augean stables, and because he lay with fifty girls in one night.

Above all take care not to establish a cult for rascals who have no merit but ignorance, hysteria and dirt, who have made a duty and a glory of idleness and mendicity. Do those whose lives were at best useless deserve apotheosis after their deaths?

Note that the most superstitious times have always been those of the most horrible crimes.

II

The superstitious man is to the rascal what the slave is to the tyrant. There is more: the superstitious man is dominated by the fanatic, and becomes one. Superstition, born in pagan-ism, adopted by Judaism, infected the Christian church from the earliest times. All the fathers of the church, without exception, believed in the power of magic. The church always condemned magic, but always believed in it. It did not excommunicate sorcerers as deluded fools but as men who really had dealings with devils.

Today half of Europe believes that the other half has long been and still is superstitious. Protestants regard relics, indulgences, mortifications, prayers for the dead, holy water, and nearly all the rites of the Roman church as superstitious dementia. According to them superstition consists of taking useless practices to be necessary practices. Among the Roman catholics there are some, more enlightened than their ancestors, who have given up many of these once sacred practices: and they defend those they have kept by saying: 'They are unimportant, and what is of no importance cannot be an evil.'

It is difficult to fix the limits of superstition. A Frenchman travelling in Italy finds everything superstitious, and is not mistaken. The archbishop of Canterbury maintains that the archbishop of Paris is superstitious. The Presbyterians bring the same charge against his lordship of Canterbury, and are in their turn called superstitious by the Quakers, who are the most superstitious of all in the eyes of the other Christians.

Thus in Christian communities nobody agrees about the nature of superstition. The sect which appears to be the least attacked by this mental illness is that which has the fewest rites. But if, having few ceremonies, it is strongly attached to an absurd belief, this absurd belief is by itself equivalent to all the superstitious practices recorded since Simon Magus down to the priest Gauffridi.

It is therefore evident that it is the heart of the religion of one sect that is considered by another to be a superstition. The Moslems always accuse all Christian societies of it, and are so accused by them. Who will judge this great cause? Will it be reason? But each sect claims to have reason on its side. So it is force that will judge, until reason has penetrated a sufficient number of heads to disarm force.

For instance, there was a time in Christian Europe when newly married couples were not allowed to enjoy the privileges of marriage until they had bought this privilege from the bishop and the priest.

Whoever failed to leave part of his estate to the church in his will was excommunicated and deprived of burial. That was called dying unshriven, that is, not confessing the Christian religion. And when a Christian died intestate the church relieved the dead man of his excommunication by making his will for him, stipulating and exacting the pious legacy the deceased should have made.

This is why pope Gregory IX and saint Louis declared nul, after the council of Narbonne held in 1235, every will in the making of which a priest had not participated; and the pope decreed that the testator and the notary be excommunicated.

The tax on sins was, if possible, still more scandalous. The superstition of the peoples submitted to these laws, which were sustained by force; and only reason caused these shameful vexations to be abolished in time, though it allowed so many others to subsist.

How far does public policy permit the destruction of superstition? It is a very thorny question. It is like asking how far one should go in tapping a dropsical man, who may die during the operation. This depends on the doctor's prudence.

Can a people exist free from all superstitious prejudices? It is like asking: Can a people of philosophers exist? It is said that there is no superstition in the magistracy of China. It is likely that none will remain in the magistracy of some European cities.

Then these magistrates will prevent the superstition of the people from being dangerous. The example of these magistrates will not enlighten the rabble, but it will be restrained by the leaders of the middle class. Formerly the middle class had a hand in nearly every public disturbance, every religious outrage, because the middle class was then the rabble, but reason and time have changed them. Their gentler ways will soften those of the vilest and most ferocious populace. We have seen striking examples of this in more than one country. In a word, less superstition means less fanaticism; and less fanaticism means fewer calamities.

Théiste: Theist[1]

The theist is a man firmly convinced of the existence of a supreme being as good as he is powerful, who has created all extended, vegetating, sentient and thinking beings, who perpetuates their species, who punishes crimes without cruelty, and benevolently rewards virtuous behaviour.

The theist does not know how god punishes, how he encourages, how he forgives, for he is not rash enough to flatter himself that he knows how god acts, but he knows that god does act and that he is just. The difficulties presented by the idea of providence do not shake him in his faith because they are only great difficulties and not proofs against the idea. He submits to this providence although he perceives only some of its effects and appearances, and, judging the things he does not see by those he does see, he thinks that this providence extends to all places and times.

United in this principle with the rest of the universe, he does not embrace any of the sects, which all contradict each other. His religion is the most ancient and the most widespread, for the simple worship of one god preceded all the world's systems. He speaks a language all peoples understand though they do not understand one another. He has brothers from Peking to Cayenne, counting all wise men as his brothers. He holds that religion consists neither in the opinions of an unintelligible metaphysic nor in a vain apparatus, but in worship and justice. To do good, that is his cult. To submit to god, that is his doctrine. The Mohammedan cries out to him: 'Take care if you don't make the pilgrimage to Mecca!' 'Woe to you,' he is told by a Recollet, 'if you don't make the journey to our lady of Loretto!' He laughs at Loretto and Mecca, but he helps the poor and he defends the oppressed.

1. Voltaire's use of 'theism' and 'deism' is interchangeable; see Theodore Besterman, *Voltaire* (1969), pp. 212–13.

Théologien: Theologian

I once knew a true theologian. He had mastered the oriental languages, and was as well informed as possible about the rites of the ancient nations. He knew the Brahmans, the Chaldeans, the fire-worshippers, the Sabeans, the Syrians, the Egyptians as well as the Jews. He was familiar with the variant texts of the *Bible*. For thirty years he had tried to reconcile the gospels, and bring the fathers into union. He investigated the precise date of composition of the creed attributed to the apostles, and that given out under the name of Athanasius; how the sacraments were instituted one after the other; what the difference was between the synaxis and the mass; how the Christian church was divided after its birth into different parties, and how the dominant group stigmatized all others as heretics. He sounded the depths of the politics which always took part in these quarrels; and he distinguished between expediency and wisdom, between the pride that seeks to subjugate the minds of men and the desire to enlighten one-self, between zeal and fanaticism.

The difficulty of organizing in his head so many things whose nature is to be confused, and to throw a little light into so many dark clouds, often disheartened him, but as these researches were his professional duties, he devoted himself to them in spite of his disgust. He finally attained to knowledge unknown to most of his colleagues. The more truly learned he became, the more he doubted all he knew. So long as he lived he was tolerant, and as he died he confessed that he had uselessly worn out his life.

Tolérance: Toleration

I

What is toleration? It is the prerogative of humanity. We are all steeped in weaknesses and errors: let us forgive one another's follies, it is the first law of nature.

The Parsee, the Hindu, the Jew, the Mohammedan, the

Chinese deist, the Brahman, the Greek Christian, the Roman Christian, the Protestant Christian, the Quaker Christian trade with each another in the stock exchanges of Amsterdam, London, Surat or Basra: they do not raise their daggers against one another to win souls for their religions. Why then have we butchered each other almost without interruption since the first council of Nicaea?

Constantine began by issuing an edict which permitted all religions, but he ended by persecuting. Before him the authorities acted against the Christians only because they started to form a party in the state. The Romans permitted all cults, even those of the Jews and Egyptians, for which they had so much contempt. Why did Rome tolerate these cults? It was because neither the Egyptians, nor even the Jews, tried to exterminate the ancient religion of the empire. They did not run up and down the earth to make proselytes: they thought only of making money. But the Christians unquestionably wanted their religion to predominate. The Jews did not want the statue of Jupiter in Jerusalem, but the Christians did not want it in the capitol. Saint Thomas had the honesty to admit that if the Christians did not dethrone the emperors it was because they could not. It was their opinion that the whole world should be Christian. So they were necessarily the enemies of the whole world until it was converted.

They were also each others enemies in every detail of their controversies. Should Jesus Christ be regarded above all as god? Those who denied it were anathematized by the name of Ebionites, who anathematized the worshippers of Jesus. Some of them wanted all property to be owned in common, as it is alleged it was in the time of the apostles. Their adversaries called them Nicolaitans, and accused them of the most infamous crimes. Others adhered to a mystical devotion. They were called gnostics, and they were attacked with fury. Marcion discussed the trinity, and he was called idolator.

Tertullian, Praxeas, Origen, Novatus, Novatian, Sabellius, Donatus were all persecuted by their brothers before Constantine; hardly had Constantine made the Christian religion prevail than the Athanasians and the Eusebians tore each other to pieces. Since then, and to this day, the Christian church has streamed with blood.

I admit that the Jewish people was very barbarous. It butchered without pity all the inhabitants of a wretched little country to which it had no more right than it has to Paris or London. Nevertheless when Naaman was cured of his leprosy by plunging seven times into the Jordan, when, as an acknowledgement to Elisha, who had taught him this secret, he told him that he would worship the god of the Jews out of gratitude, he reserved to himself the right to worship also his king's god, he asked Elisha's permission to do so, and the prophet did not hesitate to give it to him. The Jews worshipped their god, but they were never surprised that each people had its own. They thought it proper that Chemosh should give a certain district to the Moabites, provided that god gave them one also. Jacob did not hesitate to marry the daughter of an idolator. Laban had his god as Jacob had his. Here we have examples of toleration among the most intolerant and the most cruel people of all antiquity. We have imitated it in its absurd frenzies, and not in its forbearance.

It is clear that every individual who persecutes a man, his brother, because he does not agree with him, is a monster. This is obvious enough. But the government, the magistrates, the princes, how should they behave to those who have a different form of worship? If they are powerful foreigners it is certain that a prince will contract an alliance with them. François I, most Christian,[1] joined with the Moslems against Charles V, most Catholic.[1] François II gave money to the German Lutherans to help them in their rebellion against the emperor; but he started off according to custom by burning the Lutherans in his own country. He subsidized them in Saxony for political reasons, he burned them for political reasons in Paris. But what happened? Persecutions make proselytes: France was soon full of new Protestants. At first

1. These were the epithets applied to the kings of France and Spain respectively: '*roi très chrétien*' and '*roi très catholique*'.

they submitted to being hanged, and then they took to hanging in their turn. Civil wars followed, then the saint Bartholomew, and this corner of the world was soon worse than everything the ancients and the moderns have ever said about hell.

Senseless people, who have never been able to offer up a pure worship to the god who made you! Wretches, who have never allowed yourselves to be guided by the examples of the Noachids, the educated Chinese, the Parsees, and all wise men! Monsters, who need superstitions as the gizzards of the ravens need carrion! I have already told you, and I have nothing else to tell you: if you have two religions in your midst they will cut each other's throats; if you have thirty, they will live in peace. Look at the Grand Turk: he governs Parsees, Hindus, Greek Christians, Nestorians, Roman Catholics. The first man who tries to make trouble is impaled, and everybody is peaceful.

II

Of all religions the Christian is undoubtedly that which should instil the greatest toleration, although so far the Christians have been the most intolerant of all men.

Jesus having deigned to be born in poverty and a low condition, like his brothers, never condescended to practise the art of writing. The Jews had a legal system written down in the greatest detail, and we do not have a single line from the hand of Jesus. The apostles disagreed on a number of points. Saint Peter and saint Barnabas ate forbidden meat with new Christians who were foreigners, and abstained with Jewish Christians. Saint Paul reproached them for this conduct, and this same Pharisee saint Paul, disciple of the Pharisee Gamaliel, this same saint Paul who had furiously persecuted the Christians, and who, having broken with Gamaliel, himself became a Christian, nevertheless after that sacrificed in the temple of Jerusalem during his apostolate. For a week he publicly observed all the ceremonies of the Jewish law he had renounced. He even added superfluous devotions and purifications. He judaized completely. For a week the greatest apostle of the Christians did the very things for which men are condemned to the stake by most Christian peoples.

Theodas and Judas had called themselves messiahs before Jesus. Dositheus, Simon, Menander called themselves messiahs after Jesus. A score of sects existed in Judea by the first century of the church, even before the name of Christian was known. The contemplative gnostics, the Dositheans, the Corinthians existed before the disciples of Jesus had taken the name of Christians. There were soon thirty gospels, each of which belonged to a different community, and by the end of the first century thirty sects of Christians could be counted in Asia Minor, Syria, Alexandria, and even in Rome.

All these sects, despised by the Roman government and hidden by their obscurity, nevertheless persecuted each other, which is all they could do in their abject condition. They were nearly all composed of the scum of the people.

When at last a few Christians embraced the dogmas of Plato and injected a little philosophy into their religions, which they separated from Judaism, they gradually grew in importance, though still divided into several sects. There has never been a single moment when the Christian church was united. It had its birth in the midst of the divisions of the Jews, Samaritans, Pharisees, Sadducees, Essenes, Judaites, disciples of John, Therapeutes. It was divided in its cradle, it was divided even in the persecutions it occasionally suffered under the first emperors. A martyr was often regarded by his brothers as an apostate, and the Carpocratian Christian expired under the sword of the Roman executioner, excommunicated by the Ebionite Christian, which Ebionite was anathematized by the Sabellian.

This horrible discord, which has lasted for so many centuries, is a most striking lesson that we should mutually forgive our errors. Dissension is the great evil of mankind, and toleration is its only remedy.

There is nobody who does not agree with this truth, whether he meditates calmly in his study, or whether he peacefully examines the truth with his friends. Why then do the same men who in private approve forbearance, beneficence, justice, so vehemently denounce these virtues in public? Why? Because self-interest is their god, because they sacrifice everything to this monster they worship.

I possess a rank and a power created by ignorance and credulity. I step on the heads of the men who are prostrate at my feet; if they get up and look me in the face, I am lost; I must therefore keep them fastened to the ground with chains of iron.

Thus have reasoned men made powerful by centuries of fanaticism. They have other powerful men under them, and these have still others, all of whom enrich themselves at the expense of the poor, fatten on their blood, and laugh at their stupidity. They all detest toleration, just as politicians enriched at the public's expense fear to submit their accounts, and just as tyrants dread the word liberty. Finally, to crown all, they bribe fanatics who loudly shout: 'Respect my master's absurdities, tremble, pay, and be silent.'

This was for long the practice in a large part of the world, but now that so many sects rival each others' power, what should be our attitude to them? We know that every sect is a guarantee of error. There are no sects of geometricians, algebraists, arithmeticians, because all the propositions of geometry, algebra, arithmetic are true. We can make mistakes in every other science. What Thomist or Scotist theologian would dare to say seriously that he is sure of what he says?

If there is any sect that recalls the times of the first Christians, it is undoubtedly that of the Quakers. Nothing more resembles the apostles. The apostles received the spirit, and the Quakers receive the spirit. Three or four of the apostles and disciples spoke at once in the assembly on the third floor; the Quakers do as much on the ground floor. According to saint Paul women were allowed to preach, and according to the same saint Paul they were forbidden to preach; female Quakers preach by virtue of the first permission.

The apostles and disciples swore by yes and by no, the Quakers do not swear otherwise.

No rank, no finery distinguished the disciples and apostles;

the Quakers have sleeves without buttons; and all are dressed in the same way.

Jesus Christ did not baptize any of his apostles; the Quakers are not baptized.

It would be easy to press the parallel further. It would be still easier to show how the Christian religion of today differs from the religion practised by Jesus. Jesus was a Jew, and we are not Jews. Jesus abstained from pork because it is unclean, and from rabbit because it ruminates and does not have a cloven foot; we boldly eat pork because to us it is not unclean, and we eat rabbit which has a cloven foot and does not ruminate.

Jesus was circumcised, and we keep our foreskins. Jesus ate the paschal lamb with lettuce, he kept the feast of tabernacles, and we do not. He observed the sabbath, and we have changed it. He sacrificed, and we do not sacrifice.

Jesus always concealed the mystery of his incarnation and his status. He did not say that he was god's equal. Saint Paul says expressly in his *Epistle to the Hebrews* that god created Jesus lower than the angels. And in spite of all the words of saint Paul the council of Nicaea acknowledged Jesus to be god.

Jesus gave the pope neither the marches of Ancona nor the duchy of Spoleto; and yet the pope possesses them by divine right.

Jesus did not make a sacrament of marriage and the diaconate; and with us the diaconate and marriage are sacraments.

If we look at the matter at all closely we see that the catholic, apostolic and Roman religion is the opposite of the religion of Jesus in all its ceremonies and in all its dogmas.

But then must we all judaize because Jesus judaized all his life?

If it were permissible to reason consistently in matters of religion, it would be clear that we should all become Jews because our saviour Jesus Christ was born a Jew, lived a Jew, and died a Jew, and because he said expressly that he accomplished, that he fulfilled the Jewish religion. But it is even clearer that we should tolerate each other because we are all weak, inconsistent, subject to mutability and to error. Would a reed laid into the mud by the wind say to a neighbouring reed bent in the opposite direction: 'Creep in my fashion, wretch, or I shall petition to have you torn up and burned?'

Torture

Although there are few articles on jurisprudence in these respectable alphabetical reflections, a word must nevertheless be said about torture, otherwise named the question. It is a strange way to question one. Yet it was not invented by the merely curious. It would appear that this part of our legislation owes its first origin to a highwayman. Most of these gentlemen are still in the habit of squeezing thumbs, burning the feet of those who refuse to tell them where they have put their money, and questioning them by means of other torments.

The conquerors, having succeeded these thieves, found this invention of the greatest utility. They put it into practice when they suspected that some vile plot was being hatched against them, as, for instance, that of being free, a crime of divine and human *lèse-majesté*. The accomplices had to be known; and to arrive at this knowledge those who were suspected were made to suffer a thousand deaths, because according to the jurisprudence of these first heroes anyone suspected of having had so much as a disrespectful thought about them was worthy of death. And once a man has thus deserved death it matters little whether appalling torments are added for a few days or even several weeks. All this even had something of the divine about it. Providence sometimes tortures us by means of the stone, gravel, gout, scurvy, leprosy, pox great and small, griping of the bowels, nervous convulsions, and other executants of the vengeance of providence.

Now since the first despots were images of divinity, as all their courtiers freely admitted, they imitated it so far as they could.

What is very strange is that the Jewish books never mention the question, torture. It is a great pity that so gentle, so upright, so compassionate a people did not know this method for learning the truth. In my opinion the reason was that they had no need of it. God always made the truth known to his cherished people. Sometimes they learned the truth by throwing three dice, the suspected person always getting three sixes. Sometimes they went to the high priest, who promptly consulted god by the *urim* and *thummim*. Sometimes they addressed themselves to the seer, the prophet, and it will readily be believed that the seer and the prophet discovered all the most hidden things just as well as the high priest's *urim* and *thummim*. The people of god were not reduced like us to question and conjecture; hence torture could not become a practice in their midst. It was the only custom the sacred people lacked.

The Romans inflicted torture only on the slaves, but the slaves were not reckoned to be human. Nor does it appear that a judge of the Tournelle regards as a fellow man the haggard, pale, broken individual who is brought before him dull-eyed, with a long and dirty beard, covered with the vermin that have been preying on him in a dungeon. He gives himself the pleasure of putting him to major and minor torture, in the presence of a surgeon who feels his pulse until he is in danger of death, after which they set to again; and as the comedy of the *Plaideurs* says very well: 'It always helps to pass an hour or two.'[1]

The grave magistrate who has bought for a little money the right to conduct these experiments on his fellow creatures tells his wife at dinner what happened during the morning. The first time her ladyship is revolted, the second time she acquires a taste for it, for after all women are curious, and then the first thing she says to him when he comes home in his robes is: 'My angel, did you give anyone the question today?'

The French, who are considered to be a very humane people, I do not know why, are astonished that the English, who have had the inhumanity to take the whole of Canada from us, have renounced the pleasure of applying the question.

1. Racine, *Les Plaideurs*, III. iv.

When the *chevalier* de La Barre, grandson of a lieutenant-general, a very intelligent and promising young man, but with all the thoughtlessness of wild youth, was convicted of singing impious songs and even of passing a procession of Capuchins without taking his hat off, the judges of Abbeville, people comparable to Roman senators, ordered not only that his tongue be torn out, his hand cut off, and his body burned on a slow fire, but they also put him to the torture, to discover exactly how many songs he had sung, and how many processions he had watched with his hat on.[1]

This adventure did not occur in the thirteenth or fourteenth century, but in the eighteenth. Foreign nations judge France by her theatre, her novels, her charming verse, the girls of her opera, whose morals are very agreeable, the dancers of her opera, who are graceful, by mlle Clairon, who declaims verse ravishingly. They do not know that there is no nation more cruel at bottom than the French.

In 1700 the Russians were regarded as barbarians. We are now only in 1769, and an empress has just given this vast state laws that would have done honour to Minos, to Numa, and to Solon if they had had enough intelligence to compose them. The most remarkable of them is universal toleration, the second is the abolition of torture. Justice and humanity guided her pen, she has reformed everything. Woe to a nation which, long civilized, is still led by atrocious ancient practices! 'Why should we change our jurisprudence?' it asks. 'Europe uses our cooks, our tailors, our wig-makers; therefore our laws are good.'

---

1. The whole article 'Torture' was added by Voltaire in the 1769 edition of the *Dictionnaire philosophique*, primarily, I believe, to enable him to print these comments on the La Barre case. None of the victims of injustice for whom he worked so hard and so long, not even Calas and Sirven, distressed Voltaire so deeply as this; and it is not irrelevant to note that his copy of the first edition of the *Dictionnaire philosophique* was burned with La Barre.

Transsubstantiation: Transubstantiation

The Protestants, and most of all Protestant philosophers, regard transubstantiation as the uttermost limit of monkish impudence and lay imbecility. They are quite unrestrained about this belief, which they call monstrous. They do not even think that a single sensible man could embrace it seriously after reflection. It is, they say, so absurd, so opposed to all the laws of physics, so self-contradictory that not even god could perform this operation, because it is in effect to annihilate god to suppose that he does contradictory things. Not only a god in bread, but a god in place of bread; a hundred thousand crumbs become in a flash as many gods, this inummerable crowd of gods forming only one god; whiteness without a white body; roundness without a round body; wine changed into blood which has the taste of wine; bread changed into flesh and fibre which have the taste of bread: all this inspires so much horror and contempt in the enemies of the catholic, apostolic and Roman religion that this excess of horror and contempt has sometimes become rage.

Their horror increases when they are told that in Catholic countries one sees every day priests and monks who, leaving an incestuous bed and without so much as washing their hands soiled with impurities, manufacture gods by the hundred, eat and drink their god, shit and piss their god. But when they reflect that this superstition, a hundred times more absurd and more sacrilegious than all those of the Egyptians is worth an annual income of 15 to 20 million to an Italian priest, and the domination of a country extending 100 miles in length and width, they would all like to take up arms to drive out this priest who has seized the palace of the Caesars. I do not know whether I shall take part in the journey, for I love peace; but when they are settled in Rome, I shall certainly go to visit them.[1]

1. Voltaire added one of his fictitious attributions: 'By M. Guillaume, Protestant minister.'

Tyrannie: Tyranny

The sovereign who knows no laws but his own whim, who seizes the property of his subjects, and who then enlists them to seize that of his neighbours is called a tyrant. There are no such tyrants in Europe.

The tyranny of one is distinguished from that of several. This tyranny of several is that of a body which invades the rights of other bodies, and which exercises despotism thanks to laws it has perverted. There are no tyrants in Europe of this kind either.

Under which tyranny would you like to live? Under none, but if I had to choose I should detest less the tyranny of one than the tyranny of several. A despot always has some good moments, an assembly of despots never has any. If a tyrant does me an injustice I can disarm him through his mistress, his confessor or his page; but a company of grave tyrants is inaccessible to all seductions. When it is not unjust, it is at least harsh, and it never distributes favours.

If I have only one despot I can get off by drawing back against the wall when I see him pass, or by prostrating myself or by striking the ground with my forehead, whichever is the custom of the country. But if there is a company of a hundred despots I am in danger of having to repeat this ceremony a hundred times a day, which is very boring in the long run if one's knees are not supple. If I have a farm in the neighbourhood of one of our lords, I am crushed. If I sue a relative of one of our lords, I am ruined. What can be done? I fear that in this world we are condemned to be anvil or hammer: happy the man who escapes this alternative!

Vertu: Virtue

What is virtue? Doing good to one's neighbour. Can I call virtue anything other than what does me good? I am poor, you are liberal; I am in danger, you come to my help; I am deceived, you tell me the truth; I am neglected, you console

me; I am ignorant, you instruct me: I do not find it difficult
to call you virtuous. But what about the cardinal and theological virtues? Some will remain in the schools.

What do I care whether you are temperate? You are
observing a rule of health; it will make you feel better, and I
congratulate you for it. You have faith and hope; I congratulate you even more for that, they will procure you eternal
life. Your theological virtues are heavenly gifts. Your cardinal
virtues are excellent qualities which help to guide you, but
they are not virtues in respect of your fellow man. The
prudent man seeks his own good, the virtuous man does good
to others. Saint Paul was right when he told you that charity
outweighs faith and hope.

But come, should we really acknowledge as virtues only
those that are useful to our fellow men? Well, how can I
acknowledge others? We live in society, so there is no true
good for us but what is good for society. A solitary is sober
and pious, he wears a hair-shirt: very well, he is a saint. But I
shall not call him virtuous until he has performed some
virtuous act from which other men have benefited. So long
as he is alone he is neither beneficent nor maleficent: he is
nothing to us. If saint Bruno brought peace to families, if he
helped the indigent, he was virtuous. If he fasted and prayed
in solitude, he was a saint. Virtue between men is a commerce of beneficence. No account should be taken of any man
who had no part in this commerce. If this saint were in the
world he would no doubt do good in it; but so long as he is
not, the world will be right not to call him virtuous: he will
be beneficial to himself, and not to us.

But, you tell me, if a solitary is a glutton, a drunkard, given
over to secret debauch with himself, he is vicious. Therefore
he is virtuous if he has the contrary qualities. I cannot agree.
He is a very scurvy fellow if he has the faults you mention,
but he is not vicious, wicked, punishable in relation to
society, to which his infamies have done no harm. We must
presume that if he returns to society he will harm it, that he
will be very vicious in it. It is even much more probable that
he will be a wicked man than it is certain that the temperate

and chaste solitary will be an upright man: for in society faults increase and good qualities diminish.

A much stronger objection is made: Nero, pope Alexander VI, and other monsters of this kind scattered good deeds. I answer boldly that they were virtuous on that day.

Some theologians say that the divine emperor Marcus Aurelius was not virtuous, that he was an obstinate Stoic, who, not satisfied with commanding men, wanted also to be esteemed by them; that he benefited himself from the good he did to mankind; that all his life he was just, laborious, beneficent out of vanity, and that his virtues served only to dupe mankind. On which I exclaim: 'Dear god, give us often such rascals!'